P9-EDC-052

HOCKEY
A PEOPLE'S HISTORY

HOCKEY
A PEOPLE'S HISTORY

Michael McKinley

McCLELLAND & STEWART

CBC

In grateful memory of James Creighton, the father of Canada's game.

Copyright © 2006 by Canadian Broadcasting Corporation
Updated edition copyright © 2009 by Canadian Broadcasting Corporation

All rights reserved. The use of any part of this publication reproduced, transmitted in any form
or by any means, electronic, mechanical, photocopying, recording, or otherwise, or stored in a
retrieval system, without the prior written consent of the publisher – or, in case of photocopying
or other reprographic copying, a licence from the Canadian Copyright Licensing Agency – is an
infringement of the copyright law.

Library and Archives Canada Cataloguing in Publication

McKinley, Michael, 1961-
    Hockey : a people's history / Michael McKinley.

Originally published to accompany the CBC television
    series: Hockey: a people's history.
ISBN 978-0-7710-5771-7

    1. Hockey--History. 2. Hockey--Canada--History.
3. Hockey players--Biography. I. Title.

GV846.5.M248 2009   796.96209   C2009-901628-1

We acknowledge the financial support of the Government of Canada through the Book
Publishing Industry Development Program and that of the Government of Ontario through the
Ontario Media Development Corporation's Ontario Book Initiative. We further acknowledge
the support of the Canada Council for the Arts and the Ontario Arts Council for our publishing
program.

Typeset in Minion, Meta Plus and Bank Gothic by M&S, Toronto
Text design and layout by Tania Craan
Printed in China

McClelland & Stewart Ltd.
75 Sherbourne Street
Toronto, Ontario
M5A 2P9
www.mcclelland.com

1   2   3   4   5   13   12   11   10   09

CONTENTS

On a fine Sunday afternoon in the middle of February 2005, more than three hundred Vancouverites blocked off the city's eclectic Commercial Drive to protest the expansion of the Trans-Canada Highway, which they feared would bring more traffic into their lively neighbourhood, given its proximity to Canada's national autoroute. What could have been just another street protest was made striking by how the protesters chose to express themselves: they played a game of street hockey.

With the sun of an early spring beating down on the asphalt, players as young as five years old tried to put the puck – a tennis ball – into the net during the friendly match, a net moved only upon the cry of "Bus!" since the perfidious car, bane of road hockey, had been banished from the street for the protest. Vancouver's finest guarded the perimeter, just to make sure no car drivers tried to sneak through by claiming to be Zambonis.

The participants saw a good old-fashioned road hockey game as their most potent tool for social protest. It spoke to the government and its citizens in a way that banners and angry chanting could not. It was creative, and it was fun. Hockey, to paraphrase the 1960s slogan, was the power of the people.

Coincidentally, this protest happened on the same day as the last bargaining window opened to save the 2004–05 National Hockey League season. The window would shut three days later, draped in the black bunting of national lament, and with the NHL embarrassedly admitting that, yes, it was the first professional sports league in North America to cancel an entire season, thanks to an impasse between players and owners over just who makes how much money from the game.

The collision of these two realities – people playing hockey to save their neighbourhood, professionals unable to agree on the payment for play and willing to risk destroying their league over the issue – poses as many questions as it answers about how the game matters to Canadians, who have, for more than a century now, claimed it as one of the essential elements in the chemistry of their national identity.

From its earliest days, hockey has found a way to rouse Canadian passion, for its heat and speed offer relief from the freezing inertia of winter and the promise of life in the season of death. Once upon a time, hockey itself was the source of protest and it took two singular men to transform the game from being a riotous pond affair into what some poets have called our winter religion – one by giving the game a temple, and the other by giving it a chalice.

CHAPTER 1

THE TEMPLE AND THE CHALICE

"Hockey ought to be sternly forbidden, as it is not only annoying but dangerous. In its right place, hockey is a noble game, and deserving of every encouragement, but on the ice it is in its wrong place, and should be prohibited." *Halifax Morning Sun*

HOCKEY: A PEOPLE'S HISTORY

A teenaged Haligonian named James George Alwyn Creighton may have read the Halifax paper's admonition on January 25, 1864, but in all likelihood, he was too busy, out on the ice, contributing to the fall of society. His only contact with the newspaper may have been to stuff it in his skates for warmth. The idea, though, that hockey did not belong outdoors, is something that Creighton would store in his fertile brain. Soon, his answer to the problem would change everything.

Born in 1850, Creighton had inherited his father William's figure-skating talents, honing them on the frozen Northwest Arm of Halifax Harbour close to his family's home on Hollis Street. He probably skated indoors as well, for Halifax opened its first covered skating rink in 1862, the same year that Montreal unveiled its ten-thousand-square-foot Victoria Skating Rink. It was in this Montreal rink that James Creighton performed an act on ice so extraordinary it created a whole new social dimension to Canada, which, at the time the Halifax editorial writers were getting lathered about hockey on ice, was not yet even a nation.

Creighton moved to Montreal in 1872. With a B.A. in engineering from Dalhousie University, and work experience on the Maritimes' Intercolonial Railway, Creighton was lured west by the engineering opportunities offered by the building of the Lachine Canal. Once in Montreal, Creighton introduced himself to society, joining a rugby club and the Victoria Skating Rink, where he was welcomed as an expert figure-skating judge. But Creighton's real gift to the

Though ice hockey has no prime mover, James Creighton (fourth from left) is as close as it gets to a founding father of the modern game. After staging the world's first indoor hockey game in Montreal and helping write the rules for hockey, Creighton moved to Ottawa and played for the Rideau Rebels along with two of the sons of Lord Stanley – the man who would give hockey its greatest prize, the Stanley Cup. (*Library and Archives Canada, C-79289*)

Ice hockey's ancestry stretches back for millennia. This kouros (c. 600-480 BCE), from ancient Greece's culturally vibrant Archaic Period, depicts an early ball-and-stick game. (*Nimatallah/Art Resource, NY, ART32693*)

Victoria Rink – and to the nation – was ice hockey. He taught his Montreal friends his version of the game, importing from his native province, at forty-five cents a dozen, hockey sticks made by Mi'kmaq craftsmen from the wood of the hornbeam tree.

Creighton also brought hockey skates with him. In 1863, in Dartmouth, Nova Scotia, John Forbes and Thomas Bateman of Starr Manufacturing had invented Spring Skates, which clamped the skate blade to a skater's boots with a metal lever. This did away with the leather strap that held skates to shoes in a sometimes clumsy and painful manner. Three years later, the Starr company modified its Spring Skates into patent-worthy hockey skates, featuring a rounded blade that helped players make the quick changes in speed and direction that ice hockey demands. Within a few years, Starr was employing one hundred men, working a fourteen-hour shift to supply the world with hockey skates, while Mi'kmaq carvers had to switch to using yellow birch, having logged the hornbeam tree to the edge of extinction.

The game that Creighton loved to play had its origins in the ball-and-stick games that people had played for thousands of years, games that began in the various cradles of civilization: Egypt or Persia or possibly later in Greece. In Athens, 400 years BCE, the artists sculpting the marble friezes for the Parthenon depicted a ball-and-stick game, with two players hunched down in a faceoff position over the ball.

As civilization spread westward, so did ball-and-stick games, finding a congenial home among the tribes of the British Isles, where, over the next millennium, the game acquired English and Celtic names – bandy, shinty, hurley – and styles of play. The sticks acquired curves and planes, allowing the passing of the ball to become more accurate, and the games, faster.

And then came ice skating. The word *skate* comes from the Old English word *sceanca*, shinbone, which medieval hunters would tie to their feet in order to speed across the ice after their prey. By the seventeenth century, shinbones had given way to metal blades, hunting had become playing, and Pieter Bruegel painted scenes of the Dutch playing *colve* (golf) on ice. In Scotland, the Edinburgh Skating Club was formed in 1642, which makes it the oldest in the world. A century later, in Ireland, the *Dublin Evening Post* reported on January 29 and February 2 of 1740 that two teams of gentlemen played "a match of hurling" on the frozen River Shannon.

During the next century, Europeans continued humanity's migration westward, and they brought their games with them across the Atlantic Ocean. These early settlers in the New World may have been surprised to discover that the aboriginal peoples of North America played ball-and-stick games too.

The Iroquois of Quebec played *baggataway*, a game French settlers called lacrosse, after the crozier carried by Catholic bishops, and the Mi'kmaqs of Nova Scotia played a ball-and-stick game called *oochamkunutk*, after the bat or stick with which it was played. When the Mi'kmaq joined the settlers for games of hurley on ice, they called the game *alchamadijik*. The Teton-Sioux (of what is now South Dakota) played a ball-and-stick game on ice, using two sharp pieces of carved buffalo shoulder bone attached to flat birchwood runners as skates.

The word *hockey* either comes from the French *hoquet* – a shepherd's crook – or from the Iroquois *hoghee*, meaning a tree branch, which was often used as a stick in these games. There is even a story that the name comes from a British Army officer named Colonel Hockey, who was stationed at Fort Edward, built in 1750, near Windsor, Nova Scotia. But hockey was played as a game on grass long before it was played on ice, and field hockey is still popular in Europe and South Asia, as well as parts of North America.

Windsor and Halifax in Nova Scotia and Kingston in Ontario have for years waged a mostly friendly debate over which town can claim to be the birthplace of hockey, and there is evidence that soldiers and schoolboys played it in all three places – especially in Nova Scotia. No matter where hockey was born, it was in Montreal that the sport took on its modern form when, on March 3, 1875, James Creighton advertised in the Montreal *Gazette*: "A game of hockey will be played at the Victoria Skating Rink this evening between two nines chosen from among the members. Good fun may be expected as some of the players are reported to be exceedingly excellent at the game."

The players were excellent because Creighton had been making them practise. As a valued member of the Victoria Skating Rink, Creighton held some sway with the rink's caretaker, and that, helped by cash bribes, had allowed him and his friends to play hockey inside for months before his public debut of the indoor game.

Players face off in a rink on Quebec City's Grand Allée at the end of the nineteenth century. There were no nets yet, and metal spikes served to mark the goals. The players competing for the puck faced the side of the rink, not the goals. (*McCord Museum*)

To calm fears that this hockey game might be dangerous due to "the ball flying about in too lively a manner, to the imminent danger of lookers on," the *Gazette* reported that Creighton had a solution, something he knew well from his Halifax boyhood. He would replace the ball with "a flat, circular piece of wood, thus preventing all danger of its leaving the ice." This piece of wood was a rudimentary puck, though the word would not enter the hockey lexicon until the following year.

Until now, hockey had been a loose outdoor game, played on any sized ice surface by players who sometimes numbered in the dozens. The Victoria Rink's ice surface was only 80 feet wide and 204 feet long, presenting a challenge that Creighton met by restricting the two teams to nine men a side. The tight space also meant that rules would have to be imposed to avoid anarchy. Creighton resorted to the rules he had learned in Halifax, ones that regulated a game quite different to the modern eye: the puck was not allowed to leave the ice, there was no forward passing ahead of the puck carrier, and goalies could not fall or kneel to make saves. The sixty-minute match would have an intermission in the middle, partly for the players to recover, as no substitutions would be allowed during

HOCKEY ON ICE.

A Match for a dinner—Some good sport, and a lively Scene.

Yesterday afternoon eight gentlemen of the St. James' and eight of the Metropolitan Clubs took part in a Hockey match at the Victoria Skating Rink for the above object.

The names of the St. James' men were Messrs. E. A. Whitehead (Captain), Fred. Hart (Goal-keeper), J. A. Gordon, F. M. David, Lutherland, G. T. Galt, George Hope and Frank Bond.

Metropolitan Club : Messrs. J. G. A. Creighton (Captain), R. S. Esdaile (Goal-keeper), W. Barnston, J. B. Abbott, Hy. Joseph, G. G. Geddes and C. Gilder. It will be noted this Club played one man short.

Umpires: For the St. James' Col. Hutton ; For the Metropolitan Mr. D. H. Andrews.

Referee :—Mr. C. E. Torrance.

Colors: St. James' blue and white ; Metropolitan, red and black.

Following were

THE RULES OF THE GAME

1. The game shall be commenced and renewed by a Bully in the centre of the ground. Goals shall be changed after each game.

2. When a player hits the ball, any one of the same side who at such a moment of hitting is nearer to the opponents' goal line is out of play, and may not touch the ball himself, or in any way whatever prevent any other player from doing so, until the ball has been played. A player must always be on his own side of the ball.

3. The ball may be stopped, but not carried or knocked on by any part of the body. No player shall raise his stick above his shoulder. Charging from behind, tripping, collaring, kicking or shinning shall not be allowed.

4. When the ball is hit behind the goal line by the attacking side, it shall be brought out straight 15 yards, and started again by a Bully ; but, if hit behind by any of the side whose goal line it is, a player of the opposite side shall it out from within one yard of the nearest corner, no player of the attacking side at that time shall be within 20 yards of the goal line, and the defenders, with the exception of the goal-keeper, must be behind their goal line.

5. When the ball goes off at the side, a player of the opposite side to that which hit it out shall roll it out from the point on the boundary line at which it went off at right angles with the boundary line, and it shall not be in play until it has touched the ice, and the player rolling it in shall not play it until it has been played by another player, every player being then behind the ball.

6. On the infringement of any of the above rules, the ball shall be brought back and a Bully shall take place.

7. All disputes shall be settled by the Umpires, or in the event of their disagreement, by the Referee.

Early Rules

When hockey moved from the pond to the arena, the confined space made formal rules for the game crucial. The Halifax Rules, hockey's first and unofficial regulations, decreed, among other things, that games had to consist of two thirty-minute periods, with a ten-minute break for the players, who played the entire match. Teams changed ends after each goal, and goalies had to stand at all times, which they did between two metal posts, as goal nets didn't come into play until the turn of the twentieth century. With the game's rapid growth in Montreal, the Halifax Rules were soon replaced by hockey's first official Montreal Rules, written in 1877. These abandoned the forward pass, which had been allowed in Halifax, permitted injured players to be replaced, and set team sizes at seven players a side and rink dimensions at a minimum of 112 by 58 feet. Goalies still had to stand, but they were allowed to drop to their knees to stop a shot in the "Colored League" in Nova Scotia in the early 1900s, and then in the Pacific Coast Hockey Association in 1912. Teams moved from nine men a side to seven in the 1880s, when a team showed up two men short at the Montreal Winter Carnival, and their opponents discarded two players to accommodate them. The teams liked the way this opened up the ice, with the seventh man playing the position of "rover" – a position that was finally dropped by the NHL in 1917 and by the Pacific Coast league in 1922, when hockey became the six-player-a-side game that it is today. (*Hockey Hall of Fame*) the game. Everyone played the full hour, unless removed due to injury or penalty – and, in either case, players were not replaced.

March 3, 1875, was an eventful night. In London, Gilbert and Sullivan premiered *Trial by Jury*, their first comic opera success. In Paris, Georges Bizet debuted the tragic opera *Carmen* – his last success, for he would die later that year. And in Montreal, the Victoria Rink hosted what the *Gazette* called "a very large crowd" of forty people, who braved a cold night (the day's high had been a frigid nine degrees Fahrenheit) to see what would become a kind of Canadian opera, with heroes and villains, with triumph and tragedy, and an in-built beauty to every performance: no scripted endings.

Under the light cast by the Victoria Rink's gas lamps, these intrepid Montrealers, likely warmed by flasks of brandy and kept out of harm's way by standing on a platform eight inches above the ice it surrounded, watched James Creighton and his seventeen friends take to the ice. Wearing rugby club jerseys, shorts, long woollen stockings, and no protective padding, the players were all from the Victoria Rink and the Montreal Football Club. They wore Starr skates and used Mic-Mac sticks, and shortly after 8:00 p.m., the first ever indoor hockey game began. An hour later, James Creighton had captained his team to a 2–1 victory.

The next day's *Gazette* featured the world's first report on the indoor game: "The game is like lacrosse in one sense – the block [of wood] having to go through flags placed about 8 feet apart in the same manner as the rubber ball – but in the main the old country game of shinty gives the best idea of hockey." The following day, Kingston's *British Whig Standard* was the first newspaper to wag a finger at the violence already endemic to the game: "A disgraceful sight took place at Montreal in the Victoria Rink over a game of hockey. Shins and heads were battered, benches smashed, and the lady spectators fled in confusion." The *Gazette* failed to mention this brawl, which was not between the teams, but between the players and Victoria Skating Club members, who had seen enough of this new game and wanted their ice back.

The newspapers paid attention to James Creighton's indoor game most likely because of the pedigree of the players – English Montrealers all: Torrance, Meagher, Potter, Goff, Barnston, Gardner,

In this advertisement from the early twentieth century, the player wears a new line of Starr clamp-on skates, which were lighter and provided better support for the foot than strap-on skates, allowing players greater mobility and speeding up the game. He also sports Starr's Mic-Mac hockey stick, named after the Mi'kmaq carvers who pioneered the hockey stick.

(Nova Scotia Sports Hall of Fame)

Giffin, Jarvis, Whiting, Campbell, Campbell, Esdaile, Joseph, Henshaw, Chapman, Powell, Clouston, and, of course, Creighton.

The world's first indoor hockey game was the beginning of the sport's rapid development in Montreal, where James Creighton was studying law at McGill, playing more indoor games at the Victoria Rink, and helping to develop the Montreal Rules, which were published in 1877. After earning his law degree, Creighton moved to Ottawa, where he became law clerk and Master in Chancery to the Senate and a member of the Rideau Rebels, an Ottawa ice-hockey team, one that was begun by the Stanley brothers, whose father had fallen in love with the game. He, too, would change everything.

In Ottawa on March 12, 1892, seventeen years after James Creighton staged his revolutionary hockey game in Montreal, another sports revolution happened, though this one was disguised as a sportsmen's banquet. At the posh Rideau Club, Ottawa athletes and their friends gathered to celebrate the Ottawas hockey club, champions of the two-year-old Ontario Hockey Association.

The team had a royal pedigree of sorts, being the favourite hockey team of the sixth governor general of Canada, the Right Honourable Sir Frederick Arthur Stanley. Freddy Stanley, as he was known to Queen Victoria, for whom he was subbing as head of state in Canada, had been beguiled by ice hockey; the game had stolen his heart – and opened his pocketbook. Stanley owned shares in the Ottawa rink where his favourite hockey team played, though that was not the prime reason for what he was about to do. Or rather, what he was about to do in proxy, as Stanley had another engagement that night, which must have pained him, for he loved a good time as much as he loved hockey. He sent a message to the banquet via his aide Frédéric Lambert (Lord Kilcoursie), a member of the Rideau Rebels.

Lambert read the missive to the sportsmen: "I have for some time been thinking that it would be a good thing if there were a challenge cup which should be held from year to year by the champion hockey team in the Dominion of Canada," wrote Stanley. "There does not appear to be any such outward sign of a championship at present, and considering the general interest which matches now elicit, and the importance of having the game played fairly and under rules generally recognized, I am willing to give a cup which shall be held from year to year by the winning team."

And so the Dominion Challenge Trophy was born, its name reflecting Canada's status as a "dominion," or self-governing territory in the British Empire. About the size of a football, the cup was made of silver and nickel alloy, decorated with a wavy seashell pattern and a plain band on which was etched "From Stanley of Preston." This little trophy, which would come to capture the

The Right Honourable Sir Frederick Arthur Stanley, Earl of Derby, Baron Stanley of Preston

Born in London on January 15, 1841, Frederick Stanley followed the well-worn aristocratic path through Eton and on to the Grenadier Guards, which he left at age twenty-four for the family business: politics. The younger son of a three-time prime minister of England, Frederick Stanley was elected as a Conservative member of Parliament for Preston in 1865 and served in the House of Commons for various constituencies for two decades, including a term as secretary of state for the colonies in 1885–86.

On June 11, 1888, he succeeded the Marquis of Lansdowne as Canada's governor general. Upon moving to Canada, he quickly established that he was a sporting man and built a large summer home called Stanley House on the Gaspé Peninsula in order to fish. He loved his wife, Constance, the surviving eight of their ten children, horse racing, bad jokes, sailing, his hunting beagles, playing chess – and ice hockey.

(*Library and Archives Canada, PA-025686*)

imagination of the hockey-playing world, was no self-aggrandizing gesture from a pompous, condescending aristocrat, but a gesture of love.

Stanley had received his first official taste of the game at the Montreal Winter Carnival in 1889. He, his wife, Constance, two of their children – their eldest son, Capt. Edward Stanley, and fourteen-year-old daughter, Isobel – and an entourage arrived in the middle of a hockey match between Montreal's Victorias and the Amateur Athletic Association in the bunting-filled Victoria Rink – the very spot where James Creighton had made history fourteen years earlier.

The Montreal Winter Carnival was one of the great parties on the planet in a city that had turned winter into something not to endure, but to celebrate. People converged on Montreal from across the continent to take part in the skating balls and winter games and the general social parade that the Carnival offered up – jamming the streets with sleighs, as Montreal journalist P.D. Ross reported in the *Toronto Daily Mail* in 1883: "There must have been between a thousand and fifteen hundred sleighs and cutters on the street between 3 and 4 o'clock . . . and people of all description in them glide along to the endless music of their bells. . . . Montreal is today the best advertised city on the continent, remarked an American newspaperman: You can scarcely conceive the interest that is taken in it throughout the United States."

The Carnival's pièce de résistance was a palace raised from ten thousand blocks of ice hacked from the St. Lawrence River, its main tower standing 76 feet high, or 24 feet higher than the Victoria Skating Rink, whose evening fancy-dress balls saw a fantastic collection of worlds and eras glide across its ice, with masqueraders dressed, Ross said, as "Kings, queens, courtiers, pages, Indian chiefs and Arab sheiks, Highland lasses and gentlemen of the eighteenth and every other century, fairies, witches, elfs."

Hockey first appeared at the Winter Carnival in 1883. A set of rules had been published in the McGill *Gazette* in 1877 – possibly written by James Creighton, who worked for the newspaper at the time, as they elaborated the Halifax Rules of his youth. By the early 1880s, there were about one hundred players in several hockey teams in Montreal and Quebec City. At the world's first official hockey championship, McGill defeated the Victorias 1–0 and tied Quebec 2–2 to win a silver trophy, the Birks Winter Carnival Cup, then valued at $750. (The cup is now housed at the McCord Museum in Montreal.)

The idea that players could and would compete for a trophy – and a valuable one, worth nearly twenty thousand dollars in today's money – reveals just how quickly hockey had taken hold of the Canadian imagination, especially for those lucky enough to live within striking distance of seeing a game, or able to play at its highest level, as white gentlemen of British Isles stock.

Frederick Stanley was no different when he first saw organized indoor hockey at the 1889 Winter Carnival. This exciting sport of speed and skill, strength and imagination, this game that roused life in the season of death, symbolized the muscular spirit of this young country. Stanley loved it.

In Ottawa, he built a rink on the grounds of Rideau Hall, and even tried to play hockey himself one winter Sunday afternoon, word of which moved a

Montreal's Amateur Athletic Association, winners of the first Stanley Cup, play a match in Montreal's Victoria Rink in 1893, the first year of Stanley Cup competition. The ten-thousand-square-foot rink, which opened in 1862, was designed for pleasure skating, and not for ice hockey. As a result, spectators crowded at the edge of the ice, with no protection from flying pucks and players. The MAAA's logo of a wheel with a wing inspired their nickname, the Winged Wheelmen. (*Library and Archives Canada/Molson Archives collection, PA-139443*)

Isobel Stanley

Stanley's daughter, Isobel, played on a
Government House team against the Rideau
ladies in 1889, and the first recorded women's
ice hockey match was staged at the Rideau
rink in Ottawa on February 10, 1891. The
Ottawa Citizen mentioned the game, but only
listed the names of the players as a social
register. When the Stanleys returned to
England in 1893, a contemporary, Emily
Lytton, ventured that Isobel's time in a wild
colony had left her "too much inclined to be
like a boy and has in consequence lost much
of her charm." *(Library and Archives Canada, nlc-5953)*

New York newspaper to report that the Queen's representative had blasphemed on the Lord's Day.

Stanley's sons Arthur and Algernon played on a five-a-side team, essentially the governor general's house team, known as the Rideau Rebels, who, in addition to James Creighton, also featured four members of the Coldstream Guards on their nine-member squad. Perhaps as a gesture to the Coldstreamers, famed for their red tunics and bearskin hats, the team wore bright red jerseys, and when they travelled to play in Toronto, they rode in Lord Stanley's private rail car.

Toronto came late to the game in 1887, when Montreal Amateur Athletic Association goalkeeper Tom Paton visited his industrialist friend Hart Massey, of the family of whom Ogden Nash would quip, "Canada has no social classes except the Masseys and the masses." The *Dominion Illustrated Monthly* reported that Paton "happened to mention to Mr. Massey and Mr. C. McHenry the fact that hockey was fast becoming the leading game in winter in Montreal, and suggested the idea of getting Torontonians interested in it."

Massey was so taken by his Montreal friend's tales from the front lines that he sent a cable to Montreal ordering eighteen hockey sticks, a puck, and a set of rules. "On receipt of the material the next evening, some ten skaters turned out on the Granite [Club] ice and had a little game. For the next few evenings they turned out again. Their elbows and hip-bones must have been sore after this and a few fingers skinless, for we hear no regular games being played until the winter of '89."

The winter following Massey's initiative, the *Toronto Daily Mail*, hopeful that Torontonians would give hockey another chance, reported on January 16 that the previous season's efforts had been abandoned because it was too close to the spring thaw. The *Mail* gave the new enterprise a little nudge, saying that "a [hockey] match between the Toronto Lacrosse Club and the Athletic Club is on the tapis" and more importantly, "it would be satisfactory to hear the success of these arrangements and that a game equalling lacrosse in interest would be introduced to enliven the pleasures of the winter season in Toronto athletic circles."

A week later the *Toronto Globe* was even more encouraging, reminding residents, "Hockey is a game in Montreal which holds the same place in the hearts of the people as lacrosse does in the summer," and that during the past week two teams "have been organized by well-known athletes to introduce to the Toronto public this fine sport."

In late February 1889, hockey finally made its Toronto debut, with the Granites defeating their fellow Torontonians, the Caledonians, 4 –1. A year later, the Toronto Granites thought themselves ready to take on the Rideau Rebels. According to the *Toronto Daily Mail*, the competition was not immune from hockey's dark side: "It is greatly to be regretted that, in a match between ama- teur teams, some players should so forget themselves before such a number of spectators, a good proportion of whom were ladies, as to indulge in fisticuffs."

64   THE DOMINION ILLUSTRATED MONTHLY.

A Desperate Struggle.—Skeletons vs. Sawed-offs.

By 1893, the game had become so rooted in the popular imagination that it was even lampooned. The "burlesque games" staged in Montreal's Victoria Rink featured clownish teams called Skeletons battling against the Sawed-offs, the Buffers took on the Duffers, and, in a nod to the colo- nial temper of the times, the Ethiopians faced the Fatherlands. Mock scraps were frequent features of these entertain- ments, and the *Dominion Illustrated Monthly* reported that if the referee became too officious, "he is promptly 'put to sleep' by the united efforts of both combatants." (*Dominion Illustrated Monthly, February 1893*)

While hockey became formalized by moving indoors – with rules, trophies, and eventually, professional leagues – the outdoor game remained accessible to all Canadians in winter. Most, if not all, of the early game's greatest stars learned their hockey in freewheeling pond or river games, where men and women often played together.

(Library and Archives Canada, 2536-10)

Despite the hot passion it aroused – or because of it – hockey took such a hold of the Canadian imagination that the *Dominion Illustrated Monthly* in February 1893 declared hockey both popular and permanent: "The season of play extends over about four months, and the covered skating rinks, found in every city and town throughout the Dominion, render play possible in all kinds of weather, so that the hockey-player has no longer to hang up his skates and put away his stick after a deep fall of snow."

The covered rinks – which had been in existence for curling and figure skating since the middle of the century – were also, according to the *Dominion Illustrated Monthly*, of comfort to those who preferred to watch: "The rinks have done much to encourage the attendance of the spectator. From the vantage ground of the platform or gallery he can, in comparative comfort, watch every move in the game, without having, as of old, to encourage the circulation in his extremities by a frantic war dance to the accompaniment of the vigorous arm movement technically known as the 'milkman's slap.'"

The magazine also mentioned a technical innovation of benefit to spectator and player alike: "The introduction of electric lighting made rink play possible at night, and all the great matches now take place in the evening." The *Dominion*'s writer concluded, "All these advantages combine to lift hockey above all others in Canada as the National Winter Game."

By the time Lord Stanley's sons discussed the idea of a national championship trophy with their father, hockey's popularity could happily accommodate such an award, though Stanley's gift to the New World was doubtless influenced by the Old. At a meeting of England's Football Association in

London in July 1871, it was agreed "that a Challenge Cup should be established in connection with the Association, for which all clubs belonging to the Association should be invited to compete," thus giving birth to the FA Cup.

While Stanley likely wanted the Dominion Challenge Trophy's first winner to be his beloved Ottawa Hockey Club, champions of the 1892–93 season, in an effort to keep competition fair, he created the original "two-referee system" by establishing two trustees for the Cup, whose job it was to prevent it from being hijacked by any one team, and so defeat its purpose.

The Cup's first custodians, Ottawa sportsmen Sheriff John Sweetland and journalist P.D. Ross, a Rideau Rebel, also took seriously Stanley's notion that the trophy was to be won by the "champion hockey team in the Dominion," and in the late winter of 1893, they decreed that the Ottawas should play Toronto's Osgoode Hall team for the championship – in Toronto, no less. Ottawa, furious at this insult to their status as champions, refused. And so, the first Dominion Challenge Trophy competition is a ripe asterisk in Canada's sporting history: it did not take place when it should have.

In May 1893, in what was perhaps an effort to publicize the spirit of the prize, the Montreal *Gazette* clarified Lord Stanley's intentions. "The Cup shall remain a challenge cup and will not become the property of any team, even if won more than once," the paper explained, renaming it "The Stanley Hockey Championship Cup."

That fall, Ottawa reconsidered its position. After sweeping four Quebec teams, they had reason to believe that hockey's newest, greatest prize would finally be theirs – until they lost to the Montreal Amateur Athletic Association (MAAA). Now there was another problem, and a rather embarrassing one. The Montreal team that won the "first" Stanley Cup refused to accept it.

Although the Montreal Hockey Club, the team whose sweat had actually won the Cup, had "connected club" status with the MAAA, it had no voice in the official affairs of the association. It resented that a bunch of well-fed MAAA executives was now eager to accept Lord Stanley's trophy on its behalf. The Cup's trustees tried to patch up the dispute, but when Sheriff Sweetland travelled to Montreal to present the trophy to the team, the chairman of the Montreal Hockey Club was nowhere to be found, and so the MAAA happily accepted the trophy for him. This infuriated the Montreal Hockey Club, who claimed the Cup's trustees had not contacted them directly, thus doubly injuring them.

The officials of the MAAA called a special meeting of the directors, recording their mortification in their official history: "In order not to offend the former governor-general of Canada and not to seem ungreatful [*sic*] in the public's eye, the directors decided to retain possession of The Stanley Cup." And in a gesture

When Lord Stanley donated his famous trophy to hockey in 1892, he wanted to encourage regional competition, and so he called it a Dominion Challenge Trophy. One of his adjutants, Captain Charles Colville, bought the silver bowl at G.H. Collis, Silversmith, on London's Regent Street, for ten guineas. Stanley hoped that desire to win the trophy would unite teams and their fans across the Dominion of Canada, and in so doing, unite the huge, sparsely populated country. (*Hockey Hall of Fame*)

The Montreal Amateur Athletic Association (MAAA) won the first Stanley Cup in 1893 by finishing first in the Amateur Hockey Association's standings with a record of 7–1–0. While Stanley's cup was supposed to be a challenge trophy, no other team took on Montreal, who were not entirely satisfied with their prize. While they represented the MAAA, they had no voice in the club's official affairs and resented its executives claiming the Cup on their behalf. The following year, the MAAA defeated a team of challengers from Ottawa to win the Stanley Cup in the first true challenge series.

(Hockey Hall of Fame)

that speaks to hockey's popularity in those early days, "The public was never informed of the dispute." So the "first" Stanley Cup was won by a committee, in secret. This episode innocently foreshadowed all the political disputes over the game to come.

The first Stanley Cup series that resulted in a happy ending was played on March 22, 1894, two years after Stanley endowed the prize. Five thousand people, the largest crowd that had yet watched a hockey game, crammed onto a platform a foot above the ice of Montreal's Victoria Rink to watch Montreal, in blue jerseys crested by a twin-winged wheel, defeat Ottawa 3–1. "Every lady almost in the rink wore the favors of their particular club," said the Montreal *Gazette*, "and never did belted knight in joust or tourney fight harder than the hockey men." The anonymous reporter found room, however, to lodge what would become familiar post-game gripes: the referee was "not nearly strict enough"; the ice conditions could be "much improved upon" by holding the games earlier in the winter; and violence was ever present. "Hockey," said the reporter, "is not necessarily synonymous with homicide."

The victors were carried off the rink on the shoulders of their delighted fans, and the referee, Mr. H. Scott of Quebec City, made it safely home, the bowler hat that he wore while officiating the match safe on his unharmed head. The names of the champions were the first to be engraved on Lord

Stanley's silver bowl: "Tom Paton, James Stewart, Allan Cameron, Alex Irving, Haviland Routh, Archie Hodgson, Joe Lowe, Bill Barlow, and A.B. Kingan." A tradition had begun – finally. And hockey had its Holy Grail.

In the early part of the winter of 1890, a Winnipeg schoolboy was skating with friends on an outdoor rink when he saw a strange sight. "A couple of young men, both strangers to me, armed with curved sticks of more regularity in contour than the average improvised shinny club of the small boy, but designed upon somewhat similar lines, were indulging in a good-natured contest for the possession of a dark, dish-shaped object on the ice."

The schoolboy, whose remembrance of this fateful day appears under the mysterious byline "W.D." in the March 1895 issue of *Athletic Life*, asked the two men just what they were doing and learned they "were members of one of the new athletic clubs just formed in the city, who were playing some new game called hockey."

It was the Alberta-born Marshall McLuhan who said that "The Westerner doesn't have a point of view. He has a vast panorama; he has such a tremendous space around him." He also had tremendous opportunities in the vast panorama of Manitoba, where hockey found its next home. The province had seen two decades of war, followed by rapid growth, since it joined Confederation in 1870, and in the national imagination it was a place of adventure, of possibility – and of dangerous men, such as the self-proclaimed

Early hockey players seemed seriously under-protected by today's standards. Until hockey gloves appeared circa 1904, followed by hockey "gauntlets" in 1915, players wore winter gloves, or played barehanded. From the 1880s until the first decade of the twentieth century, hockey pants were knee-length and sometimes padded, then shortened for better mobility. While early goalies had worn cricket pads, the new century saw other players wearing shin guards, which were little more than padding sewn into their socks. Jerseys were first worn for warmth, but over time these thick wool turtlenecks had padding sewn into their shoulders and elbows, and then grew lighter and looser-fitting to accommodate the safety equipment beneath them. Here, the goal judge in his fur coat was probably the warmest man on ice. *(Hockey Hall of Fame)*

Collège Ste-Marie

Despite the prominence of French-Canadian players in hockey's history, francophones, like other non-English minorities, came late to the game. Montreal's Collège Ste-Marie, founded in 1848 by the Jesuits, a Roman Catholic teaching order, was an important way station for both francophone and Irish hockey players. In 1900, the liberal weekly newspaper *La Patrie* called it a "veritable [hockey] talent breeding ground" with its own league composed of four or five teams. While some Irish students went on to play for the Montreal Shamrocks, the francophone players produced by the school were crucial to the development of French-Canadian hockey. The Millaire brothers, Edouard and Albert, sons of a Montreal tavern owner, not only played on the school team, but became hockey pioneers in Quebec's first francophone teams – the Nationals, the Montagnards, and the Montreal Canadiens. (*Collège Ste-Marie*)

"prophet of the New World" Louis Riel, whose crusade to preserve the rights of the Catholic, French-speaking Métis ended in the Northwest Rebellion, and in Riel's hanging, both in 1885.

In 1881, the government of Canada, after a decade of debate and payola, had begun construction of what Liberal Opposition leader Alexander Mackenzie called "an act of insane recklessness": a railway linking Canada from east to west. Hacked through the primordial rock of the Canadian Shield, laid flat across the endless Prairies, then climbing through the seemingly impenetrable Rockies toward the balmy Pacific Coast, the national railway was the physical embodiment of the idea of Canada. It was also going to make a lot of money for its investors – and determine the demographic pattern of the country's future, for Canada's major cities grew up along the route of the railway. And Winnipeg, in the early 1880s, was booming. The railway had put the city on the world's map, with newspapers in New York and London agog at the frenzied land speculation in this new metropolis of the prairie. And along with the newcomers heading west in search of a better life or a fast fortune came the game that had seduced Canadian hearts in the east: hockey.

Fred Ashe, a Quebec hockey player who had gone west to seek his fortune, helped put a team together called the Winnipegs, and Eastern Canadian soldiers who had come to serve at the province's garrisons also started hockey teams, teaching the game to the locals.

On November 3, 1890 – about the same time that the Winnipeg schoolboy first saw hockey – a group of Winnipeg sportsmen convened to form the first

The Winnipeg Victorias won their first Stanley Cup on Valentine's Day, 1896, the first team outside Montreal to take hockey's premier trophy. Led by Dan Bain, a robust scoring and playmaking centreman, and goalie Cecil "Whitey" Merritt, the Victorias won the Cup twice more in 1901 and 1902.

(*Library and Archives Canada/Patent and Copyright Office collection/C-024328*)

hockey club in Manitoba. In honour of the Queen (not the Montreal team of the same name), they called themselves the Victoria Hockey Club, and shortly afterward, the Winnipegs obliged them by becoming their only opposition. On November 11, 1892, the Manitoba Hockey Association was born. The game of hockey had come to stay in Manitoba.

In 1893, the Victorias were the Manitoba champions, but that only made them want to test themselves in hockey's heartland. Allying themselves with their rival Winnipegs, they made a bold overture to their eastern cousins: a combined squad of Manitoba all-stars would come to Ontario and play against the province's best.

Even though the Ontario Hockey Association had been formed only in the same year as the one in Manitoba, the success of the game in Ottawa, Kingston, and more recently, Toronto, led the Ontarians to believe that they would defeat the Manitobans handily – and make some easy money from this hockey circus.

The Winnipeggers' tour began badly when a fire wiped out the hometown rink where they stored their equipment and uniforms. So Winnipeg merchants who had funded the tour dug deeper into their pockets for new skates, sticks, and for improvised uniforms of black trousers and white jerseys, with crossed hockey sticks forming a W on the proud chests of the Winnipeg All-Stars, who now took the train east.

Led by speedskating champion Jack McCulloch, a quicksilver goalscorer for the Winnipeg Victorias, the Manitobans defeated Toronto's Victorias, a team from Osgoode Hall, and a Queen's University team by a combined score of 23–10, and went on to win eight of their eleven games. Kingston's *Daily British Whig Standard* newspaper expressed the depth of wounded Ontario pride. "What would you expect," it asked, "from fellows who have ice to practice upon the whole year?"

The Winnipeg teams had tasted success, but their real object of desire was the trophy that, until now, had lived in Montreal. On February 8, 1896, the *Winnipeg Daily Tribune* announced that the city had reached the hockey big time. The Victorias were leaving for Montreal "to meet the champion eastern team at the Victoria rink, and then Vics will be pitted against Vics for the honor of the Stanley Cup and the Championship of Canada." In case anyone doubted the import of the mission, the *Tribune* added: "Our men are leaving this city carrying the confidence of the Winnipeg public, who believe that the western cyclone is again capable of teaching the eastern hockeyists what a whirlwind on ice means."

The night of February 14 was cold, and the ice was good in Montreal's Victoria Rink when Winnipeg skated out in bright scarlet jerseys splashed with a yellow Manitoba bison crest. The twenty-five Winnipeg fans who made the journey with them applauded their goalie, George "Whitey" Merritt, a native of Goderich, Ontario, who had first tried his hand at hockey as an eleven-year-old, in 1873, and who augmented his uniform with white cricket pads and a luxurious walrus moustache.

Playing in front of Merritt was a team of multi-sport athletes, very common at the time when athletes changed sports with the seasons. On cover point – or defence – was Roddy Flett, a twenty-three-year-old Manitoba native who excelled at football, rugby, lacrosse, curling, baseball, and who would represent Manitoba in rowing at Henley-on-Thames come the summer. Team captain J.C. Armytage, a twenty-five-year-old forward, was also the squad's trainer, and Dan Bain, also twenty-three, was the team's speedy forward.

Bain was one of early hockey's first stars, and his athletic prowess was considerable. At age thirteen, he won a three-mile race to become the roller-skating champion of Manitoba. At seventeen, he took first prize in the city's gymnastics competition. And at twenty, he won the first of three consecutive cycling championships. During the course of his sporting life, Bain would add to that a pairs figure-skating crown, medals in lacrosse and snowshoeing, and the Dominion trapshooting championship. Bain was sanguine about his accomplishments, assessing his success as a function of skill – and fickleness: "I couldn't see any sense in participating in a game unless I was good. I kept at a sport just long enough to nab a championship, then I'd try something else."

Bain had joined the Winnipeg Victorias in 1895 after answering an ad in a local newspaper for new players and made the team in the first five minutes of the tryout. The only thing wrong with his game was his stick, which was held together by wire. The Victorias took it away from him. "It nearly broke my heart to lose it," he said.

The only thing the Winnipeggers lost on this historic night, when the Vics played the Vics, was Dan Bain to penalties as they went on to win the game, 2–0. Back home, crowds gathered in the Manitoba, Queens, and Clarendon hotels, listening to hockey's first play-by-play coming down the Canadian Pacific Railway telegraph wires. The *Winnipeg Free Press* reported, "Superintendent Jenkins and Mr. Thos. Masters of the C.P. Telegraphs manipulated the keyboard, while Manager Tait, in clarion tones, but with a distinct Scotch accent, sang out the bulletins," as the Winnipeg seven – the new size of a hockey team – defeated their Montreal hosts.

As the *Free Press* gleefully announced, the Stanley Cup wasn't the only thing that the Montreal Victorias lost that night: "Alas for the frailty of human hopes, Montreal to-night is clothed in sackcloth and ashes, and the sports [*sic*] have gone to sleepless beds with empty pocketbooks. The 'Peg' contingent on the other hand have enough money to start a private bank. No less than two thousand cold plunkers were passed over the Windsor hotel counter after the match to-night, and went down into the jeans of the Winnipeg supporters."

Later that night, or early the next morning, another hockey tradition was indulged, the paper reported, when "the winning of the Stanley Cup was celebrated in a worthy manner. It holds some two gallons of drink, but the Winnipeg crowd were a big, dry crowd, and the cup had to be filled more than once to clear their throats efficiently."

When the Winnipeg seven returned home, a huge crowd had gathered at the CPR depot to welcome them. The front of the locomotive was draped with a Union Jack, and both sides of the fuel car were decorated with hockey sticks trailing streamers. The players were carried off to a feast at the Manitoba Hotel in open sleighs, the Stanley Cup glinting in the winter light for all who had gathered along the victory route to see.

The Montreal Victorias were one of early hockey's first dynasties, winning the Stanley Cup five times between 1895 and 1899. The Vics were captained by Mike Grant (back row, centre), a speed skating and lacrosse champion who was one of hockey's first rushing defence-men. He was further distinguished by being the son of a blacksmith, defying the class barrier of organized hockey in late-nineteenth-century Montreal.

(Hockey Hall of Fame)

Ten months later the Montreal Victorias headed west to win back the Cup in what the local newspapers called "the greatest sporting event in the history of Winnipeg," with tickets selling for a whopping twelve dollars – enough to buy both teams a lavish dinner.

The Montrealers had some adjustments to make to their play before the championship game. Winnipeg's McIntyre Rink had higher boards and slightly rounded end boards, which made the puck bounce differently. Seven hundred fans – as many as would come to games in Montreal – showed up to watch the Easterners practise.

The Montreal Victorias also found time to attend a performance by the Columbia Opera Company, which they were reported to have enjoyed as much as the locals had. They told a reporter that they considered Winnipeg a "true sporting city," a consideration not hurt by the fact that they won the Cup and took it "home" to Montreal, less than a year after it had arrived in the West.

Winnipeg competed for the Cup again in 1900, losing to the powerful Montreal Shamrocks, and later that year, the Halifax Crescents came to Montreal to try to take the Cup from the Shamrocks but wound up on the wrong end of an 11–0 score. They went back east empty-handed, but left behind their practice of draping fishing nets over the goal posts. The goal net was born.

Dan Bain played in two more Stanley Cup challenge matches for Winnipeg, bringing the Cup back west in February 1901. Named Canada's All-Round Athlete of the nineteenth century, in his old age he looked back wistfully on hockey in its pioneer days: "When we passed the puck it never left the ice and if a wingman wasn't there to receive it, it was because he had a broken leg. There was no suggestion of any money being paid to the Victorias during the years that I was associated with them, and for many years later. Those were the days of real athletes." (*Globe and Mail*, November 11, 1949)

The early years of the Stanley Cup championships gave hockey in Canada a definition, as who competed for it was as important as who did not or could not. The trophy could be won by any team, or rather, any white, male, English-speaking team, worthy of the challenge.

Although Montreal owned the Stanley Cup for its early years, the city's francophones were largely excluded, something the founder of the modern Olympic Games, the Baron Pierre de Coubertin, noticed on a visit to the city in 1889. Commenting on the numerous clubs and associations the English community had founded, de Coubertin said, "In all these associations, the few French Canadians who like exercise and the outdoors receive a warm welcome, but only English is spoken and all that is English dominates."

French Canadians were not completely left out of hockey circles. Charles Lamothe was the captain of the Montreal Victorias in 1883, one of seven French-speaking players in the Montreal league at the time. In 1872, he won four skating competitions at the Victoria Rink, and was also a league lacrosse player in 1877 and 1878. But he was very much an exception to the rule.

Montreal's expansion at the turn of the century provided its growing francophone middle-class with money to spend and, on Saturdays, the leisure time to spend it. In 1895, the city's first francophone team, the Nationals, was formed, its players taught the game by Montreal's Irish-Catholics – the two groups having their Catholicism and their mutual distrust of the English in common. The Montagnards were born in 1898, but the two clubs never won the Stanley Cup, because they could not. They were never admitted to the

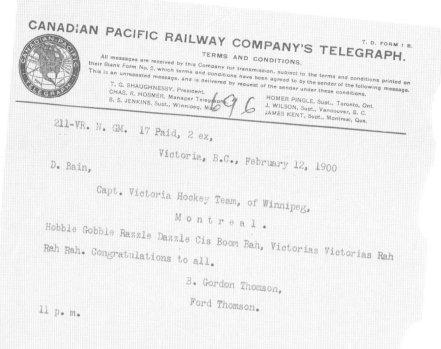

This telegram, congratulating the Winnipeg Victorias and their captain, Dan Bain, came after Winnipeg's victory in the first game of their Stanley Cup challenge against the Montreal Shamrocks in 1900. The cheers were premature, as the Shamrocks rallied to take the next two games, and keep the Cup in Montreal. Winnipeg successfully challenged the Shamrocks the following season to win their second Stanley Cup.

(*Hockey Hall of Fame*)

English leagues, such as the Amateur Hockey Association and the Canadian Amateur Hockey League, and so the prize remained out of reach.

Hockey had become a lucrative game for the "amateur" athletic clubs. The Montreal Amateur Athletic Association, nicknamed the "Little Men of Iron," earned a hearty average annual net profit of two thousand dollars from hockey revenue in rink fees and gate receipts. Gambling was also a source of revenue, with players and fans alike betting. There was none of the social opprobrium that later descended upon players who bet on their own sport – or any sport. And hockey was rampantly popular among all social classes. In the last decade of the nineteenth century, working men's clubs across Canada put teams on the ice, as did miners and barristers. Banks iced teams in bank leagues, partly to engage in friendly competition, partly to do business, as the *Dominion Illustrated Monthly* revealed in March 1893: "The Bankers of Toronto have taken the sport up, and have a league of their own. They have been playing systematically for the last four winters. . . . The Bankers' annual hockey dinner is one of the events of the season, when the Seniors and Juniors interchange convivial ideas on ice and drafts."

Women also played organized hockey. They had played the game on the pond for as long as men had, but they still faced social obstacles when they tried to arrange competition. In 1894, a Queen's University women's team angered a local cleric, who felt the women's desire to play hockey offended the divinely ordained universe. The women took his warning into consideration and called themselves the "Love-Me-Littles." They played in long skirts, which their stickhandlers used to conceal the puck and their goalies to stop it. By the turn of the twentieth century, there were women's hockey leagues in eastern universities and cities, on the Pacific in Vancouver, and as far north as Dawson City. They were also now rating newspaper coverage, one of the hallmarks of the process by which a game becomes a sport.

In February 1906, a reporter from the *Halifax Recorder* covered a match between women's teams from Windsor and Halifax, noting that the boys from King's College, Windsor, who turned out to cheer on their team gave Miss Handsombody college yells when she potted one for the side. Still, victory was not to be theirs: "The Halifax ladies rushed their opponents in the seconds, and soon Miss Edith Ritchie scored. She again rushed the puck down from the face-off, and quickly scored another. Windsor now made a gallant fight, and soon Miss Grace Smith evened the score. Miss E. Ritchie got the goal for Halifax, winning the game."

Nova Scotia, so critical to the origins and development of hockey in Canada, was also home to another pioneering ice-hockey league, again because the players had no other choice but to form their own. Nova Scotia's large black population – descended from Americans who came north during the War of Independence or to escape slavery – had its own Colored League, which iced teams against other black Maritime squads.

In February 1902, twelve hundred Haligonians crowded into the city's Empire Rink to see the West End Rangers, "the colored champions of P.E. Island" skate out in gold and black jerseys to take on the Africville Seasides, the champions of black Nova Scotia. The Seasides' and the Rangers' skill and finesse caused the *Halifax Recorder* to observe "there was not a person there who was not pleased that they were present to witness such a fine contest and such good sport." The account's surprised tone suggests the black teams were as good as those in the white leagues in which they were not allowed to play. When the Seasides' goalie, William Carvery, "stopped shot after shot," the reporter noted, "Even in the senior league better work would not be seen."

For all his admiration, the writer could not transcend the racist attitude that segregated Maritime hockey. The Seasides boasted three Carvery and three Dixon brothers, while the Rangers had four Mills brothers, of whom he felt compelled to note: "Under ordinary circumstances, it would be impossible to distinguish the players, but with a quartette [*sic*] of Mills on one team and a trio of Carverys, and the same of Dixons, it was all the more difficult."

The Seasides won the match 3–2, but two nights later the visiting P.E.I. Rangers defeated the Halifax Eurekas 2–1. After the game, the Eurekas hosted the Rangers at their club on Halifax's Creighton Street. The next day, it was reported that the Rangers "spoke in glowing terms of the treatment they received in Halifax, and hoped next season to again visit our city."

It was a scene of fellowship in stark counterpoint to the sentiment of a "Prince Edward Island poet" in his un-nuanced verse about the Rangers' special skills when compared to other Maritime teams, published in the *Halifax Recorder*: "It's all very well to talk about the Abbies; / And it's all very well to talk about the Vics; / But for tough old hockey fightin' / The kind we take delight in, / Yer orter see the Rangers use their sticks." The verse spoke of an unpleasant truth about hockey. An ancillary effect of speed and the heat of competition, violence by now sometimes seemed to be the game's *raison d'être*.

One Montreal newspaper described hockey as "a saturnalia of butchery," with brawling not limited to the ice, but breaking out among fans, and between players and fans. In 1886, the first game ever played for the title

The racism of the Victorian era meant that, to play competitively, black hockey players in Canada had to start their own hockey league: the Colored Hockey League of the Maritimes, formed in 1900. Ironically, league games regularly attracted more white fans than "white" league games did, but even so, no trophy commemorates the championship of the Colored League. In 1921, the championship was won by the West End Rangers from Charlottetown, PEI, who were famous for their exciting, rushing style of hockey. (*Black Islanders, Jim Hornby, Institute of Studies, 1990*)

Dominion Champions was a vicious and bloody affair. The fighting and stick-work claimed so many casualties that the visiting team from Quebec City had to forfeit the match when it couldn't field enough healthy players to finish the game. The Montreal Crystals, by virtue of having more men standing, won the title by default.

In 1905, a French-Canadian player named Alcide Laurin was killed by a stick blow to the head. Witnesses told police that nineteen-year-old Allan Loney from Maxville, Ontario, had swung the stick, and Loney was charged with manslaughter. But when the case went to trial, according to Wayne Scanlan in *Grace Under Fire*, the prosecutor, in a refrain that sounds startlingly current, said that Allan Loney stood in the dock with a co-accused: "Not only is the prisoner at the bar on trial, but the game of hockey itself is on trial."

As if to prove the prosecution's point, Loney's lawyer argued that he had acted in self-defence, and that Laurin's death was accidental. The jury made its decision in four hours, and the Montreal *Gazette* reported the foreman's unsentimental message to the court, to the sport, and to the nation: "We cannot too strongly condemn the increasingly brutal methods and roughness associated with the game of hockey," he said. "We believe that unless these growing tendencies can be permanently eliminated from these games, they should be prohibited by the Legislature and put on a par with bull fights and cock-fighting." Despite the hard words, the jury found Loney not guilty.

Two years later, hockey violence was as bad as ever, if not worse. After a particularly vicious game in Richmond, Quebec, in 1907, a *La Presse* reporter chronicled the bloody aftermath between the teams and their five hundred fans: "They beat on each other with hockey sticks, planks ripped from the boards around the rink, chunks of ice . . . everything became a weapon. . . . About 20 people were knocked down, unconscious and bathed in blood." The mayor of Richmond banned hockey for the rest of the season.

Had the sport been shocked into a reflection – or stringent self-policing – then perhaps a far greater shock across the river in Cornwall, Ontario, would have been prevented a month later on March 6, 1907, when things turned ugly during a match between the Cornwall Hockey Club and the Ottawa Victorias. "The most rough and tumble play ever seen in Cornwall," reported the *Gazette*. "Tripping, slashing and cross-checking was rampant in the first half. And the second half was hardly started when there was a regular donnybrook."

Owen McCourt, a twenty-three-year-old scoring wizard with Cornwall, staggered from the melee, bleeding from the head. He was carried from the rink, and the referee, a local man named Barney Quinn, followed. Two days later, the *Ottawa Citizen* quoted Quinn: "When I went into the dressing room to see him after he had gone off, I saw him lying on the slab where his wounds were being sewn up and he seemed to suffer greatly. So I told the [Cornwall captain] not to let him go out on the ice again."

McCourt would never go out on the ice again. He slipped into a coma and died the morning after the game. Cornwall police arrested Ottawa player Charles Masson, and charged him with manslaughter. A coroner's jury ruled that McCourt had been killed by a blow to the head from a hockey stick, and in a revealing observation about the way the game was played, said that he had not provoked "the blow at the hands of the said Charles Masson," adding, "After hearing the evidence, your jury further recommends that legislation be enacted whereby players or spectators encouraging or engaging in rough or foul play must be severely punished."

Masson's manslaughter trial made headlines around the country, but the evidence presented was confused and contradictory. Even Owen McCourt's mother argued that his death had been an accident, telling a reporter from *La Presse*, "What is the point of this process? Masson never intended to kill or wound my son, and if poor Owen was here, he would say the same thing."

The jury agreed and acquitted Masson. Indeed, they couldn't reckon which blow had killed McCourt – there had been so many. Hockey had been characterized, in the sober arena of the courtroom, as a sport in need of help from the law to prevent manslaughter from becoming an integral part of the game, and to punish those who transgressed. It would be a problem, and a refrain, for the next century.

While the sport had found itself in trouble with the law, the Stanley Cup managed to transcend the courts, remaining an unsullied beacon of hope and glory and good box office, much as it is today. The Cup represented all that was good about hockey, for to win it, you had to be the best. But you didn't have to be the best to compete for it.

In the early years of the new century, the most fanciful challenge to Lord Stanley's prize came from the land of gold: the Yukon.

Life had calmed somewhat in Dawson City since the gold rush of the late 1890s. The realization that the streets would never be paved with gold had sunk home for many of those in Dawson, and the consequent culling of the prospectors and dreamers, the hucksters and whores, brought order to the town, and winter sport flourished. As winter there lasted six months, and as a rich pool of potential talent had been drawn there by gold, Dawson City was prime hockey territory. Sophisticated prime hockey territory. There were four clubs in the Dawson Hockey League: one from the North-West Mounted Police,

The discovery of gold in 1896 turned a fishing village at the confluence of the Dawson and Yukon rivers into a boom-town. The first house was built in September 1896, and five hundred more were thrown up within the next six months. When miners bearing sacks of Yukon gold arrived in San Francisco in July 1897, another gold stampede began, and thirty thousand prospectors headed north. In the space of a few months, Dawson City exploded into the largest city west of Winnipeg, boasting the latest mod cons – telephone service, running water, and steam heat. And, at the dawn of the new century, hockey came to town. (*H.J. Woodside, Library and Archives Canada, PA-016239*)

one from the civil service, another from the Amateur Athletic Association, and one from the general population, the Eagles.

In 1902, the Dawson Athletic Club announced that it would build a covered arena. It would be state-of-the-art, powered by electricity, with hot-water pipes for flooding the rink laid above ground, inside wood casing, and insulated with manure. There would be a clubhouse, with training and dressing rooms, as well as showers, lounges, and a dining room.

The man at the centre of Dawson City's hockey world was Joseph Whiteside Boyle, one of Canada's most colourful swashbucklers. By the time he was thirty, Boyle had made his first million from prospecting, and was expanding his empire, shrewdly buying timber concessions, for trees grow slowly in the Yukon and wood's value to the mining community was almost as great as gold's, as it was used in the construction of everything from buildings and mine shafts to railways and for fuel. And for hockey rinks.

As one of Dawson's leading citizens, Boyle was behind the construction of Dawson's rink, and he managed one of the town's hockey teams. Business frequently took him to Ottawa, and it was on one of these trips that one of the more fantastic plans in hockey's Canadian odyssey took form. Boyle

Joseph Whiteside Boyle

Dawson City's hockey entrepreneur was a Confederation baby, born in Toronto on November 6, 1867, and sport was in his blood, as his father bred, trained, and raced thoroughbred horses in Woodstock, Ontario, and later in New Jersey and New York State. After graduating from Woodstock College in 1884, Boyle headed straight for New York City to work with his father and brothers, but the sport of kings wasn't fast enough for Boyle, and at age seventeen, he left Manhattan for a life at sea.

Joe Boyle sailed the globe, surviving tropical storms, and once fighting off a shark with a knife. He could also play any stringed instrument he picked up, and he touched hearts with his fine baritone voice. Back on land, Boyle first tried to mine the riches that could be made boxing, and at six feet and two hundred pounds, he was a natural, but instead of fighting, he had his eye on the gate and became a boxing promoter, lining up the talent and setting up venues. It was boxing that in the summer of 1897 took him, at age twenty-nine, to Juneau, Alaska, for an exhibition fight just as the Klondike gold rush was taking off. Boyle took up a lease on forty square miles of land along the Klondike River and had a stick pin made from the first gold nugget he mined. (*Woodstock Library*)

decided he would assemble an all-star team from Dawson City and, in December of 1904, transport them 6,500 kilometres across the country to challenge Ottawa for the Stanley Cup.

Joe Boyle's Dawson City Nuggets were advertised as an "all-star elite." Surprisingly, the hyperbole contained some small truth. Weldy Young, a civil servant who had played for Ottawa from 1893 to 1899 (and was the boyhood idol of a future star, Lester Patrick), was captain and coach, and Dr. D.R. McLennan, who worked for the territorial administration, had played rover for the Queen's University team in an 1895 Stanley Cup challenge against the Montreal Victorias. But that was it. Norman Watt, George "Sureshot" Kennedy, and Hec Smith, who had all come to Dawson in search of a fortune in 1898, would now try their fortunes again as the left-winger, right-winger, and centre respectively of the hockey prospectors. J.K. Johnstone, a former Mountie who worked in the post office, played point; and cover point Lorne Hannay would be picked up at the station when the Nuggets' train passed through his home-town of Brandon, Manitoba. Archie Martin, who worked in Boyle's timber operation was the spare man and trainer, and Quebec native Albert Forrest, just seventeen years old, was the Nuggets' man in goal. They would be testing their gold-dusted selves against the most glittering team of Canada's hockey elite: the Ottawa "Silver Seven" and their golden boy, Frank McGee.

The centre and rover for the Ottawa Senators (nicknamed the Silver Seven) was Frank McGee (back row, far right), an Ottawa aristocrat. Frank's father, John, was Clerk of the Privy Council, and his uncle, Thomas D'Arcy McGee, was one of the Fathers of Confederation and also Canada's first victim of political assassination when he was shot by a gunman from the Irish "liberation movement," the Fenians, in 1868.

McGee was tough and fast and fearless, earning this assessment from no less an authority than Frank Patrick, who made his hockey debut for the Montreal Victorias in 1904 on his way to becoming one of hockey's guiding geniuses: "He was even better than they said he was. He had everything – speed, stickhandling, scoring ability and he was a punishing checker. He was strongly built but beautifully proportioned, and he had almost an animal rhythm. When he walked around the dressing room you could see his muscles ripple. They weren't the blacksmith's muscles either. They were the long muscles of the great athlete. You don't see many like him."

(A. Podnieks et al., *Kings of the Ice*) (*Library and Archives Canada/Thomas Patrick Gorman collection, PA-091046*)

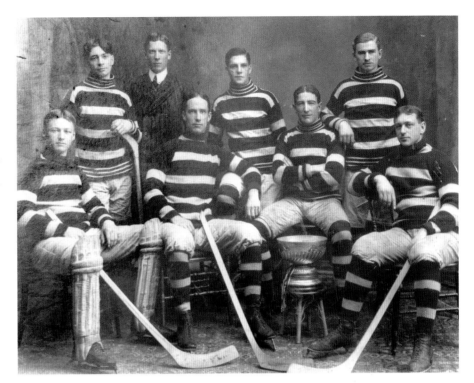

McGee has been called hockey's first real star, and while the jury is out on whether he was first (as the professional league then nascent in the United States featured superstars of its own), McGee's hockey supremacy is undisputed. A brilliant athlete, what made McGee even more remarkable as a player was that he had only one eye, having sacrificed the other to hockey. On March 21, 1900, in Hawkesbury, Ontario, during an exhibition game to raise money for Canada's effort in the Boer War, McGee took a nasty blow to his left eye from an opponent's stick. The rink was small and dark, lit by three coal oil lamps, and so initial newspaper reports erred when they said he had only been cut over the eye. Later that year, it became clear that McGee's injury was much worse than a cut, and in January 1901, the *Ottawa Citizen* wrote his hockey obituary: "The team will be short one glistening star in the person of Frank McGee, whose hockey ability was known and admired by everyone who saw him play."

The one-eyed McGee retired to a job where perfect vision clearly wasn't necessary: he became a referee. But it only made him miss playing, and so, putting his remaining eye at considerable risk, given the propensity for stick-swinging melees in the early sport, he came back to play hockey.

During the next five years, McGee led the Ottawa Senators to their first Stanley Cup, in 1903, and to the successful defence of it on an unprecedented ten consecutive occasions. The Senators left a map of Canada's expanding hockey landscape in their wake as they defeated the Rat Portage Thistles, the

Winnipeg Rowing Club, the Toronto Marlboros, the Brandon Wheat Kings, and the Montreal Wanderers en route to winning their nickname the Silver Seven as the finest team in the land.

McGee became the enemy of goaltenders everywhere, thanks to his instinct for putting the puck in the net, which led to superlative statistics such as twenty-one goals in eight Stanley Cup playoff games in 1904, and eighteen during four games in 1906. But it was his performance against the Dawson City Nuggets in January 1905 that enshrined McGee in hockey lore and Canadian mythology.

The Nuggets arrived in Ottawa two days before their match, which was ominously scheduled for Friday, January 13, 1905. They had been on the road – or rather, on bicycle, foot, train, boat, and train again – since December 19, 1904, making the trek from Dawson City to Skagway, then down to Vancouver and by train across the country. They had been bedevilled by the weather, though not as one might expect: in the Yukon, the weather had been so warm that the team didn't have any ice to practise on. Yukoners, looking for an explanation for Nature's caprice, blamed the artillery barrages from the war between China and Russia.

The warm spell also left the roads a muddy mess, so the Nuggets soon abandoned their bicycles and shouldered their gear for the walk to Whitehorse, nearly five hundred kilometres away, poignantly spending Christmas in a police shed eighty kilometres short of their destination as a blizzard raged outside. More blizzards delayed their passage to Skagway at the foot of the White Pass, and they missed their ship to Vancouver by a demoralizing two hours; the next ship, the S.S. *Dolphin* was rocked by heavy seas all the way to Vancouver, where fog stopped it from docking. It was fogged out again in Victoria, and so the ship headed south to Seattle, where the Nuggets boarded a train to take them back to Vancouver to catch the transcontinental to Ottawa.

Joe Boyle had planned a meticulous schedule for his team, and now they were perilously late – five days behind schedule – and exhausted. Boyle, who was on business in Detroit, was planning to join the team in Ottawa, leaving the players to keep in shape as their train made the final leg of their extraordinary journey. So the Nuggets trained en route in a specially outfitted rail car, and did wind sprints on station platforms as they whistle-stopped their way across the country, cheered onward by the curious and chronicled in the nation's press.

The *Ottawa Citizen* had reported the Nuggets' departure by saying: "The Dawson City hockey team left Dawson yesterday . . . to win fame and the Stanley Cup. They feel confident they can wrest the trophy from the eastern teams and

The Dawson City Nuggets pose with their creator and manager Joseph Boyle, in Ottawa in 1905. Boyle formed the Nuggets out of Yukon hockey all-stars, partly as proof that quality hockey was being played in Canada's Far North, but mainly as a way to make a tidy profit from the novelty of having the team travel thousands of miles to challenge the mighty Ottawa Silver Seven for the Stanley Cup silver. Though the Nuggets were unsentimentally walloped by Ottawa, their epic quest captured headlines across the country, and goalie Albert Forrest, just seventeen years old, was praised for his play in net.

(Glenbow Museum)

bring it back with them to glitter amid the ice and snowclad hills of the Golden North." The paper's correspondent in Vancouver reported the Nuggets' arrival there rather unenthusiastically, saying only that the players "were in pretty good condition," but the Montreal *Gazette* reminded its readers that the "Dawson hockey team state their challenge for the Stanley Cup is no joke."

Late on the afternoon of January 11, 1905, the Nuggets arrived in Ottawa. The *Citizen* reported on January 8, "On account of the delays and hard luck, the team will ask for a postponement of the first game for three or four days in order to get into condition." They asked and the answer was no. Governor General Earl Grey would "face" the puck as scheduled at 8:30 p.m. on Friday, January 13.

Joe Boyle caught up with his men on the morning of the twelfth, and they had every reason to be disheartened. Their captain, Weldy Young, had been detained on election duty back in the Yukon. The team was unused to their new uniforms and gear. Dey's Rink in Ottawa was twenty-five feet longer than the one they played in back home. And they were bone weary after their twenty-four-day quest for the Stanley Cup. Still, those who witnessed their morning practice saw the Nuggets go through a "swift limbering up workout," according to the *Citizen*, which added that those in the know – or those with an interest in the gate, perhaps – regarded the Klondikers as "one of the most dangerous teams yet sent after the cup."

That night, Frank McGee and his Silver Seven treated the Nuggets to a banquet at the Ottawa Amateur Athletic Club and gave the visitors honorary membership for as long as they were in town. It was the feast before the slaughter.

To the 2,200 people who crowded into Dey's Rink that Friday, the Nuggets looked good in their smart black sweaters trimmed with gold, but the Silver Seven looked better as their red, black, and white uniforms were the familiar colours of Stanley Cup champions.

The Nuggets played hard for the opening third of the match, and were trailing only 3–1 when halftime was called at thirty minutes. But in the second half all hell broke loose, with a stick-swinging duel between Dawson's Norman Watt and Ottawa's Alf Moore, earning each of them a fifteen-minute banishment to cool down – in these early years of the game, the referee could send players off the ice for however long he thought their offence merited. When the match was over, Dawson City was on the wrong end of a 9–2 loss, despite goalie Albert Forrest's complaint that at least six Ottawa goals were offside.

The prolific goal scorer Frank McGee had managed only one goal against the Nuggets, and one Yukon player ventured, aloud, that McGee didn't seem anything like the greatest goal scorer in the game. So, in the second match of the series, Frank McGee responded by leaving his hospitality rinkside and barraged the Nuggets' net. His achievement still stands – and probably always will – as a single-game record for a Stanley Cup match: fourteen goals, eight of them in an eight-minute-and-twenty-second onslaught.

In its report of Ottawa's 23–2 humiliation of the Klondikers, the *Citizen* made special mention of goalie Albert Forrest, whose ability in the net against McGee's scoring orgy prevented even greater embarrassment. "The only man on the Dawson team who played a really fine game of hockey was Forrest, who in goal gave as fine an exhibition as the most exacting could desire. But for him Ottawa's figures might have been doubled."

The *Toronto Telegram*, though, couldn't resist raining on the remarkable feat of both Forrest and McGee, sneering that the Yukon team was "hockey junk," the likes of which had never been seen "to come over the rails of the CPR." The insult didn't matter to Ottawa, who had retained the Stanley Cup. After a well-oiled victory banquet, they celebrated by drop-kicking hockey's greatest prize into the Rideau Canal, which, luckily, was frozen solid at the time.

Joe Boyle, who had been filing dispatches to the Dawson *Daily News*, explained the Nuggets' loss as the consequence of being worn down by the first game, and of being "in no condition to play in such a game as was put up against them." To recoup ten thousand dollars' worth of investors' money,

The Dawsons and the Victorias womens' hockey teams pose in the Dawson Amateur Athletic Association Rink in April 1904. Dawson's rink was state-of-the-art: powered by electricity, with insulated hot water pipes to prevent freezing, a clubhouse, training and dressing rooms, showers and lounges, and a dining room. Dawson's modern rink, its men's and women's teams, and its strong contingent of fans reveal the rapid progress of hockey as Canada's national winter sport. *(Library and Archives Canada, NA-2883-31)*

Boyle took the Nuggets, with captain Weldy Young finally back in the squad, on a barnstorming tour from Cape Breton to Manitoba, playing matches – and actually winning some. Then it was spring, and the thaw forced cancellation of further matches on the Prairies and in British Columbia. The team dispersed in Brandon. Only Albert Forrest went back to Dawson City, having a lot of time to reflect on his extraordinary adventure as he made the long walk in from Whitehorse. Alone.

Just why the Stanley Cup's Trustees ever agreed to this whimsical challenge isn't known, though Joe Boyle did have a tight connection with journalist, former Rideau Rebel, and now Stanley Cup Trustee, P.D. Ross. Perhaps it was just that, combined with the chance to make some money and to raise some much-needed publicity for the championship. There were healthy box-office receipts from the two matches, and the series captured national attention at a time when the game's code of amateurism was threatened by a development in the United States: a professional league that began in 1904. Canadian players were flocking south of the border to play pro, and it could be that the Stanley Cup's Trustees used the madcap series to redirect public attention to the sport at home.

The Dawson City challenge lit up the staggering difference in skill among teams playing the game at the most senior level, and the trustees tightened up the rules after Dawson City's adventure. Now, any team that wished to take on the reigning Cup champs would have to have proven their ability to do so against established teams. Never again would an unknown and untested hockey crew step off a train after an epic transcontinental journey and take on the best in the country.

Lord Stanley's opinions on the Dawson City challenge have not been left to us. He never saw a game played for his prize, having returned to England upon the death of his brother in the spring of 1893 to become the 16th Earl of Derby. It seems likely, though, that he would have approved, for the Nuggets' quest was the stuff of myth – the kind of myth a big, young country needs to understand itself.

The challenges that the Dawson City crew received on their post-Cup tour show just how far the game had come in the twelve short years since Lord Stanley had endowed his prize. Teams in Saskatchewan, Alberta, and British Columbia all felt confident that they, too, could take an honourable crack at the team that took a crack at the Ottawa Senators, the only thing preventing them being quintessentially Canadian: the thaw.

The Ottawa Silver Seven were eventually stopped when the Montreal Wanderers ended their remarkable dynasty in 1906. Frank McGee retired in the early winter of 1906, aged twenty-five, and took a job in the Interior Department of the federal government.

Joe Boyle continued cutting an epic swath through the world. He was a British intelligence agent in Russia during the First World War, setting up a network to resist the Germans. During the Russian Revolution, he helped save members of the Russian royal family from the Bolsheviks, aided many refugees, set up relief operations, and found time to win the heart of Queen Marie of Romania.

And hockey was about to go through a major revolution of its own. Though still a nominally amateur affair in Canada, players had been paid under the table for several years as both they and club managers realized the lucrative power of this distinctly Canadian winter sport. And, early in the new century, J.L. "Doc" Gibson, a young dentist from Berlin, Ontario, had taken the game across the border. Thanks to his talent and the Americans' money, hockey was about to become more than an amateur sport in pursuit of Lord Stanley's silverware. Now, there would be gold in the game, too.

CHAPTER 2

GOLD AFTER SILVER

It was a prize too good to pass up: a new pair of five-dollar skates at a time when five dollars was the weekly wage at the local piano factory. Fred Taylor coveted those skates, and he knew a thing or two about skating. So fast that he was nicknamed the Whirlwind, the fourteen-year-old Taylor regularly brought hockey-mad crowds to their feet with his spectacular play in the new arena of Listowel, Ontario. And now, in the winter of 1900, he had his chance to get some new blades on his quick feet. All he had to do was beat an American speed skater in a quarter-mile race at the local arena – with the American, Norval Baptie, skating backward.

Baptie was born in Bethany, Ontario, but moved to North Dakota with his family as an infant, and by the time he was ten, he was winning skating races – giving the first prize he won, five dollars, to his mother. Four years later, he was racing the Great Northern Train on a frozen ditch alongside the rails. And now, at age twenty-one, he had set so many speed-skating records and had won so many races that there was only one thing to do: make his talent his profession.

So Baptie made barnstorming tours of Canada and the United States, competing for the "entertainment" dollar with travelling minstrels and nickelodeon shows by putting on a show himself, one that would eventually evolve into the Ice Capades. "The show consisted of seven acts," Baptie said later. "First I would help the ticket taker at the gate. Then I would loosen up with an exhibition of speed skating just to get some of the 20 below weather out of my bones. Then I would jump a few barrels. Then I would take on some local lights in an exhibition of speed at any distance they preferred."

Taylor, the brightest of the local lights, later recalled that while he was in awe of Baptie – "the first world champion of any kind that we'd ever seen" – he was also "pretty fast" himself. Baptie got a thirty-foot head start, and before the two skaters had made two turns of the rink, Taylor had figured out how he was going to lose. "Each time I'd get close enough to pass, he'd swing out just enough to block me off, just a little shift and a subtle move of the hips," he recalled in Eric Whitehead's splendid biography of his life, *Cyclone Taylor: A Hockey Legend*. "Right away, I began to appreciate the art of skating backwards. The trick wasn't the speed but the balance and maneuverability. Right then and there, I told myself I was going to learn to become as good at it as he was."

Taylor had also learned more than that. He had seen first-hand how this world champion had used his superlative talent – and his canniness – to make a buck. And Taylor soon would become known as a canny talent who liked to make a buck. The problem for players such as the "Whirlwind" from Listowel, in turn-of-the-twentieth-century Canada, was that they couldn't make a penny from playing hockey. The codes surrounding Canada's amateur athletic clubs had been forged in the smithy of British Victorian idealism – one owned by the upper class, which could afford to engage in sport solely for the honour of competition and for the love of the game. At least on paper.

Canada's workers were increasingly living in cities, and their leisure time was something they chose how to spend. If they wanted to play hockey, they could join an organized athletic league befitting their social station – such as the bank tellers' or coal miners' hockey leagues – or they could spend some of their wage on watching hockey. There was no shortage of people who would pay to see the best play, for this fast, rough, beautiful game was heat itself in the Canadian winter.

First Artificial Ice in the United States

The first ice rink featuring mechanically refrigerated, artificial ice was built in 1876, in London, England, in the fashionable Chelsea district, and was called the Glaciarium. In 1894, Baltimore opened the first artificial ice rink in the United States, and by the turn of the twentieth century, there were artificial ice arenas in Philadelphia, Pittsburgh, and Boston. The technology was ingenious but simple: water pipes beneath the surface would flood the rink, and then a cooling fluid pumped through the pipes froze the water. The most spectacular artificial ice rink was the St. Nicholas Rink, in Manhattan, built in the late 1890s, its three-hundred-thousand-dollar tab paid for by New York financial titans such as the Vanderbilts, the Astors, the Choates, and the Morgans. The seventy-five-foot-high ice palace, built of ornamented brick, boasted a spectators' gallery, clubrooms, a grill-room and restaurant, but its main attraction was its sixteen thousand square feet of ice.

(*Private collection: Tom Sorra*)

Now that the game had been roofed and ruled, and a hierarchy of excellence, trophies, and teams had developed, Canada's amateur athletic associations were enjoying the money they made from charging admission to games in the rinks they owned. Amateur players might be given new skates or silver nuggets for playing, but these gifts were gilded with the righteousness of the amateur ideal, and were not in any way payment, because gentlemen did not take money for playing sport. It was a nakedly hypocritical sentiment at a time when ice showmen such as Baptie could book a rink and tease a local amateur with a five-dollar pair of skates and then leave with a percentage of the gate. But Canada's rink owners saw hockey as a golden goose and were certain that the surest way to kill it would be to pay the players.

Such was the power of the men behind the amateur hockey associations that they could twist the code to consolidate their power and enrich themselves. Fred Taylor found this out the hard way when he tried to put money in front of hockey, though it was money that he would be losing if he obeyed William Hewitt's command to come to Toronto and play for the Marlboroughs.

William "Billy" Hewitt, a Toronto newspaperman (and father of Foster, the future first voice of *Hockey Night in Canada*), was the powerful secretary of the Ontario Hockey Association. Word of Taylor's hockey prowess had reached Toronto, after Taylor had gone to Detroit, Michigan, in the winter of 1902–3 to visit friends from Listowel who were studying dentistry there, and

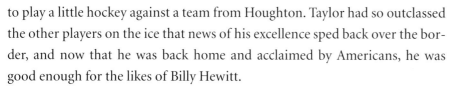

Louis Hurtubise and Louis Viau

By January 1902, the Shamrocks, an Irish Montreal team, had already won two Stanley Cups. Now, in the face of a game against the new champions, the Ottawa Silver Seven, the Shamrocks enlisted two French Canadians, forward Louis Hurtubise (left) and defenceman Louis Viau (right), graduates of Montreal's francophone hockey powerhouse, Collège Ste-Marie, and star players with the Montagnards. After the Shamrocks won, the francophone press were ecstatic: "Étonnant! Les champions battus par les Shamrocks," wrote *La Presse* on January 13. "Il fallait la présence de deux Canadiens-français pour en arriver à cette fin!" (Astonishing! The champions beaten by the Shamrocks. It took the presence of two French Canadians to do it!). (*McCord Museum*)

to play a little hockey against a team from Houghton. Taylor had so outclassed the other players on the ice that news of his excellence sped back over the border, and now that he was back home and acclaimed by Americans, he was good enough for the likes of Billy Hewitt.

Taylor later said, "I was flattered and I wanted to go. After all, it was my chance to move up into big-time hockey, but then I had second thoughts." Thoughts about money. The Marlies were offering glory, and Taylor liked the prospect of that, but it would come at a price: his job in the Morris piano factory in Listowel added twenty dollars a month to the seventy-five dollars his father brought in, so Taylor's departure for Toronto would hurt his parents and four siblings. He said no.

Hewitt was not the kind of man who was used to hearing the word *no* from hockey players, especially those out in the sticks. He gave Taylor another chance to correct his mistake, but Taylor again refused. So Hewitt showed the fist beneath the glove of hockey's genteel amateur code and told Taylor "If you won't play for the Marlies, then you won't play anywhere." He meant it. When Taylor tried to test the ban by playing in Thessalon, a town just south of Sault Ste. Marie, and far from Listowel, Billy Hewitt found out and ratcheted up the pressure by promising to ban any team in the OHA that gave the apostate Taylor refuge, unless, of course, it was the Toronto Marlboroughs. The most promising player in Ontario was effectively bullied out of provincial play at age eighteen.

Ernie "Moose" Johnson began his long pro career in 1905 as a nineteen-year-old with the Montreal Wanderers and finished it in 1931 with the San Francisco Tigers. Along the way, the left-winger took advantage of early hockey's silence on the matter of stick-length, and gave himself a 2.5-metre reach. He won eight Stanley Cups with the Montreal Wanderers, then was lured west in 1911 to play the inaugural season of the new Pacific Coast league. When he retired from the Victoria Aristocrats in 1922, he claimed that they buried his stick.

(Hockey Hall of Fame)

Taylor sat out for a year and hated it. Ever since he had first gone skating as a five-year-old with the town's barber, a speed skater named Jack Riggs, on the river of his hometown of Tara, Ontario, Taylor knew the ice belonged to him. And so, in the winter of 1905, he did the very thing that Hewitt had tried to make him do: he left home to play hockey. But the stubborn Taylor wasn't going to let Hewitt win. He left home for Manitoba, out of the OHA's reach, to play in Portage la Prairie. And once Taylor had tasted life in the great beyond, he was unstoppable.

Though Portage la Prairie was not much bigger than Listowel, its hockey team played in the Manitoba Hockey League, which, with the formidable player and hockey innovator Art Ross playing for the Brandon Elks, and Si Griffis and Tom Phillips playing for Rat Portage, just across the border in Ontario, was just one of several amateur leagues competing for talent. The Federal Amateur Hockey League featured Edouard "Newsy" Lalonde in Cornwall, while the Eastern Canada Amateur Hockey Association starred Russell Bowie and the ninety-nine-inch poke-checking reach of Ernie "Moose" Johnson, who had played for the Montreal AAA of the Canadian Amateur Hockey League in 1904–5, before moving to the ECAHA the following season.

In his first game for Portage la Prairie, Taylor quickly showed that his year away from the game had not harmed his natural talent, scoring two goals against Winnipeg and following that up with three goals against the Rat Portage Thistles, who touted that they were the fastest team in hockey. After the game, Thistles stars Si Griffis and Tommy Phillips waited for Taylor outside his dressing room and invited him out to a local café. There they made him an offer he could scarcely believe. A year ago, Taylor was *persona non grata* in

Ernie "Moose" Johnson
Reach 99 inches
Portland Hockey Team
1914-15

Photo by
Woodruff & Raymond

Ontario hockey. Now an Ontario team was inviting him to join their challenge for the Stanley Cup in Montreal against the mighty Wanderers, champions of the Federal Amateur Hockey League in 1904, who were now gunning for their first Cup.

But the day before he was about to catch the train to Montreal to play for hockey's greatest prize, Fred Taylor got an ominous phone call from a sheriff in Michigan, who had a long memory. Taylor was a wanted man, and there was a bounty involved: four hundred dollars plus expenses, promised John McNaughton, Sheriff of Houghton County, Michigan, and manager of the Portage Lake hockey team. All Taylor had to do to earn it was join his team for the rest of the season and beat their rivals Pittsburgh for the championship of the International Hockey League. A professional hockey team in a professional league.

Taylor thought about it. The Stanley Cup was silver, and this was gold. Taylor changed his train ticket. Hockey would never be the same.

The International Hockey League, the world's first professional league, was also the product of Canadian amateur hockey hypocrisy, one that cut deeply into the psyche of a young Ontario hockey star named Jack Gibson.

Gibson was thirteen years old in 1893 when hockey made its debut in his hometown of Berlin, Ontario, and he was of that breed of athletes common a century ago who excelled at many sports. In 1897–98 he won the Western Ontario half-mile and five-mile single sculls rowing title; the half-mile, mile, and five-mile skating and swimming championships; and he also starred at lacrosse and football and played a mean game of soccer.

When it came to hockey, the six-foot, two-hundred-pound Gibson commanded the ice at point (defence), delivering such clean bodychecks that even his opponents had to admire him as he skated away after levelling them. He personified the amateur ideal, and in the winter of 1898, he was punished for it.

When Gibson's Berlin team shut out their archrivals from Waterloo 3–0, Berlin's proud mayor rewarded Gibson and his teammates – including the sons of the Seagram distillery family – with gold pieces as trophies. The Eastern Ontario Amateur Hockey Association viewed this as the thin end of the professional wedge and suspended the entire Berlin team for the rest of the season for "taking money," even though the team protested that they were going to have the coins converted into watch fobs.

The experience embittered Gibson. You could pay to watch games, and you could wager large amounts of money on them, but you were damned if your hockey trophy could be spent. Gibson took the memory of this insult with him to the United States, where he studied dentistry in Detroit. By 1902,

John L. "Doc" Gibson, a multi-sport star in his hometown of Berlin, Ontario, is arguably the founder of professional hockey. In 1904, Gibson, a dentist practising in the mining country of northwest Michigan, and local businessmen formed the International Hockey League – the world's first professional hockey league. (*Doon Heritage Crossroads, Regional Municipality of Waterloo, Kitchener, Ontario*)

he was a dentist in Houghton, a town in the copper country of Michigan on the southern shore of Lake Superior, where the winter winds were so cold that the region was jokingly referred to as the Canada of the United States – the place with two seasons: winter's here and winter's coming.

At the turn of the century, Houghton was a mining boomtown. Ten trains a day called there en route to Chicago or Minneapolis, Milwaukee or Detroit. The hundred thousand people who called Houghton County home could read twenty local newspapers in four languages, send their children to any one of thirty schools, find God in thirty churches – or more than sixty bars – and spend their leisure time sampling the cultural offerings of the seven theatres and two opera houses in Houghton and Calumet, a town ten miles up the road.

James R. Dee saw the possibility of making money in Houghton County, not from the copper mines but by mining the miners. He was thinking of the money that could come from hockey. Dee was a local businessman who hadn't paid much attention to the sport until Jack "Doc" Gibson hung out his dentist's shingle and became a pillar of the Houghton community: a member of three fraternal orders, of the Light Infantry of the Michigan National Guard, and the local football team. Gibson also captained the county at bowling and had organized the Portage Lake Hockey Club, named after the lake that separated Houghton from the nearby town of Hancock. In what was possibly an act of both sentimentality and revenge, Gibson's Portage Lakers wore the same green and white colours of his old Berlin team, and they were good at winning. The 1902–3 Portage Lake team didn't lose a single game, and by the end of the season, they were the United States champion.

James Dee was smitten with the sport and saw huge potential in the Portage Lakers. A group of local businessmen headed by Dee formed the Houghton Warehouse Company, and in the fall of 1901 began building a new indoor arena that could hold thousands and showcase, among other things, the hockey talents of Doc Gibson and his Portage Lake squad. The arena was completed early the following year and named the Amphidrome in a contest that awarded the winner a gold coin. The Houghton *Mining Gazette* was suitably impressed by the new arena, reporting that, outside of Pittsburgh, Brooklyn, and New York, "there is not a rink or hockey business in the United States run on as high a scale as that of Mr. Dee."

It's worth noting that the Houghton newspaper compared this new multipurpose arena to others in the United States, not to those in Canada. And while Doc Gibson would soon go on a recruiting jag across the border to woo some of Canada's greatest players, ice skating and hockey were no strangers to the United States. Indeed, the morning after James Creighton's historic game in Montreal nearly three decades earlier, the Montreal *Gazette* had remarked,

"The game of hockey, though much in vogue on the ice in New England and other parts of the United States, is not much known here."

While Canadians may well claim hockey as a national treasure, the patterns of colonization and immigration in the eighteenth and nineteenth centuries saw ball-and-stick games merge with ice skating on both sides of the border. In 1783, a British Army colonel based in New York City reported a group of skaters "bearing down in a body in pursuit of the ball driven before them by their hurlies," and by the time Doc Gibson and James Dee had joined forces, ice polo – which had gone south with the Acadians when they were expelled from Canada in 1755 – had become something of an American phenomenon.

Such was the popularity of ice polo that New York City built a swank new indoor rink in 1895 to showcase it and other ice games. When it opened, the St. Nicholas Rink was the largest artificial-ice arena of its kind in the world, though its manager Frank Swift made clear to the *New York Times* that the rink's sixteen thousand square feet of synthetic ice was not for everyone: "We expect to start the season briskly with polo games. Teams from most of the larger colleges will compete, although a definite schedule has not been made. The class of patrons we expect is very select, and we intend to keep it so. I have advised the raising of the admission fee from 75 cents to $1. This will prevent an undesirable crowd gaining access to the ice without financial loss."

An enclosed rink at 107th Street and Lexington Avenue, the Ice Palace, had opened just before the St. Nicholas Rink, but St. Nick's was a club, open to the public from Tuesday through Saturday but reserved for its 450 members on Sundays and Mondays. The *Times* reported that a corps of grey-uniformed attendants cleared the ice on the two-hundred-by-ninety-foot rink, and that the club had its own team for ice hockey, a sport that had "come to be quite the vogue."

New Yorkers had a chance to see the new sport at its finest when two Montreal powerhouses, the MAAA's "Winged Wheelmen" and the Montreal Shamrocks, came to town in 1896 to play American college teams at St. Nick's – the same year the United States saw its first intercollegiate hockey match between Yale and Johns Hopkins, and nine years after Canadians at Oxford and Cambridge played the world's first intercollegiate match in St. Moritz, Switzerland.

It took American capital and Canadian talent and a shared appreciation of the profit motive to make hockey into a professional sport. To that, Gibson added the democratic ideal of a game that anyone could play. As he explained to Houghton's *Mining Gazette*: "The zest of it, the snap of it, the rapid changes, the ever varying scenes and incidents, the clash of honourable rivalry, the breathless rushes, the sudden turns and curves, the friendly battles of young men trained and disciplined, all in earnest, all full of best impulses. . . . It is cheap and inexpensive for the players, and even the poorest boy can hold his own at hockey against the belted heir of an earl or the son of a millionaire." Gibson's vision of hockey appealed to the republican American mind. And what appealed to Canadian players was the money he was prepared to pay them for a game they were obliged to play for free at home.

In the late winter of 1904, Portage Lake defeated the Pittsburgh Bankers for the championship of the United States, and in their opponents, they saw the future. The Bankers, so called because one of their players, Arthur Sixsmith, was secretary to Pittsburgh financier Andrew Mellon, were already paying their Canadian players. Former Ottawa star William Hodgson "Hod" Stuart could make fifteen to twenty dollars a week playing semi-pro hockey, and even more from the day job the team threw in.

James Dee gave Gibson and his Portage Lakers one hundred dollars for a victory party to celebrate their championship, but Dee and Gibson had more than a lavish banquet on their minds. Now that they had won the United States championship, they wanted to be the best in the world, and that meant winning the Stanley Cup.

The Montreal AAA, the "Little Men of Iron," who had won the Stanley Cup in 1902, declined Portage Lake's challenge, and the following year, Frank McGee and his Ottawa Silver Seven (who had won the Cup twice in 1903 and four more times in 1904 en route to ten straight Cup titles), also turned down this chance to test themselves against an American team. If the taint of American money was the worry, the Montreal Wanderers held their noses long enough to take on the Portage Lake team in a two-game series in March 1904 at the Amphidrome, billed as the "World Championship." They lost. They were in good company.

The Portage Lake team of 1903–4 has been called the "first truly professional hockey team" by historian Bill Sproule, and its record that season showed that money indeed spoke the language of a champion: 24 wins, 2 losses, and a goals advantage against their opponents of 273–48.

Doc Gibson had begun recruiting before the start of the 1903–4 season, landing Hod Stuart from Pittsburgh, as well as his younger brother Bruce. Bruce had followed Hod to Pittsburgh from Ottawa, where both had played for the Senators in the 1898–99 season. Historian Daniel Mason has called Hod "one of hockey's first great defencemen"; today, he would be called a franchise player. He rushed for thirteen goals in fifteen games, while Bruce led the team with forty-six goals, to the delight of crowds of upward of four thousand fans or "puckeys," as they were called in Houghton.

Milton "Riley" Hern, an Ontario native who had been backstopping the Pittsburgh Keystones, came over to the Portage Lake team, freely admitting in the November 16, 1903, *Toronto Globe* that the only reason he signed with Gibson's team was because it was offering him more money. In his first season with Portage Lake, Hern shut out the opposition five times.

The money flowing in copper country, and the fans cramming into the Amphidrome to see Portage Lake win, showed James Dee just how much more could be made. In the autumn of 1904, he went to Chicago to meet with other rink operators and team presidents and sell them on the next, logical step: a professional hockey league, which could make all of them some serious money. It wasn't a hard sell.

So the International Hockey League was born, with Dee serving as secretary, treasurer, and scheduler. Teams would play in Houghton and neighbouring Calumet, in Pittsburgh, and in Sault Ste. Marie, Michigan. The "international" component would come from Sault Ste. Marie, Ontario – known as the Canadian Soo to distinguish it from its American counterpart.

Players quickly caught on to the possibilities offered by the world's first professional league, which began play in the winter of 1904–5. Hod Stuart showed his grasp of free agency by signing with Calumet as a playing coach and manager, for $1,800 a season. This time his brother Bruce did not follow, remaining a Portage Laker and adding a fraternal dimension to a rivalry already strengthened by proximity. The competition was good for the gate, but not necessarily good for the Stuarts' health. As Norman Gillespie told the *Winnipeg Tribune* magazine in March 1933, the competition between the Stuart brothers was fierce: "Before the game you would see them talking to their mother, apparently quite a family party. Five minutes later the referee would ring his bell, face off the puck, and they would be seen lustily socking one another over the head or elsewhere with their hockey sticks."

Fred Taylor, the Listowel Whirlwind, had taken the train from Manitoba to Michigan in January 1906 after Sheriff McNaughton's phone call, so consumed with loneliness and trepidation that he forgot to bring his skates. He soon learned too well the roughness of the IHL, and was saved, as ever, by his

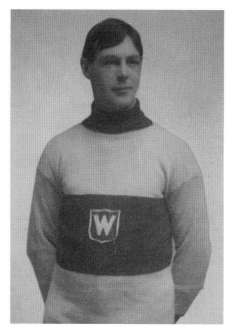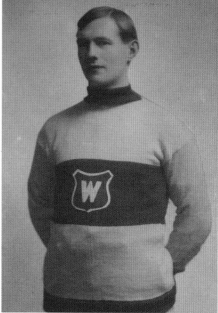

William Hodgson "Hod" Stuart (left) and his younger brother Bruce (right) pose in their Montreal Wanderers' jerseys. The brothers learned the game in the Ottawa Valley, but like many Canadian players, went to the United States to play pro. Hod Stuart campaigned for fair wages and an end to on-ice violence, which he attracted as a player of uncommon talent at point.
(*Hockey Hall of Fame*)

speed and imagination. Houghton's *Mining Gazette* simultaneously managed to reassure and worry its readers while lauding the play of the latest Canadian genius: "The other teams are doing all they can to stop Taylor or at least slow him down, and they don't mind how they go about it. They are using elbows and sticks and going at him any way they can, but so far he is too slippery for them. It is a marvel that he remains unhurt."

The teenaged five-foot-eight-inch Taylor, who weighed just 165 pounds, didn't leave much to chance. As the star he was so frequently the target of opponents that he improvised protection for himself, using the stays from his mother's whalebone corset in homemade thigh padding. In his first season with Portage Lake he scored eleven goals in just six games to boost the team to its first IHL title, and earn himself the top spot on the IHL's all-star team.

In Canada, Taylor's old nemesis, the Ontario Amateur Hockey Association, was apoplectic at the migration of Canadian talent in search of American gold, and its president, MP John Ross Robertson, issued another self-serving statement: "For self protection, the stand of the Ontario Hockey Association against the professionalism of Pittsburgh, Houghton, Calumet, and the Soo must be uncompromisingly antagonistic. . . . Any hockey player who figures on any of these teams must be banished from Ontario Hockey."

Players went to Michigan anyway. Joe Hall, a native of Staffordshire, England, who had grown up in Manitoba, moved to Portage Lake as a "right forward." He made life difficult for opponents by playing a robust game, fuelled by an incendiary and oft-regretted temper, which won him his nickname, "Bad" Joe. But Hall was much more than a goon. In twenty games with the Portage Lakers, he scored thirty-three goals – the most on the team – and won an all-star selection in that position.

It was not just players from Ontario and Manitoba who saw the wisdom of selling their hockey talent. Jean Baptiste "Jack" Laviolette and Didier Pitre had played for the pioneering Montreal Nationals, formed in 1894, and one of the city's

Joe Hall (middle, right), a defenceman whose riotous temper earned him the nickname "Bad" Joe, was also a skilled player much in demand by teams north and south of the border. Hall felt badly about his outbursts on the ice and would often enter the opponents' dressing room after a game to apologize for his violent behaviour, which over the course of his career earned him league suspensions and a suspended sentence for a stick-swinging incident in Toronto. He was killed by the Spanish Influenza pandemic while playing for the Montreal Canadiens during the 1919 Stanley Cup series against Seattle, which forced the cancellation of the final for the first of only two times in Cup history.

(*Hockey Hall of Fame*)

two francophone teams (the Montagnards followed in 1898). The smooth-talking Laviolette convinced Pitre of the wisdom of joining the IHL, where stars were making one hundred dollars a week, four times what a man could comfortably live on for a month.

Laviolette had already tested the professional waters in 1904, winning an all-star ranking with the Michigan Soo Indians, and when he returned to Montreal to tell his younger friend about the wonders of the league down south, the Montreal Nationals' management did something far more practical than wag the finger of amateur righteousness at Laviolette. They took Pitre and hid him. This was an impressive feat, as Pitre was hard to hide, weighing more than two hundred pounds at a time when the average playing weight was forty pounds less. Nicknamed "Cannonball" for his hard, accurate shot, Pitre was famous throughout the city for his hockey prowess, and it didn't take Laviolette long to tumble to his whereabouts and convince him to join the adventure in the IHL.

The Montreal Nationals' management was not going to give up so easily, and their intelligence was excellent. On the day Laviolette was rumoured to be leaving for Michigan, the club's manager and directors were waiting for him at Windsor Station. Laviolette admitted that, yes, he was trying to lure Pitre away to the IHL, but the problem in his plan was Pitre himself, who hadn't shown up for the train. As Laviolette climbed on the train alone, the Montreal officials had a good laugh at his expense, thinking that, while he was a fine hockey player, he was not much for subterfuge. Laviolette, meanwhile, jumped off the moving train from the other side, went back into the city, found Pitre, signed him to a contract, and hid him in the basement of the train station until the next train was ready to depart. Once aboard, just in case Montreal's management had spies aboard the train, Laviolette stashed Pitre in a sleeper berth and told the inquisitive that his friend had the 'flu – then, as now, a potentially fatal disease. They were left alone and made it safely to Sault Ste. Marie, Michigan, where Pitre won all-star honours in each of his three seasons in the IHL.

Edouard "Newsy" Lalonde, a feisty, gifted rover – a seventh man in the team structure of the time, who could roam the ice at will, unfettered by the restrictions and responsibilities placed on the other positions – and a gifted lacrosse player, experienced no such drama when he escaped his job as a printer's devil, or apprentice, with the *Cornwall Free Press* to play for the Canadian Soo for thirty-five dollars a week. All he had was a one-way train ticket, sixteen dollars from the team, and a considerable amount of nerve. "Friends attempted to dissuade me from trying out for professional hockey," he later recalled. "They said the game was too rough for an eighteen-year-old, and that I'd get

Didier Pitre, nicknamed Cannonball because of his powerful shot, was one of early hockey's first French-Canadian stars. Although he was unusually large for the era at six feet tall and pushing two hundred pounds, Pitre was a fast skater and eventually changed positions from defence to forward. Pitre first played pro hockey in the IHL for Sault Ste. Marie, Michigan, and became the first man signed by the Montreal Canadiens. He later went west to play in Vancouver, where he further added to his colourful reputation by drinking a pint of champagne to revive himself between periods. (*Hockey Hall of Fame*)

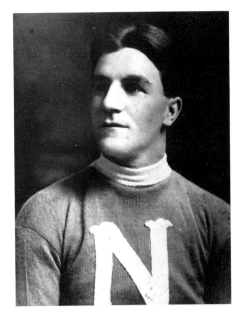

Jean-Baptiste "Jack" Laviolette played for the Montreal Nationals, one of early hockey's first French-Canadian teams, in 1903–4, then moved to the United States to play professionally. He was asked to play for the first Montreal Canadiens team in 1909, and after he moved up from defence to play forward, his speed at right-wing, together with the talents of linemates Didier Pitre and Edouard "Newsy" Lalonde, earned the team the sobriquet the Flying Frenchmen. (*Hockey Hall of Fame*)

myself killed. . . . In spite of well-meant advice, I left Cornwall by train one evening, rode all night, and arrived in the Soo at eight o'clock the next evening. A game was scheduled for eight-thirty the same night."

Lalonde had planned to spend the first game just watching and getting the hang of the pro league, but barely an hour after arriving in the Soo, the team's star, Marty Walsh, broke his leg. Lalonde was drafted into play and was soon rushing up the ice as if he'd been there for weeks. Then he ran smack into a rink fence and went down as if he'd taken an uppercut to the chin from a heavy-weight. Fortunately, a local boxer came to the rescue. Jack Hammond was at the game, and he had brought two hip flasks. He handed the gasping Lalonde the one that he thought had whisky in it. He was wrong. "It burned my mouth and my gums and my throat," Lalonde later said of the agony of drinking the pure ammonia that the boxer's hip flask contained. "I thought I was a goner."

The ammonia – used to revive knocked-out boxers via their sense of smell, not taste – worked anyway, propelling the tough Lalonde back on his skates and onto the ice. He scored two goals in the game and earned a pay raise to fifty dollars a week. Although Lalonde added twenty-four more goals to his tally over eighteen games that season, he was a "goner" the following season, accepting an offer to return to Canada to play with Toronto – of the Ontario Professional Hockey League, the country's first pro league, which began play in January 1908.

Another player who left the IHL for Canada is one upon whom the finicky eye of history has not lingered. Lorne Campbell was so talented that historian Daniel Mason considers him "the most dominant player in the I.H.L.'s brief existence," a man worthy of consideration for the Hockey Hall of Fame – if only more were known about him than mentions in Michigan newspaper stories of the time.

Campbell, a centre, finished as one of the top three goal scorers in the IHL for each of his three seasons, playing for Portage Lake, Calumet, and Pittsburgh from 1905 until 1907. Former Little Man of Iron Dickie Boon was so impressed by him that he tried to woo Campbell to Montreal to play for the team he now managed, but Campbell turned him down, preferring to remain paid and in the IHL, where he won the goal-scoring championship in 1907.

If Campbell had accepted Boon's offer, it's tempting to think there might be an award named after him today. Campbell played a few games in Manitoba for the Winnipeg Maple Leafs in 1907–8, scoring six goals for the Leafs in a match two days before they won the league championship. And then his trail just disappears into the winter of a century ago.

The return home of players such as Hod Stuart, who joined the Montreal Wanderers and attracted six thousand fans to his first game, Newsy Lalonde, and Lorne Campbell happened only because their Canadian teams were finally being paid, if quietly. The owners had realized that professional hockey could be more lucrative than the amateur game.

The 1906–7 season was the IHL's last, with Fred Taylor still dazzling crowds, his impish face showing his amusement as he scored goals at will. Doc Gibson came out of retirement for two games to help Portage Lake defeat Pittsburgh for their second IHL title. Gibson had put on his skates not for reasons of sentiment, but because the IHL was having trouble attracting players now that Canada was paying them too. Shortly after the victorious Portage Lakers were paraded through streets decorated in the team's green and white colours, a recession hit the U.S. economy, and copper prices fell sharply. There was no more money to pay people to play games, and the IHL's owners now looked at their league in the cold light of any professional enterprise: it was just another failed business.

On a hot afternoon in June 1907, Hod Stuart, who had returned home from his American hockey triumphs to Belleville, Ontario, to take a construction job with his father, went down to Grand Junction dock to cool off with some friends. Stuart swam out into the Bay of Quinte to a lighthouse half a kilometre from shore, climbed up on its platform, then dove off. His friends waited for him to surface, but they waited in vain. As the Montreal *Star* later reported, "He had dived head first on to a lot of jagged rocks, there was [a] terrible gash in his head, and his neck was broken."

Stuart's father broke down completely upon hearing of the death of his beloved eldest son, whose Wanderers he had cheered to their Stanley Cup triumph only three months earlier. The man who the *Star* reported had been "the most talked about player in the whole of America" the winter before was just twenty-eight years old when he died.

The following year, hockey held its first benefit game to help Stuart's family, and the Montreal Wanderers beat a team of challengers 10–7. Nearly four thousand people attended the Hod Stuart Memorial Match, and the Montreal *Gazette* reported that nearly two thousand dollars in gate receipts went to "Stuart's widow and two little children without any deduction for the expenses either of the clubs or the rink management."

The fact that the *Gazette* even mentioned that this time there would be no division of money shows the increasing role of Mammon in hockey. The game that had attracted forty curious onlookers to the Victoria Rink in Montreal thirty years earlier was now big business in Canada, and it was at a volatile point.

Just the year before, in 1906, Francis Nelson, the sports editor of the *Toronto Globe*, remarked that the backbiting between teams and officials had

Tommy Phillips

One of early hockey's first stars whose career spans Canada, Phillips learned to play hockey in the northwestern Ontario town of Rat Portage (renamed Kenora in 1905) but didn't see action in his first organized league until 1901, when, as an eighteen-year-old, he travelled to Montreal and played for the Shamrocks. Two years later, Phillips won the Stanley Cup as a member of the Montreal Amateur Athletic Association's "Winged Wheelmen" (whose club logo of a wing emerging from a wheel eventually found its way onto the sweaters of the Detroit Red Wings). A tenacious backchecker as well as a speedy winger, Phillips returned to Rat Portage to captain the Thistles. When professional hockey came north from the United States, Phillips played first with Ottawa, then followed the Patrick brothers to the West Coast to play pro for the Vancouver Millionaires in 1911–12, scoring seventeen goals in seventeen games. (*Hockey Hall of Fame*)

become so acrimonious that, while "the Stanley Cup provides a fine spectacle and makes money for the teams and the rink proprietors, . . . the competition does not advance the interests of the national sport." As if to prove his point, in 1907, the Thistles of Kenora, Ontario, population 10,000, defeated the mighty Montreal Wanderers to win Lord Stanley's challenge trophy. It was the triumph of the virtuous amateur over the mercenary professional, for just five years earlier, the Thistles had been a schoolboy team (and their town had been called Rat Portage. It was renamed in 1905). At the time, hockey's rugby-like forward movement, and absence of a forward passing zone, encouraged a dump-and-chase style. The Thistles had seen an opportunity and brought speed and precision passing to the game. Fred Taylor, who was not given to excess except on the ice, said Kenora had revolutionized hockey. "The Thistles, by skating fast, turned the game wide open, and by 1903, every senior team in the country had changed to that pleasing style."

Led by future Hall of Famers Billy McGimsie, Tom Phillips, Tom Hooper, Si Griffis, and Art Ross, the underdog Thistles defeated the Wanderers 4–2 in the first match, and then doubled up on them 8–6 in the second. The victory was especially sweet for Kenora: not only was it their third attempt to win the Cup, they were now – and remain – the smallest town to ever win hockey's Holy Grail.

At a time when there could be as many as four challenges for the Cup in a season, the Thistles basked in the Cup's reflected glory for all of two months before the Wanderers took it home to Montreal amid a good deal of noisy acrimony. There were accusations of ringers and mercenaries that wound up being discussed in Parliament and on the front pages of newspapers. Kenora, in addition to being the smallest town ever to win the Cup, was also the last amateur team to do so – the Wanderers had declared themselves professionals. The

After winning the Stanley Cup in 1907, the Kenora Thistles were feted in the town's Opera House, with the Cup centre stage, and the Thistles sitting like gods above it in the boxes. There were speeches, songs, gifts of silverware (a loving cup to each of the nine players), and a song was especially composed for the occasion by Mrs. W.J. Gunne:

We love to hear you praised, boys,
    we value what they mean,
When every message tells us,
    "Kenora men play clean."
It's words like this we prize, boys –
    the words we least could spare.
'Twas great to win the Cup, boys,
    but best you have won it fair.
The Thistles are at home again,
    our bravest and our best,
We are not perhaps the biggest town,
    but the proudest in the west.

(*Hockey Hall of Fame*)

Thistles' triumph, of the kind Lord Stanley had in mind when he donated his trophy, marked the end of such challenges. Now if a small-town team wanted to play for hockey's greatest prize, they had to find a professional league that would let them join.

This was the problem in the winter of 1909, when industrialist Michael O'Brien dispatched his son Ambrose to Montreal to try to win a place for his hockey team from the little town of Renfrew in the big world of corporate hockey. If a small town such as Kenora could win the Cup as amateurs, O'Brien reasoned, then so could Renfrew – but as professionals, because Renfrew had money.

Senator Michael J. O'Brien was a self-made man whose climb to the top of Canadian society began in 1866, when his father was crippled by an accident. Responsibility for supporting the family fell on Michael's fifteen-year-old shoulders. As a water-boy working the steam engine on Nova Scotia's Truro-to-Pictou railway, O'Brien saved as much as he could from the ten cents a pail he received, and dreamed of escaping. Four years later he had risen to become a subcontractor, and he had his eyes on opportunities in Ontario, where railway building was a growth industry. O'Brien won the bid to build the last leg of the K and P (nicknamed the Kick and Push) railway from Kingston to Pembroke, and while walking the land through which he would build his portion, he met the woman who would become his wife. Teamed with the estimable Jenny Barry, O'Brien settled in Renfrew to begin to conquer the world. And he almost did.

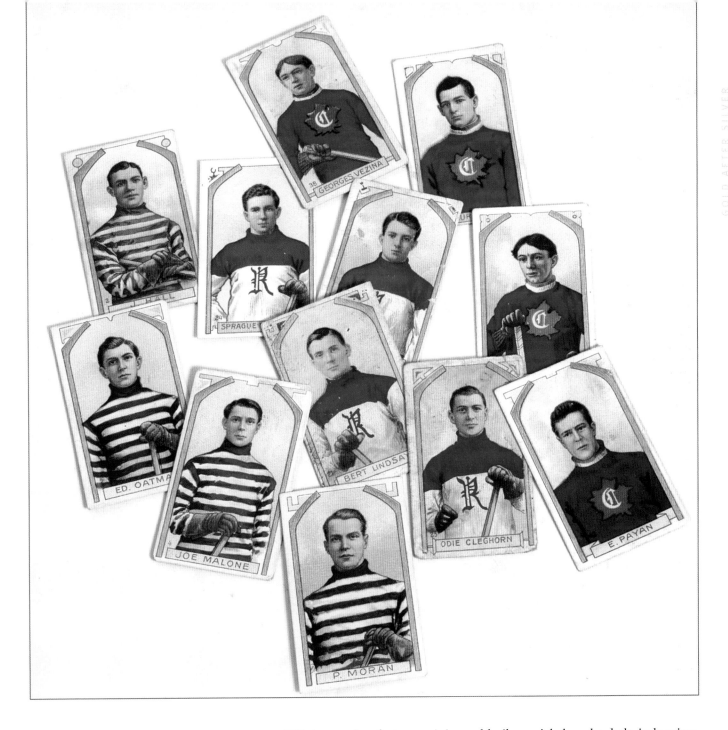

Hockey cards debuted in 1910, when the British America Tobacco Company printed a colour set of players from the National Hockey Association. By 1913, the cards were so popular that three different tobacco companies were including them in their cigarette packages. (*Hockey Hall of Fame*)

O'Brien made a fortune mining gold, silver, nickel, and cobalt, in logging, in woollen mills, and, eventually, in arms production during the First World War. Like many rich men, more than money, he wanted triumph and glory. He wanted his baby, the Renfrew hockey team, to win the most glittering prize of the Stanley Cup. Then Renfrew would be known for something other than being just another dairy town in the Ottawa Valley, even if its butter was sublime.

Despite the lobbying efforts of their local MP, Tom Low – also a self-made titan of industry – Renfrew could not get into a recognized league, the only way they could compete for the Cup. So they started their own. It included teams from other small towns – Smith's Falls, Cornwall, and

Brockville – and, with a federal nod, Ottawa's Victorias. They offended Upper Canada sensibilities by calling it the Federal League and rubbed it in by winning the league championship, which led the *Renfrew Journal* to wonder when the town would have its shot at the big time. Stanley Cup Trustee William Foran publicly promised "next year," but when next year came, the promise had vanished into thin air.

O'Brien sent his twenty-four-year-old son, Ambrose, to Montreal to convince the Eastern Canada Hockey Association to admit Renfrew into its league. Ambrose, with his University of Toronto degree, was used to his father's money opening doors, and so he showed up in Montreal on November 25, 1909, expecting a receptive audience. The directors from Montreal's Shamrocks and Wanderers, along with those from the Ottawa Senators and Quebec Bulldogs, had several matters on their mind, and Ambrose O'Brien was not one of them. They were arguing about money. They were going to lose a lot of it if J.P. Doran, who had bought the Montreal Wanderers in 1908, succeeded in moving his team from its current arena on Wood Street to the smaller Jubilee Rink, which he just happened to own. This would mean that the 40-per-cent share of profits the team owners took from each other's gate receipts would shrink. They now had to pay their players, and they were not about to dig into their profits to do it.

Their solution to the problem reflects just how cutthroat the early pro game could be. They dissolved their league and formed another one, with franchises in Ottawa, Quebec, and three in Montreal. J.P. "Pat" Doran could move his Wanderers into any rink he chose, it just wouldn't be in their new league, which they called the Canadian Hockey Association. As far as they were concerned, J.P. Doran and his Wanderers were history.

Indeed, they were, though not in the way anyone imagined when Wanderers' player and team official Jimmy Gardner came storming out of the meeting. Ambrose later recalled, "He was so mad he could hardly do anything but swear – and then turned to me and said 'Ambrose, why don't you and I form a league? You've got Haileybury, Cobalt, and Renfrew. We have the Wanderers. And I think if a team of all Frenchmen was formed in Montreal it would be a real draw. We could give it a French-Canadian name.'"

And so ambition and revenge combined to create the Montreal Canadiens, a hockey club whose rather shabby, back-handed origins did not presage its future as one of the most successful franchises in professional sport.

Though francophone Quebec had seen two teams enter league play, the teams had been treated as not quite good enough to play with the Anglo elite. This attitude was evident when the new hockey venture was announced

Club de Hockey — Le Canadien 1909-10

Skinner Poulin · Jos. Cattarinich · Eddy. McCafferty · Jack. Laviolette Capt. · Newsy Lalonde · Art. Bernier · Ed. Chapleau · Ed. Millaire M.D. · Rich. Duckett · D. Pitre · Moss Chartrand · Ed. Decary · Albert Dumas Photo

The Montreal Canadiens were invented by English-Canadian millionaires in 1909 after a business argument. Their first season saw them wearing blue jerseys and finishing in last place in the new National Hockey Association, with an embarrassing 2–10 record. The following season they switched to red sweaters, but the Canadiens' famous logo of an H inside a C (to represent Club de Hockey) didn't feature on their jerseys until 1917–18, the season after their first Stanley Cup championship.

(*Hockey Hall of Fame*)

to the world on December 3, 1909. *La Presse* reported that the new team would bear *"le nom de Canadien"* and published a photo of the Canadiens' manager, Jack Laviolette – who not so long ago had been the scourge of management in Montreal – while the *Gazette* admonished francophones not to get any ideas above their station, as "French-Canadian players of class are not numerous."

Which is not to say that there was no French-Canadian presence in the world of Montreal hockey. By 1910 francophones made up 54.8 per cent of Montreal residents, and there were 55 French-Canadian clubs out of a total of 159. Fifteen years earlier, there had hardly been any, but francophones had allied with the city's Irish-Catholics, who had managed to crack the Anglo-Protestant world of Montreal hockey and help the francophones through the door. The francophone community was now more than ready for its own professional team, and once again, the Irish, in the form of the O'Briens and

Pat Doran and Jimmy Gardner were ready to help out. Even if they had to spend a little money to make it happen.

The new "French-Canadian" team would play in the optimistically named National Hockey Association, whose notion of national was to add teams from big-city Montreal – the Wanderers and Canadiens – to the Federal League's small-town teams. The *Gazette* predicted a bidding war ahead, given that the Canadiens had to stock their team with francophone talent, and what talent there was had already signed contracts elsewhere.

Jack Laviolette knew this would be a problem, having been down this road before with his prize quarry, Didier Pitre. Or rather, down the rail track. The Montreal *Daily Star* told the story of his quest to sign Pitre for this new team on December 13, 1909, under the headline "Race By Train," as if it were a scene from a spy novel: "There was a race for a man during the last forty-eight hours. . . . Both the National and the Canadiens clubs heard that Pitre was coming to Montreal on Saturday. President Lecour of the National Club had the notice first and slipped away from a lacrosse meeting, taking the train to North Bay. Manager Jack Laviolette, of the Canadiens hockey team, heard the rumour next and took the last train to Ottawa. Mr. Lecour, however, got hold of Pitre first, and he became his."

The little detail of having already signed a contract with the Nationals didn't stop Pitre from signing another one with Laviolette's Canadiens, news of which surfaced three days later. The Nationals, all too aware of Pitre's proclivities for bolting, won a writ of injunction on December 22, 1909, to stop him from playing for the Canadiens, and he soon found himself standing in a Montreal courtroom, listening along with Mr. Justice Bruneau as the Nationals' counsel argued just why the big cover-point should belong to them. The contract Pitre had signed with the Nationals would pay him $1,100 for an eleven-week season. There was even provision to cut his salary in half should he "not make good in that position."

Outside the courtroom, Pitre was alternately humble and swaggering. He told a *Daily Star* photographer who wanted to take his picture, "What's the use? . . . I'll be in jail tomorrow," while a few days later he told *La Presse* that he would only be fined: "And don't go thinking the amount will come out of my pocket. Le Canadien knew what they were doing when they signed me and they'll be the ones to pay up."

The courts had not dealt with a breached hockey contract before, and the lawyers had to reach into the exotic worlds of Canadian theatre and American baseball for a precedent. Pitre's counsel argued that he was induced to play for the Nationals because it would be an all-star team, including other francophone

Hobey Baker

Hobart "Hobey" Baker, hockey's first American superstar, was the amateur ideal in full flight, a handsome, superlatively talented athlete who played for the love of the game. A smitten fellow Princetonian, F. Scott Fitzgerald, used Baker as his model for the character of the football hero Allenby in his debut novel, *This Side of Paradise*, later writing, "He was an ideal worthy of everything in my enthusiastic admiration, yet consummated and expressed in a human being who stood within ten feet of me." Baker played the position of rover and made his name on both sides of the border, playing matches in Canada with the Princeton Tigers, and in New York City's St. Nicholas Rink, whose marquee would boast "Hobey Baker Plays Here Tonight." After graduating, Baker joined the St. Nicholas Rink's amateur hockey team, and when Baker and the St. Nick's team played the Montreal Stars for the Ross Cup on December 11, 1915, Baker scored twice and set up three goals to lead St. Nick's to a 6–2 victory. Baker was offered $3,500 to come to Canada and turn pro, but he refused – he played only for the love of the game. Baker became a pilot in the First World War and won the Croix de Guerre for his courage under fire. Shortly after the war ended, the twenty-six-year-old Baker was killed when the airplane he piloted for a post-repair flight crashed. He is commemorated with the award for the best American college hockey player, which bears his name.

(*Hockey Hall of Fame*)

talents such as Newsy Lalonde and Georges "Skinner" Poulin. In a nice bit of sophistry, the lawyers argued that Pitre's original contract was worthless, since he wouldn't be playing with the team members he had been promised – neglecting to mention this was because the Canadiens had already poached some of those all-stars for their own devious purposes, including Lalonde and Poulin.

In an irony to be savoured by any professional player who has endured ego-wounding salary arbitration, when teams routinely disparage the worth of the player seeking a raise, Pitre answered the Nationals' claim that he was unique by arguing that "there are many others in the city who are able to occupy the position of cover point." The judge agreed, ruling that a citizen could not be forced to act against his will, and so Pitre could play for whomever he wished.

That night, the Cannonball suited up for the Canadiens as they took on Cobalt at Montreal's Jubilee Rink – the venue once deemed too small for profit by the Canadian Hockey Association owners. The Cobalt team, rumoured to take their pay in silver nuggets from the local mine, fell behind 4–0, then performed a bit of hockey alchemy by quickly turning their leaden performance into gold, with six unanswered goals. The Canadiens, whose future owner, Joe Cattarinich, was playing goal, fought back. Art Bernier, Skinner Poulin, and Newsy Lalonde each scored two goals for the Canadiens, but it was Jack Laviolette – appropriately, after all he had been through – who won the game in overtime for Montreal. *La Presse* was exuberant, running a banner headline the next day announcing, "Le Canadien Gagne Une Grande Partie." The article claimed that, fittingly, "Laviolette and Pitre shone brightest in the Canadiens'" firmament. Laviolette soon earned the nickname Speed Merchant and such was the Canadiens' team élan that sportswriters would eventually christen them the "Flying Frenchmen."

Yet the Canadiens could scarcely get airborne during their first year of existence, winning just two of their twelve games. As the *Gazette* had predicted, competition for players was stiff, and with the O'Brien family's deep pockets bankrolling the entire league save for the Wanderers, the upstart National Hockey Association went shopping, returning with the Canadian Hockey Association's greatest stars.

The Renfrew Creamery Kings signed the Montreal Wanderers' Lester Patrick for $3,000 a season. Patrick had made a name as a "rushing defenceman" at a time when the rearguard was expected to dump the puck down the ice and let the forwards chase it. Showing the same kind of shrewd, take-charge instinct with which he and his younger brother Frank would reshape professional hockey during the next half century, Patrick made his participation in this new league conditional on the signing of his brother, also a defenceman, for another $2,000. The Haileybury Comets picked up Art Ross, who had starred for Kenora and who would go on to be one of the sport's great managers and innovators, for $2,700. But the greatest prize of all was Fred Taylor, who was no longer a "Whirlwind" but had now become a full-blown "Cyclone."

Taylor had earned the sobriquet while starring for the Ottawa Senators, after returning from the IHL. When the team offered him five hundred dollars for a ten-game season, he threw in a thirty-five-dollar-a-week job with the Canadian government's immigration department. Though Taylor had been making four hundred dollars in the IHL for a shorter season, he knew the value of security, and he took the sure thing. He was twenty-two, he had time to raise his market value, and he also had his eye on an Ottawa blueblood named Thirza Cook. And the eyes of Ottawa were on Taylor.

When Taylor led the Senators to their first Stanley Cup since the glory days of the Silver Seven with a three-goal game, and on a right foot badly sliced in

The Renfrew Millionaires were not just the centrepiece team of the National Hockey Association, but their name reflected both the wealth of their owner, Ambrose O'Brien, and the richness of their talent. Edouard "Newsy" Lalonde, Fred "Cyclone" Taylor, Frank Patrick, and Lester Patrick were elected to the Hockey Hall of Fame, and together they form early hockey's pantheon. (Left to right: Bobby Rowe, Herb Jordan, Fred Whitcroft, Lalonde, Taylor, F. Patrick, Larry Gilmour, L. Patrick.) *(BC Sports Hall of Fame and Museum)*

the previous game, the 7,500 people crammed into Dey's Rink in March 1909, people from as far away as Halifax and Philadelphia, thought the Cyclone would be Ottawa's one-man Stanley Cup storm for years to come. But Taylor thought otherwise.

Taylor was as subtle and slippery with a contract negotiation as he was on the ice. When the wealthy Renfrew team came calling, he was listening. After all, he had negotiated with them while under contract to Ottawa the previous season, although he had not signed their extraordinary offer of $2,000 – at the time, more than anyone was earning to play hockey in Canada. He had just listened, and then calculated how much he would one day be worth on the market. Which was why he was laughing now at the $1,500 the O'Briens were offering for his Stanley Cup leadership, and the kind of talent that could bring thousands of people to their feet. By the time the Cyclone was finished negotiating with the O'Briens, they were begging him to take $5,200 for a twelve-game season. At the time, Prime Minister Wilfrid Laurier was earning $2,500 a year to keep united a country divided by tensions between French and English, between immigrants and British subjects, and a passionate debate about free trade with the United States. Hockey players of the calibre of Taylor and the Patricks were worth more to the marketplace than prime ministers because not only could they make money for team owners, they could do what politicians couldn't: they could turn the owners into heroes by winning the Stanley Cup.

The Renfrew Creamery Kings decided they now needed a team name that reflected the exalted professional world they had entered. So, with a bit of boastful wit, they called themselves the "Millionaires."

Charlotte Whitton, who would become mayor of Ottawa, was a twelve-year-old Renfrew girl when the Millionaires played their first game. The team bought her a ticket to their match for her thirteenth birthday and accorded her pride of place in their VIP box. Whitton remembers that the players, who generously spent time coaching the local children, frequently got thirsty. According to O'Brien's biographer, when the weather was good, the team liked nothing better than a little al fresco boozing: "The street by the *Mercury* [newspaper] had the best sunlight in town and every day that was half-way decent that's where they would be found, sitting there in the sun like graven images."

Renfrew had a reputation as a hard-drinking place, and the town's temperance activists were campaigning to rid their community of the demon drink. Around the time that young Charlotte was being feted by the Millionaires, the town held a referendum on the liquor question. To the chagrin of the drinkers, the prohibitionists won, and Renfrew became a dry town, which caused the *Ottawa Citizen* to observe it was lucky that the O'Briens got their franchise before temperance came to town, as no right-thinking hockey person would ever allow the Stanley Cup to go to a place where the win could not be "properly celebrated."

Despite this hurdle, or perhaps because of it, the Millionaires began their quest to fill the Cup with the local milk by losing their first match 11–9 to

FRED TAYLOR IN ACTION

After watching him score four spectacular goals for Ottawa on January 11, 1908, Earl Grey, Canada's governor general, declared, "Fred Taylor was a cyclone, if ever I saw one" and "Cyclone" Taylor was born. The nickname was one of many worn by the man whom Frank Patrick called hockey's first superstar, for it seemed that only a force of Nature could describe his talent. Previously, Taylor was known as a "Whirlwind" and a "Tornado" and even a "Pistol."
(*Hockey Hall of Fame*)

Fred "Cyclone" Taylor poses in his Ottawa
uniform, but Ottawa would remember
him as the man who unspeakably
betrayed them. Taylor, one of hockey's
canniest negotiators, took delight in
playing one team off against the other,
and when he jumped from Ottawa to the
upstart Renfrew Millionaires of the
National Hockey Association, he did so
for a salary more than twice that of the
country's prime minister. (BC Sports Hall of
Fame and Museum)

Cobalt. Still, the *Mercury*'s hockey man had reason to hope, noting "the clever,
elusive style" of Lester Patrick, and that Taylor was "very good," but his rushes,
"while very spectacular, lacked result because of the failure of the forwards
combination."

The Millionaires fared better when the Canadiens came to town, winning
their second outing 9–4. This time the *Mercury* reporter was impressed by the
opponents, especially by Newsy Lalonde, who "towered above" the other
"Frenchmen" so highly he could almost be a Millionaire. "Lalonde's rushes were
in the Taylor class," said the paper. "'Stop him! Stop him!' yelled the crowd every
time Lalonde went down the ice." Before the month was out, that same Renfrew
crowd was urging Lalonde onward, as he was now wearing the red and white of
the Millionaires, but the Stanley Cup stayed beyond the team's reach.

Despite their failure to win the Cup, the Millionaires remain one of the
most significant teams of early professional hockey for raising the sport's
profile on both sides of the border and creating a mythology around the
players. When Fred Taylor returned to Ottawa to play against his old team in
February 1910, the feeling that he had betrayed the Senators ran high, and
Taylor exploited it by joking – in the *Ottawa Citizen* newsroom, accompanied by Ottawa's goalie, no less – that he would score a goal against his old
club while skating backward.

Taylor was pelted with rotten lemons and horse manure and empty bottles by seven thousand screaming Ottawa fans when he skated out to play
against his former team. The hero was now a villain. While Renfrew won the
match in overtime, Taylor didn't score any backward goal – which, of course,
only stoked the appetite and box office for his return visit on March 8, where
he brought the boast home in a humiliating 17–2 defeat of the Senators.
"Taylor got the puck on a pass," reported the *Mercury*, "and skating down the
ice in his usual fine fashion, he turned, going backwards, he skated a piece
and then sent the shot home to the Ottawa nets with skill and swiftness."
Decades later, Taylor revealed that he knew exactly what he was doing when
he made the boast, and then let it marinate, but never revealed the truth. "So
many different versions have been written," he said, "that I don't want to spoil
anybody's story."

Taylor understood the power of his own myth as the country's premier
hockey player in the way that, generations later, Wayne Gretzky understood
his, and fuelled it at every chance. Like Gretzky, Taylor's fame transcended
Canada. When he made a trip to New York City in March 1910 with Renfrew,
he was greeted as "the Ty Cobb of hockey," a sobriquet bestowed on him by the
New York Times while Taylor was touring Manhattan with the Senators two
years earlier.

Such was his star power that New York promoters wouldn't back a hockey tour of Canada's best in the St. Nicholas Rink unless Taylor was part of the package. The Millionaires swept a team of all-stars from Montreal and Ottawa in a three-game series, and the New York *Evening Telegram* reminded its readers of Taylor's power in a way the American public would appreciate when it described Taylor as "the man who is paid more than $10 for every minute he is on the ice. Considering that he is paid $5,000 for playing just a dozen games, he is unquestionably the highest paid player in team sport. His salary shames what is paid our star baseball players for a full 154-game season."

ARTHUR ROSS

Art Ross was a player, coach, and an inventor, whose legacy to the game influences it to the present. One of early hockey's first rushing defencemen, Ross grew up in Montreal with Frank and Lester Patrick, and like them, was a well-travelled player who moved from the amateur leagues to the pros, picking up two Stanley Cups as a player and three more as the coach and general manager of the Boston Bruins. Ross tried to form a players' league and was nearly suspended from hockey, so turned his innovative mind to the game. Among his inventions are the B-shaped goal net, a truer, faster puck with bevelled edges (still used by the league), a protective device for vulnerable Achilles tendons, and the Art Ross helmet. Today, the NHL's top point-scorer wins the Art Ross Trophy, the most valued NHL prize after the Stanley Cup.

(*Hockey Hall of Fame*)

The Millionaires took home fifteen hundred dollars in prize money, but they could not take the prize that they had been bought to capture: the Stanley Cup, which was won in 1910 by the Montreal Wanderers. Worse, they finished the 1910 season with a twenty-thousand-dollar team debt, and in November, worried NHA owners met to try to find a way to get their ledgers back in the black.

They agreed on corporate sponsorship, adopting the Spalding puck as the official puck of the NHA, they redesigned league matches into three twenty-minute periods, hoping to increase concession sales with two intermissions instead of one, and then they did something that haunts professional hockey to this day: they tried to impose a salary cap. Under the scheme, each club would spend a maximum of five thousand dollars on players' salaries per season, which would mean high rollers like Renfrew could ice teams consisting of just the two Patrick brothers, or 96 per cent of one Cyclone Taylor. The players, who had seen the NHA as a windfall of perpetual bounty, were not prepared to accept this unilateral retrenchment, nor did they believe the owners were in as much financial pain as they claimed.

Amid rumours of a hockey strike, the Montreal *Herald* published a letter from Montreal Wanderer Art Ross: "The Wanderers have paid on the average from $10,000 to $14,000 a year in salaries since they first started the pro game.

Ottawa has paid from $10,000 to $25,000 and yet Wanderers and Ottawa have never been in the hole. As a matter of fact, they have or should have made money. All the players want is a fair deal. . . . The players are not trying to bulldoze the N.H.A., but we want to know where we get off at."

Ambrose O'Brien responded to the players' discontent by suggesting that the salary cap could be raised to eight thousand dollars, but the players had grown bold with the sense of their earning power that the NHA had given them, and looked into forming their own player-run league. There was only one problem: the rinks were all under contract to the NHA.

But the financial troubles of the NHA could not be fixed either by salary caps or by player-run leagues. The once mighty Renfrew Millionaires dropped out of the league after finishing third in the 1911 season, and Cobalt and Haileybury went with them. Toronto's Blueshirts and Tecumsehs replaced them. When the new teams competed for the NHA's O'Brien Cup in the league's 1912 season, it was a tangible reminder to Michael O'Brien and his fellow millionaire league owners that, fanciful team names and lofty player salaries notwithstanding, the Stanley Cup could not be bought.

Yet the league was notable in many ways: for the creation of the Montreal Canadiens, for the marketing of the sport's first superstars, and for providing the foundations for the league that succeeded it, the National Hockey League. The NHA was also responsible for putting ideas in the heads of two of its young stars, the Patrick brothers, who believed that, with well-paid players and sound management, hockey could thrive anywhere. As luck would have it, their father had just sold his timber business in British Columbia for nearly half a million dollars. Hockey's future, for the Patricks, was on the Pacific Coast.

In the winter of 1910, Lester Patrick, his father, and their guide were staking timber claims in the great forested mountains north of Nelson, British Columbia, when a hungry bear ate their ten-day ration supply. Lester had to hunt for food but soon found himself on the wrong end of another man's rifle when he stumbled onto the property of a mountain man named McDaniel. McDaniel demanded to know the stranger's business. The young Patrick introduced himself, and McDaniel lowered his gun. Not only did he know that Lester was a great hockey player, but he had been in a Montreal arena two years earlier when Lester had lifted the crowds out of their seats with three goals against Quebec. Lester and his father were invited to dine with McDaniel, three ex-Quebeckers briefly united by chance, and hockey, in the middle of the promised land. It augured well for hockey in the West.

At the time, the British Columbia government was practically giving away timber land to attract investment, and as M. Allerdale Grainger describes it in his 1908 novel *Woodsmen of the West*, the process was remarkably free from bureaucracy: "A man could go anywhere on unoccupied Crown lands, put in a corner post, compose a rough description of one square mile of forest measured from that post, and thus secure from the Government exclusive right to the timber of that square mile, subject to the payment of a rent of one hundred and fourteen dollars a year. Such a square mile of forest is known as a timber claim."

As the lumber industry boomed, so did the Patrick family's fortunes in Nelson, and they spearheaded a funding drive to build the town an indoor rink. Lester and Frank christened the eight-hundred-seat arena by starring on the Nelson hockey team, while their sisters Cynda and Dora played for the Nelson Ladies Hockey Club. It was the Patricks' first foray into dynasty building, and they would soon get an opportunity to try again.

In 1911, Joe Patrick sold his lumber business for $440,000 – a fortune at a time when $25,000 would buy a ten-room house in the fashionable West End of Vancouver, on Beach Avenue, no less, with an unobstructed view of English Bay. That still left a good chunk of money for Joe's sons to pursue something they'd been thinking about for a while. Frank, the visionary romantic, imagined a hockey rink on the Pacific Coast, and a league to go with it. Coastal British Columbians had largely ignored hockey, an Eastern Canadian game, because they so rarely got natural ice. The Patrick brothers decided to solve that problem with a little fakery.

Frank Patrick had been deeply impressed during his Renfrew Millionaires' barnstorming tour of New York City by the artificial ice of the St. Nick Rink, which allowed thousands to get a taste for hockey. And the south coast of British Columbia had thousands of patrons. Vancouver already boasted 100,000 people, and another 50,000 in the suburbs, with 1,000 more moving to the region each month. Professional hockey's potential was huge, and while Lester Patrick felt cautious about throwing the family fortune at a game, Frank Patrick convinced his father to make a huge bet on the sport: he would wager his fortune on artificial ice and pro hockey in Vancouver.

On December 7, 1911, the Patrick brothers announced the formation of the Pacific Coast Hockey Association, with teams in Vancouver, Victoria, and New Westminster. For $27,000, Joe Patrick bought land at the corner of Denman and West Georgia streets, overlooking Coal Harbour and the Coast Mountains, and the lush magnificence of Stanley Park – Lord Stanley's other great gift to the country. The Patricks planned to enlist subscribers to pay for the new Vancouver Arena, but Vancouverites already proved to be very good spectators: they would watch the Patricks do it themselves. The Pile, as it would become known, cost $275,000 and could seat 10,500 people – beating

It was Frank Patrick's idea to turn his father's lumber fortune into a professional hockey league on North America's Pacific Coast, and Frank Patrick had no shortage of inspired ideas. In addition to being a multi-sport athlete who earned varsity letters in track, football, and hockey while studying for his BA at McGill, Patrick was also one of hockey's first rushing defencemen. He was considered so hockey-savvy that he was asked to referee a Stanley Cup match when he was just twenty years old. That savvy and his own fertile imagination combined to earn him the sobriquet "the brains of modern hockey" for the twenty-two innovations credited to him, including the blue line, the penalty shot, a playoff system, numbered jerseys, and line changes. (*BC Sports Hall of Fame and Museum*)

the world's largest artificial ice arena, Madison Square Garden, by 500 seats. The Patricks also built the Victoria Arena, capacity 4,200, for $125,000.

The brothers took central management positions in their new Pacific Coast Hockey league. Frank, twenty-six, would be the president, and also manage and coach the Vancouver team, while Lester, twenty-eight, would operate the Victoria club. In order to fill the teams, the brothers did what the O'Briens had taught them to do: they raided the other leagues, taking particular glee in the fact that sixteen of their first twenty-three players came from the NHA. And the players weren't coming for the temperate winter climate. As Lester admitted, the Patricks lured pro hockey players to the western edge of the continent with "more money than they could dare refuse."

The new league gained instant credibility and space in the newspapers across the country by signing their biggest star, Newsy Lalonde, who quit the Montreal Canadiens to suit up as a Vancouver Millionaire – the team name was another borrowing from O'Brien's league. Jimmy Gardner, the three-time Stanley Cup winner with Montreal's AAAs and Wanderers, coached the New Westminster Royals and played left wing.

The first professional hockey game ever played west of Ontario and Michigan took place at the Victoria Arena on the evening of January 2, 1912. British Columbia's lieutenant-governor dropped the puck for the ceremonial faceoff, and the Patrick brothers' parents, Joe and Grace, were in the stands, along with a far from full house of twenty-five hundred. The Victoria Aristocrats, in red and white, lost 8–3 to New Westminster, wearing black and orange. Despite the home team's loss, the Victoria *Times Colonist* gave the new game an effusive endorsement, saying, "Ice hockey [delivered] all the thrills the west had heard of."

Across the Strait of Georgia in Vancouver, excitement rose as Frank's Millionaires prepared for their debut three nights later. The *Province* stoked Vancouverites' interest with a droll tease: "With all due reverence for cricket, we think hockey is a trifle faster; Lacrosse is a pretty swift game, but it is a funeral procession in comparison with hockey; Ice hockey in Victoria – in a real live rink too. What would our forefathers think?" On the day of the Vancouver opener, the *Province* explained the nature and rules of the game, reminding its readers, "Only a small percentage of the city's population has been privileged to see the game played in other parts of Canada." For more than half of them "the game will be very much a novelty."

It was no novelty for the Vancouver Millionaires, a veteran, star-studded squad boasting the great Lalond, as well as Si Griffis and Tommy Phillips, who had been crucial to the Kenora Thistles' Cup victory in 1907, and Frank Patrick on defence. But, despite the talent and the hype, the Pile was half empty when

the Millionaires played their home opener on Friday, January 5, 1912, defeating New Westminster (who also played *their* home games in the Vancouver rink) 8–3. The *Province*'s observation that the fans were novices was right, but they were also quick studies, becoming, the paper reported, "ardent enthusiasts long before the finish . . . up on their toes, and cheering wildly at the spectacular work shown. After last night's exhibition there is no doubt about the popularity of ice hockey here."

Popular to a point. The Patrick brothers still had seen 7,200 empty seats – nearly 50 per cent of their capacity – for the debut games of a new sport in a new league in the most urbanized province in Canada. There was only one answer to the problem: Cyclone Taylor.

It took the Patricks the better part of a year to lure Taylor west, and true to his habit of testing the waters – frozen or otherwise – to gauge his worth, Taylor skated for the East All-Stars against those from the Patricks' league in

To promote the legitimacy of their new league, the Patrick brothers proposed an exhibition series between the best players of the National Hockey Association and those of the Pacific Coast Hockey Association. So, at the close of the 1911–12 season, the East All-Stars arrived on the West Coast for a three-game contest. Though easily defeated in the first two games by the westerners, the eastern stars unleashed Cyclone Taylor (top row, second from left) for the third game. Despite nursing a left hand so badly gashed that he could barely hold a hockey stick, Taylor broke a 3–3 tie with two spectacular goals, the last of which earned him a two-minute standing ovation. (*Andrews-Newton Photograph, International Hockey Hall of Fame and Museum*)

Vancouver in March 1912, but only for the third period. The twenty-six-year-old Taylor was content to give the eight thousand fans a taste of what could be theirs, by setting up the winning goal in a 3–3 tie, then he returned to the East, leaving people clamouring for more.

Taylor had waged his own brand of off-ice fun that 1911–12 season by launching a contractual war between the Montreal Wanderers, who "won" Taylor's rights when Renfrew folded, and the Senators in Ottawa, a town where he could enjoy the charms of his fiancée, Thirza Cook, and his job with the government. He even played for Ottawa in an exhibition game in Boston, and the Wanderers reacted by convincing the NHA to suspend Taylor for the entire season. Free agency was a disease that must be crushed.

Taylor responded by trying to convince the Senators to pay him $1,200 to serve his suspension in Ottawa, or else he might just find reason to travel elsewhere. They paid, but he departed anyway, answering Frank Patrick's pithy telegram overture – "Dear Fred: Having a wonderful time. Wish you were here" – by joining the Pacific league for the 1912–13 season. Taylor would once again be the highest paid player in the game at $1,800 a season, a serious pay cut from three years earlier when he was paid nearly triple that amount. Hockey's owners had learned their lessons well (or at least had learned how to collude) from the NHA's profligate spending.

It was a huge coup for the new league to land the most celebrated player in the game in his prime, a player who, with just one Stanley Cup to his name, had a hunger to win more. But, given Taylor's history of contractual fickleness, his journey out West for the 1912–13 season was chronicled in the Vancouver press. The *Vancouver Sun* on Tuesday, November 29, 1912, assured readers that Taylor had indeed taken the train from Ottawa the previous Saturday and would be arriving in town that week; on Friday the papers published proof that he had done so, with a photo of a glowering Taylor over a caption that said the "sensational Ottawa hockey player" had shown "flashes of his brilliant . . . form at the big work-out" held the day before.

B.C. Electric ran extra trolley cars to transport five hundred New Westminster fans to Vancouver to watch Taylor's debut against their Royals. In an inspired move, Frank Patrick moved the Cyclone from defence up to the forward line, making him a rover in order to exploit his natural gifts and iconoclastic tendencies. Taylor emerged as "Hero of the Game," said the *Sun*. "Times innumerable he engineered a Vancouver attack, simply through his wonderful manipulation of the rubber, but more particularly through his lightning speed and clever stick-handling. It was Taylor here and Taylor there, throughout the entire game. Truly he lived up to his cognomen of the Cyclone many, many times."

The Millionaires' next home game again proved the Patricks had been right. For the first time since it opened, 10,500 people filled the Vancouver Arena to capacity, making it the largest audience ever to watch a hockey game.

Though they lost $9,000 on their first year of Pacific hockey operations, the Patricks were still thinking big. Frank won the right to stage ice hockey at the 1915 San Francisco World's Fair, in exchange for $250,000. The First World War ultimately cancelled that plan, but the Patricks had their eye on the United States, and, at the time, their bid captured the public's imagination. "The breaking up of the National Hockey Association by the Patricks only proved a light lunch for the progressive spirits of the Coast magnates," crowed the *Sun* on December 2, 1912, "but a more stupendous feat could hardly be imagined than that which Frank Patrick announced yesterday afternoon."

The Patricks were also busy retooling the game and over the next few years, other leagues adopted their innovations. In 1912, inspired by a British magazine showing cross-country runners wearing numbers on their singlets,

Hockey's "Royal Family" celebrates patriarch Joe Patrick's sixty-seventh birthday on August 12, 1924, at his home in Victoria, BC. It was Joe Patrick's lumber fortune, and his sons' Frank and Lester's vision and talent that brought professional hockey to the Pacific Coast in 1911. However, by the time of this birthday party, the West Coast hockey dream had turned sour. The Pacific Coast Hockey Association had folded that year, after bringing some of the brightest hockey lights, and two Stanley Cup championships, to the West.

(*BC Sports Hall of Fame and Museum*)

After Cyclone Taylor's bravura display of hockey in the late winter of 1912, the Patrick brothers knew that to make their league a true contender, they needed to put the Cyclone in a Pacific Coast Hockey Association uniform. Taylor, who had managed to have himself declared a free agent, was contemplating a fat contract with Ottawa when Frank Patrick wooed him West with an offer of $1,800 – then the richest in pro hockey. Taylor made his debut as a Vancouver Millionaire on December 10, 1912, in Victoria, and scored a dazzling goal in a 7–4 win. After the game, he returned to his hospital bed to continue his recovery from the appendicitis that had hit him two days before the match.

(Vancouver Sun, November 29, 1912)

FRED "CYCLONE" TAYLOR.

Sensational Ottawa hockey player, who arrived in the city yesterday and who showed flashes of his brilliant old-time form at the big workout held at the Arena yesterday afternoon.

the Patricks introduced numbered hockey jerseys. That same year, they freed goalies to leave their feet to stop the puck. The following year, after being frustrated by a series of momentum-killing offside calls in the World Series against Quebec, the Patricks conceived of dividing the ice into three zones with blue lines sixty-seven feet apart. Forward passing would be allowed in this zone, designed to open up the game.

The Patricks continued to lure stars out West, one way or another. In 1914, Didier Pitre arrived with his board-splintering wrist shot and toasted fans between periods with a pint of chilled champagne, which he drank to restore his lost fluids. He came as compensation for Newsy Lalonde, who went back to Montreal, but this enforced spell on the Pacific Coast didn't bother Pitre, who managed to reinvent himself as a forward and score thirteen goals in fourteen games for the Millionaires, tying for the team lead.

In the late winter of 1914, the Patricks were within striking distance of the Stanley Cup, when Victoria played the Toronto Blueshirts in a three-game series. Although Toronto won the series, the Patricks captured the Cup the following season. After sweeping the Ottawa Senators in three games, and outscoring them 26–8, the Millionaires were, as the Vancouver *Province* announced in a banner headline, world champions.

A mere four years after they had launched their Pacific Coast league, the Patricks and their all-stars had won hockey's highest prize. Professional hockey was now national, and with the sale of their New Westminster team to Portland, Oregon, and the birth of a franchise in Seattle the following year, the Patricks made it international. The Patricks had risked their father's fortune on the venture, but they had won. They had iced star-studded teams that entertained huge numbers of fans, they had changed the game with innovations, and they had managed to achieve glamour and respectability – and stay solvent. Hockey was firmly a business, now, and the Patricks had raised the stakes by thinking big.

But hockey wasn't only a business. When Frank and Lester Patrick tried to enlist to fight in the war that had begun in August 1914, the government turned them down. Frank Patrick proposed creating a Sportsmen's Battalion to the Irish Fusiliers in Vancouver in the spring of 1915, but two weeks later, a letter arrived from the federal government rejecting the proposal. The Patricks and their game were, it said, "crucial to sustaining morale during the war." Even a government engaged in fighting overseas could see the obvious: in just four decades, hockey had become essential to the health of the nation. The Patricks would stay put. The country needed hockey.

CHAPTER 3

BLOOD
AND CHAMPAGNE

"To you from failing hands we throw / The torch; be yours to hold it high" are the lines painted on the dressing-room wall of the Montreal Canadiens. They come from the poem "In Flanders Fields," written by Major John McCrae, a surgeon with the Canadian Field Artillery, on May 3, 1915, during the Second Battle of Ypres, the day after he had presided over the funeral of a friend. After several rejections, "In Flanders Fields" was published anonymously in the British magazine *Punch* and became the most popular English poem about the mass slaughter that was the First World War, a war that killed nearly 30 million people worldwide from combat, disease, and starvation.

That a hockey team would choose to inspire its young men with lines advocating violent death reveals more about the effect of what was then called the Great War on the country than it does about the literary sensibilities of hockey teams. When Canada's governor general, the Duke of Connaught, received a telegram at 8:55 p.m. on August 4, 1914, announcing that Britain was at war with Germany, Canada, not yet independent of the British Empire, was at war, too.

People across the land, both French and English, did not question their obligation to defend France, or Belgium, or England from German attack, and hundreds of thousands of Canadians answered the call to arms with an enthusiasm that, in hindsight, seems to be not only from another age, but another world. Today, the fate of many of these young men can be found on obelisks and cenotaphs seemingly in every settlement, no matter how small, across the land.

Despite daily newspaper reports on the home front of heavy casualties and news that, in addition to the use of poison gas and artillery bombardments and raking machine guns, the Germans had actually crucified a Canadian soldier, recruiters had no problem finding volunteers. The rhetoric of recruitment drew from the amateur athletic ideal of the previous century and cast war as the ultimate game an athlete could play. Captain James Sutherland, president of the Canadian Amateur Hockey Association, used hockey to inspire players to sign up. "With every man doing his bit, Canada will raise an army of brain and brawn from our hockey enthusiasts the likes of which the world has never seen. The bell has rung. Let every man play the greatest game of his life." An appeal in the Montreal *Gazette* showed a wounded soldier imagining a stadium filled with fans back in Canada, and asked, "Why be a spectator here when you should play a mans [*sic*] part in the real game overseas?"

So Canadian hockey players traded their hockey uniforms for the army's. From the MAAA alone 965 men went to Europe to "take up the quarrel" with soldiers they would otherwise have played sport against had things been different. (Famously they did play together, in soccer matches between Germans and the Allies during an impromptu Christmas Day truce in 1914, which so outraged senior British officers that they promised to shoot anyone who tried such a stunt again. The "game" metaphor for war only went so far.)

"One-Eyed" Frank McGee, the best of the magnificent Ottawa Silver Seven, managed to enlist in the army as a

Sport and battle were twinned in the language and imagery of the First World War, as young athletes were encouraged to join in the "real game" of war. The Victorian ideal, borrowed from the Greeks, of the individual being able to make all the difference to both a game and a battle might have filled the dreams of Army recruiters and those who responded to their call, but the mechanized carnage of trench warfare quickly destroyed that notion – and a generation of athletes. (*Canadian Museum of Civilization*)

lieutenant, despite having lost his left eye while playing in a charity hockey match supporting an earlier war, the Boer. During his army physical, McGee passed the sight test by merely switching the hand covering his left eye when asked to read from the chart. The doctor who examined McGee couldn't quite bring himself to play along with the hockey star's ruse – McGee's blind left eye had been an essential part of his legend – and wrote "good" on McGee's medical chart, as his assessment of McGee's right eye, and left the space describing his blind eye blank.

McGee was no impressionable youth, but a thirty-six-year-old man when he joined up in November 1915. A month later he was in an armoured car in Belgium that was hit by a bursting shell. McGee suffered a small puncture wound to his knee, which became so swollen he spent the next nine months recuperating in England, and was then offered a desk job. He wrote to his brother D'Arcy that he had turned it down and would rejoin his unit. On September 16, 1916, the man who had lit up the rinks of Eastern Canada with his brilliance was killed in action at Courcelette, another one of the 624,000 Allied troops who gave their lives in the Battle of the Somme.

Despite the colossal casualties, or perhaps because of them, his obituary in the *Ottawa Citizen* on September 25, 1916, continued the hockey metaphor, commending McGee for his "jump into the greater and grimmer game of war," and added a recruiting pitch, just in case his death should scare off lesser mortals. "And just as in his sporting career he was always to be found in the thickest of the fray, there is no doubt that on the field of battle Lieut. McGee knew no fear nor shunned any danger in the performance of his duty."

For athletes, duty, adventure, and patriotism still beckoned, and hockey players continued to enlist. After winning the Varsity Championship in front of 4,500 fans in March 1915, a twenty-year-old hockey player and the rest of his University of Toronto Varsity team decided they, too, had to join the greater game of war. As he later recalled in his memoirs, "We'd been talking about it for weeks, and decided that win or lose in the hockey final, we were going to get in uniform right away. The following Monday nine of us from the hockey team went down to join up in two artillery outfits that were recruiting. By the end of the day I was Gunner C. Smythe, 25th Battery, Canadian Field Artillery."

By that autumn, Conn Smythe was a lieutenant, waiting with his men in Toronto to be shipped to Europe. Given that ten of them were among the finest hockey players in Ontario, and had some time on their hands, Smythe's gambling instinct kicked in: he applied to the Ontario Hockey Association for a charter to ice a team of soldiers. The owners in the OHA were more than happy to accommodate him, and showed their appreciation for the men prepared to get blown to bits on their behalf by giving Smythe and his soldier team a terrible schedule: four home dates before Christmas, when attendance was traditionally so low that the players could outnumber the fans. But Smythe was counting on something the owners had shown they didn't have: patriotism. When twenty-five hundred Torontonians turned out to support the soldier team in their first game, which they lost 6–1, he knew that he could make some money as soon as his players found their skating legs.

It did not take them long. After his gunners won their next two games, and after paying off the team's start-up debts, Smythe discovered they had made a $2,800 profit. Then, in the kind of dramatic irony that followed Smythe for his long life, a Toronto magnate, who had made his fortune providing steel for the bombs and shells that were killing athletes, proposed a wager. All of Smythe's profits so far, on one game. Smythe was shocked, but his commanding officer told him to do it – it would be their last game. They were going to war.

With $5,600 riding on a single match between the gunners and their nemesis, the Toronto Argos, who had previously beaten them twice in overtime, Smythe's team unleashed Quinn Butterfield, an Orillia native, who scored four goals to lead the soldiers to an 8–3 victory. Smythe's team received another $1,106 in gate receipts, as a record crowd of more than six thousand fans had turned out to watch the match, making the soldier team's take a handsome $6,706.

Smythe's soldier team caught the attention of the National Hockey Association, whose executives saw the draw of a man with two uniforms: hockey's and the army's. They started their own team, turning the 228th Battalion or Northern Fusiliers into a full-fledged NHA member, and gave them a full roster of games against other professional teams. On December 1, 1916, wearing khaki-coloured uniforms, the 228th skated onto the ice and showed they were much more than a curiosity by humbling a team of all-stars 10–0 in the presence of the Duke of Devonshire, the governor general, and five thousand paying spectators.

While Smythe's gunners were an amateur college team infused with patriotic fervour, the Northern Fusiliers were seasoned pros. Sergeant Eddie Oatman, twenty-seven, had played for the Quebec Bulldogs in 1911, then joined the Patricks' Pacific Coast league, playing for New Westminster, before signing with the Portland Rosebuds. Sergeant Samuel "Goldie" Prodgers, twenty-five, had recently scored the Stanley Cup–winning goal for the Montreal Canadiens, playing there with twenty-one-year-old Sergeant Amos Arbour, and twenty-five-year-old Captain Howard McNamara and now with them again in the 228th. Howard's older brother, Captain George McNamara, twenty-eight, had played defence for the 1912 NHA champion Toronto Tecumsehs and more recently for Toronto's Blueshirts, who won the 1914 Stanley Cup, while

While athletes were trading their hockey jerseys for army uniforms, in December 1916, a hockey team made its debut wearing military khakis. Far from being a collection of amateur athletes, the team from the 228th Battalion (known as the Northern Fusiliers) were seasoned pros who outscored their opponents forty goals to twenty in their first five games to lead the National Hockey Association by January 1917. (*Hockey Hall of Fame*)

Lieutenant Art Duncan, twenty-five, had starred for the 1916 Vancouver Millionaires. Even the amateur players on the team were exceptional, with Lieutenant Gordon Meeking being rated "the greatest little goal-getter ever seen in the O.H.A." by the *Toronto World*, and Lieutenant Rocque "Roxie" Beaudro having been a member of the 1907 Stanley Cup–winning Kenora Thistles. Oddly enough, the squad's only neophyte was the goalie, Private Howard Lockhart. But then, he had an all-star team in front of him.

The 228th outscored their first five opponents 40–20 to lead the NHA by early January, but in mid-February, the team was going off to war – or at least, their battalion was. "The soldier team is thru for all time," mourned the *World*, writing the team's obituary. "They always played clean hockey, and always put their best foot forward. One can hardly say more than this. Doing one's best is all [that] can be asked of mortals in this world of sadness." When the 228th received their marching orders, they were leading the league with seventy goals and sat in third place in the standings – with one win less and one loss more than the first-place Montreal Canadiens, who would go on to compete for the Stanley Cup.

At the same time, the *Toronto Telegram* ran a bizarre item from London announcing "a welcome falling off in the names of prominent British sportsmen killed and wounded in action on the Somme," possibly due to the fact that most of the sportsmen had already been killed. The 228th need not have worried, for their departure revealed the true nature of their patriotic enterprise. Just ten days after shipping out for France, star forwards Eddie Oatman and Gordon Meeking turned up in Montreal, having both been discharged because they "would not become efficient soldiers," an offence for which some soldiers in the front lines were court-martialled and shot at dawn. Oatman came clean and revealed he was never a "real member of the battalion," and had only been recruited to play hockey for them. He claimed they still owed him seven hundred dollars on a twelve-hundred-dollar salary. Meeking's complaint was that he had been promised a lieutenant's commission, and was even allowed to wear the appropriate uniform in anticipation of it coming through. When the battalion shipped out in February 1917, he had been ordered into a private's uniform, and having had the taste of life as a star officer hockey player, politely declined. Other players could do the dying.

In November of 1917, the Toronto papers reported that Lieutenant Conn Smythe had done just that, or rather, was "missing in action," a euphemistic way of saying that the soldier in question had probably been killed. Smythe had managed to get himself out of the trench war and into the air war, where the chances of dying were still good. Smythe was now the pilot of an artillery observation plane, one whose design was so flawed it was nicknamed the "Incinerator." But he was lucky: his plane didn't spontaneously burst into flames, as other planes of the same design had done. Instead, he was shot down and captured, whereupon his scrappy manner managed to so offend the German soldier who was trying to take him into custody that the German shot him twice, at point-blank range. Smythe was saved by his thick flying coat, but it was really another instance of the magical luck that would colour his life. He would spend the rest of the

war in the safety of a prison camp, though it took a month for news to reach Smythe's mourning father that his son had not been killed. Conn Smythe would soon be home, reminding people that he had been resurrected once, and would do it again. And he would do it in hockey.

While their young men were away at war, Canadian women finally got a chance to improve their lot. When the war began, Canada's women couldn't vote, nor they could own property. By 1917, women with male relatives serving in the armed forces could vote on their behalf, and by the time the war ended in 1918, women had won the right to vote in federal elections – as long as they were British subjects, and at least twenty-one years old.

The war also offered women skilled jobs, more often than not in the industry then powering the country's economic engine, munitions. While Canada's young men were off in Europe getting killed or maimed by shells and bombs, and using them to kill, Canada's young women were making them. "Twelve months ago, in Canada, no thought of woman labour was in the mind of any manufacturer," reported the Imperial Munitions Board in 1916. "Experience has proved that there is no operation on shell work that a woman cannot do, and as a matter of fact, is doing."

The maple leaf may have been used as a symbol for Canada as early as 1700, and in 1867, a patriotic song was composed in its honour, "The Maple Leaf Forever." By 1914, it was used extensively on Canadian military badges, coats of arms, and coins. Canadian soldiers wore the maple leaf badge on their tunics, and soon it truly permeated the Canadian consciousness as a national symbol, inspiring Conn Smythe to name his hockey team after it. (*Hockey Hall of Fame*)

The Birth of the NHL

The National Hockey League came into existence "to perpetuate the game of hockey," because of a dispute among businessmen. The directors of the National Hockey Association met at Montreal's Windsor Hotel in November 1917 because the league was in trouble. Quebec City's franchise had money problems and, at the same time, the other owners found Eddie Livingstone, who owned the Toronto club, "difficult." The NHA owners came up with a simple solution to the last problem: they would form a new league, the National Hockey League, that would exclude Toronto. As the meeting was nearing its end, timely news arrived that Eddie Livingstone had just sold his Toronto franchise. The financially strapped Quebec owner offered to withdraw from the new league to make room for the Livingstone-free Toronto team – but only if he was allowed to sell his players for seven hundred dollars a man. He was, and he did. And so the National Hockey League was born.

Transplanted British schoolteacher and sportswriter Frank Calder was elected president and secretary-treasurer of the "new" league at an annual salary of eight hundred dollars, first making sure that the new league accepted the president's decision as final. In the hotel corridor after the meeting broke up, a young *Montreal Herald* sports reporter, Elmer Ferguson, asked Calder what had happened to professional hockey in Canada. "Not too much, Fergie," Calder replied. (*Imperial Oil – Turofsky/Hockey Hall of Fame*)

By 1917, the government's Imperial Munitions Board was Canada's biggest business, earning $2 million a day from its more than six hundred weapons factories. Munitions production was at its height, and thirty-five thousand women were employed in munitions plants alone in Ontario and Quebec, though their salaries were still between 50 and 80 per cent of what men doing similar work earned.

The war cohabited with civilian life in a jarringly ordinary way – casualty reports and clothing sales took up equal billing in many newspapers, while the daily sports section briefly eulogized the local athletes who had died young amid the sports scores and news of the world of games. But the world of games wasn't doing too well. With many players at war, hockey was suffering. In Montreal, the Wanderers made the patriotic gesture of offering free tickets to servicemen and their families in a desperate attempt to put fans in seats, though, on the miserly and macabre condition that the soldiers in question had to have been wounded. But hockey's woes were yet another chance for women to step – or skate – forward.

Halifax Explosion

On December 15, 1917, Montreal's Canadiens and Wanderers played the NHL's first exhibition game, in aid of the victims of the explosion that had levelled much of Halifax ten days earlier. One of those victims was Charlie Vaughan, who was killed instantly when the French munitions ship *Mont Blanc* exploded after colliding in Halifax Harbour with a Belgian relief ship. Vaughan had played semi-pro with the Halifax Socials in 1916, winning the local championship and then defeating Glace Bay for the regional title. He signed with the city's Crescents in 1917, and his obituary mourns him as "one of the best wing men in the Maritime Province." The explosion also killed Vaughan's wife, his five-year-old son, his sister, and his mother – along with nearly 2,000 other Haligonians in a city of 50,000 people. (*Library and Archives Canada, C-166585*)

The Montreal *Daily Star* of January 18, 1916, reported: "Casualties were heavy. Miss Hill of North End Stanley received a blow with a stick across the face. Miss Allbutt of Telegraph gained a black eye. Miss May Doloro of Maisonneuve stopped the puck with her forehead and sports a fine big bump, and Miss Thompson of Telegraph hurt her arm when she fell in a mix-up with another young lady on top of her." In an effort to reassure its readers that the women's match was "real hockey," the reporter added, "There is a tremendous interest being taken in ladies' hockey just now." The women's game had a real star too, in the person of twenty-six-year-old Albertine Lapensée, who played for the Victorias in Cornwall, Ontario. She knew how to put the puck in the net – and paying customers into the rink.

"Perfect ice is promised, and it is probable that the match will attract the largest crowd that has ever witnessed a girls' game in Ottawa," the *Ottawa Citizen* reported on March 4, 1916. The reason was that "Miss Albertine Lapensée will be the centre of attention when the Cornwall team skates out. The gallant little lady has gained fame as the queen of all lady hockeyists. She scored fifteen goals in a recent game."

Her coach, Cornwall promoter Ernie Runions, called her his Miracle Maid, but ever since Lapensée's debut for Cornwall in a game against Ottawa in January 1916, scoring all three Cornwall goals in their victory, there had been questions about her. Ottawa players complained after the match that Albertine was really a man, and the accusation resurfaced the following week when Lapensée scored four goals in an 8 – 0 shutout of the Montreal Westerns before a crowd of three thousand.

The *Daily Star* reported "Miss Lapensée's shots were the hardest and she was such a superior player that for a while the Western players and their supporters thought she really was a boy in girls clothing." The Montreal goalkeeper had been warned about her and wore a baseball catcher's mask to protect herself – a decade ahead of Queen's University's Elizabeth Graham, who donned a fencing cage and is usually credited with wearing the first goalie mask.

The rumours of Lapensée's Y chromosome spurred the *Cornwall Standard* to run an extraordinary "investigative" piece on February 17, 1916, in response to the demand for evidence from the sports editor of the *Daily Star*, proving that Lapensée was, in fact, a woman. The piece explains that she had "played more with her brothers and other boys than with her girlfriends, and this accounts for the masculine style of play she has developed. Scores of people in East Cornwall have known her since her infancy." The paper also reported that players on the Montreal Westerns had yanked off Lapensée's toque in a recent match "to ascertain the length of her hair and in doing so caused it to fall in long braids down over her shoulders. There is no question about it, Miss Lapensée is a girl."

Lapensée even behaved like a male player off the ice, nearly causing a riot by refusing to play until she had been paid. As the *Ottawa Citizen* reported, the matter was quickly resolved and "the Ty Cobb of the Cornwall team, conspicuous with a little blue fringe around her toque, skated out amidst cheers. And she more than made good."

The manager of the Montreal Westerns, Len Porteous, frustrated that his star, Agnès Vautier, was no match for Lapensée, seemed to have found his answer to the Cornwall scoring machine in the form of Ada Lalond. As a local newspaper reported in March 1917 the seventeen-year-old Lalond was a "hockey prodigy" and "all those who saw her play . . . proclaimed her Lapensée's rival." Hope was short-lived, however, as the next day's edition revealed that Ada Lalond was not who she said she was. A young man had confessed that "he dressed as a girl because he wanted to play against Lapensée. . . . The young boy, dressed in bloomers and a jersey top, definitely looked like a girl and even fooled Len Porteous during the first practice."

There was talk, though, that some of the women hockey players would be drafted into the men's professional leagues. "It is said that Miss Hart, goalkeeper for Maisonneuve Stanley, has been offered a contract by some N.H.A. team," reported the Montreal *Daily Star* on January 26, 1916, and taking a dim view of it, called the promoters "wolves trying to enter the sheepfold of ladies hockey." It went on to reassure readers worried that this might happen, "Thus far the emissaries have met with absolute non-success, and it is more than likely that if they persist they may have to deal with some of the mothers and male friends of the young ladies."

And the clergy. "Quebec Priests Do Not Approve of Ladies' Hockey" was the headline of a March 1916 report in the *Daily Star* revealing that young women of St. Patrick's parish had been warned to stay out of women's hockey because it was "not for ladies." It was, however, for the public, and promoters were soon talking of a tour of the United States, of the kind male stars such as Cyclone Taylor and the Patrick brothers had made.

On March 3, 1916, American investors came to Montreal hoping to entice the Westerns to undertake a six-week tour of the States. The project made headlines for days, as convention held that it was inconceivable for ladies, even chaperoned, to go on such a trip, The *Star* editorial of March 4 supported "short pleasure trips out of town to play against other established ladies teams under the guardianship of older ladies as chaperones" but objected to the "commercial barnstorming trips which are simply undertaken to put money in the pockets of certain promoters and are liable to do the young ladies harm in various ways. . . . Young ladies going on these sorts of trips put themselves in competition with professional actresses, burlesque performers and vaudeville and [could expect] to be treated as such."

A week later, the entire Montreal Westerns team wrote to the newspaper's editor, expressing outrage. "As members of the Western Ladies Hockey Club of Montreal who saw in last Saturday's *Star* dispatch about lady hockey players going 'trooping' to the States, and in which some of the Western players were mentioned as taking the trip, we beg to say that we strongly object to such treatment and do not wish to be in any way connected with this trip." It was left to Ottawa and to Albertine Lapensée's Cornwall Victorias to satisfy American curiosity about women's hockey. Because of the threat to public morals their trip evidently presented, the two teams departed for a three-game exhibition in Cleveland, Ohio, in the middle of the night. The Montreal papers happily reported that women's hockey was treated as "burlesque" in Cleveland.

Albertine Lapensée scored 80 per cent of her team goals in that 1916–17 season, but the following year, she disappeared. Family lore has it that in 1918 the Miracle Maid went to New York and had a sex-change operation, settled down, and opened a gas station near Cornwall, adopting the name Albert Smythe.

Albertine Lapensée and the first surge of popularity for women's hockey came from necessity. When the war ended, so did the craze for women's hockey. It would be another two decades, in the prelude to another world war, before women's hockey once again captured national attention.

Professional hockey was still hurting. The 1916 Stanley Cup match between the Portland Rosebuds and the Montreal Canadiens was so poorly attended,

In 1916, the Portland Rosebuds of the Patrick brothers' Pacific Coast Hockey Association became the first American team to play for the Stanley Cup. The Vancouver Millionaires had won it the year before, and the Rosebuds hoped to keep the Cup in the West. The series against National Hockey Association champions the Montreal Canadiens went the full five games, with the Canadiens edging the Rosebuds to win hockey's top prize, but the Pacific Coast league had served notice that it was a serious contender. The following season, the Seattle Metropolitans became the first American team to win Lord Stanley's Dominion Challenge Cup.

(Hockey Hall of Fame)

the Montreal *Gazette* wondered if people were scared off by the increased ticket prices, or perhaps had "grown tired of hockey through the prolonged season." After initial nervousness in the fifth and final match of the series, both teams put on a splendid show, and with less than four minutes to go, the score was tied at one. Then Montreal forward Goldie Prodgers took the puck in his own end and steamrolled a couple of Rosebuds before faking out the last defender, drawing the goalie out of his net, skating around him, and lobbing the puck home. The Montreal Canadiens had just won their first Stanley Cup.

Without taking a breath after reporting their triumph, the *Gazette* indulged in a carping no Montreal team has escaped since, adding, "Through mistakes from their bench in the fourth game, they made it necessary for the series to go the full five games before a winner was determined."

In March 1917, professional hockey saw another first, as the Montreal Canadiens travelled west to play the Seattle Metropolitans of the Patrick brothers' Pacific league for the Stanley Cup – highly symbolic in light of the United States' entry into the war just two weeks later. The Metropolitans were the darlings of Seattle, whose citizens hoped the unofficially transplanted Toronto Blueshirts would bring the Emerald City its first professional sports championship. The Montreal *Gazette* of March 19, 1917, reported that "Thousands of frenzied hockey fans" from all over the Pacific Northwest and southern British Columbia turned out to cheer the series, pitting the 1916 Stanley Cup champion Canadiens against a Seattle team that was confident and sleek.

Despite their long train ride to the West Coast, and despite playing the first game under the Patricks' unfamiliar Pacific league rules, which allowed forward passing and falling goalies, Didier "Cannonball" Pitre blasted four of Montreal's eight goals past Seattle's Hap Holmes. Montreal's Georges Vézina fared better in goal, displaying, the *Gazette* reporter said, "one of the best games of netguarding that the American fans have ever seen. . . . Again and again he stopped some hard close-in shots with apparent ease and the Canadiens can shower most of their congratulations upon him for tonight's victory."

Vézina had been discovered by the Canadiens before the 1911 season when the team toured the Quebec hinterland and were shut out in a game against Chicoutimi. The nineteen-year-old Chicoutimi goalie, who had learned to skate only the year before and played in his boots, so impressed the Canadiens that manager Joe Cattarinich hired him on the spot – even though it meant Cattarinich would lose his job as the team's goalie. Vézina possessed such coolness under fire that he soon earned the nickname the "Chicoutimi Cucumber."

The Metropolitans, duly provoked, put six pucks past Vézina in the next game, and seeing that his feet were back in boots of clay, pressed harder, taking the last two games by a combined score of 13–2. Seattle forward Bernie Morris, who had made his professional debut with Victoria in 1915, went on a goal-scoring orgy, putting nine of his fourteen series goals past Vézina in the last two games alone – the greatest display of Stanley Cup scoring virtuosity since the days of Frank McGee. The Metropolitans' fans were exuberant, the *Seattle Times* reported, cheering their heroes "until the iron girders of the roof rattled as the Seattle team left the ice with the world's title safely won." So on March 25, 1917, an American-based team became champions of the professional hockey world for the very first time. No matter that all the players were Canadians, an American city's team had won Lord Stanley's Dominion Challenge Trophy.

Two years later, the same clubs met again in Seattle for the Stanley Cup final, while the world was no longer being ravaged by war, but by a pandemic so virulent that it would kill as many as 50 million people. It was as if Nature were taking revenge for the four-year assault she had suffered on the battle-fields of Europe. By March of 1919, the killer virus had caught up with the Montreal Canadiens in Victoria, where it sent seven members of the Victoria Aristocrats to hospital. When Montreal's Joe Hall, Newsy Lalonde, Louis Berlinquette, Billy Couture, Jack McDonald, and owner George Kennedy were afflicted during the Cup final, the Seattle management feared the worst, and began dismantling the arena's ice in order to convert the building into a roller rink for the spring and summer.

The Stanley Cup series was tied at two wins and one draw when on April 5, "Bad" Joe Hall, aged thirty-six, was killed by the pneumonia that came with the 'flu. Despite his rough reputation, Hall was "one of the jolliest, best-hearted, most popular men who ever played," said Frank Patrick. His death left a grim legacy, for the 1919 Stanley Cup championship was the only one ever cancelled – until eighty-six years later, when it was cancelled not because players were dying, but because of money.

Soldiers who survived the war and the 'flu returned to a Canada that was much changed, and if they were expecting endless victory parades, they were disappointed. While they were away, Canada had become more restrictive, adopting both passports and income taxes for all, and the consumption of liquor except for "medicinal purposes" was now banned, a prohibition that must have seemed unreal to soldiers who had been to hell and back.

The war, as wars are, had been good for business, but now that it was over, munitions factories were shutting down, and bankruptcies and unemployment rose. So did the cost of living, as products that had been rationed were now in demand, and housing that had been promised the returning veterans was scarce, making rents depressingly high and adding to the wounds, both mental and physical, the soldiers already bore.

Georges Vézina guarded the net for the Montreal Canadiens from 1910, the year after they were formed, until 1925, playing 367 straight regular season and playoff games until tuberculosis forced him from the net on November 28, 1925. Here, he poses in the style in which he played: standing up. Until 1922, or for most of his career, goalies in the Eastern professional leagues were not allowed to drop to the ice to make saves and had to remain standing throughout the game. Despite this restriction (which affected his goals-against statistics in comparison to later goalies), Vézina was considered such a fine netminder that the Canadiens donated a celebrated goaltending trophy in his name, and the Hockey Hall of Fame selected him as one of its original twelve members. (*Hockey Hall of Fame*)

Frank Frederickson was another hockey player who signed up in 1916, enlisting in the 196th Western Universities Battalion before transferring to the 223rd Scandinavian Battalion along with several of his Winnipeg Falcons teammates, whom Frederickson had captained and led to a league title in 1915. The 223rd also iced a soldier team during the 1916–17 season in Winnipeg before being sent overseas. Frederickson nearly became a casualty en route to Egypt, where he was to join the Royal Flying Corps, when his ship was torpedoed by a German submarine. A Japanese destroyer found him floating in a life raft in the Mediterranean, clad only in his pyjamas and clutching his violin, which he played as expertly as he played centre ice. (*BC Sports Hall of Fame and Museum*)

Frank Frederickson was one of those returning veterans, another hockey player who had signed up in 1916. When he arrived back in Winnipeg in 1919, he wanted to play hockey again, as did his teammates in the Falcons, who, with the exception of one player, Allan Woodman, were all of Icelandic descent. Despite the fact the Falcons had gone off to fight for Canada in 1916, they were still Scandinavian boys – or in the bigoted language of the time, "goolies," and the Manitoba senior league wouldn't let them play. Frederickson later explained, "We found that the reason we couldn't get into the senior league was because the players were from well-to-do families and wanted no part of us. But they couldn't quite get away from us that easily."

Frederickson, who learned English as a child by playing in local hockey games, now spoke it so eloquently that he convinced Bill Finlay, then the sports editor of the *Winnipeg Free Press*, to help him form an independent league so that the Falcons could play someone, anyone. "Bill was a bit dubious of our motley ragamuffin team," Frederickson later said. "No two players wore the same coloured socks, sweaters, or pants, and most had been off skates entirely during the war." But Finlay agreed to help and enlisted Fred "Steamer" Maxwell to coach the Falcons, and enticed two other teams, the Winnipeg Selkirks and one from Brandon, into the new Manitoba Hockey League. "By the end of the season, Steamer had welded us into a great team," Frederickson remembered. "We whipped the Manitoba league champions and later the Lakehead winner to enter the Allan Cup against Toronto Varsity."

The Allan Cup had been endowed in 1908 by the Montreal financier Sir Hugh Allan as a response to the professionalism that had claimed the Stanley Cup. The Allan Cup would be the prize for the best senior men's amateur hockey team. The ragtag second-class Falcons were considered lucky to be on the same ice as the highly favoured Toronto team, who had their eye on an even greater prize: the Olympic Games.

In January 1920, the International Olympic Committee announced that the games would be revived (they had been cancelled in 1916 due to the war), and that although they would be summer games, ice hockey would be included for the first time – because the owners of the Palais de Glace in Antwerp, which had been awarded the Games because of the city's suffering during the war, refused to allow figure skating unless they got ice hockey, too. As there was no time to round up a Canadian all-star team, Canada's amateur hockey brain trust decided that the winners of the Allan Cup would represent Canada. More

The International Ice Hockey Federation

The International Ice Hockey Federation was founded in 1908 as the Ligue International de Hockey sur Glace as the world's governing body for ice hockey (and became the IIHF in 1911). At the time, the IIHF "world" consisted of charter members Belgium, Bohemia (later Czechoslovakia), England, France, and Switzerland, with Germany joining the following year. Canada and the United States, respectively the birthplaces of the amateur and the professional games, did not join until 1920. *(Hockey Hall of Fame)*

than eight thousand fans paid as much as twenty-five dollars a ticket to see the Falcons play the University of Toronto Varsity Grads in March 1920 – though a former U of T hockey stalwart, Conn Smythe, wasn't on the team, he was on his honeymoon.

The Winnipeg war veterans not only won the two-game series easily, they won respect. "The Icelanders [Falcons] displayed more class than has been seen on the Toronto arena this year," said the *Winnipeg Free Press*. "The performance of the Westerns was a revelation to the eastern bugs, and their wonderful speed and puck carrying had the immense crowd gasping with amazement. Frank Frederickson, the clever center and captain of the team, and Mike Goodman, the speed king, gave a marvelous exhibition of skating and puck carrying, the like of which has never been seen here during a winter of sensational hockey."

The Falcons had no time to return to Winnipeg before they sailed off to represent Canada in Antwerp, so, with twenty-five dollars for new clothes in their pockets, the players shipped overseas one more time, although this time their weapons were hockey sticks, which the ship's carpenter patriotically made for them from wood especially purchased in Montreal.

The trip back to the continent where the Falcons had recently been fighting a war was made frustratingly banal by the presence on their ship of members of the Women's Christian Temperance Union, who seemed to find their way on deck whenever the Falcons were training. "They do their best to make things miserable for everybody," Alan Woodman wrote to his mother. "Lord I'll be glad to get off this boat because I find the novelty wears off after the first three or four days. And eight days is all together too long in one place."

The winter component of the Games was held in April, ten weeks before the Summer Olympics started. Construction delays meant that the athletes

In 1916, the Winnipeg Falcons had set sail for Europe to fight for Canada in the First World War. Four years later, they embarked once again, this time in relative peace, armed only with hockey sticks. They were en route to Antwerp's Palais de Glace, site of the 1920 Olympic hockey competition, which the Falcons would dominate. *(Courtesy Brian Johannesson)*

had to sleep on cots, but the Palais de Glace was a marvel that sports editor and team manager Bill Hewitt, former scourge of Cyclone Taylor, played up for his readers back in Canada. "Chairs and tables remained on elevations on the other side, and spectators dined and drank as they watched the various nations play hockey," he wrote. "A really good orchestra played tirelessly from early morning until late at night."

Attendance at this Olympics was low – the war had made the cost of admission beyond the reach of most citizens. Hockey, however, was a hot ticket, as everyone wanted to see the Canadians play – or rather, play along. "All through the tournament we tried to limit ourselves to 14 or 15 goals a game against the European teams," Frederickson said. "Believe me, it was difficult, but we managed to stay within reasonable bounds." The Europeans loved the Canadians to the point of star worship, crowding outside the Palais de Glace from the early afternoon onward to await the Falcons, who had to be escorted to their dressing room by soldiers when they did arrive. A posse of adoring Europeans appointed themselves valets to Falcons' speedster Mike Goodman, whom they called "Monsieur le Canadien." They would accompany him to the rink, to ensure his safe passage through the adoring hordes.

Bill Hewitt reported, "Goodman was so fast and elusive that Europeans thought he had some kind of secret power in his boots and skates," but the war had also made them cold-eyed realists. "To discover that magic influence they offered as high as $100 a pair for Mike's equipment." Money was also offered by the American team, the only squad that could give the Canadians a scare. "One of the Americans was sure they'd beat us and offered a good-sized bet," Frederickson said later. "Our treasurer never told us, but he took him up on that wager." The Canadians beat the U.S. team 2–0, and the delighted treasurer presented each Falcon with a new suit of clothes. The Canadian Olympic program head found out and was furious – the ideal of amateurism had been tainted by filthy lucre. "He wanted to have us deprived of our title and medals for having accepted those gifts," Frederickson said, "but nothing happened."

The Canadians had defeated their opponents by a combined score of 29–1, and the one goal they did allow was to the Swedes, whom the Canadians thought were the best of the European teams. Frederickson later said, "I guess it's safe to confess that we gave [the goal] to them. The Swedes went wild. They were yelling and cheering, shaking hands with themselves, shaking hands with us. It was great."

Five years later the International Olympic Committee returned the favour, deciding that the Winter Games were official only from 1924 onward. Frederickson's gold medal no longer counted. But the Falcons – and Canada – had indisputably won the first World Championship. In the years to come, the public would expect nothing less.

After years of death and deprivation, in the 1920s the Jazz Age popped its champagne cork, and North America entered a time of garish prosperity and limitless ambition. Now, more than ever, people looked to sport to provide them with heroes. Hockey was happy to oblige, producing some of the game's most exalted players.

In Montreal, the Canadiens' boss, Leo Dandurand, saw the future, and it was one filled with infinite possibility and no small box office thanks to Howie Morenz, a young hockey wizard from Stratford, Ontario. Morenz had survived the war by being too young to serve, though that had not stopped him from sneaking off to Toronto in 1917 to enlist. When he failed to show for both lunch and dinner, his mother called the police, and off she went with them to Toronto to rescue her fourteen-year-old son from the Governor General's Horse Guards, who had already enlisted him.

In the spring of 1922, Leo Dandurand wanted to sign him up too. When Morenz scored nine goals for Stratford's Canadian National Railway team in the Montreal Canadiens' old home, the Mount Royal Arena, the referee, who had once played amateur hockey for the Canadiens' coach, Cecil Hart, called his friend with the news of the talented kid from Stratford. Hart relayed the

In 1906, four-year-old Howie Morenz's curiosity moved him to look into a pan of potatoes cooking on the stove. The pan tipped, splashing boiling water on his legs and scalding him so badly that his older sister Gertrude said, "We never thought he'd walk again, let alone play hockey." Howie Morenz did walk again, and on ice, he flew – earning the moniker the Stratford Streak and personifying the speedy élan of the Montreal Canadiens in the 1920s and 1930s. (*Hockey Hall of Fame*)

H.R.H. PRINCE OF WALES TROPHY
CHAMPIONSHIP EMBLEM
of the
NATIONAL HOCKEY LEAGUE

TRUSTEES
FRANK CALDER CHAIRMAN
WILLIAM FORAN   JOSEPH HANNON
W.T.COLLINS ·   JOHN S. HAMMOND

The Byng, Hart, Vezina, and Prince of Wales Trophies

The 1920s saw the creation of some of the game's great trophies as the NHL became the world's premier professional hockey league. In 1924, the Prince of Wales continued the aristocratic tradition of endowing hockey with prizes when he donated an eponymous trophy to the champions of the NHL in the multi-league system. The coveted Hart Trophy was born in the 1923–24 season courtesy of David Hart, the father of Montreal Canadiens' three-time Stanley Cup–winning manager Cecil Hart. Dr. Hart's trophy, which recognizes the player judged the "most valuable" in the league, soon became the most desired individual award in the game. Frank Nighbor of the Ottawa Senators won the first Hart Trophy in 1924 and in January 1925 was invited by Lady Byng of Vimy, wife of Canada's governor general, Sir Julian Byng, to drop by Rideau Hall. Lady Byng, a Senators fan, was especially keen on Nighbor's civilized and skilful play, and she showed him a huge two-handled silver goblet, asking him if he thought the NHL would accept the trophy as a token of her love for the game. Nighbor believed that they would, and so she handed him the trophy for being the most sportsmanlike player of 1925. "You have given me so many furiously thrilling hours at hockey," she wrote in a letter accompanying the award, "that I would like to take this opportunity of telling all the team what a real delight those evenings have been and how much I look forward to them."

(*Hockey Hall of Fame*)

referee's praise to Dandurand, who was at first skeptical: if Morenz was so good, how come no one else had signed him up? It was an uncharacteristic hesitation from the Canadiens' owner, who had bought the team that would become known as "les Glorieux" at the estate sale of its previous owner, George Kennedy. Or rather, Cecil Hart had bought the team while Dandurand and his partners "Little" Louis Letourneau, a Montreal fishmonger, and Joe Cattarinich, who once played goal for the Canadiens and now owned a tobacco business with Dandurand, were at the horse races in Cleveland, Ohio, where they owned a racetrack.

Dandurand and his partners wanted to transform the Canadiens into a team as distinctive as the city and culture from which they came, because it would be good for business. The Canadiens' style of play would come to be called "firewagon hockey," a fast, creative, elegant, and, when needed, tough game that turned Montreal into the standard by which all other teams measured themselves. Dandurand changed the team chemistry – and provoked

Leo Dandurand (right) and his partners, Louis Letourneau (middle) and Joe Cattarinich (left), or the Three Musketeers, as they were known, loved to gamble, and eventually owned seventeen racetracks across North America. (In the 1930s, Dandurand invented the daily double, and the photo finish.) Dandurand, the trio's gregarious leader, came to Montreal in 1905 as a sixteen-year-old from Bourbonnais, Illinois, and quickly assimilated thanks to his francophone heritage. He enrolled in the Jesuit Collège Ste-Marie and played for the school team, who voted him best player in 1907 and 1909, the year he graduated.

Dandurand made his first foray into the management world with the Nationals, an extremely successful French-Canadian lacrosse team, at the age of twenty – not even of legal voting age by club rules – and by the time he was thirty-two, he was the proud owner of the Canadiens, which he and his partners bought for eleven thousand dollars in November 1921, beating out none other than Frank Calder, the president of the National Hockey League.

(Hockey Hall of Fame)

howls of outrage among both Montreal fans and NHL owners who wanted a crack at him – by trading charter-member Newsy Lalonde to Saskatoon for the promising left-winger Aurèle Joliat. A twenty-one-year-old dynamo from Ottawa, Joliat turned to hockey after breaking his leg in football – an injury that was not surprising given his five-foot-six, 140-pound stature. And less than a year later, Dandurand was trying to sign up the player who together with Joliat would light up the Jazz Age and make the Montreal Canadiens synonymous with hockey excellence.

There was a problem with Dandurand's plan. The young saviour he was hoping to sign, Howie Morenz, was reluctant. Like Cyclone Taylor before him, he had a steady job – as a CNR machinist – and pride of place in his small-town hockey world as "the Stratford Streak." He didn't want to leave home. Young Morenz also had money troubles: he owed $800 as a result of spending habits that were as exuberant as his hockey. Dandurand saw an opening and offered Morenz an $850 signing bonus – enough to pay off the debt, or perhaps buy a stylish new car – on a contract of $2,500 a year. Because Morenz was only twenty, and thus underage, Morenz's father had to co-sign the contract with him. A month later, Morenz sent Dandurand a polite note cancelling the deal. "Dear Sir, I am enclosing a cheque and contract to play hockey with your club. Owing to several reasons, of which family and work are the most to consider, I find it impossible to leave Stratford. I am sorry if I have caused you expense

HOWIE MORENZ

When Howie Morenz was standing still, he looked tentative and slightly surprised to be in the uniform of the Montreal Canadiens. When he was moving on the ice, however, his genius not only lifted fans from their seats in delight and awe, it enshrined his Canadiens as the true Flying Frenchmen. *(Hockey Hall of Fame)*

and inconvenience, and trust you will accept the returned contract in a sportsmanlike way."

Dandurand would do no such thing and summoned Morenz to Montreal. At the meeting Morenz begged Dandurand to set him free and save him from public embarrassment. He wasn't good enough, he wasn't tough enough, and in a plea that reveals the power of the amateur ideal that still lingered, he claimed that playing for the professional team would kill his future as an amateur. "My whole life," he told Dandurand, in tears, "will be ruined." Dandurand gave Morenz a ticket back to Stratford – and some food for thought: he was confident that Morenz was good enough to hold his own in the NHL. Besides, he had signed a contract. His life would be ruined if he *didn't* play for the Canadiens.

Morenz's first shift with the Flying Frenchmen was on Boxing Day 1923, in Ottawa's new rink. Before a record crowd of 8,300 fans, he scored the first of the 270 goals that he would tally in the NHL. "Morenz skated right at me, going like hell, shot the puck, and knocked me on my ass," recalled young Frank "King" Clancy, who was on defence for Ottawa. "I told him if he tried it again, I would cut his head off. He laughed and said he planned to do it again. Know what? He did."

After beating Vancouver, champions of the Pacific Coast Hockey Association, Morenz and the Canadiens took on the Calgary Tigers for the 1924 Stanley Cup championship. With the "Little Giant" Aurèle Joliat and Billy Boucher on his wings, Morenz centred a blazingly fast line. In two games against the Tigers, the Joliat–Morenz–Boucher line accounted for eight of the Canadiens' nine goals. Georges Vézina allowed only six goals in six playoff games, and earned two shutouts. Aurèle Joliat came in third in playoff scoring, Billy Boucher came second, and Howie Morenz came first, with seven goals. The man who didn't want to play professional hockey – and certainly not in Montreal – wound up drinking champagne from the Cup in his first season as a professional.

In the autumn of 1924, the NHL, just seven years old, had one franchise in Hamilton that it considered "unstable," and three dependable teams: the Canadiens, the Toronto St. Patricks, and the Ottawa Senators. Twenty years earlier, the United States had transformed hockey into a professional sport. Now, the NHL believed, it was time for the sport to return to its professional roots but not for reasons of sentiment. The NHL knew it had an entertaining product, and the United States had a lot of money to spend on entertainment.

The United States of the 1920s was paradise for those looking for a marketable, profitable commodity to monopolize. Reduced business taxes and government tariffs protected American manufacturers, and new ways to increase the generation of electricity made mass production an even more powerful beast. The supply of and demand for cars, mechanized washing machines, phonographs, and radios soared, and Hollywood presented to the world the idea that America was the land of endless opportunity. Sport of all stripes was an essential component of the American experience. That most cherished of American freedoms, the individual will, could bring glory and fortune to those with talent and those who promoted them. And the population of the leviathan – then close to 120 million, compared to 10 million in Canada – meant that winners won very big indeed.

So, in December of 1925, fur coats and pearls brushed with top hats and tails as Park Avenue mingled with the belles of Broadway – and some two thousand Canadian swells – to see the debut of professional hockey in Manhattan. "Two charming debutantes will be formally presented to the sporting society tonight," the *New York Evening Post* wittily announced. "They are Madison Square Garden, darling of Tex Rickard's heart, and professional hockey, favourite child of Canada." What the paper didn't report was that hockey had made it to New York because George "Tex" Rickard, saloon keep, soldier of fortune, boxing promoter, and prime mover behind the new arena (built in 1925 to replace its 1890 predecessor), had seen Howie Morenz play. That, and a bit of good old-fashioned labour scandal.

The Hamilton Tigers, who had finished in first place during the 1924–25 season, went on strike after they learned that the "suffering" Tigers had made a $24,000 profit. Earlier, the owners had refused the players additional playoff pay of $200 a man. During the 1920s, strikes were more often than not portrayed as the work of socialist radicals, and for a group of hockey players to take such action was both a bold and an unpopular move. Still, the strike leaders Billy Burch and Wilfred "Shorty" Green remained firm, even though some of their teammates wanted to give in after NHL president Frank Calder threatened them with fines, suspensions, and a lawsuit.

The last thing Calder and the NHL owners needed as they advanced into the brave new American market was an ugly public labour dispute, and

When Newsy Lalonde was traded to the Saskatoon Sheiks by the Canadiens in exchange for Aurèle Joliat on November 3, 1922, there were howls of outrage in Montreal. But the five-foot-seven Joliat, nicknamed the Little Giant, soon had Montrealers cheering at the sight of his trademark black peaked cap, as he raced down the left wing to set up his linemates Howie Morenz and Billy Boucher. Toronto defenceman Babe Dye, frustrated by trying to catch Joliat, told Canadiens' owner Leo Dandurand that if he "moved Joliat to centre and held a mirror to each side of him, he'd have the fastest line in hockey." (*Hockey Hall of Fame*)

Lionel Conacher

Although Lionel Conacher, who was so large that he was nicknamed the Big Train, didn't start skating until he was sixteen, by the time he was eighteen he had won a Memorial Cup with the Toronto Canoe Club hockey team. That same year, 1920, he hit the winning home run in a baseball game, then travelled by taxi across town to suit up for his lacrosse team, the Toronto Maitlands, and bail out their 3–0 deficit by scoring four goals. The following year he scored four touchdowns for the Toronto Argonauts to win them the Grey Cup championship of football. He even played in the first hockey game to be broadcast on radio in 1923.

Both Toronto and Montreal coveted the big defenceman, but Conacher wanted an education, so he stayed amateur long enough to win an athletic scholarship to college in Pittsburgh. From there he made his NHL debut in 1925 with the Pittsburgh Pirates, and scored their first goal in franchise history. Conacher played for the New York Americans, and won Stanley Cups with the Montreal Maroons and Chicago Black Hawks. Upon his retirement in 1937, he turned to politics and was elected to the Ontario legislature that year, and in 1949, went as an MP to Ottawa. In 1954, while running the bases in a charity baseball game, the Big Train finally ran out of steam, when he collapsed and died. Conacher is a member of Canada's Sports, Football, Lacrosse, and Hockey halls of fame, and was named Canada's top athlete of the first half of the twentieth century by sportswriters in 1950. Today, Canada's top male athlete receives a trophy named after him. (*Hockey Hall of Fame*)

so the NHL did something ugly to crush their upstart players. Invoking the dictatorial power he insisted upon when he took the president's job in 1917, Calder suspended the entire team indefinitely, without leave to appeal, and fined them each $200 – the amount they had sought in compensation. Then, in 1925, the NHL sold the team to New York bootlegger William V. Dwyer for $80,000. The striking Hamilton Tigers had just become the New York Americans.

Dwyer loved hockey, having learned the game from a Canadian friend, and when his partner, Montreal Maroons director Tom Duggan, a reputed bootlegger, found out that Tex Rickard shared no such affection for the game and, shockingly, had no plan for hockey in Madison Square Garden, he had a solution. He invited Tex to Montreal to see the game as it should be played, and to wet his dry throat in post-Prohibition Canada. By the time the game started, Rickard was afloat on a sea of high-proof goodwill, and in the mood to watch Howie Morenz work his magic against the Ottawa Senators. When the game was over, Rickard had agreed to put ice in Madison Square Garden, but on one condition: the wizard Howie Morenz would have to play in the opening game.

And so he did. Morenz played before the crème of New York society in a charity benefit game sponsored – fittingly, given hockey's record of head injuries – by the city's Neurological Institute. Patrons such as Quincy S. Cabot

In 1925, George "Tex" Rickard, a cowboy, gold prospector, and boxing promoter, drove the final rivet into the new Madison Square Garden, whose construction he spearheaded, and which was quickly nicknamed the House That Tex Built. Initially Rickard had no plans to put ice in the new facility, then he saw Howie Morenz play hockey and changed his mind. New York City entered the National Hockey League that year with the creation of the New York Americans.

(Corbis/Bettmann)

Jr. and Mr. and Mrs. E.F. Hutton, financiers to the world, paid $11.50 for box seats, while the rabble forked out $1.50 for a perch in the gods. The prices were inflated for the evening from the usual $1.10–$3.85 a seat. The *New York Times* reported, "Much water will flow under the Brooklyn Bridge before New York witnesses a sporting carnival with so much fuss and ostentation." Mrs. Franklin D. Roosevelt was there too, as were Mrs. Charles Scribner and Mrs. Charles Tiffany, and circus tycoons John Ringling and William Barnum. When Aurèle Joliat saw the New York Americans skate out in their star-spangled uniforms, he thought that "they looked like they had come right out of a circus. We didn't know whether to play hockey against them or ask them to dance."

Professional hockey fit so nicely into this world of "pearls, patricians and playboys" because the city's St. Nicholas Rink, which had opened a quarter of a century earlier, had routinely showcased the talents of upper-crust Ivy Leaguers. Most Canadian boys started playing on frozen sloughs and ponds and rivers, but American boys more often than not learned the game at Groton, or Exeter, or St. Paul's, and carried it on to Harvard, Princeton, and Yale. So it was unsurprising that their supporters should come to the games in limousines. Both amateur and professional Canadian teams had made regular pilgrimages to New York to top up their bank accounts, and New Yorkers regarded these games as a guaranteed display of dazzle, skill, and flash.

Howie Morenz would not disappoint them, though Morenz didn't look like much. Balding already, and a slender five-foot-nine at 160 pounds, with a five o'clock shadow that seemed to appear five minutes after he had shaved, the twenty-three-year-old Morenz often seemed to be in his own world while out on the ice, following in his mind's eye a puck whose position bore no obvious relationship to the puck on the ice. Much as Wayne Gretzky would famously "see" the ice in his head sixty years later, Morenz could see the game unfold before it did and would anticipate where his linemates Joliat and Boucher would be before they knew it themselves. In their crimson uniforms, and with their firewagon style, Morenz and the Canadiens represented the exotic francophone north, even if Morenz was a German kid from Ontario, Joliat the son of a Swiss Protestant, and Boucher three-quarters Irish. Their line combined for all of Montreal's goals as they defeated the Americans 3–1. "The red coats met the Americans last night in a new revolution," gushed the *Evening Post*. "They met on ice – not the ice of the Delaware but the ice of the hockey rink in the new Madison Square Garden . . . and the soul of the new garden awoke."

Tex Rickard's soul awoke, too. The American papers, so captivated by Morenz that they cast him in the only terms they could understand, calling him "the Babe Ruth of Hockey," had put the NHL under the limelight in the

Lorne Chabot

At six-foot-one and 185 pounds, Lorne Chabot filled much of the goal net. He made his professional debut with the New York Rangers on November 27, 1926, posting a 2–0 shutout against the Toronto Maple Leafs. After fighting for Canada on the Western Front in the First World War, and a subsequent stint in the Royal Canadian Mounted Police, Chabot came to the attention of Conn Smythe when he backstopped Port Arthur to two Allan Cup championships. Smythe made Chabot the centrepiece of the first New York Rangers team. Soon the team's first press agent, Johnny Bruno, proposed renaming Lorne Chabot, a French Canadian, "Lorne Chabotsky" to give the Rangers ethnic cachet in New York's large Jewish community. Team coach and general manager Lester Patrick angrily quashed the rechristening when he saw the new names published in the game report, and when Johnny Bruno proposed "kidnapping" Rangers captain Bill Cook (and returning him just before the game) to generate headlines, Patrick sent him packing. Chabot was gone too after he was hit in the eye with a puck, which Patrick thought had made him skittish. Conn Smythe snapped him up for the Leafs in 1928–29, when Chabot posted a stingy 1.61 goals-against average and had twelve shutouts in forty-three games. He won the Stanley Cup with the Leafs in 1932, and the Vezina Trophy as the NHL's best goalie in 1935. (*Hockey Hall of Fame*)

Big Apple, and now the city wanted more. Tex Rickard would provide it, but, not before another war veteran found it.

When Conn Smythe finally stepped onto the platform of Toronto's Rosedale Station after being released from his German prisoner-of-war camp, he felt both cheated and impatient. "Four years of my life were gone that I would never get back," he said in his autobiography, *If You Can't Beat Them in the Alley*. "I was twenty-four and hadn't done a thing yet. But I was going to make up for it. Of that I was damn sure." There was still work for him in the gravel business, but his father had remarried and moved house, and he had a new baby sister. Canada had changed, but Smythe's nose for hockey talent had not, and it was his shrewdness and his prickly self-confidence that put him on the hockey map.

In 1924, Smythe took his University of Toronto Varsity squad on a college hockey tour to Boston, where the NHL had sold its first franchise to grocery tycoon Charles Weston in 1924, and promptly began a lifelong feud with Boston Bruins coach Art Ross. When asked what he thought of the lamentable Bruins, who had won only two games in the first half of a thirty-game schedule, Smythe bluntly replied that his college boys could certainly beat the Bruins, but, as amateurs, they had to settle for defeating Boston college teams. They did just that while drawing crowds so large that those who couldn't get into Boston Garden to see them in action had to be restrained by mounted police.

By 1926, the NHL had teams in Boston, Pittsburgh, Detroit, Chicago, and New York, and after witnessing the financial success of the New York Americans, who finished the season second from the bottom but with great box office, Tex Rickard reckoned there was room in New York for a second professional hockey team. The NHL agreed and sold him a franchise. One of Rickard's New York sportswriter pals jokingly gave the team their name – Tex's Rangers. And so the New York Rangers were born, much to the consternation of the Americans' owner, "Bootleg" Bill Dwyer, who had not agreed to a duet, yet couldn't do much about it from a Georgia prison, where he was serving time for tax evasion.

Rickard's problem was that while he had the NHL's blessing, and while his team had a name, he didn't actually have a team, so Charles Weston advised him to hire the guy who had put on such a show in Boston – Conn Smythe. But although Smythe had been going to the Toronto St. Patricks' games, and knew the book on all the players in the NHL, his real advantage was his amateur hockey experience. Smythe had watched players on their way up to the pros, and when he took his amateur teams on tours to places the NHL thought too out-of-the-way, he saw players who would otherwise have been missed altogether. He took the job in New York, and by the time he was finished, he had put together the New York Rangers for only $32,000 – an astonishing bargain, considering the Americans had cost $80,000, and Major Frederic McLaughlin had recently paid $120,000 to put a team in Chicago when he bought the Portland Rosebuds from the Patrick brothers. (The Patricks had moved their two surviving Pacific teams to the Western Canada Hockey League in 1924, and now that the WCHL had folded too, they sold off their players.)

Smythe built the Rangers with talent from Toronto, making forays into the hinterland to woo players whom he couldn't see in town, and always lamenting one who got away: Mike Goodman, the speed skater who had so dazzled the Europeans at the 1920 Antwerp Olympics and now refused to play for Smythe or anyone in the NHL, simply because he didn't want to. Another player who caused Smythe grief was St. Patricks' scoring machine Cecil "Babe" Dye, for there were those in New York who said that had Smythe been serious about

building a big-city team, he would have gone after Dye instead of serving up a team of amateurs from the boonies (an attitude that has plagued New York over the years). The gossip made Smythe burn, for he felt that he had created a team – not a backup chorus for an egocentric player like Dye.

Shortly after the Rangers opened their 1926 training camp at Toronto's Ravina Rink, Smythe was summoned to a meeting at Union Station. There to greet him were the Rangers' president, Colonel John Hammond, and the

The New York Rangers received their nickname as a play on the Texas Rangers, after George "Tex" Rickard, the man who brought pro hockey to Madison Square Garden. But the man who brought the Rangers to New York was Conn Smythe, whose knowledge of Canadian hockey talent helped him stock the new team at the bargain price of $32,000. The strategy only got him fired for being "provincial," and in the autumn of 1926, Lester Patrick stepped in to take over the Rangers for the outrageous sum of $18,000 a year. With Smythe's lineup of hockey talent, and Patrick's hockey acumen, the Rangers won the Stanley Cup in just their second season of play. (*Hockey Hall of Fame*)

team's new coach, Lester Patrick, who, after selling off the family league had landed on his feet in New York, at Smythe's expense. The Rangers were firing Smythe for not serving up enough glamour. As if that weren't bad enough, Hammond announced he was withholding a quarter of Smythe's $10,000 fee. The money, he said, had been meant to cover that cost of Smythe's move to New York, but Smythe had snubbed the city by staying put in Toronto. He would take $7,500, or he would take nothing.

Smythe took the reduced sum, vowing to have nothing more to do with the Rangers, but his wife, Irene, had other ideas when an invitation arrived from Tex Rickard for an all-expenses paid trip to New York City for the Rangers' home opener. While Smythe had been out scouting players for the Rangers, she had been at home looking after their children. She wanted a vacation, and this was going to be it. Smythe's wounded pride started to heal rapidly as he sat in Rickard's private box and watched the team that he had built defeat the Montreal Maroons in their debut game. A delighted Rickard offered Smythe a job as the team's vice president, and it was then Smythe realized that Rickard didn't know he had been cheated. Once he found out, Rickard ordered Colonel Hammond to pay Smythe the $2,500 they owed him. Smythe then did what came naturally to him: he bet it all on a football match between Toronto and McGill University. He doubled his money. When the Rangers came to town to play the St. Pats, Smythe took advantage of bookies who pegged the New Yorkers as a fluke, and secured 5–1 odds on the Rangers, who won. In three days, Smythe had parlayed $2,500 into $10,000.

Smythe knew he could build a team, and now he wanted to get involved with one on a more permanent basis – as an owner. So he approached J.P. Bickell, owner of the St. Pats, who were being wooed south by Philadelphia interests. Smythe played the patriotism card, arguing that if Toronto lost its only pro hockey team because Bickell had sold it to the United States, it could be a good long while before it saw another one. Bickell liked Smythe's nerve, and his eye. He agreed to put up $40,000 if the thirty-one-year-old hotshot could raise the other $160,000 he was asking for the team from investors. And if he did that, there was another condition: Smythe would have to take over the team. Smythe put down his $10,000 proceeds from gambling and found enough investors to front the rest of the cash.

As the son of a Belfast Orangeman, he thought the name and the green and white livery of the St. Patricks was too sectarian, too old world. He wanted something Canadian, something that would capture the hearts of English Canada in the way that the Montreal Canadiens had secured the affections of

Conn Smythe fell for Irene Sands at first sight when he was almost seventeen years old and she, a bit younger. For the next fifty-three years, until she died in 1965, she was his muse and he, her contrarian hero. When an invitation to sit in Tex Rickard's box at the New York Rangers' debut (together with tickets to Broadway shows) arrived at their house in the autumn of 1926, Smythe, still angry at how the Rangers had treated him, dismissed it. But Irene was determined to go, saying, "It'll help make up for all the nights I spent alone when you were out with hockey." They went.

(Courtesy Dr. Hugh Smythe)

the francophones. So, taking the colour scheme from his gravel business trucks, which he in turn had borrowed from his alma mater, the U of T, he dressed his crew in blue and white. Since there was already a minor hockey team called the Maple Leaves, he renamed his team the distinctively ungrammatical Maple Leafs after the emblem that meant so much to him, the one Canadian soldiers wore and made famous as a sign of valour during the war. And the young gambler who had given four years of his life to that war made another wager, this time betting that in five years, he and his Maple Leafs would win the greatest prize he could imagine, the Stanley Cup.

CHAPTER 4

THE
DUSTBOWL DREAM

It was a beginning, and an end. On March 30, 1926, the Montreal Forum, that great temple to the Montreal Canadiens, which, when it closed its doors seventy years later, seemed to have gilded its rafters with Stanley Cup banners, saw its first Stanley Cup game. But on that chilly Tuesday night, the *bleu, blanc et rouge* were not playing for Lord Stanley's prize. Though they had been the Cup champions the year before, the Canadiens had finished last in the standings in 1926, and they were in mourning, not so much for their failed season, but for the reason behind it: Georges Vézina.

On November 28, 1925, after one period of shutout hockey against Pittsburgh, the Canadiens' goalie Georges Vézina collapsed in front of his net, bleeding from the mouth, and racked with chest pains and fever. Vézina, who had played 325 consecutive regular season games in his pro career with the Canadiens, had tuberculosis. The disease, a bacterial infection of the lungs then morbidly known as the White Plague, was incurable. It would be twenty years before the discovery of the anti-microbial drugs that would make it, if not curable, then manageable. Vézina had known he was afflicted with the dreaded TB for some time, but he hadn't told his teammates. Now they knew.

In late March 1926, shortly before the Stanley Cup series began, Vézina arrived at the Canadiens' dressing room at his usual game-day time. He had once been a stocky five-foot-six and 185 pounds, but now he was scrawny and wheezing, his lungs ravaged. He sat in his usual spot in the dressing room and slowly looked around it, taking it all in, as if he would never see it again. Then he began to weep. "I glanced at him as he sat there, and saw tears rolling down his cheeks," Leo Dandurand said. "He was looking at his old pads and skates that Eddie Dufour had arranged in Georges's corner, thinking he would don them that night. Then he asked one little favour – the sweater he wore in the last world series." On March 26, a few days after his visit to his old dressing room, Georges Vézina died at age thirty-nine. The Canadiens' owners, Dandurand, Louis Letourneau, and Joe Cattarinich, who had discovered him fifteen years earlier, immortalized the great Vézina with a trophy in his name, the highest award an NHL goalie can win.

While the Canadiens were in mourning, the Victoria Cougars were hoping to celebrate. They had been following the progress of the Ottawa Senators–Montreal Maroons series from their Pullman car as their train chugged eastward. During a brief stop in Winnipeg, Frank Patrick hustled over to the station's telegraph office and brought back news – of the good and profitable kind. As playoff champions of the renamed Western Hockey League and reigning Stanley Cup holders, the Cougars were now going to play the NHL champion Maroons in the new Montreal Forum, whose eleven-thousand capacity (counting standing room) meant that the Cougars would double their take from the gate receipts. And they needed the money.

The Patrick brothers' experiment with professional hockey on the west coast of North America had expanded eastward to become a "Western" hockey league, with teams in Edmonton, Calgary, and Saskatoon, along with a relocated Regina franchise in Portland, and the surviving Pacific league duo of Vancouver and Victoria. Although Edmonton and Saskatoon had finished one-two in the western standings, professional hockey in the Prairies was suffering from low attendance, and it was an open secret that the Western

How to Become a
HOCKEY STAR
by T. P. (Tommy) GORMAN
Manager of 1935 Stanley Cup Winners
in collaboration with F. J. (Shag) Shaughnessy
With the Compliments of
The CANADA STARCH COMPANY Limited
Montreal · Toronto

Tommy Gorman

Tommy Gorman is one of professional hockey's most colourful and enduring characters. A fine athlete himself, Gorman turned his attention to hockey when his family bought the NHA's Ottawa Senators during the First World War. When the NHA became the NHL, Gorman became a founding member of the new league, and during his three-decade career, he coached or managed seven Stanley Cup winners, guiding the Ottawa Senators to three, the Montreal Canadiens to two, and the Chicago Black Hawks and Montreal Maroons to one each. He then moved on to amateur hockey, where he bought senior hockey's Ottawa Senators and managed them to an Allan Cup title. He also loved horse racing and baseball, and made regular ventures into both. Despite his time in Montreal, Gorman's French was as impoverished as his English was rich. Nevertheless, the Montreal *Star* reported "If he only said 'oui' he said it with an air as though he could run the gamut of the whole French language." (*Hockey Hall of Fame*)

Hockey League's skating legs were nearly worn out. It was something the Patrick brothers hoped they could fix, one way or another, in Montreal.

The NHL's Maroons, on the other hand, found themselves in the Stanley Cup final in only their second year of existence, after a predictably disastrous rookie season, when they finished last with only nine wins in a thirty-game schedule. But they had come back strong with new players in new uniforms – featuring a bold white "M" on their maroon sweaters – and they were playing in the Forum, which, although it would become synonymous with the Canadiens, was actually built for the Maroons.

The Maroons were born in 1924 from a mix of English pride, French largesse, a good dose of irony, and a fire. English Montreal had been the prime mover in hockey's development as a sport, and its elite had kept hockey their almost exclusive preserve for more than three decades. When the city's Westmount Arena burned down on January 2, 1918, its tenants, the storied Wanderers, whose nine Stanley Cups had been the catalyst for the creation of the Montreal Canadiens, were forced to abandon the NHL and professional hockey. Or so the story goes. The Wanderers were in financial trouble, and even though Hamilton had offered to take them in, the Wanderers' volatile owner, Sam Lichtenhein, used the fire (which had started in the Wanderers' dressing room) as an excuse to fold the franchise. The Canadiens, who had been sharing the rink with the Wanderers, were forced to move to the much smaller Jubilee Rink, with a capacity of just 3,000 – a far cry from the Westmount's capacity of 8,500. And Montreal was without an English team.

So the French came to the rescue. In March 1922, Donat Raymond was a Montreal financier and Liberal party fundraiser (whose success at the latter endeavour was rewarded with a seat in the Canadian Senate by Prime Minister Mackenzie King four years later) who saw Montreal's need – or market potential – for a new English team. So did Leo Dandurand, owner of the Canadiens. Dandurand agreed to sell his territorial rights if Raymond could get someone to build a big new arena and let his Canadiens become joint tenants when their lease ran out on the Mount Royal Arena. *Et voilà*, there would be two professional teams, one English, one French, with lots of room in the new building for paying customers. It would be very good for business.

Raymond enlisted William Northey, former manager of the Westmount Arena, and the duo approached Sir Edward Beatty, president of the Canadian Pacific Railway for financing help. The railway company, which had done so much to spread hockey across the country, colonizing land as it moved westward, saw sense in Raymond's proposal to tap into an underserved market. So the Canadian Arena Company was formed in January 1924 to build a new rink at the corner of Atwater and St. Catherine. Construction began in the spring, and 159 days later, the Montreal Forum was open for business.

In the meantime, Raymond went into partnership with James Strachan, founder of the Montreal Wanderers, to obtain an NHL franchise, which they

Contrary to national mythology, the Montreal Forum was not built as a francophone shrine to the Canadiens. It was built to house the Montreal Maroons, a team created for the city's English hockey fans in 1924. The Forum opened that same year on November 29, after being built in a record 159 days. After the demise of the Maroons in 1938, it became the domain of the Canadiens – and hockey's francophone shrine. (*Library and Archives Canada, PA-202809*)

OFFICIAL HOCKEY PROGRAMME
ARENA GARDENS PRICE 10¢
FASTEST SPORT IN THE WORLD.

When the Mutual Street Arena opened in 1912 as the Arena Gardens, it featured eight thousand seats, making it the second-largest indoor rink in Canada after the Patrick brothers' Denman Street Arena in Vancouver.

(*Hockey Hall of Fame*)

got for $15,000 on November 1, 1924. The new team, the Montreal Maroons, had a new $1.2-million building to play in, though destiny stepped in early, for it was the Montreal Canadiens who played the first game in the Forum on November 29, because the natural ice of their Mount Royal Arena had not yet frozen.

When Frank and Lester Patrick rolled into Montreal with the Cougars to take on the Maroons in the 1926 Stanley Cup final, the brothers saw the future all too clearly. Not only did the Maroons take the best-of-five series and win their and the Forum's first Stanley Cup, they took the Patrick brothers' breath away with their financial clout. "Frank, these Easterners are out of our league," Lester complained to his brother, revealing that he'd learned some of the Maroons were making close to ten thousand dollars a season, and team owners were throwing their money around like confetti. When Lester dropped into the Maroons' dressing room, he saw their star player, Nels Stewart, he told his brother, "standing with a wad of bills big enough to choke a horse. Somebody had walked in and slipped him $1,000, as a bonus for his play in tonight's game. My goodness, Frank, it's immoral."

The Patricks, who not so long ago had thrown money around like confetti themselves, now saw that the power of the NHL was too much for their league, with its top salary at just four thousand dollars. Earlier that season Frank Patrick had tried to quell the stirrings of labour unrest in his league when he dismissed reports of large NHL salaries as "bunkum," but the brothers knew the jig was up. After all, they had lured players from a competing league with lavish amounts of money, so before that could happen to them, they showed their undiminished ability to innovate by selling their Western League players to the NHL for $317,000. The rights to the Victoria Cougars' players, who had won the Cup in 1925, were bought by Detroit (and the team eventually became the Red Wings). The Portland Rosebuds' players rights were bought by the new franchise in Chicago, the Black Hawks. Players had been sold before when leagues folded, but not on this scale, and the Patricks' fire sale reflected the muscle of the NHL, who would now take sole possession of the Stanley Cup. Now that the NHL owned professional hockey in both Eastern and Western Canada, there was only one way to grow: export the game to the United States, where hockey had begun its professional life more than two decades earlier.

Murray and the Hounds of Notre Dame
The year the young priest James Athol Murray turned thirty, he was sent "on loan" to the Regina diocese. The loan turned out to be permanent after Murray founded one of Canada's most revered hockey high schools, the College of Notre Dame in Wilcox, Saskatchewan, home to the fabled Hounds. The original Hounds of 1927 were the fifteen Regina boys who played hockey, lacrosse, baseball, and football under the auspices of Murray's Argos club, and moved to Wilcox with him. Soon the College was attracting students from across the continent. Murray's basic admission requirement was simple: students had to want to learn and to play sports, under the school's motto of *Luctor et Emergo* – Struggle and Emerge. *(Notre Dame College)*

In time for the 1926–27 season, the NHL reorganized into ten teams in two divisions, five Canadian and five American. In case anyone missed the point of this internationalization of the sport, the New York Americans moved into the Canadian Division the following year to make room for the Rangers. The United States, with its muscular prosperity, and its burgeoning mass culture that both advertised and fulfilled the American dream, was the friend everyone wanted to have.

By May 1929, when the NHL directors met in the Sun Life Building in Montreal – the largest building in the British Empire – life was good and looking to become even better. During the past year, the NHL had doubled its profits to a staggering $2.5 million, thanks to the heat of American money flowing into the Canadian game. In an effort to expand their fortunes, they voted to allow forward passing, the Patrick brothers' innovation, to add speed and offence to the game and further persuade fans to part with their money.

People had money – but, increasingly, just on paper. After the stunning cruelties of the war and the Spanish Flu pandemic, the gods were smiling again, and in Canada, stock prices tripled between 1918 and 1929. Frank Selke, the general manager of the Toronto Maple Leafs in that tumultuous year of 1929, saw how the stock market craze affected hockey. "Players spent their hockey earnings buying stocks on margin, despite constant warnings . . . that

New York Americans

In 1926, after the demise of the World Hockey League, because of its inability to compete with the increasingly rich salaries offered by the National Hockey League, the only remaining professional hockey league in North America organized itself into two divisions based on a team's home country. The anomaly of the New York Americans appearing in the Canadian division is a justice of sorts: the previous season the team were the Hamilton Tigers, but had been sold en masse to American interests when they went on strike for playoff pay.

(*Library and Archives Canada, PA–194592*)

they return to sanity and put their cash in the bank," he said. "In the [Montreal] Maroons' dressing-room, this craze for stock-market profits became so strong that, on occasion when coach Eddie Gerrard called a practice, only one or two boys showed up. The rest were downtown, counting their riches in the rising markets."

It was easy to play the market because for those who didn't have money, there was always the magic of credit, which extended to buying stocks "on margin," a risky venture that allows the buyer to purchase stocks with money borrowed at beguilingly low interest rates from a brokerage house, using the stocks themselves as collateral. But the riches weren't real. Corporate profit expectations were vastly inflated, and the rampant speculation was driving stocks up as much as forty times their value. Companies responded by issuing more stock, and the bubble just got bigger. Then, on October 29, it burst.

That day, the *New York Times* front-page headline read: "Thousands of accounts wiped out, with traders in dark as to event on exchange." Less than a month after the market crash, the Associated Press's man in New York used the language of market speculation to predict a green future for the professional game: "A new hockey season, one which promises to be the biggest and most profitable and certainly the most interesting since the National Hockey League took its present form, gets underway tonight." While a new season for the only remaining professional hockey league on the continent was getting underway, so too were the effects of the market crash on Canadians. Canada's economy, long enjoying the same ride as that of the United States, plunged. By the time of the first snowfall of 1929, nearly 30 per cent of the population was unemployed. One in five Canadians were on government handouts – and if you were Chinese, you got one-third of what a white man received. Historians and economists do not pin the blame for all of what would become known as the Great Depression on "Black Thursday," but it was certainly the catalyst for a decade of often brutal deprivation, both economic and natural.

People no longer lined up at the doors of hockey arenas; they were lining up at soup kitchens. Or, before they took that humiliating step, they were selling their possessions to their neighbours. In the middle of a Saskatchewan winter, one such peddler knocked on the door of the Howe family. "My mom gave a couple of dollars to a woman who was in desperate need of milk for her family," Gordie Howe said later. "In return, the woman gave my mom a gunny-sack full of things, including a pair of skates. My sister Edna grabbed one, and I got the other. We went outside and push-glided around an ice pond. When Edna got cold and took her skate off, I put it on my other foot."

For Howe, that simple act of neighbourly charity in the depths of the Depression opened up a whole new world. "From that moment on, I loved skating," Howe said. "As a boy, I even ate meals with my skates on. Hockey meant everything to me. I'd go off the ice straight into the kitchen. My mom put some papers down so that I wouldn't mark up the linoleum. As soon as I finished eating, I'd go right back on the ice, missing only a couple of shifts. . . . I think the two dollars my mom gave that woman was the down payment on my career."

In the Cariboo country of British Columbia, another young man had fallen in love with the sport, too, and while the Alkali Lake Ranch where he worked was relatively insulated from the hardships of the Depression, Alec Antoine was both a cowboy and an Indian, and as such, knew all about deprivation. Whenever Antoine's Alkali Lake hockey team made the twelve-hour sled journey in subzero temperatures into the town of Williams Lake, fifty-six kilometres away, to play hockey against white teams, their welcome was even colder than the weather. The Alkali Lake team, who were all members of the Shuswap nation, were barred from staying in a hotel, or eating in a restaurant, by the colour

The Alkali Lake Braves were a team made up of aboriginal players from the Cariboo District of British Columbia. Their centre, Alec Antoine (back row, middle), also known as Se'leste or Sylista (his first name was Célestin), was a power skater with tremendous speed and a skilled stickhandler. "He skated backward with the puck better than most of the players could carry it going forward," said one observer, the young Englishman Hilary Place. "He had a natural talent for shooting as well; the players regularly lined up bottles or tin cans on the backboards and Sylista picked off each one of them from the blue line. His accuracy was uncanny."

(*Courtesy Barbara Poirier*)

barrier. So, after watering their horses at the creek, they would make their way up a hill to the outdoor rink on Third Avenue, where they shovelled snow to clear a place to pitch their tents, build a fire, cook a supper of deer meat and boiled potatoes, and then sleep next to the campfire for warmth.

The next day they would suit up in their much patched green and white uniforms, a gift from the Woodward Department Store owner, who was married to the daughter of the Alkali Lake rancher, and they would play hockey so beautifully that it moved a young English immigrant, Hilary Place, to write about them. "The Indians loved the game. It gave them an opportunity to prove they were the best at a highly demanding sport. But winning the game was not the only thing that counted. For them, the sheer joy of the contest of skills was important: a quick turn around the opposing player; skating, turning, stickhandling, all the skills that made hockey the fastest, toughest, and most elegant game ever devised by man were their delight. They played the game not only with grace and power and skill, but with their souls as well."

The Alkali Lake Braves, led by the stocky, powerful Antoine at centre, were such a fine, clean team that they won the Northern B.C. amateur league title in 1930–31. At a time when aboriginal children were being forcibly removed from their homes and placed into white-run residential schools, the Braves received an invitation to come, of their own free will, to Vancouver, where their hockey success had been noted by Andy Paull, chief of the Squamish nation. Paull arranged for them to play two matches against a team of all-stars selected from the semi-professional Commercial League (the Commercks). For Paull, the game was about much more than hockey, as he was also president of the North

American Indian Brotherhood – the first effort to group aboriginals into a political force. The Brotherhood had organized the tournament to get a little good ink for the Alkali Lake Braves, and in so doing, to get a little good ink for all aboriginals. It wasn't quite the same as Joe Boyle's Dawson City Nuggets heading to Ottawa to prospect for Stanley Cup silver, but the curiosity in Vancouver was high, stoked by a little good-natured taunting from Chief Paull, reported in the *Vancouver Sun*.

"Squamish Indians are making preparations for the entertainment of the boys from the frigid Cariboo and will house them at the North Shore reservation," the newspaper read on January 9, 1932. "'It will be the Indians' night to howl, we hope' said Andy 'and we of the Squamish will have a 40-piece band at the game. We hope to play our boys off the ice to the strains of "See the Conquering Heroes."' One of the Alkali players is 50, and a grandfather. Yet, Mr. Paul [*sic*] says he has the meticulous word of Harry Taylor, Northern Indian agent, that it takes a darn fast skater to even catch pieces of this hardy ancient of the north as he flits hither and yon on the steel blades."

The Braves, who played on average only eight games per season on outdoor rinks, found themselves face to face with a star team three times their size – and in an artificial ice rink holding four thousand fans. The series was highly anticipated back in the Cariboo, where people turned on their radios to listen to the matches, though the mountainous landscape was no friend to radio waves. "Reception was terrible and the station kept fading in and out," recalled Hilary Place. "Just when you heard that Alkali was starting down the ice, the radio faded out and the results of the rush were lost in the statics. The last big fade-out happened at the very end of the game. When we heard the final score, Alkali had been beaten by one goal. Vancouver sportswriters had predicted a walkover, with scores of 15 to 1 for the Vancouver team, so we Cariboo people were more satisfied with the showing."

The Vancouver press were harder to please, and typical of the attitudes of the time, assessed the Braves' performance by making it racial: "The Alkalis of today start in pursuit of the puck when the whistle goes off and they never cease until the period ends" reported the *Sun*. "There is little system to their attack. Just dogged pursuit. They are still a primitive people, these silent, shadowy folk of the northland and they take their sport in the same way." By the time the second match also ended with the Braves losing by a goal to the pros, more than eight thousand Vancouverites had seen for themselves that the Braves were playing the game as it was meant to be played, including the *Vancouver Sun* reporter. "They did teach Vancouver one lesson. Hockey can be played absolutely without malice. . . . They were beaten last night and they took it with a smile and three lusty cheers. The crowd seemed to like that. Don't you?"

No less an authority than Lester Patrick, now the general manager of the New York Rangers, liked what he saw so much that he tried to convince Antoine to come to Manhattan, where he would make him the toast of Broadway. But Alec Antoine said no thanks to NHL stardom. He already had a sure thing at fifteen dollars a week and went home to his life as a cowboy on the Alkali Lake Ranch.

January 1932 saw other Canadians making long trips from home to play hockey for people who looked upon them and the sport they played with intense curiosity. The previous autumn, Ottawa amateur hockey broker Cecil Duncan put together a team of Ottawa–Hull all-stars to play an exhibition series in Europe, where the Ligue International de Hockey Sur Glace (later the IIHF) had been formed in 1908 by France, England, Switzerland, and Belgium.

Centred by future Hart Trophy winner Bill Cowley, then a nineteen-year-old junior star with Ottawa Primrose, the Canadians played their way through France, Switzerland, Poland, Czechoslovakia, and England. European promoters,

As one of seven teams in the English League, the Grosvenor House Canadians, founded in 1929, played their home matches at the Park Lane Rink, in the basement of the Grosvenor House Hotel, in London's posh Mayfair district. The rink, which opened in 1927, could hold fifteen hundred spectators, and featured an ice surface smaller than the Canadians were used to at home – 171 feet long and 71 feet wide.

A 1932 match in the hotel's basement between touring colonials and the U.K.–based Canadians was distinguished by being the first hockey game broadcast on radio in Great Britain, though the sport was too fast for the medium: "[It was] one of the fastest games ever seen at Grosvenor House, so fast indeed that on several occasions I believe, the wireless commentator who was broadcasting a running commentary on the match, was baffled for words," reported the *Skating Times*.

(Courtesy Grosvenor House Hotel)

The Ice Rink

BE not perturbed if you notice, on a warm, sultry afternoon, people walking down Park Lane carrying ice skates—they are merely wending their way to Grosvenor House for an hour or so on the Ice Rink, one of the first of its kind in this country.

impressed by the visiting Canadians' hockey skill invited other Canadians to follow them across the Atlantic on a more permanent basis. For young Canadian men looking for work in the Depression, the offer was too good to pass up. Jacques Moussette, who had played for the Ottawa All-Stars on their tour was invited to join a French league, eventually winding up on the Français Volants (Flying Frenchmen) in Paris in 1933. The Français Volants were almost entirely Québécois and captained by Roger Gaudette, a left-winger from Saint-Jean-sur-Richelieu, described by a British hockey program as "caged lightning with a burst of speed that puts him with the speediest puckchasers in Europe."

Gaudette recalled that although playing for a team based in Paris had its obvious pleasures, playing in Europe posed a new kind of challenge when it came to road games. "We played everywhere, in the great capital cities: Prague, Vienna, Budapest, Berlin, London and Paris. We played 24 games a season, running from one place to the other. It wasn't always easy! We'd often attract crowds of 20,000 spectators." Those spectators weren't always drawn by the game. European ice hockey was part sport, and part show business, with live music, skating exhibitions during intermission, and the chance to mingle with

During the Depression years, Canadian hockey players flocked to Europe to pursue jobs with European clubs. Les Français Volants (the Flying Frenchmen) of Paris, established in 1933, offered French Canadians the chance to be paid well for playing hockey in the great cities of Europe, sometimes before crowds of twenty thousand people. Financial troubles forced the Volants to decamp to play in England in 1936, but their joie de vivre was dampened both by the English weather and the fact they were now playing, as they were told, more for "glory" than money.

(Courtesy Philippe Lacarrière)

celebrities at rinks such as the one in Wembley, where patrons could watch the game from a restaurant. When the Français Volants played at Wembley's Empire Pool and Sports Arena in November 1935, the promoters had arranged for a half-hour display of women's figure skating between periods, which, while good for the crowds, was bad for the players. "During this time we were hot, we were cold, we lost our élan," Gaudette recalled. "It wasn't very motivating."

While Canadian amateur players were looking for work in Europe, Conn Smythe was building the Toronto Maple Leafs a new hockey arena, one, he said, which people could dress up and go to as if they were attending the opera or the theatre. Smythe had made a promise in 1927 that his Maple Leafs would win the Stanley Cup in five years, and now, with the Great Depression in full swing, the marker was about to be called in.

Smythe's Leafs were doing well – but not quite well enough. Although they were filling their home rink, the Mutual Street Arena, about half the time, it was too small to give Smythe enough revenue to mount a challenge for the silver jug. He needed to put two more pieces in place, a bigger rink and a star player. That player just happened to be public enemy number one in Toronto: Francis "King" Clancy.

Clancy was an Ottawa sportsman to the core of his being. His father, an American immigrant, had switched from playing football to rugby when he

In 1932, the Toronto Maple Leafs won their first Stanley Cup, just five years after Conn Smythe invented them. Key to their triumph were Francis "King" Clancy, a small but fearless defence-man, and former New York Rangers goalie Lorne Chabot. (Back row: Tim Daly, Clancy, Andrew Blair, Red Horner, Chabot, Alex Levinsky, Joe Primeau, Harvey Jackson, Harold Darragh, Harold Cotton. Front row: Charlie Conacher, Frank Finnigan, Hap Day, Smythe, Dick Irvin, Frank Selke, Ace Bailey, Bob Gracie.) *(Imperial Oil – Turofsky/Hockey Hall of Fame)*

moved north, and became so good at rolling the rugby ball out of the scrum with his heel that he was nicknamed the "King of the Heelers" in 1890s Ottawa. His son, Frank, joked that this must make him "King of the Heels" but when people saw him play hockey, they just called him King. Unless they were Toronto Maple Leafs fans.

Clancy, who had broken into the NHL with the Ottawa Senators in 1921 at age seventeen, was one of the smallest pro defencemen to play the game, just five-foot-seven and 155 pounds, though his playing weight might have been bumped up in case opponents got the wrong idea, for the garrulous Clancy later said, "A sportswriter once described me as '135 pounds of muscle and conversation.'" Those opponents who thought they could push Clancy around soon found out how wrong they were. Not only could he play hockey, running on his skates to get up a head of steam, he was fearless, challenging much bigger players and never backing down from a fight. Clancy was just the type of man that Conn Smythe, himself about the same size as Clancy, wanted on his team. But there was a problem: popular wisdom had Clancy preferring to play in hell than for Toronto, and the Leafs captain, the gentlemanly Clarence "Hap" Day, would gladly have used some of his knowledge as a U of T pharmacy grad to send him there, for Clancy's biggest feud was with Day.

When Smythe heard that the financially troubled Ottawa Senators had put Clancy up for sale in the autumn of 1930, for a hefty $35,000, he thought he didn't have a chance. The best the Leafs could offer was $25,000, plus there was the feud with Day, and the fact that the Montreal Maroons were rumoured to be eager to get Clancy, too. And then, Conn Smythe remembered that he had a racehorse. He entered the horse in the Coronation Futurity at odds of 106–1. Fuelled with brandy, Rare Jewel won its one and only race, and Smythe had enough to buy a King.

When someone finally got around to asking Clancy about his playing preferences, it turned out that he had no problem at all playing for Toronto, and he joined a team that would go down in Leafs history as one of their finest. Ace Bailey, an aggressive right-winger, and Hap Day, a defenceman and natural leader, had been part of the original 1927 crew. "Gentleman" Joe Primeau was a young centre whose clean play would win him the Lady Byng Trophy and fame as the middleman of the celebrated Kid Line. Charlie "the Big Bomber" Conacher, a Toronto boy from an immigrant Irish family of eleven children, so poor, he said, "we didn't have enough money to buy toothpaste," had come up from the junior ranks. At six-foot-one and two hundred pounds, with a board-splintering shot, he made for a fearsome presence on right wing, while on left, Harvey "Busher" Jackson was a silky skater whom Leafs general manager Frank Selke remembered as being as "good-looking as a movie idol, six feet

The only thing rare about Conn Smythe's thoroughbred, Rare Jewel, was its ability to win. The horse had never finished first past the post, nor had Smythe's horse trainer, Bill Campbell, ever saddled a winner at Woodbine Racetrack. Indeed, he even warned Smythe against entering the Coronation Futurity, where Rare Jewel's odds were 106–1. For the gambler in Smythe, the odds were perfect. He bet sixty dollars on his filly, and both the horse's trainer and a gambling buddy of Smythe's each secretly slipped the horse a flask of brandy. Running on fermented grapes, Rare Jewel won her first race (she never won another), and Smythe found himself nearly $11,000 richer from his wager, with another $3,750 from the winner's purse.

(Courtesy Dr. Hugh Smythe)

tall, weighing some 202 pounds . . . as light on his feet as a ballet dancer. He could pivot on a dime, stickhandle through an entire team . . . and shoot like a bullet, either forehand or backhand." (Jackson's life would end badly, as a penniless alcoholic panhandling outside the Toronto arena he used to light up. Conn Smythe never forgave him for his alcohol and domestic abuses troubles, considering them moral failings. He blackballed efforts to elect Jackson to the Hockey Hall of Fame until 1971, five years after Jackson's death.)

Smythe also brought his favourite goalie, Lorne Chabot, back from New York. The Rangers were happy to let Chabot go because they thought he had lost his nerve after taking a puck to the face. Smythe paid eight thousand dollars to Pittsburgh for the tough, backchecking left-winger Harold "Baldy" Cotton (who had once challenged referee Cooper Smeaton to a fight and was saved from eternal banishment only by NHL president Frank Calder), and he added Reginald "Red" Horner, a big defenceman with a hard shot and a punishing physical style. Smythe called him "the greatest bodychecker I ever saw."

Smythe planned to put this collection of champions-in-waiting in a new arena at the corner of Church and Carlton streets, where the Eaton's department store chain had sold him a piece of land for $350,000 and a stock option. Eaton's came through again when Smythe was trying to decide where in the new arena to put the booth for the team's radio broadcasts. The "Voice of the Leafs," Foster Hewitt, went from floor to floor of the new Eaton's building at College and Yonge, looking down on the pedestrians below until he found the perfect height to see the whole action clearly without being too far away. The fifth floor would provide the altitude for Foster's perch in Maple Leaf Gardens in a booth soon nicknamed the Gondola.

It was a long way up from Hewitt's vantage point for his first radio broadcast of a hockey game in 1923, when he was a twenty-three-year-old cub reporter calling the action from a glass box at ice level in the Mutual Street Arena for CFCA. Like many radio stations at the time, CFCA was owned by a newspaper – the Star Printing and Publishing Company, publisher of the *Toronto Star*, where Hewitt's father, William, the amateur hockey czar, was

Ground was broken for Maple Leaf Gardens on June 1, 1931, and five-and-a-half months later crowds gathered in English Canada's new hockey temple to watch the Leafs lose to the Chicago Black Hawks. Despite this stumble, that season the Leafs won their first Stanley Cup. (*City of Toronto Archives, 25377*)

sports editor. The station's first broadcast was the final period of a hockey game between North Toronto and Midland from the Toronto Mutual Street Arena on February 8, 1923 – but Hewitt was not the play-by-play man. Hewitt Jr., who also worked for the *Star*, made his first broadcast from the arena on February 16. The booth he was in was so cramped that his own breath fogged the glass, and he had to keep wiping it to see the play. Describing it was difficult, too, as Hewitt had to phone in his commentary to the station and was constantly interrupted by operators demanding to know what number he was calling.

But by 1931, both Hewitt and radio had come a long way. Radio was cheap entertainment during the Depression, and hockey on radio was especially popular. "Our little world was brightened by those broadcasts," recalled Toronto sportswriter Dick Beddoes. "They were money from home at a time when there was no money at home or anywhere else. We didn't know how rich we were to be so well entertained on Saturday nights." By 1936, there were nearly 900,000 radio sets in Canada – with an estimated four people listening to each one of them, for a potential audience of almost 3.5 million.

Advertisers liked radio, too, among them the St. Lawrence Starch Company, which took advantage of the fact that newspapers did not regularly feature photographs of the professional game's greats and came out with a promotion. In exchange for proof of purchase of a bottle of Bee Hive Corn Syrup, the company would send out cards featuring players whom those 9 million Canadians living outside the NHL cities only knew through radio – players

"The first place some visitors to Toronto headed was to Carlton and Church," said Conn Smythe, "just to stand there and look at the place they imagined around their radios every winter Saturday night after Foster Hewitt had called out his excitement-filled 'Hello Canada' to the farthest corners of the land." When Conn Smythe built Maple Leaf Gardens, he granted Foster Hewitt Productions the lucrative exclusive broadcasting rights to every event under its roof, but it was hockey that made Hewitt, and from his perch in his famous "gondola," suspended some twenty metres above the ice, he was the voice of the game for generations. *(Imperial Oil – Turofsky/Hockey Hall of Fame)*

such as Clancy, Morenz, and Joliat. "I know that it was in hockey that we found our heroes," recalled Canadian journalist and future hockey chronicler Peter Gzowski. "We collected their images on Bee Hive Golden Corn Syrup cards and tore their history from the pages of the newspapers and magazines we delivered."

A young boy growing up in Montreal also remembered the effect of the Bee Hive cards on his young imagination. "Dans mes rêves les plus fous, je me voyais, moi aussi, figurer un jour sur une carte, comme mes idoles. (In my craziest dreams, I saw my own face on a card one day, like my idols.) Denis Brodeur's vision wasn't so crazy after all, as he went on to be a celebrated hockey photographer whose images stoked the dreams of young players. Among them was his son, Martin, who would grow up to realize his ambition of being a Stanley Cup–winning goaltender.

On June 1, 1931, workers broke the ground for Smythe's dream, the ice palace in Depression-ridden Toronto. The gamblers among them took their wages in shares of the new building. On November 12 that year, bands from the Royal Grenadiers and the 48th Highlanders played "Happy Days Are Here Again" at the building's opening to an audience of more than thirteen thousand hockey fans, many of them wearing evening dress in response to Smythe's stated purpose of creating a temple for a national art form.

The Leafs lost that first game in Maple Leaf Gardens to the Chicago Black Hawks, but they made it to the Stanley Cup finals in 1932, their first full year in

Gordie Drillon

Gordie Drillon, from Moncton, New Brunswick, played just seven seasons in the NHL – six with Toronto and one with Montreal – but his talents were enough to win him a place in the Hockey Hall of Fame and the worship of fans across the Maritimes, as well as in his NHL cities. A six-foot-two, 180-pound right-winger, Drillon was big for the era, fast, and he had sure hands, working his magic with Toronto Maple Leafs centre Syl Apps, with whom he would practise for hours deflecting pucks against Toronto goalie Walter "Turk" Broda. "I spent ten years playing in the slot before anyone invented a name for it," Drillon said. Broda saw him as much more than a deflection artist. "I don't think there's a player in hockey who can shoot the puck more accurately," he said. "Even if you leave him an opening [only] the size of the puck, he'll hit it every time." Drillon won the Art Ross Trophy as the NHL's top scorer in the 1938–39 season, with 26 goals and 26 assists, and when he went off to war in 1943, he had won the Stanley Cup, three All-Star Team selections, and had scored 155 goals – an annual average of 22. He also won a Lady Byng Trophy for gentlemanly play, never spending more than fifteen minutes in the penalty box in any of his NHL seasons. *(Hockey Hall of Fame)*

their new home. Fittingly, their opponents were the New York Rangers, the team that Smythe had built. The Leafs outscored the Rangers 18–10 to win three straight games, the last one in Toronto. Almost five years to the day that Conn Smythe had promised his new team would win the Stanley Cup within five years, they had done so. Foster Hewitt mythologized them for the continent, beginning his radio broadcast with a trademark "Hello, Canada, the United States, and Newfoundland" from his silver tube hanging in the rafters of Maple Leaf Gardens. Canadians had begun a love affair with "Canada's team," or, rather, English Canada's team. Down the railway line in Montreal, French Canada's team was in trouble.

While Conn Smythe was planning big and watching it pay off in Toronto, fuelling the escapist dreams of Canadians suffering through the Depression, other professional teams were suffering. In 1931, the faltering Ottawa Senators and Philadelphia Quakers had their operations suspended "for one year at least" by the NHL. The Quakers were effectively done, but the Senators came back in 1932–33, although they finished out of the playoffs for the next two seasons.

In 1934, the National Hockey League made a promise that Canadians have heard, in various forms, many times since. President Frank Calder swore that the historic, essential Senators would never leave hockey's birthplace of

HE SHOOTS
HE SCORES

Broadcasting from Maple Leaf
Gardens on March 10, 1934

Foster Hewitt Said:

"By Actual check, 25 out of 33 'All-Star' hockey players taking part in the 'Ace Bailey' Benefit Game wore C.C.M. Skates. In various N.H.L. games played, all but one player of the Maroons, the Red Wings and the Canadiens, used C.C.M.'s. All but two of the Senators, Bruins and the Maple Leafs wore C.C.M.'s. This certainly puts C.C.M.'s in the 'All-Star class.'"

The reason C.C.M. Skates are the "Choice of Champions" is not hard to find. They have proved their superiority on the ice. They have the lightness, the speed, the strength, EVERYTHING that the pros want and everything that YOU could want.

The last word in hockey skates is the new C.C.M. "Prolite". Ask your dealer to show it to you.

C·C·M· *true-value* **SKATE & SHOE OUTFITS**

Ace Bailey Benefit Game

On December 13, 1933, Boston Bruins defenceman Eddie Shore, in a daze after being levelled by a check from Toronto's rugged defenceman Red Horner, mistakenly thought he had been hit by the Maple Leafs' star right-winger Ace Bailey. Bailey had taken over the defence position when d-man King Clancy took the puck up the ice. Shore retaliated by charging Bailey from behind, upending him with a heavy shoulder butt. Bailey's head hit the ice with such force that, after being given last rites, the convulsing and bleeding Bailey was rushed to a Boston hospital with a suspected fractured skull. A renowned neurosurgeon, Donald Munro, performed two risky operations to relieve pressure on Bailey's brain, and the player was given last rites again. Despite the grim odds, Bailey recovered, and though his hockey career was finished, the NHL celebrated his survival by staging the Ace Bailey Benefit Game on February 14, 1934, featuring the Maple Leafs against a team of NHL All-Stars, with the proceeds going to Bailey and his family. Bailey was at centre ice to present the players with their game jerseys, and when Eddie Shore skated up to receive his, the tense crowd exploded in cheers when Bailey offered his hand to Shore, and the two men shook in the spirit of sporting forgiveness. The game raised more than twenty thousand dollars for Bailey, and the Leafs added to the bounty by defeating Shore and the All-Stars by a score of 7–3. (Hockey Hall of Fame)

Canada. But the truth was that the Senators, a team that had won four Stanley Cups in the Roaring Twenties, was about to splash the most American of symbols across their jerseys as the St. Louis Eagles. The Eagles lasted one season, and then asked the league for permission to suspend their operations until happy days were here again. The NHL refused, bought the franchise, and dispersed the players throughout the league.

The NHL also lowered its salary cap to $62,500 per team, and a maximum of $7,000 per player. In Montreal, Leo Dandurand had once joked with his superstar Howie Morenz that, because the team had lost money, Morenz's salary was going to drop by $4,000. Morenz, the man whose hockey genius had put ice in Madison Square Garden, showed a deference to management that has long characterized hockey, and said that the pay cut would be fine with him. As Dandurand recalled, "Not until he was leaving the house that night did I tell him: 'This is the real figure. You get $11,500 again this year.' He thanked me and there were tears in his eyes. And that was our real contract, a verbal one."

Tears were appropriate. The Canadiens had severe box office problems – only two thousand people were attending their games in a building that could hold five times that number – and it was a heavily mortgaged building, at that. A few months after making his promise to Morenz, Dandurand had to do the unthinkable: he broke his verbal contract with Morenz, the man who had come to define the Montreal Canadiens. In October 1934, he traded Morenz, a Canadien – and a Canadian – icon, to the Chicago Black Hawks, along with Lorne Chabot and Marty Burke, in exchange for Leroy Goldsworthy, Lionel Conacher, and Roger Jenkins. Montrealers were outraged, as if Dandurand had single-handedly robbed them of their one hope for glory. "I received hundreds of phone calls every day," he recalled. "They accosted me on the streets and each person felt the need to tell me what they thought. Basically, I got royally told off."

In truth, Dandurand got something for a player he felt was a fading asset. From 1926 to 1933, Morenz had led the Canadiens in goals; to back-to-back Stanley Cups in 1930 and 1931; had won three Hart Trophies as the NHL's most valuable player; and was twice the league's leading scorer. But the speedy genius who once had made people leap from their seats, their brains just catching up with what their eyes had just seen the Stratford Streak do, was now thirty-two years old. And he was not a young thirty-two. He was injured, both from playing and from hard living during those periods of intense light or intense darkness between games, when Morenz walked the streets, floating on whisky, or sinking in it.

Dandurand's desperate attempt to save the team by jettisoning the high-priced superstar came back to bite him less than a year later when the team deficit hit $45,000. The original musketeer and his surviving partner, Joe Cattarinich, finally faced facts and sold the Canadiens in September 1935 for $165,000 to the Canadian Arena Company. Montreal pro hockey was a small world: the Arena Company was owned by Donat Raymond, the financier who put together the syndicate to build the Forum, and who was now a senator. Raymond's company also owned the Montreal Maroons, and while having both an English and a French professional hockey team in Montreal was a good idea in the Roaring Twenties, it was no longer working out. One of them had to go.

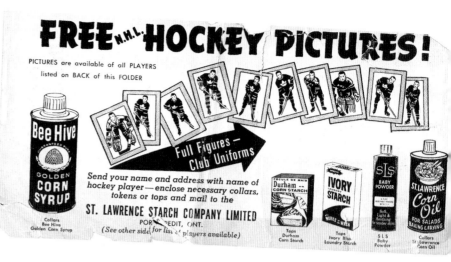

In 1934, the St. Lawrence Starch Company Ltd, makers of Bee Hive Golden Corn Syrup and other products, hired a photographer to shoot Toronto Maple Leafs star players for a promotion campaign for their syrup. Fans could get a "free" black and white player photo by redeeming a coupon on any St. Lawrence Starch Co. product, and for the next thirty-three years, a generation of hockey-loving kids collected their favourite players, whom they knew only from radio. But by 1967, the cards got too expensive: the NHL expansion that decade, the new, smaller, coloured hockey cards that had hit the market, and higher postage rates together persuaded the St. Lawrence Starch Co. to end a Canadian institution.

(Courtesy Rev. Glen Goodhand)

Financial woes moved Montreal Canadiens boss Leo Dandurand to trade Howie Morenz, the man who had defined the Canadiens for a decade, to the Chicago Black Hawks prior to the 1934–35 season. Dandurand saw Morenz, now thirty-two, as an asset with rapidly diminishing value, but Montreal fans felt betrayed. In the final game of that season, Morenz returned to the Montreal Forum for the first time in his pro career wearing a jersey other than the *bleu, blanc et rouge* of the Canadiens. When he scored a goal against his beloved Habs, the crowd in the Forum gave him a standing ovation.

(Hockey Hall of Fame)

Morenz's departure, on the other hand, was working out. In the last game of the 1935 season, he returned to the Montreal Forum for the first time since the trade and scored a goal against the team he had defined. In a gesture both sporting and defiant, the crowd in the Forum rose to give him a standing ovation. Their message was clear: Management was wrong, Morenz was right. In the end, the fans are always on the side of genius.

Midway through the 1935–36 season, Chicago traded Morenz to the city that had always worshipped him, New York. Although the Rangers finished out of the playoffs that year, the speed and magic of New York City revived both qualities in Morenz. Now it seemed as if the Montreal Canadiens might have been hasty in their dismissal of him. Morenz wasn't lighting up the scoring charts any more, but he still had star power, and the Canadiens, who finished not just last in the Canadian Division in 1936 but last in the entire league, needed just that. Morenz's old coach, Cecil Hart, who had guided Morenz and the Canadiens to back-to-back Stanley Cups earlier in the decade, was brought back to Montreal and made Morenz's return to the *bleu, blanc et rouge* a condition of his return to the Canadiens' bench. He was convinced that, together, they could win that third Stanley Cup.

The Montreal fans and Morenz fell in love all over again. Now that Morenz was back playing on a line with his friend and acolyte Aurèle Joliat, the hockey world was in order, even if the world beyond its margins was suffering terribly. People who saw Morenz play against the Black Hawks on the night of January 28, 1937, witnessed the star whom many had thought was gone forever, a half-smile playing at the corners of his mouth, as he pictured a play in his head that they couldn't see quite yet. When he burst through the Chicago defence at full speed, hunting down a loose puck that had slid into the end boards, the fans rose to their feet, as they had done so many times before. Something was going to happen, something because of Morenz. Something did happen. Chicago defenceman "Big" Earl Seibert chased him, but Morenz was too fast. "There was no way I could catch up with him, but I was able to force him behind the net," Seibert recalled. "Then he tripped and the tip of his skate got caught in the boards, and I hit him. There was no other way of stopping him." The fans in the Forum could hear Morenz's bones snap when Seibert crashed into his trapped left leg. But they had no way of knowing that he would never skate again.

The newspapers tried to keep it that way, reassuring their readers in both French and English that Morenz was through only for the season, and that the four broken bones in his leg would heal. But Aurèle Joliat knew differently. "I cried that night. I knew he wouldn't be back," Joliat recalled thirty-four years later. "We were very close, and I knew that Howie was worried about the fact that he might burn himself out early . . . but . . . he could only play full-out. When his leg shattered that night, I knew there was no way he could come back. He was through and we all knew it."

To ward off the grim, unspoken prognosis, Morenz held merry court from his bed in St. Luke's Hospital, joking with visiting players, and drinking the supply of whisky and beer that they brought. In a letter to his wife and children, Morenz tried to keep up a brave front, saying, "I sure would have liked to finish the season, but fate gave me quite a blow. You can bet it's not going to get me down." But the man who had a hard time accepting loss in a hockey game was, in fact, reeling from the very real loss of his entire identity. He had a nervous breakdown, and for a while, he was in hospital in a straitjacket. He confessed to Joliat that his lavish lifestyle had left little money for his family – in his head, where he could always see the play before it happened, he was dead already. Pointing to heaven, the tears streaming down his face, he said, "I'll be up there watching you in the playoffs."

On the evening of March 8, 1937, Howie Morenz got out of his hospital bed to use the bathroom and dropped dead. The medical verdict was that a coronary embolism had killed him at age thirty-four, but Aurèle Joliat had a simpler, yet more profound, explanation for his friend's death. "Howie loved to play hockey more than anyone ever loved anything, and when he realized that he would never play again, he couldn't live with it," said Joliat. "I think Howie died of a broken heart."

The hockey world on both sides of the border was stunned by the news of Morenz's death, and the response showed just how much the sport and one of its legends meant to people. The day after he died, New York's Rangers and Americans lined up on their respective blue lines at Madison Square Garden, and ten thousand people stood in bowed silence in the stands as a lone bugler played the "Last Post." In Montreal, two thousand people filed by Morenz's casket at the funeral home, the wealthy from Westmount arriving in expensive cars and furs. Solemn little boys came clutching their hockey sticks, and tough working men held their caps to their chests as they filed past and held back their tears. It was as if they all had to see Morenz dead to believe it could be so. Then Morenz's body was moved to centre ice at the Montreal Forum, a place where he had so often stood in the spotlight after scoring a goal for the Canadiens, the cheering of thousands ringing in his ears. Four of his Canadiens' teammates formed an honour guard, and more than fifty thousand people walked past his casket in the four hours before his funeral. A quarter of a million more – many of them sobbing – lined the route to the cemetery. The funeral of the Stratford Streak, the once reluctant Canadien, was the largest public memorial of an athlete yet seen in Canada.

A disconsolate Aurèle Joliat stares at the equipment belonging to the late Howie Morenz, his linemate and great friend, with whom Joliat lit up NHL arenas with speed and skill in the 1920s and '30s. Morenz died on March 8, 1937, of complications from an injury he suffered in a game. *(Hockey Hall of Fame)*

Morenz's death cast a funereal pall over the Forum that lasted into the following season. Its shadow encompassed even the Montreal Maroons. The town wasn't big enough for both them and the Canadiens, but there was no way that the team created for French Canadians was going to be allowed to die in a city that was three-quarters francophone. When Dandurand sold the Canadiens, there had been a rumour that they would be merged with the Maroons, and then one that the Maroons would be moved to St. Louis. But the Maroons, led by the big, tough "S Line" of Babe Siebert, Nels Stewart, and Hooley Smith, and the managerial genius of Tommy Gorman, had made the relocation plan impossible by winning the Stanley Cup in 1935, and the Canadian Division title the following season, while the Canadiens had finished last.

The new owners, the Canadian Arena Company, reckoned they would help the Maroons die a natural death, and before the 1936–37 season, they shipped their star player, Hooley Smith, to Boston rather than pay him the salary he'd earned. Lionel Conacher, one of Canada's greatest multi-sport athletes and the older brother of Maple Leafs star Charlie, retired the following season. And despite the efforts of King Clancy, who had been hired as a coach

to lend the team some of his fighting spirit (he had retired from playing in 1936), the Maroons finished last, and out of the playoffs, for the first time in their nine-year history. The owners now had what they needed to pull the plug on the team. In August 1938, some of the players were moved to the Canadiens, some divvied up among the rest of the NHL. The Maroons were no more, and professional hockey was in deep trouble in the city that had invented its form. Montreal fans needed another saviour.

On a November morning in 1935, Mike Buckna found himself a long way from Trail, British Columbia, where he had starred for the Smoke Eaters, the smelter town's hockey team. Now he and a friend were in Czechoslovakia, the home-land of his parents, who had immigrated to Canada in 1898 to open a small hotel in Trail. The cityscape around him was unfamiliar, but Buckna knew all about the building in front of him: it was an ice rink. Coach Jiri Trzicka didn't know that the twenty-two-year-old Canadian, clutching a newspaper clipping about tryouts for the national team, would be the star of hockey in Czechoslovakia, but he knew that if he didn't figure something out fast, Buckna and his friend would be gone, as they were leaving for Slovakia later that morning. He frantically phoned the team's manager at home. "I was given a strict order: 'Try them and if they are good enough, call me!'" Trzicka later told the Trail Historical Society. "I lent him skates, stick and puck. I was, by myself, an examining as well as a hiring committee."

Buckna skated around on the uneven ice surface, and it was quickly appar-ent to Trzicka that the young Canadian would not be leaving for Slovakia that day. "His skating and his moves were inimitable, with lightning speed," recalled

The death of the great Howie Morenz on March 8, 1937, saw a huge outpouring of grief from Canadians. The Stratford Streak had come to personify all that was beautiful about the game, and his death hit the country hard. Fifty thousand people paid their respects at his casket in the Montreal Forum, while more than a quarter of a million more lined the route to the cemetery.

(Hockey Hall of Fame)

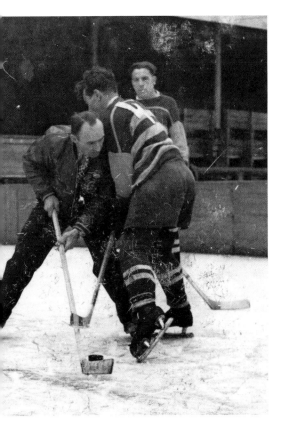

Mike Buckna had left his home in Trail, B.C., in 1935 to visit Czechoslovakia, the country his parents had come from as immigrants. When he saw an ad in a Prague newspaper offering tryouts for the Czech's national hockey team, he answered. Buckna not only made the team, but by teaching the Czechs the fluid, creative style of hockey he had learned in Canada, and coaching them to excel, he became known as the Father of Czech Hockey. (*Courtesy Mike Buckna*)

Trzicka, "and you could see how happy he was doing it, and with such a great enjoyment he did it. . . . And that was how we finally got a Canadian player and a coach whom we all well understood, and especially he understood us. We had an urge to learn again because Matej [Buckna] was on fire and totally lived for hockey." The Czechs had found their hockey saviour by accident.

Buckna was hired as the assistant playing coach for the Czech national team. He had his work cut out for him. Once players made the team, seemingly a job for life, they played hockey to pass time between stints in the pub. "One guy I got rid of," said Buckna, "was a forty-two-year-old defenceman with a stiff leg. He couldn't bend his knee." Buckna culled the lame and the aged and the drunk from the team and replaced them with young players, whom he still found passive and unimaginative when it came to hockey. "Their approach was basically soft. They weren't aggressive," he said. "They'd give up on games and even on plays. They had never heard of forechecking. Their defence never dreamed of carrying the puck or making offensive plays."

Buckna taught them how to forecheck, how to rush the puck, and how to take a man right out of the play "instead of giving him just a little push." He taught them conditioning, how to move the puck around with precision, how to break out of their own zone with speed, and how to get rid of the puck fast, to take goalies by surprise. "Basically, I taught them the kind of hockey we were playing in Trail." He also taught the Czechs a fundamental truth that all great teams know instinctively: the game is so fluid and fast that fortune's wheel can spin from despair to triumph with one inspired rush. "That's the beauty of hockey," Buckna said. "It's possible to reverse the trend of a game as long as you don't give up."

The Czechs would not let Buckna captain their Olympic team in Berlin in 1936, for, as they bluntly told him, all nationalist sentiment aside, attendance at matches for his Prague team would drop from fifteen thousand to five thousand if the league's leading scorer were off playing hockey in Nazi Germany.

In March 1939, Nazi Germany was marching on Prague, and Buckna knew that it was time to go home, with his new wife, Lola Frolikova, whom he had married the year before. A Prague newspaper issued a sad farewell, as if also saying goodbye to a way of life: "Today, on March 30, Matej Buckna is going back to Canada. During his years in Prague, he has contributed greatly to Czech hockey. As a good and decent man he will be missed by many friends he made here. The fact he chose a Czech girl as his wife proves how much he likes our country. We wish you a lot of happiness, Mike, and let us hope that we will see you back in Prague soon."

Tropical Hockey League

One of professional hockey's most fanciful experiments took place in southern Florida in 1938, when the Tropical Hockey League launched four teams in the land where ice is most commonly found in rum punch. The Miami Clippers, the Miami Beach Pirates, the Coral Gables Seminoles, and the Havana Tropicals all played out of the Metropolitan Ice Palace in the Miami suburb of Coral Gables. All but three of the players were Canadians, recruited in training camps in Winnipeg and Port Colborne, Ontario, and the playing coach of the Coral Gables team was Mike Goodman, a former Olympic star with the Winnipeg Falcons. The historic first match, played on December 10, 1938, between the Clippers and the Pirates, was advertised as "the first hockey game ever staged in the south." Before the game, the players put on a display of plays and penalties, and the second intermission featured the mambo stylings of the Caesar La Monaca Orchestra. The Clippers prevailed 4–3, and the game ended with fighting, which the promoters encouraged to attract punters. But the 9:00 p.m. start times, lack of true rivalries, and preponderance of fighting led the league to evaporate in the Florida sun after just one season. (*Hockey Hall of Fame*)

But another terrible war was coming to Europe, and this one would be much more than a bloody stalemate fought from muddy trenches. Buckna would not return to Prague until 1946. The following year, he coached the Czech national team to its first title in the World Championships.

The coming war would affect all the teams, including one whose record is so commanding that it's unlikely ever to be beaten. While Fascists were jackbooting through Europe in 1939, the Preston Rivulettes, led by star forward Hilda Ranscombe, a speedy and skilled right-winger, were tearing up Canadian ice rinks with their superlative hockey, popularizing the women's game and playing to packed arenas across the land, as they had done for much of the decade.

The Preston Rivulettes were born of a summer game. Hilda and her sister Nellie were star baseball players on a local women's softball team, and at the end of the 1930 baseball season, when Hilda was just seventeen, because they wanted to keep their team together through the winter, they decided to play a winter game. A neighbourhood boy who was within earshot laughed at the young women, telling them that girls couldn't play hockey – especially not girls who played the genteel game of baseball. It was all Nellie Ranscombe needed to hear. "That did it. Nobody can dare me to do anything and get away with it."

Women's teams had flourished in communities and colleges in the early 1920s, and the McGill University Debs even took to the ice in culottes in the spirit of the Jazz Age. The University of Saskatchewan team starred Genevra "Ginger" Catherwood, whose sister Ethel would win a gold medal in the high jump at the 1928 Olympics. The Catherwood sisters were formidable athletes, and on a two-game road trip to Manitoba in 1921, Ginger scored twenty-one goals.

Ontario women's hockey was dominated by Ottawa's Alerts, champions of Eastern Canada. In March 1922, they met a Toronto women's team in a fine exhibition series, though one a little too chippy for the *Toronto Star*, which ventured that the fans "do not want to see any roughness creep into the contests." The game was refereed by Fred Waghorne, the first referee to drop the puck for faceoffs. Waghorne also introduced the plastic whistle as a replacement for the hand bells referees had used to start and stop play, the bells having been used because metal whistles would often freeze to a referee's lips in frigid rinks.

Hilda Ranscombe was a talented multi-sport athlete who captured titles in softball and tennis, but it was hockey that made her famous. The right-winger was celebrated for her speed and stick-handling skills as she led the Preston Rivulettes to six national titles and ten Ontario and Quebec championships.

(Dave Menary)

One of the Toronto players was Fanny "Bobbie" Rosenfeld, who would go on to star for the city's Patterson Pats and win an Olympic gold medal in track-and-field in 1928. After the Pats won a playoff game in the Ontario Ladies Hockey Championship in 1927, the *Toronto Star* proclaimed that Bobbie Rosenfeld and her teammate Casey McLean "could earn a place on any OHA [men's] junior team."

In the late 1930s, when Bobbie Rosenfeld saw Hilda Ranscombe play, she knew she had seen a kindred talent. "She has all the equipment for stardom," Rosenfeld wrote in her sports column in the *Globe and Mail*. "She is an instinctive performer. In home competition or on foreign ice she is the same natural and gifted player." Even players on opposing teams were in awe of Ranscombe. Mary McGuire, who played for the Stratford Aces, remembered her as "the best female hockey player in the world. She was just marvellous to watch. . . . I can still see her weaving through the team. She would do it so smoothly. It never seemed any effort to her." Despite Ranscombe's elegant play, the women's game was just as rough as the men's, and newspapers delighted in playing up the violence for their readers.

During the women's championship match in 1935, between the Rivulettes and the Winnipeg Eatons, emotions ran high. Myrtle Cook of the Montreal *Daily Star* reported that "Helen Ransom of Winnipeg and Marm Schmuck of Preston dropped their sticks and gloves and exchanged a number of full-swing blows that had the crowd gasping." The game turned into a donnybrook: "Those lassies from the wild and woolly west, where the men are men and the women rule the roost, certainly can pick them up and set them down. [The] Rivulettes did not back up however and both teams were throwing around everything but the chairs and the box seats."

Hilda Ranscombe managed to stay above the fray, keeping focused on the task at hand – which was nothing less than establishing a dynasty. With the talents of her sister Nellie in net, and the offensive gifts of the Schmuck sisters, Marm and Helen, the Rivulettes were unstoppable. Between 1930 and 1939, they won ten championship titles in both Ontario and Quebec, as well as six national champion titles, tying games just three times and losing only twice – in 350 games. Their two losses came after a long train ride west in March 1932, when, 'flu-ridden, they took on the Edmonton Rustlers for the first Dominion Women's Hockey Championship title. The two thousand spectators who turned out saw a tough, skilled series, which further buoyed the popularity of the women's game. Cinemagoers the following week watched newsreel highlights of Edmonton playing Lethbridge at Banff, whose Winter Carnival showcased powerhouse teams like the Red Deer Amazons and put women's hockey on a level with men's.

But there was nothing like the same money involved. Throughout their career, the Rivulettes and other women's hockey teams were hard-pressed to meet travelling and equipment expenses, and the Depression only added to the difficulty. There was also a near-strike in 1937 over the hardship issue of women's teams paying entry fees to the Dominion Women's Amateur Hockey Association, and of covering their own travel costs. In the end, only teams that could afford to travel could afford to compete for the Lady Bessborough Trophy, donated by the wife of Canada's fourteenth governor general, though the championship match between the Winnipeg Falcons and the Rivulettes at the Galt Arena attracted more than three thousand spectators and gave both teams a profit after expenses.

The Rivulettes, who all held jobs in local factories, were no different from any other women's team in that they funded their own success. When they beat

The Preston Rivulettes dominated women's hockey during the 1930s, losing only two of the 350 games they played between 1930 and 1939. Despite their on-ice success, playing to enthusiastic and large crowds, the Rivulettes and other women's hockey teams struggled financially. To pay for their appearance at a championship series in Prince Edward Island, their coach, Herb Fack, mortgaged his house, and the Rivulettes themselves often paid out of pocket to finance their decade-long dynasty.
(Hockey Hall of Fame)

the Montreal (women's) Maroons in 1936, only 168 fans turned out to watch, leaving the Rivulettes short $150 in gate receipts. They had to kick in five dollars a player so that the Maroons, their hosts, could pay for their victory party.

In 1938, the Rivulettes' coach, Herb Fack, mortgaged his house so the team could play for the women's championship in Prince Edward Island. Ruth Dargel, the youngest member of the team, remembered the trip as magical, with the players billeted in a lovely Charlottetown hotel, "and taken on a tour that included the Parliament Buildings, fabulous dinner and scenery, all by horse and buggy." Even though the local bootlegger's shop was right across from the team's hotel, the Rivulettes managed to get to sleep early, and woke up to three feet of snow – an inconvenience since none of them had brought any winter gear. Then they went off to play championship hockey. "We won our games and had national coverage, but I don't recall ever seeing a trophy," said Dargel. "The crowds were enthusiastic, but the arena wasn't full. I scored a shorthanded goal and that was my highlight of the trip. I also received a rough-ing penalty. When we returned home our families were waiting, but [there was] no special reception for us. My co-workers asked about my hockey trip and then it was quickly forgotten. I put my medallion in my dresser drawer and looked at it from time to time."

The Rivulettes continued their domination of women's hockey up to the beginning of the Second World War and were about to embark on a European tour when war cancelled their plans. After rationing forced the Rivulettes to cancel their away games, and some team members took work in munitions factories, they folded in 1941. A banquet was held for them at the Preston Springs Hotel. Ruth Dargel remembered it as "very sad and yet happy as we celebrated all that we had achieved." Each of the Rivulettes was given a red silk jacket with a crest as a memento. The best women's hockey team ever was done in, not by a rival team, but by the global cataclysm that was the Second World War, for there was no female force on ice that could stop the Rivulettes. Now, just two decades after the last war to end all wars, young men and women were trading in their hockey uniforms for khaki. War would change the world once more, and after it was over, women's hockey would not be seen again for a very long time.

CHAPTER 5

A COOL MEDIUM

One snowy night in Toronto in late December 1942, the writer Morley Callaghan was walking to Maple Leaf Gardens when he saw a group of boys playing road hockey. As the streetlight caught their faces, Callaghan could see an ethnic ragout of, as he later wrote, "Anglo-Saxon faces and Scandinavian faces and Italian and Slavic faces . . . though they were all one, they were just a collection of Canadian kids playing shinny. The game held them all together. . . . And come to think of it, hockey does more for the racial unity of this country than all the speeches of all the politicians who ever pointed with pride at Ottawa. . . . It laughs at the supremacy of any racial faction."

The sight stirred Callaghan in part because the world was at war once again, with Adolf Hitler's army marching through Europe, imposing his ideology of racial purity. Hitler's world had no place for these kids playing hockey. "So I went on my way thinking how important it was that in the coming year, with the nation geared up a little tighter for total war, that hockey should not die," wrote Callaghan. "Hockey is our winter ballet and in many ways our only national drama. When the Germans were at the gates of Moscow the Russians were still listening to the plays of their classic dramatists, weren't they?"

On September 1, 1939, Germany had invaded Poland, and Canada's prime minister, William Lyon Mackenzie King, responded to the crisis by holding a séance at Kingsmere, his estate near Ottawa, around which he had conveniently bought all the land to avoid having to live next to Jewish neighbours. King conjured up his father, who told him that Hitler had been assassinated by a Pole, while his dead mother – his closest adviser – manifested along with his grandfather, William Lyon Mackenzie, and William Gladstone, the British prime minister of the past century, to tell him Hitler was alive, but desperate. King's séance was interrupted by a phone call informing him that Hitler was doing all too well and the British had given him an ultimatum: withdraw from Poland, or else.

Two days later, with the Wehrmacht nearing Warsaw, France and Britain declared war on Germany, and by September 10, Canada – despite King's reassurances from the spirit world a week and a half earlier – was at war, too. Once again, hockey players found themselves in military uniforms, heading off to a contest where losing could mean death. By the end of the year, sixty-nine thousand Canadians had enlisted, and while the NHL was getting underway with its business as usual, a convoy of Canadian troops was sailing for England, some of them not knowing that their initial mission would be fought on ice.

Gilles Turcot was a twenty-one-year-old lieutenant in the storied Royal 22nd Regiment – the Vandoos – of Quebec when he disembarked in Great Britain in December 1939. He had also been a Junior A hockey player, and hockey was a hot subject just a month after Turcot arrived, when English league hockey officials approached General Andy McNaughton, the commanding officer of Canada's 1st Division, and made him an offer he couldn't refuse. "They told him if he wanted to form a hockey league, they would pay all the expenses," recalled Turcot. "So he said yes, and they formed a league and we guys in the 22nd were in the Eastern Flyers."

When war broke out, most of the Canadian players who had been stocking the popular English League returned to Canada, and the English promoters,

Gilles Turcot (back row, second from left) was twenty-one years old when he joined Canada's celebrated 22nd Regiment – the Vandoos – in September 1939. Two months later, he was in England, where the outbreak of war had hit the professional hockey league so hard that most of its Canadian players had returned home. When British hockey promoters asked the Canadian army to fill the void, Turcot found himself playing league hockey with other Canadian soldiers in rinks such as London's Earl's Court Arena, before crowds of ten thousand people.

(Musée du Royal 22ième Régiment)

who had rinks and fans but no on-ice talent, were stuck. Now they looked upon the influx of (what eventually would be five hundred thousand) Canadians as providential, and so did the Canadian army commanders, who saw in hockey a constructive way to keep the troops occupied. And fighting fit. "Our team was made up of enlisted men and officers," recalled Turcot. "We practised once a week and played once a week. It was like a real season of hockey. In addition to playing hockey we had military training – manoeuvres and marches. We were in great shape."

The Imperial Ice Rink in Purley, south of London, was close to the Surrey camps where Canadian soldiers were stationed. Canadian airmen who fought in the Battle of Britain in the summer of 1940, played hockey to relax between sorties. Although the rink was damaged by German bombs during the bombing, by the winter of 1940–41, as many as two hundred soldiers were playing hockey daily on weekdays. And there were still some Canadian players in the United Kingdom who weren't wearing a military uniform. An anonymous pilot of the 401 Fighter Squadron, Royal Canadian Air Force, found this out the hard way and wrote in his war diary for November 8, 1940: "In the evening a hockey team composed of Squadron personnel and billed as 'Les Canadiens' for advertisement purposes played against the Ayr Raiders in the local hockey stadium. Our opponents were all Canadian hockey players who had been brought to this country some years ago to play for the town. . . . After securing a lead of seven goals to one, the Ayr Raiders lifted the pressure in order to make the game interesting, and the final score amounted to 10 to 6."

A few days later the pilot records that the non-coms, with the eternal cunning of those ranking lowest in war's hierarchy, had found a worthier opponent. "November 17: In the evening a hockey game between the officers and men resulted in a victory for the latter, 6 to 4. The officers were handicapped by having only two substitutes while their opponents had three complete forward lines." The enlisted men had shown up in force.

On December 7, 1941, the war spread to the Pacific when Japan attacked Pearl Harbor. Two days after that, ten thousand hockey fans in Boston Garden listened in grim silence to Franklin Roosevelt's radio address over the PA system. Both the Bruins and the Chicago Black Hawks sat wrapped in blankets on their respective benches as the president told his country that the United States was now at war with Japan.

In British Columbia, the response to Japan's entry into the war was swift and brutal in its own way. In January 1942, all male Japanese Canadians between the ages of eighteen and forty-five were taken to camps in the province's Interior, and the Pacific Coast was designated a "protected area." The following month, a further twenty-one thousand Japanese Canadians – virtually the entire community in Canada – were told to pack a suitcase each and herded into livestock barns to be processed for "internment." The unfounded fear was that their sympathies lay with Japan, not with Canada, and that they would destroy their fellow Canadians by signalling to Japanese submarines off the coast of Vancouver.

At the time, their fellow Canadians were being destroyed quite nicely by their own allies. When the Germans overran France in May 1940, Mackenzie King had written, "It is now left to the British peoples and those of British stock to save the world." In August 1942, with German troops massed on the coast of the English Channel, Britain took King up on the finer nuances of this offer. They dispatched predominantly Canadian troops to raid the port of Dieppe, in what was supposedly a dry run for the Allied invasion of Europe. Of the five thousand Canadians who took part in the disastrous, British-planned assault, nearly half were killed or captured by the waiting Germans.

For Conn Smythe, the man who invented the Maple Leafs, both Prime Minister Mackenzie King and the war he was waging were disasters. Smythe reckoned he knew more than the prime minister about fighting wars and tried to give him some advice. The fastidious, cautious King – the man who cabled Churchill during the Battle of Britain seeking spare rubble to decorate his Kingsmere estate – took an instant dislike to the scrappy, opinionated Smythe. The feeling was reciprocal. Smythe sent the PM goading telegrams, which likened war to sport in their suggestion that King was letting down the side because he didn't have a crackerjack team of well-trained and armed troops and commanders like others in the British Empire league – Australia, New Zealand, and South Africa.

King remembered all too well the conscription problems Wilfrid Laurier faced in Quebec in the last war, and he also knew that he could win the next election only by winning the Quebec vote. His government introduced the National Resources Mobilization Act, a kind of compromise conscription that required soldiers to serve at home and do their basic military training over thirty days on evenings and weekends.

Smythe, now a forty-five-year-old captain in the Non-Permanent Active Militia, had a brainwave: he would take a Sportsmen's Battalion to war, just as had been done a quarter of a century earlier. The government and the army eventually capitulated to the Little Pistol's plan, and in September 1941, Smythe became a major in command of the 30th Battery of the 7th Toronto Regiment. Smythe signed up the starting lineup of the Mimico Mountaineers, winners of lacrosse's Mann Cup, as well as several Ontario baseball stars, a Toronto Argonaut, and two of Canada's best golfers, Jim Boekh and Clare Chinery. Smythe even convinced two Toronto sports scribes to join his gunners: Ted Reeve of the *Telegram* and Ralph Allen of the *Globe and Mail*. Allen went on to become a war correspondent for *Maclean's* two years later.

The last thing the continent's only professional hockey league wanted was for its star players to wind up as starred names in a Book of Remembrance. So the Boston Bruins' brilliant Kraut Line of Milt Schmidt, Bobby Bauer, and Woody Dumart, who all hailed from Kitchener, Ontario, sanitized their line name to the Kitchener Kids and were recruited to the relative safety of the Royal Canadian Air Force Flyers hockey team. Fellow Bruins Milt Schmidt and Woody Dumart were sent to England as player-coaches for the Canadian Bomber Group League. Ewart Tucker, who was a motorcycle dispatch rider and then a tank driver in the Army, remembered recruiters showing up in 1942, looking for men to try out for a hockey team to tour the British Isles. "There were sixteen of us soldiers that were playing hockey, and then there was the trainer and the coach and also an officer that was in charge. That's all we did until March 26, 1943, and we toured all over England and Scotland playing exhibition hockey."

Back in Canada, an armed forces hockey rivalry began. When the Air Force team won the Allan Cup, the championship trophy of Canadian senior men's hockey, in 1942, in response the New York Rangers' coach, Frank Boucher, helped to create a Canadian Army hockey team. The Ottawa Commandos included Neil and Mac Colville, and Alex Shibicky, all members of the 1940 Stanley Cup–winning Rangers squad, as well as their goalie, "Sugar" Jim Henry. Montreal Canadiens defenceman Ken Reardon was a Commando, as was his coach, Dick Irvin, who split shifts between the soldiers and the Habs (short for the Québécois term *habitants*).

Army teams were playing senior hockey all across Canada during the war, their ranks filled by NHLers on sabbatical and men who would one day rise to the pro game. In Calgary, former Hart Trophy winner Tom "Cowboy" Anderson led his Currie barracks team along with goalie Frank McCool, who would go on to star in the NHL. Maple Leaf Nick Metz and Chicago Black Hawk Bill Carse played for the Victoria Army squad, which won the B.C. Senior Championship in 1943.

Great Lines

The practise of naming the trios who form hockey teams' line of attack dates back to the 1920s, when Bun Cook (left wing), Frank Boucher (centre), and Bill Cook (right wing) formed the New York Rangers' A Line, named after the A Train, which ran under Madison Square Garden, the team's home rink. Line-naming saw its heyday between the 1930s and the 1960s, although the 1990s produced such lines as the Legion of Doom in Philadelphia, featuring John LeClair (left wing), Eric Lindros (centre), and Mikael Renberg, and the Vancouver Canucks of the 1990s called Geoff Courtnall (left wing), Cliff Ronning (centre), and Trevor Linden the Life Line. Other historic lines, from left wing to right:

- **Bread Line:** Mac Colville, Neil Colville, Alex Shibicky. New York Rangers, 1930s–1940s. They were not named thus because of the Depression bread lines, but because they were the team's bread and butter.
- **Donut Line:** A generic term for two star wingers and a journeyman centre – or a hole in the middle.
- **French Connection:** Richard Martin, Gilbert Perreault, René Robert. Buffalo Sabres, 1970s. After the popular movie, and their francophone heritage.
- **GAG Line:** Vic Hadfield, Jean Ratelle, Rod Gilbert. New York Rangers, 1960s–1970s. They scored a goal-a-game (or hoped to).
- **Kid Line:** Harvey "Busher" Jackson, Joe Primeau, Charlie Conacher. Toronto Maple Leafs, 1930s. Their youth and inexperience made them the original and most famous Kid Line in hockey history.
- **Kraut Line** (above, left to right): Bobby Bauer, Milt Schmidt, Woody Dumart. Boston Bruins, late 1930s, early 1940s. The trio led the Bruins to a Stanley Cup in 1939, finished one-two-three in scoring in 1940, and won another Cup in 1941. The Second World War saw the line's name changed to the Kitchener Kids. Midway through the 1941–42 season, the Kids joined the air force, where they won the Allan Cup with the Ottawa–based RCAF Flyers.
- **Mafia Line:** Don Moloney, Phil Esposito, Don Murdoch. New York Rangers, 1970s–1980s. The Godfather, Esposito, and two dons.
- **Pony Line:** Doug Bentley, Max Bentley, Bill Mosienko. Chicago Black Hawks, 1940s. Small, but mighty.
- **Production Line:** Ted Lindsay, Sid Abel, Gordie Howe. Detroit Red Wings, 1940s–1950s. They could produce goals, the way the production lines of Detroit's auto industry could produce cars.
- **Punch Line:** Toe Blake, Elmer Lach, Maurice Richard. Montreal Canadiens, 1940s. They had offensive punch.
- **S-Line:** Babe Siebert, Nels Stewart, Hooley Smith. Montreal Maroons, 1929–1932. Not the most imaginative line name, using the first letter of their surnames, but they lit up the score charts for the Maroons.
- **Triple Crown Line:** Charlie Simmer, Marcel Dionne, Dave Taylor. Los Angeles Kings, 1970s–1980s. Three kings. (*Hockey Hall of Fame*)

Senior hockey, for all of its amateur status, was also good for wartime business. Conn Smythe and his fellow directors at Maple Leaf Gardens had won the right from the OHA to host all junior and senior hockey games in the Toronto area, a concession that was renewed for five years in 1942. Since the soldier teams were classified as senior hockey, even though they were stuffed with professional players, their contests made money for the Gardens – in 1943, more than doubling the 112,693 tickets sold the previous year. As it had been in the First World War, it was profitable for Conn Smythe to have hockey players in khakis and on skates.

For some players, senior hockey wasn't all fun and games away from the dangers of battle. The Oshawa Generals' Albert "Red" Tilson, Jack Fox, a Leaf prospect, and Dudley "Red" Garrett, a former New York Ranger, were all killed on "active duty."

After a stint protecting Tofino, B.C., from a Japanese invasion and keeping his battery's gunnery skills high by practise shooting at an offshore rock, Major Smythe shipped out for Europe. His Leafs lost a third of their team to the army, including their star goalie, Walter "Turk" Broda, whose enlistment made national headlines and was the subject of parliamentary debate. Broda had been arrested on October 18, 1943, by the RCMP while en route to Montreal and told he was about to breach his draft notice, even though he had already volunteered for military service in Toronto three days earlier and was in the company of an army NCO when he was arrested. He was hauled off the train and shipped back to Toronto, where he formally signed up for the army again. Now he was eligible to play goal with the Toronto Army Daggers hockey team.

Conspiracy theorists at the Montreal *Gazette* suggested that Conn Smythe was behind a plot to keep Broda from playing for the Montreal Army team, which had offered him $2,400 above his military pay. The *Calgary Herald* gave voice to the thoughts of many Canadians by calling it a national disgrace that hockey players who had enlisted one or two years earlier were still in Canada playing hockey and not fighting the war. The Army and Air Force responded to this outcry swiftly, and within months the military hockey teams were disbanded and their players sent on for advanced training in preparation for battle.

During the Second World War, the NHL didn't want any of its players killed in Europe, so those who joined the Canadian military wound up playing hockey. Army teams such as the Ottawa Commandos included Neil and Mac Colville, (front row, third from right) and Alex Shibicky (back row, second from left) – all members of the 1940 Stanley Cup–winning New York Rangers squad, as well as their goalie, "Sugar" Jim Henry. Montreal Canadiens defenceman Ken Reardon was a Commando, too, and the team won the Allan Cup in 1943 as the best in Canadian men's senior hockey.

(*Hockey Hall of Fame*)

Binoculars for the RCAF

After Japan attacked the United States on December 7, 1941, Canadians feared that the country's West Coast would be invaded. The Royal Canadian Air Force was worried that its binoculars were not powerful enough to survey the Pacific for signs of enemy aircraft. Their solution was hockey. On December 20, 1941, during the Imperial Oil Hockey Broadcast from Maple Leaf Gardens, Foster Hewitt issued an appeal for hockey fans to donate their binoculars. By Monday, January 12, 1942, the RCAF had received 400 pairs of binoculars and asked the broadcaster to suspend the appeal for a while, as the appraisers couldn't keep up with the supply. But Canadians kept sending them, and 440 of the 1,116 pairs donated were used by the air force. (*Hockey Hall of Fame*)

HOCKEY FANS "KICK IN"

FOR R.C.A.F. COASTAL PATROL

ONE afternoon late in December 1941, in an Ottawa office, an important meeting was called to order to formulate ways and means of solving a pressing problem.

The Royal Canadian Air Force *must* have binoculars and have them immediately! The problem had already been a headache to the Air Member for Supply for several months—and then, quite suddenly, it had been brought to a head by the Japanese attack on Pearl Harbor. Canada's west coast was tensely on guard, and powerful field glasses and night glasses were needed desperately to catch a first distant glimpse of an invasion fleet or marauding aircraft in case an effort was made to attack Canada immediately.

The optical industry said flatly, "No!" It could not supply binoculars, and it frankly didn't know when it would be able to. European sources of supply had long been cut off. There was already a huge backlog of unfilled and equally urgent orders in the hands of the industry on this continent. And yet the R.C.A.F. had to find the glasses. It simply HAD to find them. Immediately!

So an emergency meeting was called, to see whether a solution could be found. Senior R.C.A.F. officers were present at the meeting—and just to show how important the matter was, no less a personage than the Minister of National Defence for Air, the Hon. C. G. Power, P.C., M.C., was there. The question was surely vital enough—how to provide Canada's West Coast with "eyes."

It seemed clear from the beginning that the only way to get high-grade prismatic binoculars, and quickly, would be by getting them from private owners among the general public. Incidentally, it should be kept in mind that very few people ever trouble to equip themselves with glasses of the quality and power required for R.C.A.F. coastal patrol work. However, an appeal over the air was decided upon as the best and quickest way to reach the relatively small number of such private owners.

But the question remained: what broadcast to use? It might make a big difference.

Some bright soul suggested that sportsmen would be the likeliest owners of high-grade binoculars—and for an audience of sportsmen, what about Imperial Oil Hockey Broadcasts? So a request was telephoned at once to Imperial Oil asking the company to announce the need for binoculars on its regular hockey broadcast the following Saturday night, December 20th.

There were two things that helped to slow up the early response from listeners. One was the fact that the first three appeals were all bunched during the heart of the year-end holiday season—December 20th and 27th, and January 3rd—when people were busy on other things. The other was that the address to which the glasses were to be shipped was very long and very complicated.

However, before the end of the first week in January, parcels were arriving at a fair rate. On Monday, January 12th, the Liaison Officer to the Air Member for Supply 'phoned Imperial Oil to 'please lay off' for a week. With 400 pairs received, he explained, the appraisers (able to examine and repair only a few pairs a day) were practically snowed under.

Two days later, the Deputy Minister (Air Service) wrote to say: "I have been very impressed by the skill and imagination with which the appeal was presented over the air by Mr. Benson and your radio staff. That these appeals were most successfully effective can be seen in the quantity of over 600 binoculars which have been offered to date."

Two hundred additional pairs in just two days! Mostly high-priced binoculars!

Five days later (in spite of no further appeals being made) the total was still going up, and the Liaison Officer to the A.M.S. wrote Imperial Oil: "We have actually received to date some 850 pairs, which far exceeded our wildest expectations. The point we now wish to get across to the public is not an appeal for more binoculars but a request that they be more patient if they do not hear promptly as to the valuation on the glasses sent in."

Consequently there were no further appeals at any time after January 10th; yet when the final count was made, it was found that in all, 1,116 instruments had been submitted; and of these, 440 were found acceptable for Air Force use.

For the first time, the hockey audience had been called upon in a critical emergency. And, as the R.C.A.F. Directorate of Public Relations expressed it in reporting the facts to Imperial Oil: "It got results like a fire box does when you break the glass and pull the switch."

Even so, the hockey players did manage to get in some ice time after they had been shipped over to England, and as Montreal Canadien Ken Reardon recalled in Dick Irvin's book *The Habs*, the NHL was never too far away. "We played a game in Brighton for the Canadian Army championship. Conn Smythe was there, and he brought along Field Marshal Montgomery. Smythe was really glad to see us. He was a real military man. I think he felt every player from the NHL should have joined up."

By 1944, a total of ninety NHL players had at one time or another served in the armed forces, either because of their own patriotism, or that of their team's, but many weren't in uniform at all. The Canadian government's selective service board had issued an escape clause saying that professional athletes would receive no special treatment, but on the other hand, were to be allowed to play professional sport if their war work was of a low priority. The National Resources Mobilization Act, introduced in 1940, allowed the government to register men and women for jobs necessary to the war effort, with the guarantee they would not be shipped overseas. The Montreal Canadiens were spared military call-ups because many of their players held jobs considered essential to the war effort (as did the Leafs, but they also had Conn Smythe urging them into battle). In 1944–45, the NHL changed its constitution to prevent such players from being exempt from military service, a move that Conn Smythe was said to have spearheaded in the face of the wartime powerhouse that was the Montreal Canadiens.

The darkness of war served to shine a brighter light on the Canadiens. Great things were expected of them by a city that hadn't had a true hockey dynasty since the early years of the Stanley Cup challenge. Now, in 1942, the Canadiens had a reason to hope for glory again in the form of a twenty-three-year-old right-winger who had finally made the big club. His name was Maurice Richard. He had been rejected for military service, because his bones broke too easily, but he would become the battle standard for the city and the province.

As he had done nearly three decades earlier, Conn Smythe readily answered the call to war and again took a sportsmen's battery with him. He was badly wounded in France in July 1944, and when Smythe's attendant saw how many other injured men were being treated before him at the casualty clearing station, he told the medics who Smythe was. Fortunately, the medics were Leafs fans. (*Library and Archives Canada, PA-163191*)

Richard was in his sophomore year of NHL hockey when fellow Montreal Canadien Ray Getliffe watched him play from the bench one night. "He got the puck at the blue line, deked two guys and streaked in with that fire in his eyes to score," recalled Getliffe. "I said, 'Geez, he went in like a rocket.'" The sportswriter "Dink" Carroll overheard the remark. "That's when he publicly became Rocket Richard," said Getliffe. "One of the most famous names in all sport."

Maurice "Rocket" Richard, a five-foot-ten inch, 170-pound package of fire on ice, became much more than a famous sports figure. He became the icon of a people, and in the end, of a country. In Roch Carrier's classic story *The Hockey Sweater*, the narrator explains just what the Rocket meant to children out on Quebec's frozen ponds: "We would ask God to help us play as well as Maurice Richard. We all wore the same uniform as he, the red white and blue uniform of the Montreal Canadiens, the best hockey team in the world; we all combed our hair in the same style as Maurice Richard, and to keep it in place we used a sort of glue – a great deal of glue. We laced our skates like Maurice Richard, we taped our sticks like Maurice Richard. We cut all his pictures out of the papers. Truly, we knew everything about him."

Maurice Richard was the eldest son and second child of Onésime and Alice Richard, who came from the Gaspé to Montreal as part of the post–First World War migration of people from rural Quebec into the city. Onésime found a job as a carpenter for Canadian Pacific, and the family of nine eventually settled in the northern reaches of the city, across the Rivières des Prairies from Laval. It was on this river, and in the schoolyards of Laval, that Maurice Richard honed his hockey gifts.

Richard began playing league hockey when he was eleven. After a cup of coffee with the Verdun Junior Maple Leafs in 1938–39, he joined the Canadiens' farm team, the Senior Royals. The first Canadiens' game Richard ever saw was the one he played in, though his beginning with the team was less than auspicious. When Richard was invited to the Royals' training camp in 1940, he scored two goals in his first regular season game. But he was out of the game, and the season, after he caught his skate in a rut and broke his left ankle. The following year he broke his wrist, and in 1942–43, his first season with the Canadiens, he broke his right ankle. Rumours had it that Richard was too fragile to play in the big leagues, and his coach, Dick Irvin, openly questioned his fortitude.

Richard came back with the fire in his eyes that would one day move William Faulkner to declare in *Sports Illustrated* that the Rocket had "the passionate glittering fatal alien quality of snakes." Dick Irvin placed him on a line with silky centre Elmer Lach, and left-winger Hector "Toe" Blake, whose goal-scoring ability had earned him the nickname of the "Lamplighter." Together, the trio were known as the Punch Line because of their ability to knock out opponents with their hockey genius. They were also a microcosm of their fan base, for, at the beginning of their union, Lach spoke only English, Richard spoke only French, and Blake was bilingual. The language of the 1940s Canadiens was English – from the management through the coaches and into the dressing room, a reflection of the reality that real power in the province was held by English hands.

The language that Richard spoke most eloquently was the one on ice, with his stick and a puck. In the 1944 Stanley Cup finals against the Canadiens' natural enemy, the Toronto Maple Leafs, his hockey oratory showed just how fragile he really was. In the second game of the series, Richard declared his intentions by scoring his first two goals just seventeen seconds apart in the first two minutes of the game. He made it a natural hat trick before the period was out. The Rocket soared again in the third period, scoring twice more to tie Newsy Lalonde's 1919 record of five goals in one Stanley Cup game. The final score was the Maple Leafs 1 and Rocket Richard 5. Broadcaster Foster Hewitt picked the game's three stars: "Maurice Richard, Maurice Richard, Maurice Richard." The Stanley Cup came back to the Canadiens that year after a thirteen-year drought, and Richard was a hero to francophone Quebec.

English Canadians were not so sure. While Conn Smythe never doubted the worth of the Leafs' 1942 Stanley Cup triumph, he saw no irony in dismissing Richard's extraordinary accomplishment in 1944 as just the dividend of playing in a weak league. Smythe, who returned from the war in 1945, was not alone in questioning the quality of wartime hockey, though Frank Selke, the man he left in charge of the Leafs while he was off fighting Hitler,

The Red Line

At the beginning of the NHL's 1943–44 season, the league's Rules Committee met to see whether they could speed up the game and make it more entertaining. New York Rangers' coach Frank Boucher had a compelling idea: put another line on the ice to divide the zones further. Boucher, a centreman whose skill at stealing the puck and his clean play (he won the Lady Byng Trophy seven times in eight years, so in 1935 the NHL just gave it to him and had a copy made) led to the nickname Raffles, after the fictional gentleman thief, A.J. Raffles. Boucher's idea was that a line bisecting the ice would allow teams to pass the puck out of their own end – which they weren't previously allowed to do. The new line, the red line, sped up the game by allowing defencemen to be creative, sending wingers down the boards and into exciting rushes, and freed up the defence to sweep the puck into the "neutral zone" and out of danger. The innovation led to a scoring bonanza for NHL snipers, and the 1943–44 season saw six players in the scoring top ten notching thirty goals or more, a first for the NHL. (*Hockey Hall of Fame*)

blamed Smythe for the depletion of the pro ranks by bullying players into the armed forces.

The war years saw team scoring averages rise from 2.5 goals per game in the late 1930s to 4.08 in 1944, the year six NHL players notched thirty goals or better, a previously unheard-of achievement. The scores were not so much proof of inferior goaltending and defending than of success. At the beginning of the 1943–44 season, the NHL Rules Committee decided to speed up the game to make it more entertaining. Boston's Art Ross, a great player, coach, hockey innovater, and – to more than a few who worked for him – tyrant, teamed up with the New York Rangers' Frank Boucher to create a fundamental innovation, the red line.

Before this invention, which divided the ice in half, players could not pass the puck from their own zone; they had to skate it out across their blue line. If they were short-handed, they had to manoeuvre past the opposition while outnumbered, or pass the puck in their own zone, a dangerous move. The red line sped up the game by freeing wingers to receive passes in the middle of the rink, and then rush into the enemy zone. It also freed up the defence to sweep the puck into the new neutral zone and out of danger. The red line allowed players to be creative.

In February 1945, Conn Smythe celebrated his fiftieth birthday, and his first live NHL hockey game in three years, by going to see with his own eyes

With linemates Elmer Lach and Toe Blake making up the Punch Line, Maurice Richard terrorized NHL goalies, his eyes like lasers as he bore down on them to shoot another puck into the record books.

He scored nine goals in the 1944 Stanley Cup playoffs, including five in a semifinal game against Toronto, and then another four in a 3–2 series win against Chicago, leading Montreal to their first Stanley Cup championship in fourteen seasons.

The following year, late in the last game of the season, Richard became the first player in NHL history to score fifty goals in fifty games. It was a record that stood until Mike Bossy of the New York Islanders accomplished the feat in 1980–81. *(Hockey Hall of Fame)*

that Maurice Richard was just an overrated talent. Once he saw Richard in action, Smythe, the man who had never had a French-Canadian player on his team, and who once, astonishingly, began a speech in Montreal with the greeting "Ladies, Gentlemen and Frenchmen," wanted Richard in a blue and white sweater.

The Rocket had shot to unexplored hockey scoring heights in his red, white, and blue sweater, his own mythology rising in his afterburn. Three days after Christmas 1944, he spent the day moving into his new house – not supervising the movers, but shifting the furniture himself, including a piano. It was a game day, and Richard arrived in the Montreal dressing room exhausted, and sprawled out on the training table, as if to send a message to his teammates not to count on him that night. But he was just using the rest to gather his forces. He unleashed them that night in a five-goal, three-assist, and eventual 9–1 trouncing of the Detroit Red Wings. In a nine-game stretch in 1944, Richard fired in fifteen goals, despite every effort to stop him by his opponents, who slashed and elbowed and hooked and even draped themselves over his hurtling frame. Richard shoved them away, and if they persisted, he levelled them with a punch as powerful and as accurate as that of any heavyweight. He had to – there were no enforcers around to fight his battles for him.

The one thing he wanted more than anything was to become the first man to score fifty goals in fifty games. When Richard beat ex-Canadien Joe Malone's record of forty-five goals (set in 1918, over twenty-two games), he still had eight games to reach the magical fifty. But he couldn't get past forty-nine. Everyone wanted to stop him – no team wanted to be the one that gave him the record, to be the team everyone would remember for the wrong reason. It only fuelled Richard's obsession, and the drama on ice was operatic.

In the last period of the Canadiens' last home game of the 1944–45 season, Richard found himself alone in front of the Chicago net. A Black Hawk defenceman chopped him down, and the referee gave Richard a penalty shot. Here, surely, was number fifty – in a duel, no less. But the Chicago goalie stopped him, and Richard now had just one game to make that goal, or be forever remembered for how close he came, and how he had fallen so cruelly short. He didn't make it easy on himself, or for the millions cheering him on. Late in the third period of the last game of the season, in the hostile territory of Boston Garden, Richard scooped up a pass from Elmer Lach and fired it on Boston's net. The puck went in, and finally, he had his fifty.

To obliterate any memory of the eight-game dry spell before he made the magic number, Richard added six more goals in six games against the Maple Leafs in the Stanley Cup playoffs, making it an astonishing fifty-six goals in fifty-six games. His place in hockey mythology was assured.

Now Conn Smythe wanted Richard more than ever. He offered the Canadiens $25,000, with a $1,000 bonus to anyone who could swing the deal, but no one could manage it for one simple reason: Maurice Richard already wore the only hockey sweater he ever wanted.

For twelve-year-old Felix Gatt, sitting in a Maltese cinema watching hockey newsreels in 1950, the greatest iceman was Gordie Howe. "The way Gordie played impressed me," said Gatt. "And I fell in love with hockey." Gatt had a

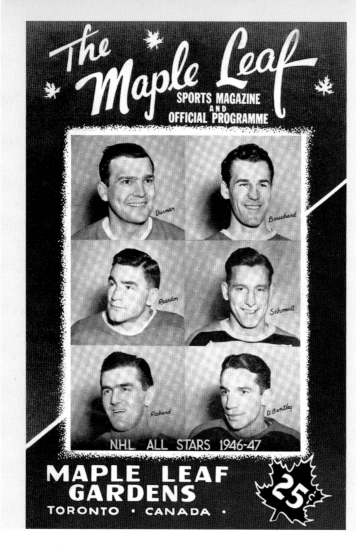

The First Official NHL All-Star Game

The NHL's first official All-Star game took place in Toronto's Maple Leaf Gardens on Monday, October 13, 1947, to raise money for the newly formed NHL Pension Society. The Leafs, as defending Stanley Cup champions, took on a team of NHL All-Stars, who had some serious firepower in their ranks, including Maurice "Rocket" Richard, Detroit's Ted Lindsay, Chicago's Pony Line of Bill Mosienko and the Bentley brothers, Doug and Max, as well as Boston's famed Kraut Line. The Leafs had their own stars in goalie Walter "Turk" Broda, forward Ted "Teeder" Kennedy, and captain Syl Apps, but the All-Stars prevailed in the inaugural game 4–3. More than twenty-five thousand dollars was raised for the Pension Society, and a significant NHL tradition had begun. In the years to come, however, the actual amount of the money raised each year became a source of bitter contention between the league and the players. (*Hockey Hall of Fame*)

personal connection with the Red Wings, Howe's team, for his father had moved to Detroit in advance of his wife and nine children, to whom he would send news of the new world. "You know, sometimes, something happens that attracts you to somebody," said Gatt. "[Howe] was the star player . . . in Detroit, and every time I used to look at the papers that my dad sent me, he was always in the headlines." When Gatt arrived to begin his new life in the United States, he had one mission more important than all others. "I could not wait to see Gordie Howe. . . . The first thing I did was . . . I started to go to games."

Howe was a six-foot, two-hundred-pounder with a physique so sculpted by his summer job hauling cement for his father's roadworks crew in Saskatoon that when Detroit owner Jim Norris first saw him naked in the Red Wings dressing room he exclaimed "I could make you heavyweight champion of the world in ten months." Howe was already a heavyweight champion on the ice, with a punch so powerful that it worried his father, Ab, when Gordie joined the pros. "I told the wife 'I hope that boy never fights. He's got a blow that can kill a man.'"

The year that young Felix Gatt fell in love with hockey was the year that Gordie Howe was nearly killed. On March 28, 1950, midway through the second

When Detroit Red Wings coach and general manager Jack Adams first saw sixteen-year-old Gordie Howe at training camp in 1944, he thought Howe the best hockey prospect he'd ever seen. Even so, and foreshadowing the Wings' shabby treatment of the man who would become known as Mr. Hockey, Adams forgot all about his promise to send Howe the Red Wings windbreaker that he so admired. The following year, when Adams offered Howe a contract, Howe remembered the broken promise and refused to sign. "You can't imagine how quickly I got that windbreaker," Adams said later. "But that's how close I came to losing him." *(Hockey Hall of Fame)*

period of the first game of the playoffs against Toronto, Leafs captain Ted "Teeder" Kennedy was rushing with the puck when, from the corner of his eye, he saw Howe, hurtling toward him at full speed. Kennedy braked, Howe tripped, sticks flew up, and a Detroit player accidentally slammed Howe into the boards. Suddenly, Number 9 was lying in a heap, blood gushing from his head onto the ice in dreadful contrast, for an innovation that season had been to paint the ice white.

The man who had scored thirty-five goals and added thirty-three assists that season, putting him in third place on the scoring charts behind linemates Sid Abel and Ted Lindsay, was carried off the ice, barely alive. Doctors drilled a hole into Howe's skull, just above his right eye, and the fluid that had been building upon Howe's brain flowed out. In Detroit that night, people said Howe was dead. In Saskatoon, Howe's mother, Katherine, listened as Red Wings manager Jack Adams told her that Gordie might not live to see his twenty-second birthday, just three days away on March 31. Radio stations in both Canada and the United States made regular news updates on Howe's condition; in Saskatoon, radio stations covered the disaster all night long.

With morning came good news. Howe would not only live, he would play again the next season. When Howe stepped onto the ice after the Wings won the 1950 Stanley Cup, his linemate Ted Lindsay gently raised his stick to Howe's head and knocked off the hat that Howe was wearing. Lindsay wanted to show the fans at Detroit's Olympia Stadium the awful scars on Howe's head. He wanted to show them how close they had all come to losing him.

Howe recovered from his head injuries well enough to play in all seventy of Detroit's regular season games the following year, scoring forty-three goals and adding forty-three assists to win the Art Ross Trophy – the first of his six NHL scoring titles. And now, in 1951, he was to become one of the hottest characters on television.

Televised hockey had been experimented with as early as February 11, 1939, when the third period of a match between Oxford and Cambridge at Earl's Court was broadcast by BBC Television. In 1940, Madison Square Garden tried an internal broadcast. But not everyone saw a happy future for hockey on television. In 1949, NHL president Clarence Campbell gave voice to the fear – and to the truth about who was going to NHL games. "Television sets are expensive and at present within the reach of only the upper and middle income tax brackets," he said. "These are the people who support hockey and if they stay home it is estimated that the six NHL clubs could lose as much as one million dollars a season in gate receipts. It is extremely doubtful if television can afford to pay us enough to make up for this lost attendance."

The Zamboni Ice Resurfacing Machine

The boxy ice-smoothing tractor seen everywhere from humble local ice rinks to NHL hockey palaces was invented out of necessity by Frank Zamboni. Zamboni's stints as an auto repairman and builder of refrigeration units for local dairies in Southern California came together when he and his cousin built the open-air Iceland Skating Rink in the Los Angeles suburb of Paramount. Iceland opened in 1940 as one of the largest rinks in the country, with twenty thousand square feet of ice, and Zamboni soon realized he needed to roof the rink to protect the ice from the California sun and wind. Even roofed, there was still the problem of keeping the ice smooth and fresh. The method then current was time-consuming and inefficient, taking three or four workers an hour to shovel up the ice shavings created by a tractor with a scraper on it, then spray fresh water on the ice, and scrape off the excess. Zamboni's idea was simple: a machine that shaves the ice, gathers the shavings, smoothes and squeegees the ice with clean cold and hot water, then filters the dirty water for reuse. Zamboni took out a patent on his invention in 1950, and the machine that is today known affectionately as the Zamboni made its NHL debut, fittingly, in a Montreal versus Toronto game in 1952. (*Frank J. Zamboni & Co., Inc.*)

Three years later, just 10 per cent of Canadians owned a television. It had not yet reached the country's three coasts, but what Canadian cultural philosopher Marshall McLuhan had famously called the cool medium had penetrated the consciousness of the continent, and its transformative cultural power was enough to persuade the Chicago Black Hawks to broadcast weekend matinee games. The first team to use television, the Hawks played matinees, fearing that Saturday night hockey couldn't compete with Saturday night television.

That year, the Canadian Broadcasting Corporation began transmitting a television signal first from Montreal on September 6, and then from Toronto on September 8. One month later, on October 11, 1952, Gerald Renaud, a twenty-four-year-old newspaper sports editor who hadn't even seen TV, produced for the new medium a hockey game between Montreal and Detroit, or rather between the two Number 9s, Rocket Richard and Gordie Howe.

Three weeks after hockey debuted on TV in Montreal, where play-by-play man René Lacavalier invented a whole new lexicon to describe the exploits of the Canadiens for the viewers, Foster Hewitt became the voice of televised hockey in English Canada. On November 1, 1952, *Hockey Night in Canada*

Since 1936, Saturday night radio broadcasts of hockey games, sponsored by Imperial Oil, had been a fixture in the lives of hockey fans. And when television started to become popular after its debut in Canada in 1952, hockey moved to the new medium, still on Saturday nights, and still sponsored by Imperial Oil. (*Hockey Hall of Fame*)

broadcasts began in the middle of the second period of a game between the Canadiens and the Leafs. Conn Smythe refused to let the first part of the game go on the air as he didn't want to give it all away for free. But then he almost did that with the Leafs' television broadcast rights, charging Imperial Oil just one hundred dollars a game for that first season. Then Smythe gauged the value of televised hockey in the marketplace, and the following season, he sold Imperial Oil three years' worth of Leafs TV games for $450,000. *Hockey Night in Canada* had made the televised sport the hottest thing in the country, even though it wasn't until 1968 that viewers saw the game from the opening faceoff.

As a boy in suburban Toronto, former Canadiens goalie and hockey author Ken Dryden used to sit down with his parents, siblings, and grandmother to watch *Hockey Night in Canada* at 9:00 p.m. sharp on Saturday nights. In an essay on the Imperial Oil website, Dryden says, "Everything about it was special. It was Saturday night. It was staying up late. It was the family all together. It was seeing adults get more excited than you ever saw them at other times (just my father and grandmother; my mother was always calm and serene), saying and doing things as impolite as things you thought only you did. It was watching a game you were beginning to know and love played by players you wanted to be. It was the one time of the week that never came fast enough. So everything and everyone associated with *Hockey Night in Canada* was special."

Conn Smythe saw television not so much as a tool for family building, but as a sales vehicle that would propel people out of their living rooms and into hockey arenas. He argued that when hockey's Cassandras had warned that radio would kill interest in the sport, the opposite had happened. "Same way with television," he reasoned. "There'll be thousands of people seeing hockey as played by the pros for the first time. They'll be sold on it because it's a great game, and they won't be satisfied to stay [at home] but will turn out to the rinks." Smythe was right. Fans kept coming to see games live. Except in Ottawa.

The Senators, once at the apex of the professional game, were now members of the Quebec Senior Hockey League, playing semi-pro men's hockey on Saturday nights, and in December 1954, no one was coming to their games. Ottawa's managing director, Tommy Gorman, who had guided three different teams to four Stanley Cups, and had resurrected the moribund Canadiens in the 1940s, fought hard before finally surrendering to the power of television. "We have no choice in the matter but to withdraw from the Quebec League without further delay as the televising of the Saturday night programs from the Maple Leaf Gardens has completely ruined our attendances," he wrote to John McLaren, the president of McLaren Advertising, the original producers of *Hockey Night in Canada*. Gorman was even more blunt in his explanation of the matter in a letter to the Western Hockey League. "We find it impossible to carry on. On Saturday nights, the Cocktail Bars and Beverage Rooms are jammed with hockey fans, watching the Toronto and Montreal games, while our auditorium has been nearly empty."

The *Ottawa Citizen* put into words what many in the national capital were thinking. "The city of Ottawa awoke today to the realization that it no longer had a big team in the national sport of the country. It's probably the first time in the memory of living man that the Capital City, once known as the cradle of hockey, has been without a senior club of some kind, amateur or professional." The truth was that all the senior leagues now had to compete with television's interest, and the camera eye was most interested in the so-called Original Six of the NHL. Once seven teams, the NHL was down to six when the New York Americans folded during the war. The NHL was now the only league that could win hockey's ultimate prize, and so it had the brightest stars to attract both viewers and advertising dollars.

The Montreal Canadiens knew this all too well. They wanted Jean Béliveau, a big, handsome, smooth-skating centre who played for the Quebec Aces and was so popular that local merchants gave him suits and hats and shirts and free steak lunches every time he scored three goals. The Aces had given the twenty-one-year-old Béliveau a twenty-thousand-dollar-a-year contract and two cars, one of them a stylish convertible with the licence plate "2B." (Quebec's all-powerful premier, Maurice Duplessis, already had the licence plate "1B.") The Canadiens already owned Béliveau's NHL rights, but he was happier in Quebec – and making more money – than he thought he would be with the NHL club. So Senator Donat Raymond, the Canadiens' owner, bought the entire Quebec Senior Hockey League, and then, as GM Frank Selke put it, "opened the vault" to put Béliveau in a red, white, and blue jersey in 1953. He would be good for business – and good for television.

Television and its radio and newspaper cousins were clearly to blame in the eyes of Detroit Red Wings coach and general manager Jack Adams on the night of March 17, 1955. Reporters caught up with him as he prepared to board a train to Detroit after the Red Wings had won – by default – a game against Montreal. "What happened tonight makes me sick and ashamed. I blame you fellows for what happened," Adams said. "You've turned Richard into an idol, a man whose suspension can turn hockey fans into shrieking idiots. Now, hear this: Richard is no hero! . . . He makes me ashamed to be connected with this

Nicknamed Le Gros Bill because of his resemblance to a big, heroic character in a French-Canadian folk song, Jean Béliveau came to embody the poise, class, and success of the Canadiens, for whom he played until 1971, spending ten seasons as captain and winning ten Stanley Cups. (*Frank Prazak/Hockey Hall of Fame*)

game." Some cultural pundits have called what happened that night one of the critical events leading up to Quebec's Quiet Revolution. It was the Richard Riot, and it changed Quebec political thinking and showed just how much hockey had come to matter to the Canadian psyche.

The riot was the result of a collision between the francophone icon, Maurice Richard, and the anglophone president of the NHL, Clarence Campbell, one laden with incendiary cultural symbolism. Richard, the fiery, working-class idol of French Canadians, had already clashed repeatedly with Campbell, the Oxford-educated supreme being of the NHL, whose rule was law. Or rather, who was willing to implement the wishes of the NHL team owners as law. "Where else," said Conn Smythe's son, Stafford, "would you find another Rhodes scholar, graduate lawyer, decorated war hero, and former prosecutor at the Nuremberg trials, who will do as he is told?"

By March 1955, Richard had already been fined $2,500 by Campbell – more than any player – and given several game misconducts for his rampages, which weren't confined to the ice. Richard believed that referees went easy on those who repeatedly fouled him on the ice, even attacking one in the lobby of the New York Hotel by grabbing the startled official by his lapels before he was restrained by his teammates.

Hugh MacLennan, author of the classic novel *Two Solitudes*, about Canada's French-English divide, explained in *Saturday Night* magazine in January 1955 that Richard could only play the way he did. "If he explodes, it's because he is too often powerless to play his best hockey because the referees don't respect the rules." Richard was regularly slashed, tripped, cross-checked, held, and goaded by rival players and coaches. And he could find no refuge on his own bench, as his coach Dick Irvin told him that people would think he was a coward if he didn't fight back against his tormentors. Earlier that season, Richard had responded to a hard check from Maple Leaf Bob Bailey by hitting him in the mouth with his stick. During the ensuing melee, referee Red Storey and his linesman George Hayes took Richard's stick away five times, and five times Richard came back with a new one. It wasn't until Storey looked at the game film afterward that he figured it out: coach Dick Irvin had been giving the Rocket new sticks from the bench.

Richard had also slapped Hayes and face-washed Storey with his glove, a serious offence in any league, but the officials gave him a break in their post-game reports. They knew that, in addition to his regular on-ice torments, for the first time in his career, he was under intense pressure to win the Art Ross Trophy – and its $1,000 cheque – as the league's leading scorer. NHL president Clarence Campbell had fined Richard $250 and promised him that, if he crossed that line again, he would be suspended from play.

Then, in Boston on March 13, Richard took a high stick in the face from the Bruins' defenceman Hal Laycoe. Richard responded in kind, hitting Laycoe in the face with his stick, and then escaping the officials who were trying to restrain him to hit Laycoe again – twice. The rookie linesman Cliff Thompson, who had once been a defenceman for the Bruins, tackled Richard, and the Rocket punched him in the face, later saying he was only defending himself, as Laycoe had been sucker-punching him while Thompson was holding him down. Three days later, Clarence Campbell made good on his promise to Richard and suspended him for the rest of the season, as well as the playoffs. Then he took a shot not just at Richard, but at all francophone Quebeckers, by saying, "The time for leniency or probation is past. Whether this type of conduct is the product of temperamental instability or wilful defiance doesn't matter."

To francophones, this was not about hockey, this was about centuries of insult and injustice at the hands of the English. People jammed radio-station switchboards to complain and wrote angry letters to Campbell suggesting that if Richard had been named Richardson, he would still be playing. One Montreal weekly newspaper published a cartoon showing Campbell's head on a platter, captioned, "This is how we'd like to see him." *La Presse*'s headline on March 17, 1955, read, "La punition jugée trop forte" (the punishment judged too strong), which was restrained, under the circumstances. In Toronto, the *Globe and Mail* parsed the situation down the national divide: "Clarence Campbell will be vilified and abused in Montreal for the disciplinary action he took against Rocket Richard. . . . In Detroit, Boston and all points north, he will be commended for the same performance of duty." There were rumours that Richard's suspension had been engineered by Detroit, who saw Richard as the greatest obstacle between them and the Stanley Cup, with the assistance of Conn Smythe, still smarting over Richard's refusal to become a Leaf a decade earlier.

When Red Storey woke up in Montreal on March 17, 1955, he heard a radio announcer ask, "Is this St. Patrick's Day, or blow up the Sun Life Building day?" – the building being the headquarters of the NHL. When Clarence Campbell showed up at the Forum that night, despite warnings from Montreal's police and Mayor Jean Drapeau to stay away, the question was answered: it was blow up the Forum day. Before the game, angry crowds milled outside the arena, some with placards attacking Campbell, and a few, in a rehearsal of the night to come, throwing bottles. Guy Robinson was at the game with his two brothers and a bag of tomatoes that they stashed beneath their seat, prepared to do battle with the enemy. "We hoped, in spite of everything, that the Canadiens would be able to beat Detroit [but] when the Canadiens started to lose, that's when things exploded."

After NHL president Clarence Campbell suspended Maurice Richard for the remainder of the 1954–55 season, and the playoffs, the Montreal police and Mayor Jean Drapeau knew there would be trouble and warned him to stay away from the next game. Campbell ignored them and, along with his secretary, Phyllis King (whom he later married), and a friend, attended the Montreal versus Detroit game on March 17, 1955. Campbell thought he'd be seen as a coward if he didn't attend the game, but he was attacked in the stands, and his presence helped spark a riot.

(Montreal Gazette)

The Canadiens played the Red Wings as if in shock, and were down 4–1 by the end of the first period. Suddenly, Clarence Campbell, who had arrived at the game late with his secretary and a female friend of hers, was more than the target of boos and catcalls. "Hockey was a religion," recalled Romeo Paré, who was at the game that night. "But it was our heroes who were massacred by Clarence Campbell – an Anglophone who had always had it in for French Canadians."

The Robinson brothers now hauled out their weapons. "We started to throw tomatoes," Guy Robinson says. "We hit people, but we didn't hit Campbell, unfortunately. My brother was angry . . . so he went up to Campbell and crushed a tomato on him." Suddenly, a tear-gas bomb – of the kind used by the Montreal police – exploded near the NHL president and the crowd began to rush for the exits. The Forum organist quickly began to play "My Heart Cries Out for You," either a perversely inspired bit of improvisation, or he had been forewarned. "It was suffocating," Robinson says. "We quickly went down the stairs, and while going down we saw women's shoes, hats. . . . There was real panic."

Clarence Campbell headed for the first-aid centre, where he consulted with the Montreal fire chief before sending Detroit a note. "Jack Adams: The game has been forfeited to Detroit. You are entitled to take your team on your way any time now. Mr. Selke agrees to the decision as the Fire Department has ordered the building closed. Clarence S. Campbell."

The panicked Forum crowd spilled onto St. Catherine Street, where they ran into the crowd that had been protesting Richard's suspension. There were

Anger at Maurice Richard's suspension on March 16, 1955, led to the venting of built-up frustration at the highhanded way the Anglo elite in Quebec had always dealt with the francophone majority. The following night, a protest of ten thousand people outside the Forum quickly became a riot that left windows smashed, stores looted, and cars overturned. The result was sixty arrests, damage estimated at one hundred thousand dollars, and the galvanizing of separatist sentiment in Quebec. (*Montreal Gazette*)

only 250 police to contain 10,000 people, and the crowd quickly became a mob – setting fires, overturning cars, smashing glass. "I saw the newsstand burning," Robinson says, "and the crowd had stopped the streetcars. It was a mess."

The riot went on until 3:00 a.m., and it had much deeper implications than the seventy arrests and more than one hundred thousand dollars' worth of damage Montreal had seen. "Mob Rule Wrecks Forum, Game," pronounced the English-language Montreal *Gazette*, characterizing the hockey mob as "just as shocking and just as violent as the hordes who screamed their defiance [in Berlin] at the close of the Second World War." The francophone papers blamed it all on Campbell, as did Jean Drapeau, who said that the riot was inexcusable, but understandable, and "provoked by Mr. Campbell's presence in the Forum."

The city feared that now the mob had tasted blood, it would come back for more. And so the man whom one side felt was responsible for it all, and the other, victimized by it, was called in to settle things down. The next night, shortly after 7:00 p.m., Richard went on radio and television to explain that while he disagreed with his sentence, he had accepted it. "I will take my punishment and come back next year. So that no further harm will be done, I would like to ask everyone to get behind the team and help the boys to win from Rangers and Detroit." Richard would later say he hadn't accepted his punishment at all, but was under intense pressure to prevent further violence, and so he said the only thing he could, if he ever wanted to speak again in the only place that mattered to him, the arena.

Montrealers listened, and there were no more demonstrations, but the Canadiens had been severely wounded. Detroit won the Stanley Cup that year, and Felix Gatt was there to see it live, not on TV. "Ted Lindsay took the cup around the rink . . . and he let the people touch the Stanley Cup when he went around. . . . It's unbelievable," he said. For the Canadiens and their fans, it was all too believable.

Two years later, Maurice Richard scored his five-hundredth goal in Montreal in front of fourteen thousand fans, who stood as one to applaud him – and themselves. Hockey was more than a religion to them, it was a battle. Richard, through his excellence, his endurance, his refusal to accept being second-best to anyone, had triumphed despite his opponents. But now hockey had a new opponent. And it wasn't English, nor was it French. It was Russian.

In 1954, the Cold War was in full swing. Two years earlier, the United States had secretly tested a hydrogen bomb in the Pacific Ocean that was a thousand times more powerful than the atomic bombs that vaporized Hiroshima and Nagasaki. In September 1954, the Soviets tested their own hydrogen bomb, and now fallout shelters were being built across North America in readiness for the nuclear apocalypse between the United States and the Soviet Union, which were apparently prepared to destroy the planet in the name of competing ideologies.

In Canada, however, one day of reckoning had already come, when the East York Lyndhursts went as the national amateur team to the World Championships in Stockholm to play the Soviet Union for the first time ever, and lost the gold medal game in a 7–2 drubbing that shocked the country to its core. The *Toronto Telegram*'s headlines pronounced "Canada's Black Eye" and "Send the Selectors to Siberia" and prescribed the gulag for the people responsible for what the Montreal *Herald*'s Elmer Ferguson called "a national calamity, a national humiliation, and a mortifying experience."

Canada thought it owned the international ice, and over the past three decades it had seemed as if any Canadian team could win gold. As diverse a roster as the University of Toronto Varsity Grads, the Winnipeg Monarchs, the Saskatoon Quakers, the Royal Canadian Air Force Flyers, and the Edmonton Mercurys had all proven themselves the best in the world. But now the Soviets had skated rings around the Canadians, showing speed, stamina, and precision passing in all directions – forward, laterally, and, astonishingly, backward to their own defencemen – to regroup and set up a play. Ironically, the Soviets had honed their hockey through watching the Czechs, who in turn had learned the Canadian game from Mike Buckna in the 1930s.

After the Lyndhursts' and the country's humiliation, the Canadian hockey world was determined to send over worthier representatives to reclaim Canada's lost honour. Conn Smythe volunteered to send over the Maple Leafs, and Toronto mayor Alan Lamport offered to pony up five thousand dollars of his own money to defray travel costs, but the IIHF would not allow Canada to send professional players, and the task of rescuing Canada's national sport from the godless Soviets fell to a team from the British Columbia orchard town of Penticton, who, as winners of the 1954 Allan Cup, were now Canada's best Senior Amateur team.

The Penticton Vees took their name from three different types of peaches that grew in the surrounding orchards – Valiant, Vedette, and Veteran. In 1955, they were sent over to Krefeld, West Germany, to challenge the Russian bear. The Vees, too, had known humiliation, but had risen above it. The Penticton *Herald* journalist Sid Godber was sure they were now worthy of their mission, describing them as "a team made up of has-beens, reinstated professionals who seemingly had had their day – and pluggers who had not what it takes to make the professional ranks. Therein lies the greatness of the Penticton Vees. . . . [They went] from league doormat in the first season to the Allan Cup final in their second season, winning the Allan Cup in their third season."

Led by playing coach Grant Warwick, a former Calder Trophy winner with the New York Rangers, and a nine-year NHL veteran, and bolstered by a rugged crew of ex-pros and skilled amateurs, the Vees knew they carried the nation's honour in their baggage, along with their hockey gear. "[The Lyndhursts] lost 7–2 and the whole country was in an uproar," recalled Billy Warwick, one of the three Warwick brothers at the heart of the Vees. "It was so political, you know, the Cold War was on and 'how can Russia come in and . . .' The whole Western world was upset over this: how could Canada lose to the communists?"

Hundreds of supporters came to the Penticton airport to send off the Vees with well-meaning advice that reflected the depth of the nation's fear. "Be sure

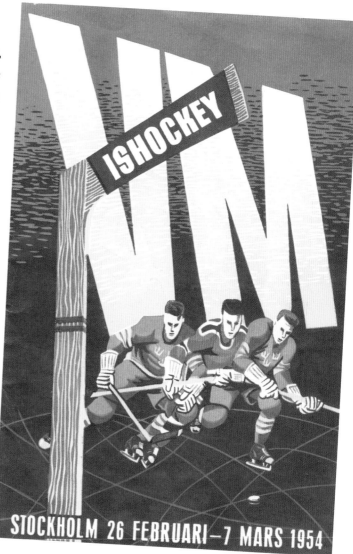

In 1954, the East York Lyndhursts were highly favoured to bring the world hockey championship back to Canada from Stockholm. After winning their first six games of the round-robin tournament, only the Moscow Dynamos stood between them and the title in the first international hockey matchup between the two countries. The Lyndhursts – and all Canadians – were shocked by the Soviets' hockey skills as they handed Canada its worst defeat since the tournament began in 1924, a 7–2 loss. (*Hockey Hall of Fame*)

After Canada was drubbed in the gold-medal game at the world hockey championship in 1954 by the Soviets, the Penticton Vees, as winners of the 1954 Allan Cup, awarded to Canada's best Senior Amateur team, went to the 1955 tournament in West Germany determined to get revenge. Led by playing coach Grant Warwick, who had won the Calder Trophy in 1932 as NHL rookie of the year with the New York Rangers, the Vees trounced the Soviets 5–0. *(Library and Archives Canada, Tribune Collection, PA-093954)*

you win," "Stay out of the penalty box," "Beat them," "Don't come home with-out it," Billy Warwick remembered them saying.

For the first time, the CBC sent crews to cover the game: Foster Hewitt, the iconic voice of the Maple Leafs, would call the action on the radio, and Steve Douglas would do the TV play-by-play. The presence of the media made the message even clearer: this was a battle that could not be lost.

The nature of the battle became apparent in a pre-championship game the Canadians played in Berlin when they spotted Soviet star Vsevolod Bobrov in the crowd. The Canadians had done their scouting homework, and now the Soviets were doing theirs. Like Cold War spies in the city literally divided by Cold War ideologies and their enforcing armies, Bobrov and his teammates were photographing the Canadians in action. "They were watching to see who was who," Billy Warwick said. "And Grant called us in the room and we all changed our sweaters. The numbers were all mixed up."

On March 6, 1955, the Vees faced off against the Soviets in the final game for the World Championship. For veteran journalist Andy O'Brien, it seemed as if the world's media had packed into the little German arena to witness this symbolic fighting of the Cold War. "The pressure build-up for the Sunday final was more intensive than I ever met in Stanley Cup, Grey Cup or world heavyweight fight super situations. In the Saturday lull before the playoff game on Sunday, the press-radio-television representation had swollen to 350 and included Sweden, Poland, Finland, Switzerland, England, the United States, Holland, France, Italy, Austria and Germany – as well of course as Canada and Russia."

The Canadians keyed in on Bobrov, stopping him from getting the puck and tying him up when he did have it, all the time hitting everything that moved. The European fans loathed the Canadians' punishing, physical play, and one man nearly beaned Warwick with an empty liquor bottle. It didn't matter at all to the Canucks as they pounded the life out of the Russians, while Foster Hewitt relayed the 5–0 rout to a relieved nation. The Vees had restored Canada to its rightful place on top of the world. They were national heroes.

"We worked a whole year for that one game," said Billy Warwick. "We could have played all day and all night. And we would have beaten anybody that day. I don't care who we played, they wouldn't have beaten us. That's just how it was. It was the pressure and it was the politics involved. It was politics. East against West and the Cold War."

Six years later, the Trail Smoke Eaters went to the World Championships and beat the Soviets 5–1. And in between, another team from the land of orchards actually went through the Iron Curtain to take on the Soviets on their own ice.

In November 1958, the Kelowna Packers became the first Canadian team to play in Russia, preceded only by a British team the year before. As Okanagan Senior Hockey champs, the Packers had fought to the seventh game of the Allan Cup finals only to lose to the Belleville McFarlands. But the Packers had been without five of their best players, and so the Canadian Amateur Hockey Association took a risk and chose the Packers to make this historic – and dangerous – trip.

The Packers landed in the middle of a very hot Cold War. Less than two years earlier, Soviet troops had brutally crushed an uprising in Hungary. Now, the Soviets, with their hydrogen bombs, were a real and frightening enemy. Upon arriving in Moscow, the Kelowna team's plane filled with menacing soldiers. The Canadian Embassy told the Packers their hotel rooms were bugged, and series MVP Bill "Bugs" Jones later recalled that the team "slept with the lights on. . . . We were afraid to turn them off."

Soviet law allowed the detention of any Russian national or their offspring, regardless of their current citizenship. No one had told the Packers anything about this and now players Greg Jablonski and Russ Kowalchuk – both of

On January 18, 1958, hockey history was made when Willie O'Ree became the first black man to play in the NHL, appearing with the Boston Bruins in a game at Montreal. O'Ree, from Fredericton, New Brunswick, played two games for the Bruins that year, then another forty-three in 1960–61 – despite being legally blind in his right eye after being hit by a puck, a detail he kept secret from the NHL or he would not have been allowed to play.

(James McCarthy/Hockey Hall of Fame)

Ukrainian parentage and who spoke good Russian – risked being sent to Siberia. The Soviets confiscated their passports, and they played the entire series fearing they would never see Canada again. The team was shadowed by KGB agents, and fraternization with their hockey opponents and curious Muscovites alike was forbidden. Moscow itself was a bleak, concrete monolith, but the Soviet passion for hockey surfaced for the five-game series, which had been sold out for weeks.

The first two games were played at the brand new, fifteen-thousand-seat Lenin Sports Palace, and the last three were held outdoors in a sixty-thousand-seat soccer stadium. Soviet coach Anatoly Tarasov was keen to learn from Jack O'Reilly, his counterpart, and despite the prohibition on socializing, doing hockey business was allowed. The two men would exhaust their interpreters, talking hockey for hours. The Soviets even filmed the Canadian practices, and players such as Mo Young suspected the Russians had set their sights higher, later saying, "They were getting ready to take on the NHL even back then. We all knew it."

In the first game, the Red Army team overcame a 3–2 deficit to beat the Canadians. The second and third games were tied, and the Packers were worried. Forward Mike Durban recalled that the speedy, well-conditioned Russians played the game "as if it was all designed on a blackboard. But when we knocked one of their guys down, the whole thing fell apart."

The Canadians found their game in the final two contests, winning them both. At the end of the last game, the Packers threw their sticks into the crowd and skated around the ice to a standing ovation for both them and their brand of hockey. Tarasov, who was not given to easy praise, said afterward what everyone in Canada wanted to hear: "The Canadians are magnificent hockey players." But the Soviets were determined to be better, and within fifteen years, Canada would be fighting another cold war on ice that would make the games of the 1950s look innocent.

On January 18, 1958, the Moncton-born Willie O'Ree played for the Boston Bruins in a game against Montreal, the first black player to suit up in the NHL. Ten years earlier, Jackie Robinson's arrival in professional baseball had shattered the sports colour bar, and now O'Ree's debut was remarkable more to him than to the media. "The Montreal Forum was different and special that night," O'Ree recalled. "The lights were brighter and the ice whiter. The fans seemed more elegant and nobody called me any names."

NHL hockey was still the undisputed preserve of white men. In 1948, Larry Kwong, the son of Chinese immigrants to British Columbia, had played one minute of one game for the New York Rangers, becoming the first "person of colour" to crack the NHL, though for Kwong, his appearance was something less than a triumph. "How can you prove yourself in a minute on the ice?" he said. "Couldn't even get warmed up!"

In the 1953–54 season, Fred Saskamoose, a Cree from Saskatchewan, played eleven games for the Chicago Black Hawks. But in the 1930s, when Herb Carnegie, who was of African heritage, played semi-pro, he was in a class by himself, and it was an all-too painful one. During the 1938–39 season, when Carnegie was beginning his career with the Toronto Rangers, his coach said something to him that would change his life: "See that man sitting in the blues? That's Conn Smythe, owner of the Toronto Maple Leafs. He says he'd take you tomorrow if he could turn you white." Smythe's brutal comment is often given an even more cynical twist – saying he'd pay ten thousand dollars to anyone who could turn Carnegie white, as if by some racial alchemy. But as it was, it motivated Carnegie to succeed in the white man's game. He paid his dues

with the Rangers, far away from his family in the remote mining towns of northern Quebec and Ontario, and then returned north to start on the first all-black line, in Timmins, Ontario, in 1941 with his brother, Ossie, and Manny McIntyre, a speedy winger from Fredericton, New Brunswick.

Herb Carnegie was a magical stickhandler, whose crisp, seeing-eye passes made the line the best in the league. When he moved on to the Quebec Aces for the 1949–50 season, he won three most valuable player awards, and the admiration of Jean Béliveau, whom Carnegie later mentored. "Herbie was a super hockey player," Béliveau recalled. "A beautiful style, a beautiful skater, a great play maker. In those days the younger ones learned from the older one. I learned from Herbie."

Carnegie was offered a tryout by the New York Rangers and then a place on their lowest-ranking farm team in New Haven, Connecticut. "They told me that if I signed with the Rangers and went to New Haven, I would make international headlines," Carnegie recalled. "I told them my family couldn't eat headlines. That was probably when the Rangers decided to forget about me."

Carnegie was so good that he easily could have played in the premier pro league at a premier salary, had the NHL been able to see beyond the racial prejudice of not just Conn Smythe, but of the era, one that professional baseball had challenged by bringing up Jackie Robinson from the Montreal Royals to

Fred Saskamoose is widely held to be the first aboriginal player to pull on an NHL jersey when the Chicago Black Hawks called him up for eleven games in 1953–54. Saskamoose, a centre, had learned hockey at St. Michael's residential school in Saskatchewan and had won the most valuable player award in the Western Hockey League as a member of the Moose Jaw Canucks in 1952–53. (*Courtesy Barbara Poirier*)

Herb Carnegie (centre), along with Mannie McIntyre (left) and brother Ossie Carnegie (right), starred for the Sherbrooke Rand team in Quebec's Provincial League shortly after the end of the Second World War. As the first all-black line integrated into white semi-pro hockey, the trio had novelty appeal, and as hockey players, they were so skilled that they became known as the Black Aces. The line dominated the league, thanks to Herb Carnegie's speed and playmaking finesse and his linemates' skill and fearlessness.

(Courtesy Frederic Zachaib)

the big-league Brooklyn Dodgers in 1947. Had Conn Smythe been a different man, he could have broken hockey's colour barrier a decade earlier and changed the history of the game.

Being white wasn't a bonus if you were female. Though the women's game had flourished during and between the wars, the new age of the nuclear family, where women were expected only to keep their suburban homes spotless while the men went out to hunt and gather in the cities, had thrown women's hockey back into the shadows.

An American woman, impressed by a televised game in the mid-1950s, took the initiative to call NHL president Clarence Campbell to propose a professional women's league. Campbell, who would take calls from drunks in bars trying to settle bets, listened to the woman's proposal, then reminded her of her place by telling her that "hockey was too rough for gals."

The newsreel short *Detroit Hockey Wives* depicted the Red Wings wives sipping tea, chatting, and occasionally glancing at a TV set showing a hockey game, while in real life the Red Wings wives, such as Colleen Howe, were being publicly humiliated by team owner Bruce Norris. At a year-end party, he drunkenly accused his star player's wife of "having affairs" on the ski trips she took with her friends and children, instead of taking her rightful place at Wings' home games to support Gordie. Colleen Howe found skiing trips to be a more appealing prospect than being a slave to the Wings' idea of wifely duties, and Norris's attack made her cry.

Norris and his half-brother, Jimmy, had actually appointed a woman to run the Red Wings when their financial interests in Chicago and other NHL rinks, as well as a congressional investigation into pro boxing in which they were heavily involved, necessitated a low profile. In 1953, the Norrises made Marguerite, Bruce's twenty-five-year-old sister, president of the Red Wings, until their troubles blew over. The hitch was, she was good at her job, and with a talented team to work with, she showed the hockey world that there was indeed room for a woman at the top. It wasn't easy for her. Conn Smythe was appalled at her presence and tried to block Marguerite from sitting on the NHL's Board of Governors, inventing a law which essentially said all governors had to be men. Marguerite outsmarted him by appointing his loathed rival, Jack Adams of the Detroit Red Wings, as her proxy, giving "Jolly Jack" hand signals during board meetings to ensure her wishes were carried out.

Smythe continued his campaign to discredit her, publicly questioning her management abilities, and even criticizing the state of the women's washrooms

Marguerite Norris, a member of the family that owned the Detroit Red Wings, took over as president of the club when legal problems obliged her brothers – who ran the Wings – to take a low profile. Norris, who had played goal in childhood games with her brothers, knew all about playing with the boys and more than held her own in the NHL boardrooms, despite opposition from Conn Smythe. In 1954, she became the only woman to have her name engraved on the Stanley Cup, when the Wings defeated Montreal to win their third Cup of the decade. *(Corbis/Bettmann)* at the Norrises' Olympia Stadium. Marguerite got him back by mentioning to a Toronto reporter that Mr. Smythe seemed to be fascinated by the condition of the ladies' rooms in her stadium. Smythe dropped the matter. And then Marguerite was dropped too, by her brother Bruce, who decided the time had come for him to be boss now that the Wings were winners. He made her executive vice president of the team – a pretty title, with no real power.

For girls who wanted to play hockey at a higher level, there was only one thing to do, and Abigail Hoffman figured out what that was when she was only eight years old. Hoffman had played hockey with her brothers since she was five. The post-war baby boom was seeing minor hockey leagues springing up everywhere. Hoffman wanted to join one; she wanted to keep playing with the boys. So, when the Toronto Little League advertised that it was looking for players, Hoffman lined up to register for the new league. "I show them my birth certificate, they ask me my name, I tell them my name, they write down the information from my birth certificate, and that's it," she said later. "My father comes back and reports that 'No, there's no girls' hockey, for sure there's no girls' hockey.'"

Despite Hoffman's birth certificate, the organizers of the league didn't twig to the fact that she was a girl. A few days later, Abby's mother, Dorothy, answered the phone. On the other end was "a very nice gentleman who said he would like our boy to play on one of the teams. We didn't have the heart to tell him that the boy was a girl and spoil her chances of playing." Abby Hoffman didn't want to spoil her chances either and went to the barbershop. "I wore my hair quite short," Hoffman recalled, "but I went and I got more or less of a brush cut in order to play." Thirty-five years earlier, a boy using the pseudonym Ada Lalond had disguised himself to play hockey during the First World War, and now a girl was doing the reverse. For the next three months, Hoffman wore her gear to the rink like the other players and took the ice to become a standout on defence for the St. Catharines Tee-Pees. Then she was selected from among four hundred players in the league to play on an all-star team. Her coach, Al Grossi, had to verify her birth certificate, and the truth came out. "I defy anyone to pick her out as a girl when the team is on the ice," Grossi told the *Toronto Star*. "She skates like a boy, plays aggressively, meets the players when they come in on defence."

Hoffman became an instant celebrity. A cartoon in the *Toronto Star* showed Hoffman defeating the Soviets was accompanied by an editorial headlined "She's a Star." *Time* and *Newsweek* magazines wanted to interview her, and she was invited by both the Montreal Canadiens and Toronto Maple Leafs to meet their teams. A Warner-Pathe documentary entitled *He's Not a He, He's a She* showed Hoffman getting ready for a game in her locker room with her

When eight-year-old Abigail Hoffman signed up to play hockey for the new Toronto Little League in 1956, she did so as a girl. But the boys' league management mistook her for a boy, and by the time their error was discovered, Hoffman was one of the league's all-stars. Hoffman became an international hockey celebrity, but the fame was bittersweet, as she was no longer allowed to play with the boys.

(*York University Archives*)

teammates, while the announcer revealed that "Abigail, Ab for short, Hoffman, nine years old, seventy-three pounds of rock'em-sock'em hockey player" had "captured the imaginations of hockey-conscious Canadians."

Now that she was known to be a girl, and as there was no girls' league to play in, Hoffman had to hang up her skates. She would go on to have a distinguished athletic career in track and field, but her pioneering gesture on ice would inspire other girls to play hockey, and led to the creation of girls' hockey leagues in the 1960s, and to the Abby Hoffman Cup, awarded to the national champions of Canadian women's hockey. When she was asked by an interviewer shortly after her story broke what she made of all the fuss about her, her reply summed up decades of women's dismay at being shut out of the national sport. "It's all a lot of nonsense," she said.

Nonsense was what Ted Lindsay, the captain of the Detroit Red Wings, thought of the state of things in the NHL as the 1950s came to a close. "There was a dictatorship. . . . There was no voice," he recalled. "The owners told you what to do. They'd say 'jump' and you'd say 'how many times do you want me to jump and how high do you want me to jump.' That was it. They ruled you."

Ted Lindsay had won the Art Ross Trophy for 1949–50 as the league's leading scorer, and led the NHL in assists in 1956–57, with thirty goals and fifty-five assists, the best by a left-winger ever. He had also made a reputation as a man who backed down from no one.

When Lindsay was appointed to the board of the NHL's Pension Society in 1952, he was at first proud to be part of a pro-hockey government that viewed the players, if not as equals to the owners, then as partners. But that pride turned into bitter disappointment when the NHL owners refused to let the players see the books belonging to the pension fund, begun five years earlier. The players were contributing 20 per cent of their annual salaries – which averaged $8,000 – to the fund, while the NHL kicked in $600 a year for a player, taking the money from their earnings from the All-Star Game, which the players played for free.

Professional baseball players in the United States had recently formed a players' association, and Lindsay flew to New York to talk to the lawyers who had helped the ball players organize. In that meeting, he learned what was starting to drive the revenues of all professional sports: television. The NHL's owners maintained that they didn't make any money from TV, or from paying customers. Theirs was barely a break-even enterprise, they claimed, but Lindsay, and his fellow Pension Society members suspected otherwise. However, communication between the owners was very good, but between the players, there was none. "The owners met four or five times a year and we never met," Lindsay said. "That was their advantage. . . . They controlled everything. There was nothing you could do."

At the beginning of the 1956 season, Lindsay did the unthinkable. He approached the Montreal Canadiens' defence star Doug Harvey during a warm-up skate at the Forum, a brave act given the hostilities between teams. (Rivalries in the six-team NHL were so intense that when the Montreal Canadiens and the Detroit Red Wings shared a train on back-to-back road trips, neither team would enter the dining car while the other was there – largely to avoid prosecution for destroying a rail car in the inevitable brawl.) Doug Harvey and Ted Lindsay were cut from the same hockey cloth – tough, talented, unsentimental players who faced their opponents without pity. They had served together on the Pension Society, and respected each other. Harvey

Red Storey

Roy Alvin "Red" Storey was one of professional hockey's most colourful and respected referees, a larger-than-life character who presided over some of the game's greatest players. Like many athletes of his era, Storey grew up in the 1920s playing hockey, lacrosse, baseball, and especially football, which he started to play professionally in 1936, at age eighteen, when he joined the Toronto Argonauts. He scored three touchdowns in the fourth quarter and set up another to lead the Argos to their 1938 Grey Cup victory – his and their second in a row. A knee injury ended Storey's football dream, so he switched to hockey, winding up on defence for the Montreal Royals of the Quebec Senior Hockey League, where he soon attracted the attention of the New York Rangers.

In 1950, another knee injury made Storey exchange his jersey for the referee's stripes of the NHL, and he quickly became widely respected for his fair handling of NHL games – and there were some wild ones. Storey was refereeing on the night of March 17, 1955, when a riot erupted in Montreal after the Canadiens' hero Maurice Richard had been suspended for the rest of the season for striking an official. Storey had also been the ref in Toronto earlier that season when Richard attempted to swing his stick at opponents and had verbally abused an official. Storey had downplayed Richard's actions in his official report in recognition of the on-ice stress endured by the game's greatest player. That courtesy was not reciprocated on the night of April 8, 1959, when fans at Chicago Stadium went berserk when he didn't call what they thought were penalties against Montreal in a playoff game, littering the ice with debris and threatening to kill Storey after the game. The next day, NHL president Clarence Campbell said Storey had "choked," and the proud referee resigned. Despite pleas from Maple Leafs owner Conn Smythe to return to the NHL, he refused, and he never refereed another NHL game. Despite his relatively brief career in the NHL, as testament to his excellence, he was inducted into the Hockey Hall of Fame in 1967.

(Imperial Oil – Turofsky/Hockey Hall of Fame)

Billy Harris

During his long NHL career, which began in Toronto in 1955 and ended in Pittsburgh in 1969, with stops in Detroit and Oakland, Billy Harris was not only a Memorial Cup–winning centre, but he was also a shutterbug, and his photographs of hockey locker-room celebrations reveal an insider's intimacy that no professional photographer could ever hope to capture. When the Leafs defeated Chicago to win the 1962 Stanley Cup, Harris dashed into the dressing room to set up his camera and missed the presentation of the Cup, but he nevertheless caught the unfettered joy of the Leafs in his photos. (*Graphic Artists/Hockey Hall of Fame*)

agreed to Lindsay's idea of establishing a hockey players' association. Other players were quick to respond, and soon representatives from all six teams were talking. When they held a press conference in New York on February 12, 1957, to announce the birth of their association, they had signed up every player in the NHL except for Toronto star Ted Kennedy, who was retiring.

Although the players were careful to present their association as a cooperative, good-for-business venture between themselves and the owners, the NHL's owners, led by Conn Smythe, painted it as communist. "I feel that anything spawned in secrecy as this association was," Smythe said, "certainly has to have some odour to it." No one hated Lindsay more than Conn Smythe, who would run along the front row of Maple Leaf Gardens to scream abuse at the smart, bold young Red Wing. What made Smythe angry was the fact that Lindsay was not a Maple Leaf. As a product of Toronto's St. Michael's College, Lindsay might well have been recruited by the Leafs, but he was injured and out of the lineup when the Leafs scouted his high-school team.

Detroit's general manager and coach, Jack Adams, used to remind players of their fragile place in the cosmos by flashing train tickets to Omaha, home of their farm club, but now he had a different punishment in mind for Lindsay. On July 24, 1957, while most hockey fans were at the beach, or at that other new symbol of post-war prosperity, the cottage, Bruce Norris, the president of the Detroit Red Wings, traded his thirty-three-year-old former captain to the dreadful Chicago Black Hawks, a team co-owned by his brother Jimmy, and that had, between 1949 and 1957, finished dead last every season but one. It was a stark punishment to Lindsay for daring to stand up to the NHL. Lindsay had lost his war, and the players took note. Gordie Howe and Red Kelly convinced the Detroit team to withdraw from the Players' Association, and others followed. It would be a decade before the players resurrected the idea, when once more, Canada's game was looking south because of a gold rush called TV revenue.

CHAPTER 6

US AND THEM

On a Tuesday night in early April 1960, Maurice Richard sat in his room in the Royal York Hotel in Toronto, smoking a cigar and watching *The Red Skelton Show* on TV. According to *Sports Illustrated*, during a commercial break, the announcer asked, "What makes Toronto tick?" and the Rocket, now a thirty-eight-year-old warrior of eighteen NHL seasons, his famous black eyes still hot, but his body battered, shot back at the TV screen, "What makes Toronto dead?" The captain of the Canadiens, who was no stranger to *la vie douce*, may have been referring to the Presbyterian qualities of the city then known as "Toronto the Good." In all likelihood though, Richard was

predicting the imminent demise of the Canadiens' natural enemies, the Toronto Maple Leafs, whom Montreal would soon meet in the Stanley Cup final.

Demise was much on Richard's mind in the spring of 1960, and he didn't want it to happen to him. "If I play bad," he said, "people will talk. I like to leave the game before people criticize me, boo me. I used to skate a little better, go around the fence a little better. I've got to watch myself. The day of the game, I'm afraid to get hit. I know when I feel that, it is getting close to the end."

After dispatching Chicago in four straight games in the Stanley Cup playoffs in late March – the last two of them shutouts – the Canadiens and Richard took on the Leafs, winning another four straight games to take their fifth Cup in five years. As the clock wound down to ten seconds in the third period of the final contest, a 4–0 Montreal shutout, the Toronto Maple Leafs' owner Conn Smythe forced his way through a crowd of photographers to the Montreal bench, where he began to shake hands with each of the victorious Canadiens, in what the *Globe and Mail* called "a hockey man's tribute to the greatest team in the history of the NHL."

It was more than that: it was a pride-swallowing bit of chivalry from the old soldier Smythe, who now explained his saluting the enemy by simply saying, "They won seven times in ten years, didn't they?" Smythe could be forgiven his math in the devastating heat of the moment, for Montreal had won six times in eight years, still a formidable average.

Richard, his eyes ablaze, hunts down the puck to score his eighty-second and final playoff goal, against the Leafs' Johnny Bower in April 1960 to lead Montreal to another Stanley Cup victory. Richard would retire later that year, having shot 544 regular season goals, the most in Canadiens history. *(Michael Burns Photography)*

Richard couldn't resist reminding the fans in Maple Leaf Gardens of the bitter rivalry between the two cities, and the fact that urbane, sophisticated Montreal was used to winning. "It's always nice to win the Cup," he said, while accepting the trophy at centre ice, "but especially nice to win it right here in Toronto." But what seemed a tease was really grateful humility. The player whom Marshall McLuhan once said responded so viscerally to the acoustical life of an arena that he "felt the puck off his stick rode on the roar of the crowd" now thanked that crowd. "Because," he continued as the fans let out a cheer, "because the people here are really nice, they give us a nice hand anytime we score and they really give us a good hand all the way during the series. Thank you very much."

As the 1960s began, Toronto and Montreal were more than hockey rivals, they were the two hearts of the country, and it seemed as if Montreal's beat with a faster, louder pulse. Montreal's vitality was so compelling that even the enemy couldn't help but be seduced. "It's like stepping into another world," said Bob Haggert, the head trainer of the Maple Leafs, comparing it to the buttoned-up Toronto of the 1950s. "And the city of Montreal – it's open 24 hours a day. Toronto is dead – on Sunday, you can't go to a movie or a restaurant. Montreal is wide open – you can hoot and holler all day and all night long. Passion for life – that is their legacy."

Montreal's passion for life was part of a renaissance that was happening throughout Quebec. Jean Lesage was elected as premier in June 1960 in a vote that was much more than the triumph of the Liberals over the Union Nationale. It was the popular endorsement of a social and political struggle that would come to be known as the "Quiet Revolution," and which saw the transformation of the French Canadians into the Québécois. Anger at Anglo-Canada's control of Quebec had found its voice in Lesage's powerful campaign slogan: "Maîtres chez nous" ("Masters in our own house"). The people of Quebec voted for Lesage and for his other campaign slogan: "Il faut que ça change." (Things have to change.)

Everything, that is, but the Montreal Canadiens. The Canadiens' domination of pro hockey was so assured that New York Rangers coach Phil Watson grumbled that science shouldn't be wasting its time sending American satellites and Soviet Sputniks into space. "There's lots of things right here on earth that science has yet to do. Science," he told a *Sports Illustrated* reporter, "has yet to find a cure for Montreal."

All through the political changes happening in Quebec in the 1960s, the Canadiens represented freedom from oppression on all sides, of winning on your own terms, and of a belief system not unlike the various creeds both sacred and secular then aswirl outside the hockey arena. "The Canadiens play

A weary, elated Richard embraces the Stanley Cup in April 1960, after the Canadiens defeated the Toronto Maple Leafs to win their fifth straight Stanley Cup. It was Richard's eighth and final Cup. (*Imperial Oil – Turofsky/Hockey Hall of Fame*)

The Curved Blade

In the early 1960s, Chicago Black Hawk All-Star centre Stan Mikita cracked his stick during a practice at Chicago Stadium. "I was pissed because I was bushed and didn't want to walk up and down those twenty-one stairs to the dressing room to get another stick," Mikita later told the *Hockey News*. "I shot the puck against the board in anger and it reacted differently. Then me and Bobby [Hull] started bending sticks." The curved sticks that soon appeared ranged from the slightly bent to the wildly torqued banana blades, and these curves made the puck's behaviour even more unpredictable for goalies. At first tolerant of the new blades, the NHL eventually regulated the curve. Mikita later regretted his innovation, even though he won the Art Ross Trophy four times as the NHL's leading point scorer while using a curved stick. "It's one of the worst inventions in hockey," he said, "because it eliminated the use of the backhand." *(Graphic Artists/Hockey Hall of Fame)*

for the French – like Notre Dame playing for the Catholics and the Irish," said Carolyn Yovic, a recent immigrant to Montreal. "We've moved from Chicago. The French Canadians are super to us, because we're not English Canadians, we're Americans. Going to the Forum to watch Montreal's great hockey team is like experiencing history."

The Canadiens on the ice as a team and off it as a symbol of city and a culture were so revered that they captured the imagination even of new immigrants. "The Canadiens have always reflected and have been attached to the people, not only of Montreal, but of the whole province," said Eric Lalonde, a distant cousin of Newsy Lalonde. "It's the French culture and the dynamic trends that we see in our team – being fast, being impulsive – being exciting. It's hockey and pride – it's always been that way – they are the very best."

The Canadiens, who in 1960 had made it to the Stanley Cup finals for ten straight years, had been the best for so long that *Sports Illustrated* was moved to beg the hockey fates: "Next season it would be refreshing if by some remarkable stroke of luck Montreal crumbled and the Stanley Cup ended up on a shelf in some other city. But then, how many years have people been hoping for the same thing?"

The hopes of those apostates who weren't Canadiens' fans were raised in September 1960, when Maurice Richard showed up at training camp and realized that his time had indeed come – his desire was gone. On September 15,

A torch passed in 1962 when Conn Smythe, prime mover behind the Toronto Maple Leafs, sold his shares in the team to his son Stafford (centre) and partners John Bassett (left), a media tycoon, and Harold Ballard (right), from the skate-manufacturing family, which had a long history in managing Canadian amateur hockey. The Leafs initially saw a string of championships under the leadership of this trio, but their relentless cost-cutting and the eccentric Ballard's eventual buyout of the others made the franchise's fortunes plummet.

(*Graphic Artists/Hockey Hall of Fame*)

1960, he retired, but before he left the ice, he put four pucks past Canadiens goalie Jacques Plante as a kind of "adieu" to his own glory, and a reminder that the man who had missed so many games in recent years due to injury, and who had scored just one goal in his last playoff campaign, could still beat the man who had led the league the previous season.

On the morning of November 23, 1961, the Toronto Maple Leafs saw the end of an era, too. Conn Smythe, the man who had invented them more than three decades earlier, sold his shares in both the team and their temple to his son Stafford. Smythe, now sixty-six, had imagined his eldest son would continue the tradition he had begun, but he was bitterly disappointed. Before the deal was done, Stafford told his father that he would be selling his shares to *Toronto Telegram* publisher John Bassett Sr., and to a swashbuckling Toronto amateur hockey fixture named Harold Ballard, who had first caught the attention of the nation when he managed the Toronto National Sea Fleas to the Allan Cup championship in 1932. The following year, Ballard took his team to the World Championships, where his Sea Fleas made history by losing the final and giving the United States its first gold medal.

When John Bassett announced the deal on the front page of his newspaper, on the morning that Conn Smythe was due to sign over his legacy, Smythe was furious with his son. "This is the kind of guy you're taking on as a partner, who can't even keep his word about an announcement deadline!" he fumed. But in the end, Smythe signed, and the minutes of meeting for the new board of directors, on which he would remain as chairman, reminded them of what he expected. "Mr. Conn Smythe then addressed the Board and stated that it had always been his hope to pass on the Company to hands who would maintain it with the prestige, dignity and character it had enjoyed in the past."

Toronto's past had become weightier with each passing spring. The Leafs had not sipped champagne from the Cup since April 1951, when their dashing young defenceman Bill Barilko left his position at the Montreal blue line to intercept a puck that had deflected off the skate of Montreal's Butch Bouchard. Barilko scooped up the puck and fired it past Gerry McNeil to break a 2–2 tie in overtime, giving the Leafs their seventh Stanley Cup. The goal was immortalized by the pioneer hockey photographer Nate Turofsky, who captured Barilko flying through the air like winged victory after taking his shot. The twenty-four-year-old Barilko was hoisted onto the shoulders of his teammates while the Gardens erupted in jubilation. Captain Ted Kennedy accepted the Cup at centre ice while the band played "Auld Lang Syne." The song was a prophetic farewell.

Four months later, on Friday, August 24, Barilko ignored his mother's pleas not to fly out on a fishing trip with an amateur pilot. Faye Barilko had a premonition as her husband and Bill's father had died on a Friday. Barilko and a friend, the Timmins, Ontario, dentist Dr. Henry Hudson, took off for Seal River, where James Bay meets Hudson Bay – named after another Henry Hudson, the explorer cast adrift by his crew in 1611 to vanish forever.

By the end of the following week, Barilko's failure to return was front-page news across the country and had launched the largest search Canada had yet seen. The Ontario Provincial Police, the Royal Canadian Air Force, and Cree hunters were all looking for the yellow Fairchild 24 two-seater. Conn Smythe had even put up a ten-thousand-dollar reward, set to expire on January 1, 1952, as if the ticking clock on the money would inspire in searchers a greater sense of urgency than they already had. But the searches proved fruitless. And ten years later, in the spring of 1962, some Leafs fans were convinced that Barilko's disappearance had cursed the team, as the Montreal Canadiens had continued their almost annual claiming of the Cup.

Since the Leafs' last Stanley Cup triumph in 1951, Montreal had won six Cups, and dominated the NHL with speed, skill, and a sense of entitlement. "The Montreal Canadiens, their nickname was the Flying Frenchmen," said Leafs trainer Bob Haggert, who saw their prowess up close from his place on

On April 21, 1951, at two minutes and fifty-three seconds of sudden death in Game 5 of the Stanley Cup final, with the Leafs pressing in the Montreal zone, Toronto's twenty-four-year-old defence-man Bill Barilko stretched to keep Howie Meeker's pass from sliding over the blue line. Off balance and about to go airborne, Barilko fired the puck into the Canadiens' net to give Toronto its fourth Stanley Cup in five years. That summer, Barilko was killed in a plane crash in Northern Ontario while on a fishing trip. It was eleven years before his body was found, and before the Leafs won another Stanley Cup.

(Imperial Oil – Turofsky/Hockey Hall of Fame)

Frank Mahovlich was such an impressive junior prospect in 1953 that several scouts from the NHL travelled to Timmins, Ontario, to try to sign the fifteen-year-old son of a miner from Croatia. The Detroit Red Wings scouts offered Peter Mahovlich a five-acre fruit farm on the Niagara Peninsula if young Frank would sign, but the elder Mahovlich hadn't toiled in the mines of Canada since stepping ashore in 1929 just so he could make money off the backs of his children. No, young Frank would take up a scholarship from St. Michael's College, and, if everything worked out, he would one day be a Leaf. That day came in 1957, when nineteen-year-old Frank Mahovlich came to the big club directly from Junior A. His parents came too, for now that Frank was making proper money, he got his father out of the mines of Timmins and into one of Toronto's gleaming neighbourhoods, Leaside. In his first season, Frank scored twenty goals and showed such brilliance that fans who thought they had seen it all jumped to their feet when he danced his ballet with the puck. Sportswriter Stan Houston nicknamed him the Big M.

(*Imperial Oil – Turofsky/Hockey Hall of Fame*)

the bench. "And their skill was moving the puck. Get it up to guys on the fly. Guys skated like they had rocket fuel. They had an awesome group of guys who could score. Sometimes games were over by the middle of the first period."

The Leafs, however, were starting to look like spoilers. They had climbed from fifty-three points and last place in the 1957–58 season to ninety points in the 1960–61 season – just one win out of first place. Playing on a line with Red Kelly and Bob Nevin, their star player, Frank Mahovlich, finished third in the scoring race, with two goals fewer than the league's scoring champ Boom Boom Geoffrion, who tied the Rocket's fifty-goal record. Rookie Dave Keon won the Calder Trophy; veteran Red Kelly, the Lady Byng; and goalie Johnny Bower pried the Vezina loose from Jacques Plante. Then disaster struck the Leafs. Their star players were suffering from numerous injuries, and the entire team scored just eight goals in five games with the mercurial Frank Mahovlich scoring just one goal. The fourth-place Detroit Red Wings knocked them out of the playoffs.

The Leafs also had "Grim" Tim, the rock-jawed, granite-bodied defenceman whose legal name was Miles Gilbert Horton, but whom everyone called Tim unless they wanted to be crumpled the way he dealt with rushing opponents along the boards, or on open ice. "Horton is the strongest player I've ever met – raw strength," recalled trainer Bob Haggert. "He's a sleeping giant – one of those guys you don't want to wake up. He'd just pick guys up and throw them away." Gordie Howe, considered the strongest man in the NHL in his prime, said that Horton was the strongest man that he'd ever played against.

Horton had been named after his two grandfathers by his own father when his mother was too ill to attend the registering of his birth, and so she called him Tim, the name she preferred, anyway. The name fit – an honest, solid, unadorned name that typified the Leafs' style in the 1960s. Like half the Toronto team, Horton came from a mining town in Northern Ontario. Cochrane had seen hard times during the Depression, and the Horton family, thought to be deserving by their neighbours, were left a hamper on their doorstep one Christmas by a local church. Horton's mother broke down in

Les Costello and the Flying Fathers

Les Costello, a speedy, talented left-winger, had won two Memorial Cups with Toronto's St. Michael's junior team, and the 1948 Stanley Cup with the Maple Leafs, when he heard the call to play for a different team. "I'd rather teach people to live with God than thrill them occasionally on Saturday nights," he said as he left hockey to become a Roman Catholic priest. But hockey called him back in 1962 when Father Brian McKee approached him to play on a team of hockey-playing priests to raise money for a sick child in his parish. The comic on-ice antics of the Flying Fathers, as they called themselves, caught the imagination of the country, and soon millions were laughing at the unorthodox playing style of the priests, abetted, at times, by Sister Mary Shooter, a mascot named Penitent, and by giving opponents penalties

for "being a Protestant." There was even a distraught woman who would appear rinkside holding a baby, while an embarrassed Father Costello hid behind a teammate, paying off the joke. Costello's ready wit was apparent off the ice as well, and once during a Vatican audience with Pope Paul VI, Costello noticed the Pope was holding a hockey stick upside down, and showed him the right way, lest people think he was "trying to stir spaghetti." The Flying Fathers have raised more than $4 million for charity, and now, in their fourth decade, are a true hockey dynasty, with nearly a thousand victories and just six losses. Their success, said Costello, was simple: "We win a lot of games because we cheat a lot." During a game in 2002, Costello fell and hit his head on the ice; a few days later, he slipped into a coma. He died on December 10, aged seventy-four. In the comedy of the Flying Fathers, Costello saw a potent way to make hockey connect to a global mission. "Laughter soothes the body and soul," he said. "Save the family and you save the world."

(Imperial Oil – Turofsky/Hockey Hall of Fame)

tears and refused to bring the hamper inside, for that would be to admit defeat. Horton inherited his mother's determination and pride, and the long cold winters of Cochrane gave Horton a vision of the future he wanted. "Guys played a lot of pond hockey there – Tim would play eight hours a day," recalled Haggert. "There was nothing else to do up north, and they knew it was the only way out."

Tim Horton has been called the strongest man to ever play in the NHL. His Spartan childhood in the rough mining towns of Northern Ontario made him into a tough, reliable defenceman. He had a punishing slapshot and an equally punishing bear hug, which he used to defuse on-ice violence, not to start it. Horton made his name as a Toronto Maple Leaf, for whom he played eighteen seasons, winning four Stanley Cups. In 1970, Horton was traded to the New York Rangers. He was then selected in the intra-league draft, moving first to Pittsburgh in 1971–72 and then Buffalo. While he was driving back home to Buffalo after a game against the Leafs in 1974, Horton was killed in an accident. The chain of coffee and doughnut shops that he began as a Leaf still bears his name. *(Imperial Oil – Turofsky/Hockey Hall of Fame)*

As a seventeen-year-old in 1947, Horton came to Toronto's St. Michael's Majors, the Catholic boys' academy that was one of the Leafs' feeder teams (along with the Marlies), a big step toward fulfilling his NHL ambitions. "The Leafs spent a lot of time bird-dogging in Northern Ontario, and the pitch to the Catholic guys, they said, 'Come play for St. Mike's,'" Haggert explained. "You were guaranteed your guy would go to school and live in residence. As for the Marlies, they'd find a place for you to live. It was a great opportunity for those guys."

After playing for Pittsburgh in the AHL, Horton was taken on by the Leafs for the 1952–53 season. Two years later, his punishing defensive play had put him on the NHL All-Star team and into a much higher salary bracket. "Guys were making five, seven, eight grand, and that was good when the average salary was sixty, seventy bucks a week," said Haggert. "That was life. You signed your contract, played hockey, and worked in the summer at another job."

Most of the Leafs worked in the off-season for Conn Smythe's gravel company, and when Horton broke his leg in 1955 and couldn't play, he worked there too, while he recovered. It was a tough life, with 6:00 a.m. starts and hard physical labour, though Horton's injured leg kept him behind a desk, working the scales. If the poor Cochrane boy needed any reminder that his hockey career could end with one bad injury, the desk job only served to make him want more, and soon.

Horton started his own businesses to give him security beyond hockey, and after a few early ventures failed, he teamed up with Ron Joyce, a former Hamilton policeman. The business was a success, and Tim Hortons would become not only the country's most successful coffee and doughnut chain, but also a Canadian tradition, much the way Conn Smythe saw the Leafs becoming when he invented "Canada's Team" in 1927. Now, in the spring of 1962, the Leafs and their city were in a confident and competitive mood. They were sure that they would soon claim bragging rights from Montreal.

Though the pews in hockey's temple in Toronto were filled with a more sober crowd than regularly filled the Forum, the Leafs' rivalry with the Canadiens was also expressed in the language of a creed. "The Toronto Maple Leafs can do no wrong," said Leafs fan Leroy Peach, whose family had moved from Cape Breton to the heartland. "The players are gods, almost – they raise hockey to a religion. I don't care what they say in Montreal, the most quintessential team in Canada is the Leafs. It's not just Toronto who owns the Maple Leafs – the whole nation owns the Toronto Maple Leafs. They are Canada."

The Chicago Black Hawks had disrupted Montreal's winning streak by taking the Cup in 1961, and they met the Canadiens again in the 1962 semifinals. The prospect of another year without Lord Stanley's gift belonging to

the Canadiens so alarmed Ken Kilander, a twenty-five-year-old lounge pianist who styled himself the Montreal Kid, that he was moved to take extreme action while watching the Canadiens on the verge of elimination in Chicago. "My Habs were getting clobbered," Kilander recalled. "I couldn't take any more of that. I jumped out of my seat and ran down into the lobby to take a look at the Stanley Cup. I couldn't resist reaching in and taking the Cup in my arms. The Hawks were about to win, and who knew when I'd ever see it again. I started carrying it across the lobby when an usher spotted me. He asked me what the hell I was doing and I said, 'I'm taking the Cup back to Montreal where it belongs.'"

Kilander was arrested, released, and sent back to Montreal on the next train out of Chicago. The Black Hawks, meanwhile, defeated the Canadiens and set their hopes for a repeat victory on beating the Leafs, who had knocked off the New York Rangers. But with the Canadiens out of the way, Toronto fans were sure the Cup would be theirs.

Toronto found a fierce opponent in Chicago. Their star, Bobby Hull, had scored fifty goals in the 1962 season; defenceman Pierre Pilote and goalie Glenn Hall had made the Second All-Star team; and Hull and Stan Mikita had made the First.

Toronto took a two-game lead in the final, but then Chicago tied the series at home. Frank Mahovlich's two goals and Bob Pulford's hat trick led the Leafs to an 8–4 blowout in the fifth game in Toronto, and the sixth was a 0–0 tie until eight minutes into the third period when Bobby Hull scored for Chicago. Exuberant Black Hawks fans showered the ice with debris in a Chicago-style

In 1962, the Chicago Black Hawks, led by Bobby Hull (nicknamed the Golden Jet), was the only team standing between the Toronto Maple Leafs and the Stanley Cup championship after an eleven-season drought in Toronto. The Leafs defeated Chicago in six games to win their eighth Cup in four decades.

(Imperial Oil – Turofsky/Hockey Hall of Fame)

US AND THEM

In October of 1962, Jim Norris, the multi-millionaire who owned the Chicago Black Hawks and the Detroit Red Wings, threw a post All-Star game party in his suite at Toronto's Royal York Hotel. At the time, Harold Ballard was in difficult negotiations with his star forward, Frank Mahovlich, who had scored forty-eight goals in the 1960–61 season but was never paid his promised bonus because it wasn't written in his contract. At the party, Ballard had an idea of how he could unload the problem and make a lot of money. He held an impromptu auction for Mahovlich's services, and soon he and Norris had a signed deal – the shaky scrawl perhaps a reflection of the success of the party – for $1 million. In the sober light of day, the Leafs tried to laugh it off, but Norris wasn't joking and wrote out a cheque. In the end, NHL president Clarence Campbell intervened, saying that no "responsible" officer of the Leafs had accepted the offer, and Mahovlich, to the great relief of the other NHL owners, who feared the consequence of this expensive precedent, stayed put. (*Hockey Hall of Fame*)

tickertape parade, but their premature gesture delayed the game for ten minutes, and what momentum the Hawks had vanished with the clean-up of the garbage on the ice. When the game resumed, Toronto's Bob Nevin tied it, and then Tim Horton set up Dick Duff's winning goal. In the dressing room afterward, Frank Mahovlich kissed the Stanley Cup for all of Toronto.

On June 6, 1962, just two months after the Leafs had won their first Cup since Bill Barilko's overtime winner in 1951, a pilot spotted the single-engine airplane that had carried him and Henry Hudson in dense forest one hundred kilometres northwest of Cochrane, Ontario – the tough railway town where Tim Horton was born. No official explanation for the crash was ever released, though speculation ranged from the banal to the fantastic: the plane had run out of fuel; its cargo of fish had been too heavy; Barilko had defected to Russia, the land of his ancestors, to teach the Russians how to play hockey. It is a mystery still.

In October that year, in a sign of the new era of "prestige, dignity and character" under Stafford Smythe and his partners, Harold Ballard – who liked a good time – went for drinks to the Royal York Hotel suite of Jim Norris, owner of the Chicago Black Hawks and the Detroit Red Wings. Norris was soon bidding upward from $250,000 for the services of the still unsigned Frank Mahovlich, and when the figure hit $1 million, Ballard said they had a deal. Norris peeled off ten one-hundred-dollar bills from his roll as a deposit. The next morning, the Leafs' high command treated the events of the night before as the kind of hijinks that can result from having an all-star drinking session with a man worth a quarter of a billion dollars. The hangover arrived in the form of Chicago's general manager Tommy Ivan, who showed up at Maple Leaf Gardens with a cheque for $1 million. Stafford Smythe said Ballard had had no authority to trade the Big M but that he could do nothing until he called a directors' meeting. Tommy Ivan immediately phoned Norris at

the Royal York to give him the news that the Leafs had reneged. Toronto coach Punch Imlach later said the enraged Norris's opinion of this double dealing could be heard all the way from Front Street to the Gardens.

Publicly, Stafford Smythe laughed off Norris's claim as a publicity stunt. "No human being is worth $1,000,000 – to buy or sell," he said, but Harold Ballard admitted that he had "$1,000 in my pocket right now confirming the deal." Fans picketed in front of Maple Leaf Gardens, and both Conn Smythe and Clarence Campbell eventually stepped in to calm things down. If the transaction were allowed, the financial future was frightening for the NHL.

Through it all, coach and general manager George "Punch" Imlach, superstitious, splenetic, and frequently profane, made it known that any credit for stopping the trade – and for the Leafs' success – was due to him. "Nobody second guesses me around here," he said. "I make the decisions myself and take full responsibility. The owners of this club know that as soon as they want to make the decisions, all they have to do is fire me. I always remember what Conn Smythe told me: 'Be sure to make your own mistakes.'"

Though he ran brutally tough practices and would ridicule players for attempting to think of life beyond hockey, lambasting Tim Horton for opening his doughnut shop, Imlach was not delusional. "There's nothing unusual in the Leafs' success," he said. "We work harder than, and practise longer than, any of the other clubs. Even the Canadiens. But the Canadiens are *the* team to beat. They are *always* the team to beat."

George "Punch" Imlach earned his nickname after being knocked out while playing hockey and then throwing punches at the trainer who was trying to revive him. Imlach became assistant general manager of the Leafs during the summer of 1958, and when the Leafs were struggling in the 1958–59 season, Imlach demanded full authority and soon was behind the bench. Stubborn, superstitious, profane, sometimes cruel, and always insistent on total loyalty, Imlach guided the Leafs to four Stanley Cups until he was fired by Stafford Smythe in 1969 after the Leafs lost four straight playoff games.

(Imperial Oil – Turofsky/Hockey Hall of Fame)

Jacques Plante, the full-time goaltender of the Montreal Canadiens from 1954–55 until he was traded to New York in June 1963, waves to fans during a Stanley Cup victory parade in 1956. While with the Canadiens, Plante won five Stanley Cups and five Vezina Trophies as the NHL's top netminder. He was also one of the more innovative members of a singular breed: the first goalie to roam out of his crease to play the puck and the first to wear a mask. He liked to knit to relax, and the toque he is wearing in this photograph was likely his creation. (*Robert Dubuc/Hockey Hall of Fame*)

When the Leafs did beat Montreal in the 1963 semifinals, en route to their second straight Stanley Cup, Montreal's usual verve gave way to self-questioning and trepidation, and not just because of hockey. A militant separatist group calling itself the Front de libération du Québec had exploded three mailbox bombs outside federal armories on the night of March 7, and the following morning released a manifesto promising that they were prepared to die, and to kill, to achieve total independence for Quebec. In the French–English cultural war, hockey triumphs would never again be enough.

Canadiens' goalie Jacques Plante, one of the most talented players the NHL has ever seen, was one victim of the Canadiens' loss of the Cup. On ice he was an extrovert, darting out of his net for the puck, marshalling his defencemen in both French and English, firing long, daring breakout passes up the ice to his forwards; on road trips, he would stay in a different hotel from the rest of the team; and for relaxation, he knitted toques, sweaters, and even his own underwear. His teammates joked that the real reason Plante liked knitting was because he was so cheap.

Plante's frugality was learned. As one of eleven children growing up in Shawinigan, there was no money for luxuries, certainly none for a radio for young Jacques to listen to the exploits of his beloved Canadiens. Still, there were thin walls. "I used to lie awake at night," he said, "listening to hockey games in the ceiling coming through from the radio upstairs that some people there owned."

Plante's bold style was born of necessity in the days when he played with the Citadelle in the Quebec Junior League. The team had four bad defencemen: two were slow, one couldn't skate backward, and another couldn't make left turns. "It was a case of me having to go and get the puck when it was shot into our end because our defencemen couldn't get there fast enough," said Plante.

He debuted with the Canadiens for three games in 1952–53, and by 1954–55 he was their starter in goal. His brilliance on ice won him comparisons to the Canadian virtuoso of the keyboard, and people called Plante "the Glenn Gould of hockey," or more familiarly, "Jake the Snake," because of his litheness and quick cunning. But it was his desire to keep his face in one piece that did him in with the Canadiens.

In 1955, Plante's right cheekbone was shattered by a shot from teammate Bert Olmstead, and he was out of action for five weeks. In 1956, another shot deflected into his face, and Plante mentioned in a TV interview that he'd be interested in trying out any masks suitable for hockey goaltenders. A man in Granby, Quebec, heard his plea and sent him a plastic model that Plante used in practice for three years. Then, in 1957, Bill Burchmore sent Plante a letter

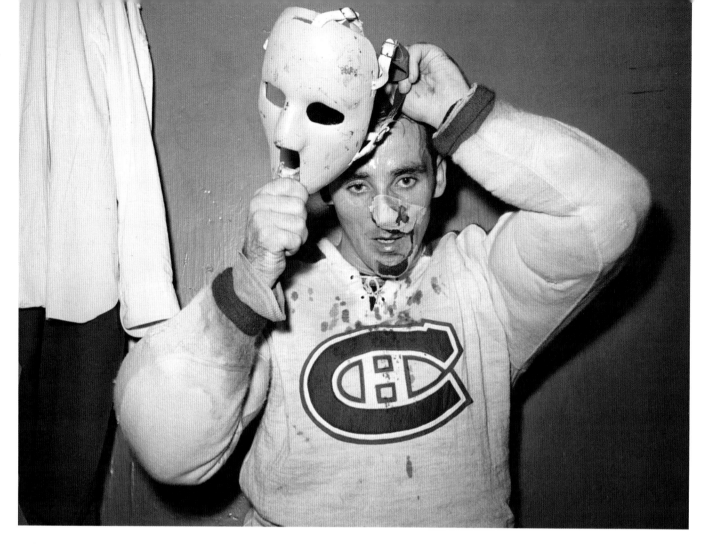

saying he had been developing a fibreglass mask that could be molded to fit his face. He and Plante perfected the design, but there remained a problem: coach Toe Blake. Like many hockey men of the era, Blake thought the face protector would impede any goalie's vision and could "take him out of the game" by making him feel safer.

All of that changed in a game against the New York Rangers at Madison Square Garden on November 1, 1959, when Plante's face was on the receiving end of an Andy Bathgate slapshot. Plante refused to go back into the game unless he was protected, so Toe Blake finally agreed to let him wear a mask. Montreal promptly went on an eleven-game unbeaten streak. When Plante's nose had healed, he took off the mask at Blake's urging, and Montreal lost. Plante recalled, "Blake came to me and said that I had a chance to win a fifth straight Vezina Trophy that year, and that if the mask would help, 'Do what you want.' So I put it back on." Plante won the Vezina, and the Canadiens won the Cup. "Before, we had control of [the puck], and that's why goalies could do without a mask," he said. "Now, a lot of guys would be hurt without a mask. It changed the game drastically." But the following three straight years of Stanley Cup failure in Montreal coincided with the years that Plante continued to

Jacques Plante was not the first NHL goalie to use a mask – in 1930, the Montreal Maroons' goalie Clint Benedict had tried a crude leather face protector but had given it up when he found that it impaired his vision. Plante had experimented with a mask in practice, but it was not until he was badly cut by a puck to the face from the stick of New York sharpshooter Andy Bathgate on November 1, 1959, that he insisted on wearing a mask during games. The Canadiens were initially concerned that the protective mask would make him less alert, but after the team went undefeated over the next ten games, Plante's mask became a permanent fixture. *(Corbis/Bettmann)*

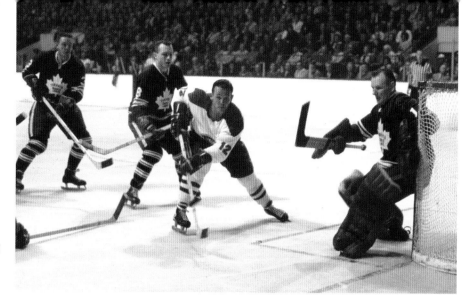

Johnny Bower was always the old guy of hockey, having just one season of NHL play under his belt (in 1953–54) before he finally left the minor leagues to join the Leafs in 1958, the year he turned thirty-four. While crossing the American border on a road trip, a Customs official scoffed at his claim to be a goalie, saying Bower was too old. He may have been old, but he was good. He won the Vezina Trophy in 1961 and shared it, at age forty-one, with fellow Leafs netminder Terry Sawchuk in 1965.

(*Imperial Oil – Turofsky/Hockey Hall of Fame*)

wear his mask, and Blake, tired of what he saw as Plante's whining, traded him to New York.

Soon other goalies started to wear masks for protection. As Bathgate said, "Everybody's become a slapshot artist, and the puck is going all over the place. That's why they put masks on." But not all goalies were keen to adopt the mask, however. Toronto's Johnny Bower, who had a permanent squint from staring pucks in the face without protection, decided that even if he could see properly through the mask, the scorn that he might face for wearing one wasn't worth it.

Bower had come to the Leafs in 1958, as a thirty-three-year-old minor league veteran. Though keenly competitive, Bower was a realist, and knew that job security for goalies in the six-team professional league – with just six netminders – was shaky. He had spent four seasons in the minors after playing one full season and parts of two others for the New York Rangers because he knew that a few bad games in the NHL could ruin his career and that life in the minors was safer. Now that he had won the Vezina Trophy and was goalie for the Leafs, he wasn't going to risk his livelihood on a speeding puck that he couldn't see through a mask. "I just made up my mind that I was going to lose teeth and have my face cut to pieces," he said. He also now had Andy Bathgate as a teammate, which improved his odds of keeping his face whole, and together they beat Montreal in the 1964 Stanley Cup semifinals – again – and celebrated Toronto's third straight Stanley Cup by beating Detroit in a hard-fought seven-game series.

The band of the 48th Highlanders piped the Cup up Bay Street during the victory parade, a display of Toronto's thanks that had begun two years earlier, and which the Leafs hoped would become an annual event. But the virtue the Leafs had brought to the city, and to those across the country who saw them as Canada's team, was in jeopardy as the new management team of Stafford Smythe and Harold Ballard made the Conn Smythe era seem prim.

Toronto sportswriter Dick Beddoes covered the Leafs' 1964 triumph, a series in which Leafs defenceman Bob Baun scored an overtime goal in Detroit while playing in pain on an injured ankle, which post-game X-rays revealed was broken. After the game on April 23, Beddoes and CKFH sportscaster Joe Morgan went to the Leafs management's suite at the Book-Cadillac Hotel, where they found Harold Ballard and Stafford Smythe partying with wine and women in celebration of Baun's series-tying goal.

While the rulers of Canada's Team drank and played, there was a man of virtue who also had hockey championships on his mind, victories that would stem from taking the best qualities of the Canadian psyche, and combining them with the country's unofficial state religion. Father David Bauer would make Canada's brand of hockey belong not to a city, but to the whole world.

Between the first and second periods of the last match of men's hockey during the 1964 Winter Olympics at Innsbruck, Austria, there was an extraordinary meeting of members of the International Ice Hockey Federation and its autocratic president, John Francis "Bunny" Ahearne. The Swedish team was defeating the Czechs and, after Canada's loss to the Soviets earlier that night, it looked as if there would be a three-way tie for second place in the standings among Canada, Sweden, and Czechoslovakia.

Under the tie-breaking system of goal differential – for and against – among the top four teams, the Canadians thought they had secured a bronze medal. But Ahearne, who had launched his hockey career by using a team of Canadians with British citizenship to win gold for the United Kingdom at the 1936 Winter Olympics, now seemed to want to thwart Canada at every turn. With the clock ticking down on the final game, he proposed a change to the medal conditions: goal differential among all eight teams would win the day. The IIHF agreed, just as Sweden won gold.

The Canadian team left a victory party at an Innsbruck hotel to pick up the bronze at the medal ceremony, but they were in for a shock. Thanks to Ahearne's machinations, the Canadians would now finish fourth, out of the medals. The team's coach, Father David Bauer, said, "Well, that's that. Let's get out of here," and so the Canadians did. But they didn't go far. They trooped to Bauer's room in the Olympic Village. Brian Conacher, a centre who would go on to play in the NHL, remembered the meeting. "Marshall Johnson [a fellow player], from Birch Hills, Saskatchewan, walked in and said, 'The shepherd and his flock have been fleeced.' Everybody chuckled at that."

Not everyone agreed. On the Monday after their loss, Dick Beddoes gave voice in the *Globe and Mail* to an opinion that has followed the Canadian National Team through its entire incarnation: It simply hadn't been good

Father David Bauer, the younger brother of Boston Bruins star Bobby Bauer, had been an NHL–calibre left-winger when he won the 1944 Memorial Cup with the Oshawa Generals. Then Bauer stunned the hockey world by deciding to become a priest, not a professional hockey player. After his ordination in 1953, he took up a teaching post at Toronto's St. Michael's College School, home to the Majors. As a member of the Basilian order of priests, Bauer had joined an ecclesiastical team of teachers whose aim was to educate a well-rounded person. "Make use of technique, but let the spirit prevail," was his philosophy, which Brian Conacher said had a visceral impact. "Finally, here's a coach, instead of saying 'up and down the ice, let's do a few mindless drills, and scrimmage for awhile,' he was the first one outside of college hockey who started to teach about the game. You were there to sweat and to think, too." After coaching the St. Michael's College School team to a Memorial Cup in 1961, Father Bauer had a vision of a national team, where players could go to university and play hockey for their country. The idea caught on, and Bauer's national team won a bronze medal at the Winter Olympic Games held in Grenoble, France, in 1968. (*Graphic Artists/Hockey Hall of Fame*)

enough. "Our decline as a hockey power is a minor piece in the West's athletic puzzle. We can continue sending semi-amateur competitors, as we did this year, or we can send our best, which are the bona fide pros in the National League. We are the only country that doesn't send its best athletes from its major sport to world tournaments. At the rate of hockey progress in Russia, pretty soon our best won't be good enough." The irony behind Beddoes's complaint was that the Canadian National Team had been formed in 1963 to establish a national standard of hockey excellence precisely because the Canadian Hockey Association thought that Canada was not sending its best when it dispatched semi-pro squads to represent the country internationally. And being second best was not the goal of David Bauer, idealist, philosopher, athlete, and Roman Catholic priest.

Bauer taught at St. Michael's College in Toronto and had coached its team, the Majors, to the 1961 Memorial Cup. Barry McKenzie, who played for him at St. Mike's and later on the national team, remembers how Bauer's worldly sensibility affected his team's performance on the ice after St. Michael's had blown a 3–0 series lead by losing two games. "We changed hotels and went up to one of the Hannigans boys' places, went out on paddle boats, and he was interviewed after the second loss. The reporters said to him, 'You must be concerned.' He said, 'I'm concerned about Cuba, and hunger in the world.' His point was to say that we should put things in perspective. So we went out, had a fun day, and won the series."

After the Memorial Cup triumph, Bauer moved in 1962 to St. Mark's College at the University of British Columbia, coaching the UBC Thunderbirds, who flew all the way to the Canadian university final, where they lost to McMaster.

When the Canadian amateur hockey power brokers were looking for a new way to play the game in the international arena, they sought Bauer's advice. He proposed a bold plan. He would create a national system for about one hundred student hockey players to receive tuition and board at the Canadian university of their choice and learn hockey while they studied academic subjects. The student teams would compete regionally and then nationally to determine the best of the best, who would be sent abroad to represent Canada. Even Bauer was daunted by the plan's challenges, and doubted his own sanity in dreaming it up. "I'm tempted to say it was a giant act of faith," he recalled. "It was crazy, and to my horror, in a way, it was accepted by the Canadian Amateur Hockey Association. We would begin in the fall of 1963. We had no uniforms, no ice, no schedule, no base, no money. Nothing!"

Former National Team player Terry O'Malley remembered that when Conn Smythe heard the news of Bauer's national hockey program, "he called him and said, 'If you get this thing off the ground, I'm going to run for prime minister, and I'm going to have you elected pope.'" Bauer's ambitions were far more humble. He wanted to create more opportunities for Canada's young hockey players, ones whose pro-hockey rights were owned by the NHL team within a fifty-mile radius of their homes, or who were trapped on junior teams by a system that Brian Conacher remembers as hidebound. "Father Bauer believed that you could be a good player and a good student as well, and you could mix the two. In the old days, the implied attitude was that if you were at school, you wouldn't turn out to be a good hockey player. Other guys, guys who came from Northern Ontario, didn't have expectations beyond hockey."

The NHL, which suspected that Bauer's national project would hurt their own business, wouldn't loan him junior prospects, but the national team's principal nemesis was Bunny Ahearne, an Irish-born travel agent who had seen his first hockey games in 1931 at London's Golders Green Rink, and who soon began booking the travel arrangements for hockey teams playing in Europe. A wily politician, Ahearne had become president of the IIHF in 1954 and had built up a cozy and questionable relationship with IIHF members, using proxy votes in hockey backwaters such as Korea to retain his hold on the presidency in exchange for a share of the profits.

Ahearne's power was absolute, as Derek Holmes, the former head of Hockey Canada and a Canadian National Team player who played in Europe in the 1960s, found out. When the British National League appeared unstable, Holmes signed a contract to play in Italy, and went into Ahearne's travel

Irish-born John Francis "Bunny" Ahearne was a London travel agent who became the autocratic head of the International Ice Hockey Federation in 1957 and remained as president until 1975. Ahearne had been the manager of the British hockey team that in 1936 became the first in history to win the European, World, and Olympic championships. It was stocked with Canadians, including the coach. (*Frank Prazak/Hockey Hall of Fame*)

agency on Piccadilly to bid him farewell. "He says, 'My good friend in Finland needs a national coach for Finland.' I said, 'What about my contract in Italy?' He says, 'Looked after.' Next day he says, 'You're on a plane to Finland.'"

At the 1966 World Championships in Ljubljana, Yugoslavia, the Canadian team was subjected to refereeing that bordered on the farcical. "You couldn't do anything without getting a penalty," recalled Barry Mackenzie, who had been coached by Bauer at St. Michael's and on the National Team. When goalie Seth Martin skated out to stop Czech player Stanislav Pryl on a breakaway, Martin stuck his glove out to take the puck away. "Pryl skated over Seth's hand, accidentally," recalled Mackenzie. "Didn't cut it, but [Pryl] fell. And Seth got two for tripping." The Canadian players threatened to quit the tournament, and Bauer brought in journalists George Gross and Jim Proudfoot to quell the rebellion, "but they just added fuel to it," recalled Mackenzie. It was the team doctor Jack Waugh who reminded the players of their obligation to their country – and of the dire consequence of disgracing the national religion. "He said, 'You guys are playing with fire here. You've been sent over by the Canadian people to represent Canada, and you might be surprised to see what might happen to you if you go home,'" recalled player Morris Mott. "'You might be suspended for life.' Which was true."

At the tournament's closing banquet, Terry O'Malley found himself sitting next to Ahearne, and spoke bluntly about the poor officiating. Ahearne's response revealed much about his attitude toward Canadian hockey. "You Canadians. You've got no right to complain," he spat at O'Malley. "You've got so little history." O'Malley's response showed the kind of mental toughness and agility that Father Bauer valued as much as physical play on the ice. "We've got enough history to know what is just, and what is not," said O'Malley, "and Canadian bodies are lying dead all over Europe. That proves it!"

Ahearne beat a hasty retreat to another table, and the following year, Canada was allowed to add some firepower to their national squad, in the person of former Toronto Maple Leafs defenceman Carl Brewer, now a reinstated amateur thanks to the intermediary efforts of the prime minister, Lester B. Pearson. But when it came to the abilities of Father Bauer's crew, many Canadians remained doubtful, a doubt Bauer saw all too clearly. "The men of the NHL have looked on this effort with a mixture of suspicion and scorn," he said. "Suspicion that this might be a real danger to themselves combined with a scorn for the idea that anybody else could hope to play really first class hockey."

Although the Canadians did win the 1967 Centennial Invitational Tournament in Winnipeg, and even beat the Soviets in the final game, Bauer's dream of winning a world title was destroyed by Bunny Ahearne. He had harshly pronounced on Canada's fate during a television interview, saying that as long as the country's international hockey program consisted of just one team, David Bauer's, "They'll never win the title, never, never, never."

After promising to allow each team to use nine minor pro players at the 1970 World Championships in Winnipeg and Montreal, Ahearne reneged, and Hockey Canada, the new governing body of the amateur national sport, pulled out of the contest. Bauer was devastated. "We could have won in 1970. . . . I knew that at the time, but I was being studiously ignored by those who were making the decisions," he said. "With the National team gone, the NHL is once again unchallenged. But the youth of Canada have been betrayed and Canada itself has lost a glorious chance to become a leader within the IIHF. And I? How could I be happy seeing all this?"

On February 15, 1965, after months of acrimonious debate, Canada got a new flag, and the Honourable Maurice Bourget, Speaker of the Senate, addressed the thousands who had gathered to witness it being raised on Parliament Hill for the first time: "The flag is the symbol of the nation's unity, for it, beyond any doubt, represents all the citizens of Canada without distinction of race, language, belief or opinion." Tellingly, the Speaker did not add "sex," even though Canadian women were starting to demand equal rights.

At the time, Katherine "Cookie" Cartwright, a law student at Queen's University, was desperately looking for some hockey uniforms to patch up so that she could get a women's university league on the ice. The total budget for women's sport at Queen's was four thousand dollars – the same figure as the cleaning bill for the men's football team's uniforms at a university that, in 1894, boasted one of the first female hockey teams, the Love-Me-Littles.

Cartwright, who grew up playing hockey on Deadman Bay, near Kingston, objected to the fact that while there were fifteen intercollegiate sports for men, there were only six for women, and hockey wasn't one of them. In 1961, she approached the women's athletics director at Queen's, Marion Ross, about the matter. "She was well aware of it, as she had battled for years for rights for women," Cartwright recalled. "Miss Ross still didn't say yes. She wanted to know how much equipment would cost and where we thought the money for it would come from. I didn't know, of course, but I stalled her for a while until I could deal with the problem."

Enrolment for women undergraduates in universities was increasing, having risen across the country from 25 per cent in 1960 to 33 per cent in 1965, and women were feeling both encouraged and a new sense of power. But women who wanted to play hockey were met with the refrain from the men who controlled the game: it was too rough. Cartwright, though, thought that their

The Chum Witch

When the Toronto Maple Leafs were faltering during the 1963–64 season, an announcer on Toronto radio station CHUM suggested, after another Leafs loss, that perhaps the team needed "a CHUM witch to put a hex on the opposition." Station executives loved the idea, and on February 15, 1964, a Toronto entertainer named Phyllis Shea made her debut as the CHUM Witch, Mabel Leaf, complete with pointy hat, black cape, and, most importantly, a magic wand. She put a "hex" on the opposition, and the Leafs won 4–1. CHUM thought that Mabel Leaf was a one-time promotion, but when the Leafs lost the next game without her, CHUM was bombarded with phone calls from listeners hankering for a return to the dark arts, and no one was more eager than the famously superstitious Leafs coach "Punch" Imlach. With Mabel Leaf in attendance, the Leafs went on an 11–2–1 run. In Game 7 of the Stanley Cup semifinals, with the Leafs up against archrival Montreal, Mabel was given some help when CHUM sales secretary Shirley Hart was enlisted as her sister, Flo de Leaf, whose job was to hex the Habs while Mabel charmed the Toronto team. It worked, and Toronto now took on the Detroit Red Wings for the Cup, though the Wings fought back with a wizard of their own. The sorceresses from Toronto were too powerful, and the Leafs won the first game, but they needed help. CHUM librarian Mary McInnes became Chicken Wing, mother to Mabel and Flo, whose job was to hex the older Wings players, such as Gordie Howe. Once again, the magic worked: Bob Baun scored an overtime goal in Game 6 with a broken bone in his leg, and the Leafs handily won Game 7 – and the Cup – 4–0. Leafs goalie Johnny Bower, in a post-game interview on television, didn't forget to acknowledge a higher power for the victory. "I want to thank the CHUM Witch, Mabel Leaf," he said. (*Courtesy The CHUM Group*)

objection to the women's game came from a deeper fear about what kind of woman hockey might attract: "The . . . women who play hockey though, don't care what other people say about them. They have to be the sort of people who think independently and who don't follow the crowd."

A men's team trainer sympathetic to Cartwright's mission showed her a treasure chest inside a rundown room in the bowels of Queen's Arena. Inside the boxes was mothballed hockey equipment dating from the 1930s, when Queen's last had a women's hockey team. "What a delight!" Cartwright recalled thinking. "With Queen's having their own arena, we were not charged for ice time. Now Miss Ross had no reason not to let us play. She conceded. We played exhibition games and became a full-fledged collegiate team." A women's university hockey league was established in 1962, and Queen's resumed its rivalry

Terry Sawchuk

One of the greatest goalies ever, Terry Sawchuk was also one of hockey's most conflicted figures, and his life played out like a Greek tragedy. Sawchuk became a goalie because there was a spare set of pads at home, ones belonging to his older brother, who had died of heart problems at age seventeen. Sawchuk turned pro with the Omaha Knights in 1947, and during a game in Houston, a stick caught him in the right eye. Instead of going out to celebrate his eighteenth birthday, Sawchuk spent the rest of the evening on an operating table. The doctor decided to remove his eye, then changed his mind – he would take another look in the morning. The delay saved Sawchuk's eye, and his career. He became the first player to win rookie-of-the-year honours in all three of his professional leagues, and he was awarded four Vezina Trophies as the NHL's top goalie, sharing his final one in 1965 with teammate Johnny Bower in Toronto.

Bent so low in the net that his shoulders practically touched his knees, Sawchuk's style was nicknamed the Gorilla Crouch, and the mobility it gave him was a precursor to the popular "butterfly" style of goaltending that followed. During the 1952 Stanley Cup playoffs with Detroit, Sawchuk posted an astonishing 0.63 goals-against record as the Wings won eight straight games, and he won his first Cup. Sawchuk won his fourth and last Stanley Cup with the 1967 Toronto Maple Leafs, and that same season recorded the hundredth of 103 career shutouts, a record that still stands. A volatile and sometimes depressed man off the ice, Sawchuk frequently got into confrontations, and during a 1970 tussle with New York Rangers teammate Ron Stewart over who would clean their rental house, Sawchuk suffered internal injuries that killed him a month later, at age forty. A year later, the Hockey Hall of Fame waived the traditional three-year waiting period and added his name to the pantheon of hockey's greatest players. (*Graphic Artists/Hockey Hall of Fame*)

with McGill, whose women had competed intensely on the ice with Queen's forty years earlier. Young girls who wanted to learn the game still had no choice but to play with boys. But, while it was one thing for them to play pond hockey with their brothers, girls who attempted to join boys' leagues were redirected to figure skating or received dire warnings that the game would damage their femininity and jeopardize their chances for marriage.

A well-meaning solution to the conflict between a girl's desire to play hockey and the obstacles in her way came from Sam Jacks, the recreation director of North Bay, Ontario. According to his widow, Agnes, "His heart lay with the poor, he was always trying to think up free skating lessons, free swimming lessons, free everything." Jacks wanted to create an inexpensive team sport for girls. So he equipped the girls with bladeless hockey sticks and figure skates, prohibited body contact, both to address concerns that hockey was too rough and could damage the girls' reproductive organs and to eliminate the need for costly gear, and transformed the dangerous puck into a harmless rubber ring. Ringette was born.

Sam Jacks's invention was both a solution and a problem, for while it offered girls a chance to taste something of the game on ice, it was predicated on the notion that girls didn't want to play hockey the way boys did. After ringette was presented to a group of municipal recreation directors in Ontario, the Espanola High School women's hockey team was asked to try the new game out. They did, but as their coach, Laurann Van Volkenburg, recalled, these young women "had already discovered the joy of playing hockey, [and] never requested to try that game again. Nobody ever said, 'Are we going to try that ringette game again?'" Nevertheless, schools across the country adopted ringette in their curriculum. But, still, women wanted to play hockey.

In Brampton, Ontario, Marge Poste overcame the stigma of wanting to play the sport by pretending that she was buying equipment for her brother. Then, inspired by other girls who wanted to play too, in 1965 she helped form the Brampton Canadettes, a team that was not only about hockey, but also about social change. "Women were saying we have rights and we have a right to play hockey," Poste said later. "There was a strong sense of camaraderie – it's us against the whole world. It was a microcosm of what was happening in Canadian society."

Taking their cue from the many women who wanted to play hockey as equals with each other, Roy Morris and Jim Tokiwa formed a Brampton girls' league, colour-coding the girls' helmets so that the red-helmeted line would play only against the red-helmeted line from the opposing team, thus ensuring that players could compete at their own level of ability and that no superior line would humiliate a weaker one.

Eventually, a second Canadettes team was created, as were teams across the country proudly featuring the feminine ending to their names: the Spudettes in Prince Edward Island, the Burlington Buffaloettes, and the Kapuskasing Kookettes.

In February 1967, in Wallaceburg, Ontario, Harold and Lila Robson, who had once taken their Lucan Leprechauns girls' team onto the *Ed Sullivan Show* in New York (reflecting more the curiosity factor of women's hockey than its accomplishments) organized the North American Girls' Hockey Championship Tournament, affectionately known as the "Lipstick Tournament." A crew from *Hockey Night in Canada* showed up to cover the sixteen girls' teams who entered, including one from Port Huron, New York, and the male broadcasters and technicians played a game against the Wallaceburg Hornettes, losing 6–2.

Lucan Leprechauns
The Leprechauns, a girls' peewee hockey team from the southwestern Ontario town of Lucan, population nine hundred, celebrated their Irish name with green uniforms and nicknamed a trio of their players the Colleens. In trying to drum up publicity for their team, the Robsons, a husband-and-wife coaching duo, sent out an appeal to another Irishman, the immensely popular American television host Ed Sullivan. His Sunday-night show was the longest-running variety series in television history, a CBS institution from 1948 to 1971, and with the luck of the Irish in play, the Leprechauns were the novelty highlight of the *Ed Sullivan Show* in New York City on St. Patrick's Day, 1958. (*Courtesy Steve Oroz Associates, NY*)

When broadcaster Bill Hewitt was tackled from behind by a Hornette, he protested, and "she gave him a peck on the cheek," says broadcaster and author Brian MacFarlane, who played in the game. "The referee gave him a two-minute penalty for 'having lipstick on his collar.'" The final was played between the Don Mills Satan's Angels and the Humberside Dairy Queens, names that innocently summed up the range of debate about the nature of women who wanted play hockey. Cookie Cartwright scored the winning goal for Humberside.

The tournament was a catalyst for the rapid development of the women's game. "Everybody was talking about how they managed to play and how they found out about it and how we can get more teams and more girls," says Fran Rider, who was a novice defenceman in 1967 and went on to become executive director of the Ontario Women's Hockey Association.

Roy Morris and Jim Tokiwa, who had already formed a Brampton girls' league, started to plan their own tournament. "There are more than 100 women's teams that we know about," said Tokiwa. "We're sending invitations to British Columbia, Alberta, Saskatchewan, Manitoba, Quebec, as well as

In 1961, Queen's University law student Katherine "Cookie" Cartwright (receiving award) resurrected the long dormant women's hockey program at the university and was a catalyst in the re-emergence of women's hockey at an elite level. In 1967, at the North American Girls Hockey Championship Tournament – known as the Lipstick Tournament – Cartwright, as a member of the Humberside Dairy Queens, scored the championship-winning goal. (*Harold Ribson/Wallaceburg Courier Press*)

some American cities. We're just getting our feet wet." Twenty-two teams responded, and the first annual Dominion Ladies Hockey Tournament was born, with players ranging from nine-year-old Lynn Franklin to Mabel Boyd, who was in her fifties. The *Toronto Star* was impressed with the level of competition. "It wasn't powder-puff hockey. The Gals skated hard, used slapshots, body-checked and even dropped their sticks for the occasional fight."

The Dominion Ladies Hockey Tournament went on to become the largest women's competition in the world. It would also become known as the Centennial Tournament, for Canada was celebrating its one-hundredth birthday in 1967. A new century in the life of the country had begun, and the nation was in the mood for a party.

As Canada turned one hundred, people across the country were encouraged to celebrate with a Centennial project, something that would put into action the core Canadian value of a community working for the betterment of all. Of the 2,301 projects funded by the federal government's Centennial Commission, 520 were recreational centres, and many of those were hockey arenas, located in communities that had previously only had ice in the winter, and had had to shovel snow from it when they wanted to play hockey.

In December 1965, the sixteen hundred people of Three Hills, Alberta, saw notice of a public meeting advertised in their local paper "for the purpose of giving information . . . on the financing of the proposed skating arena, which involves the centennial project of Three Hills." Picturesque Three Hills, surrounded by the rolling wheat fields of southern Alberta, had seen its local hockey team, the Wheat Kings, miss out on games because they lacked an indoor rink. "Hockey is about all we have in the winter," said Wheat King Bruce Somerville. "I play a lot of hockey, all outdoors, freezing yourself. Some of the bigger centres won't come to play us outdoors."

As an indoor arena would cost $80,000, the town agreed to build the new facility onto the existing outdoor dressing rooms, and without a full ice-making plant. A referendum was held, and 225 ratepayers voted 85 per cent in favour of the arena, and for the township to assume a $45,000 loan to build it rather than increase property taxes. The Centennial Commission added $9,400, and Canada's Winter Works program gave $11,600. The Elks and Kinsmen each donated $1,000 per year for five years, and the community raised cash from wrestling, bingo, Christmas tree sales, and hockey pools. People also volunteered their time. "Hockey is an important part of the community and it's just something you have to have," said Three Hills councillor Dan Shea. "We are the last ones in our area to have an enclosed arena. There isn't a lot of money to go around in the town. I am a volunteer – everybody is a volunteer."

The volunteers were not expert at working with cement, and when they had finished pouring the floor, it wasn't exactly level. "There's one particular place where we have four inches of ice and another spot where it's an inch and a half," said Shea. "But it serves its purpose." And, as the town couldn't afford a Zamboni, one was improvised from sacks and a barrel. The barrel was filled with water, towed around the ice by a farm tractor, and the sacks trailing from it dispensed the water and levelled it.

After its completion, the arena became a centre of life year round in Three Hills – hosting hockey and skating in the winter, and rodeo, lacrosse, and community events in the summer. But as Bruce Somerville saw it, this centennial project's real legacy was hockey. "It is great getting to play inside. The sport is really taking off – the arena is used all the time," he said. "There are a lot more registrations in minor hockey. Our team is getting better because we are drawing kids from other towns around here. More people come to town. We've never looked back since."

In the spring of 1967, Canadians were not only watching hockey, they were playing it – in their basements, courtesy of Donald Munro. In 1932, Munro invented the first mechanical table-hockey game using his wife's old ironing

Dick Gamble

In Depression-battered 1932, Donald Munro couldn't afford to buy his children Christmas presents, so instead he invented the first mechanical table-hockey game, using his wife's old ironing board and scrap wood and metal he scavenged in his Toronto neighbourhood. In January 1933, Munro took a second game to Eaton's department store, and soon, the game was selling in the thousands. In the 1950s, a photographer took shots of all the Montreal Canadiens as the possible "face" on Eagle Toys' table-hockey game. Left-winger Dick Gamble was chosen to represent the Canadiens. His profile was also used for the Maple Leafs table-hockey players, but Eagle Toys changed the dark-haired Gamble into a strawberry blond.

(Above and right: Courtesy Rob Raven)

board, and wood and scrap metal that he scavenged in his Toronto neighbourhood. He was inspired to do so because, with the Depression in full swing, he could not afford to buy his children Christmas presents. He also thought that he could make more than just the one game, and in January 1933, Munro took a sample to Eaton's department store, and received a $3.60 voucher in exchange. He was still riding the streetcar home when Eaton's called and told his wife that the game had sold. Soon, it was selling in the thousands as children across the country now wanted a Munro table-hockey game.

By the 1950s, the original wooden peg players representing the Leafs and the Canadiens had given way to metal, and a see-through plastic puck dropper had replaced the old plunger, adding to the excitement as players representing the Leafs or the Canadiens waited to pounce on the puck rattling its way down the dropper toward the "ice." A metal game that used a Swedish invention allowing players to pivot on metal rods was introduced by Montreal's Eagle Toys Company, and endorsed by the Canadiens. It was the first Canadian game to feature players printed in colour on tin cutouts shaped like real hockey players who stood on a surface that resembled ice. Soon, both Munro and Eagle were issuing similar games that not only had spinning players, but slots that let them slide up and down the "ice" surface.

In Mont-Joli, Quebec, Pierre Bechard was just seven years old when dire circumstances broke up his family. With his father gone, and his mother's meagre factory wage insufficient to support for two boys, Bechard wound up first in an orphanage, and then in a foster home. Yet, after his mother, Chantal, bought him a tabletop hockey game, whenever Bechard played, he wasn't in a foster home, he was on the ice. "The father here liked hockey. Each Saturday night, just before the game came on TV, we put my game on the kitchen table and we played table hockey to get into the mood. It was a great moment," recalled Bechard. "We are the players, the coach and we are the fans – we are everything – we're in control. It helped me forget everything else. Table hockey was a remedy; a peace of mind." Bechard, the table-hockey player, was on the ice for Montreal: "It is very special, like a religion. In the Quebec province, for sure Toronto is the most dangerous opponent for Montreal," he said. "They are the two kings of the NHL."

Montreal Versus . . .
Montreal's colourful mayor Jean
Drapeau at the Expo 67 site, the city's
glittering World's Fair celebrating "Man
and His World." Drapeau had staked his
re-election on it by promising that the
city would not only win the fair, but
would become the "metropolis of the
world." Perfection would have been
complete if the Canadiens had also
won the 1967 Stanley Cup.

(*Roger Varley/Canadian Press*)

The rivalry between Canada's two teams was not only a romantic duel that captured the hearts and minds of those who called the two cities home, but one that extended far beyond their boundaries. In Sault Ste. Marie, a group of Italian-Canadian kids watched Toronto and Montreal games on TV. To them, Toronto represented the ruling class, so Frank Paci and his friends became Montreal fans. "We identified with the French-Canadian players, surrounded by the English," said Paci. "The Leafs were the team to hate."

As the son of working-class immigrants, Paci couldn't expect new hockey gear from parents whose sporting allegiance was to soccer, but he persuaded them to buy him a pair of second-hand skates from the Salvation Army. As generations have done before him and since, Paci felt freedom and power on the ice, but he also felt that playing hockey was his true passport to the new world. "For us immigrant kids, hockey is the game we all want to excel in because it's the Canadian game," he said. "Hockey makes us different from our parents – it sets us apart. Playing hockey makes us feel that we belong in the new country."

. . . Toronto

Captain George Armstrong and Leaf co-owner Harold Ballard embrace the Stanley Cup, as the Toronto Maple Leafs celebrate their 1967 victory over Detroit with a parade up Bay Street – a new Leaf tradition since 1962. They were piped along by the band of the 48th Highlanders, who a generation earlier had played their pipes at the opening of Maple Leaf Gardens in 1931.

Toronto's futuristic new City Hall, designed by Finnish architect Viljo Revell, towers in the background. Not only was the Leafs' victory especially sweet in Canada's centennial year, but it was a victory over Montreal, further fuelling Toronto's aspiration to become Canada's First City. (*Canadian Press*)

The new country was feeling confident in the spring of 1967, with a new flag flying over Expo 67, the ambitious World's Fair that would attract 50 million visitors to Montreal to explore its theme of Man and His World. But in the hockey world that spring there were two nations in Canada – one wearing blue and white, and the other red, white, and blue. For the fifth time in NHL history, the Leafs and the Canadiens were meeting in the Stanley Cup final. Each team had won the Cup twice against the other, though Montreal had recovered its dynastic form to win Lord Stanley's prize in both of the past two seasons, after Toronto had won it each of the previous three.

There was also more than a touch of nostalgia in the air, for this series would mark the end of the Original Six era of the NHL. The league was doubling its size the following season, and David Molson, of the brewing family that now also owned the Canadiens, put into words what people were thinking. "With the League expanding to include twelve cities next year, this could be the last time we see two Canadian teams play in the finals." Molson's statement was disingenuous. While it was true that the NHL was adding six new teams, there could have been another Canadian Stanley Cup final because one of the expansion teams could have been in Vancouver.

NHL president Clarence Campbell had announced that Vancouver – which had won the Stanley Cup a half century earlier with Cyclone Taylor and the Millionaires – would be a serious candidate only when it had a serious arena. Toronto Maple Leafs co-owner Stafford Smythe stepped in with an offer to build and operate an $8-million facility on a downtown Vancouver site, and to use his influence to convince the NHL that it needed a team on Canada's Pacific Coast, where the Patrick brothers had once pioneered so many rules of the game now being played. Vancouverites, however, were annoyed that Smythe's deal included purchasing a $2.5-million piece of land for one dollar, and voted down his offer in a municipal referendum. Smythe was not gracious in defeat. "Vancouver lost its chance the day it turned down the referendum on our arena proposal," he said. "That proved to me the people out there aren't interested in going major league."

Clarence Campbell was both paternalistic and harsh. "It would have been in the best interests of the NHL to have another Canadian franchise," he said. "It's too bad Vancouver fumbled the ball so badly in the first place." He was also being economical with the truth. The catalyst for the NHL's expansion was television. New York Rangers owner William Jennings was instrumental in showing the other NHL teams how lucrative American television deals had changed the fortunes of professional football and baseball. Now they wanted some of that money. So the NHL expanded to major U.S. TV markets: Los Angeles, Oakland, Minneapolis–St. Paul, Philadelphia, and Pittsburgh, and in the ultimate insult to both Vancouver and Canada, St. Louis was awarded a franchise even though it had not applied. It was granted the franchise simply because Chicago Black Hawks owner Bill Wirtz owned an arena in the city. Assembling a team to play in it was a relatively minor detail, given that the NHL would secure a three-year, $3,600,000 television contract with American broadcaster CBS, which, in theory, was to be split evenly among the teams, as broadcast revenue was among the six-team NHL.

Canadians voiced their outrage. MP George Hees saw it as more American imperialism. "The whole thing stinks," he said. "The Yanks are going to line their pockets while the Canadians are shoved out in the cold in their own game." Prime Minister Pearson saw the expansion as a denial of Canada's heritage. "The NHL decision to expand only in the U.S. impinges on the sacred principles of all Canadians," he said. Toronto Maple Leafs coach Punch Imlach saw it for what it was. "Vancouver was sold out. Television is the answer to Vancouver's rejection," he said. "Montreal and Toronto would have to share their TV with Vancouver if they had let Vancouver in. Better to split the loot two ways, I guess, instead of three."

So in April 1967, Canadians looked forward to a Stanley Cup series already seasoned with nostalgia. The Canadiens were heavily favoured, even after finishing the season in second place, just two points ahead of the Leafs. They were younger, and with pugilistic John Ferguson wearing their colours for the past four seasons, they were tough. They had also come off back-to-back Cup victories, both times dispatching the Leafs in the first round, and Fergie had been a key player in the course of the victories, each time deepening his loathing of the Leafs, and they of him, which only endeared him further to Montreal fans, whose passionate hearts he had won in his first NHL game.

Like many a tough guy before and after him, Ferguson longed for the chance to prove that he could skate and shoot and score, as well as pummel opponents into submission. After the Canadiens' management felt the team had been manhandled in the 1963 playoffs by the Leafs, they were determined to get some muscle in the lineup. Canadiens scouts had checked out Ferguson while he was playing for Cleveland in the AHL, and he unequivocally established his fierce team loyalty during the pre-game warm-up by shooting a puck at a teammate who was talking to an opponent.

The Canadiens outbid Boston and New York to sign the five-foot-eleven, 190-pound right-winger, and in his first game with the Canadiens on October 8, 1963, Ferguson showed his contrary talents. Thirteen seconds into

John Ferguson joined the Montreal Canadiens in 1963–64 to give the team some muscle and to give linemate Jean Béliveau more room on the ice. Ferguson often stained the ice with the blood of his opponents as he played his tough-guy role to the delight of Forum fans, but he could put the puck in the net as well, reaching the NHL goal-scoring ace benchmark of twenty goals in the 1966–67 season. *(Corbis/Bettmann)*

the match, he got into a fight with Boston's tough guy, Ted Green, managing to land three quick haymakers. By the end of the night, he had also scored two goals and added an assist, on his way to an eighteen-goal season and a place in the Canadiens' pantheon of the 1960s.

In Canada's Centennial Year, Ferguson had his best NHL season to date, with twenty goals and twenty-two assists to go with his league-leading 177 penalty minutes. The Canadiens were hot as well, riding a fifteen-game unbeaten streak into their championship series with the Leafs – who, to deepen the drama, had been the last team to beat them, on March 8, 1967.

The Leafs were an aging crew, and some called them the Over the Hill Gang: defencemen Marcel Pronovost was thirty-six, Tim Horton, thirty-seven, and Allan Stanley, forty-one; centre Red Kelly was thirty-nine, and captain George Armstrong was thirty-six; goalie Terry Sawchuk was thirty-seven, and his counterpart, Johnny Bower, was forty-two. Thirteen of the players had at least seven years' NHL experience, and six of them had turned pro in the 1940s. When told that Johnny Bower had served in the war, twenty-nine-year-old Frank Mahovlich asked, "The Boer War?" However, in honour of the country's centennial, the old Leafs were sporting something new: a five-pointed maple leaf, just like the one on the new flag, in place of their veined eleven-point emblem. And after the Canadiens easily won the first game 6–2, it looked as if the Leafs were going to be swept.

In Montreal's Le Barbier des Sportifs, which had pictures of Canadiens on the wall and the custom of their fans, barber Menick Perazzino's Saturday salon was really a pre-game show. "Well, it was a special day, mostly, people didn't work, so they'd get here early," he recalled. "The guys would meet up. It was a bit like at the Tavern. You had the barbershop, the hairdresser elsewhere, the Tavern. The guys would tease each other, there were favourite players, favourite teams. For sure hockey was a priority." The second game had been moved to Saturday afternoon to accommodate CBS television, which didn't want hockey clogging up Saturday night's prime time, and although Montreal had handily won the first game 6–2, in the barbershop there was no sense of a brewing rout. "Toronto was a team to be wary of," Perazzino said. "They had a good team. Toronto always had good teams. They always had tough guys too. But for me, Montreal is my team."

Some of the most passionate Canadiens' fans could be found in the Czechoslovakian Pavilion at Expo 67, where a specially created Bohemian Crystal Trophy awaited the winners of the Stanley Cup in Canada's Centennial Year. Their commissioner general made no secret about the Czechs' desired outcome. "Hockey is the deepest link between Canada and Czechoslovakia, and we want to make this recognition of the Stanley Cup winner," said

Terry Sawchuk (left) and fellow goalie Johnny Bower celebrate the Leafs' 1967 Stanley Cup victory over Montreal with coach Punch Imlach. The goaltending duo, aged thirty-seven and forty-two respectively, shared the triumph equally, for each had played three games of the series, winning two games and losing one. It was their last hurrah together, as that summer Sawchuk became a Los Angeles King in the NHL expansion draft. *(Graphic Artists/Hockey Hall of Fame)*

Miroslav Galsuka. "We hope it will be Montreal." The closest thing to the hockey the Czechs at Expo 67 knew and loved was played by the Canadiens. "I have always respected the Canadiens – to me, they are hockey," said Villem Havelka, the Czech Pavilion's Director of Exhibits. "During the time we've been working in Montreal on our Pavilion for Expo, we have come to know them very well. Canada's best – Les Canadiens! We are looking forward to presenting the trophy to them."

But with the series going into its fourth game in Toronto on the opening day of Expo 67, the Leafs were making the Czechs nervous. Johnny Bower – who had shared the Vezina with Terry Sawchuk two seasons earlier – had led Toronto to a 3–0 victory in Game 2. The Over the Hill Gang came home to Toronto invigorated, and the third game was a goalies' battle, with Montreal's young Rogie Vachon stopping sixty-two shots, and Bower, fifty-four, before Bob Pulford won it for Toronto eight minutes into the second overtime period.

The Captains

Syl Apps (left), Ted Kennedy (centre), and George Armstrong (right) all captained the Maple Leafs at one point in their careers. Armstrong was the last of nine captains personally selected by Conn Smythe, who called the right-winger the "best captain, as a captain, the Leafs have ever known."

In Game 4, the Leafs showed their age when Johnny Bower injured his groin in the pre-game warm-up. The mercurial Terry Sawchuk went in as his replacement, and played as if he were in practice, which he hated because he didn't like to get hit with pucks unless there was something on the line. After Sawchuk let six pucks get past him in a 6–2 Canadiens' victory, a fan sent him a telegram asking, "How much did you get?" Sawchuk, who was as sensitive as he was tough, was deeply wounded by the fan's accusation that he could be bought, and responded in Game 5 with the kind of goaltending genius that had made him a four-time Vezina winner, giving Toronto a 4–1 win over Montreal. The Over the Hill Gang went home needing just one win to capture the prize no one thought they could take. After all, the Canadiens hadn't lost a Stanley Cup final since 1955. They had destiny on their side.

Game 6 was played in Toronto on May 2, the latest date ever for a Stanley Cup match. Louis Janetta, maître d' of the Royal York Hotel's Imperial Room juggled the staffing schedule so that he could make use of his four seats right behind the Canadiens' bench by bringing a friend and their sons to the historic

The Chief

George Armstrong was affectionately nicknamed the Chief, partly because of his Iroquois mother, and partly because Alberta's Stoney Indian tribe made him honorary Big-Chief-Shoot-the-Puck when Armstrong's senior hockey team made a western tour after winning the 1950 Allan Cup. The Chief was a great natural leader, regularly hollering encouragement to his teammates from the bench, and his strong positional play and stickhandling skills led general manager Hap Day to compare his end-to-end goal-scoring trips to those of Gordie Howe. A childhood bout with spiral meningitis had left Armstrong with a less than elegant skating stride, but he could make his way to the net, racking up 713 points in 1,187 regular season NHL games. Here, the Toronto Maple Leafs watch as Armstrong strikes a chivalric pose to kiss the prize after Toronto's 1967 Stanley Cup win, the eleventh for the franchise. (*Frank Prazak/Hockey Hall of Fame*)

game. Through his work at one of the city's premier restaurants, Janetta had come to know many NHLers. "As the Montreal players are going on the ice, they're giving me a tap with their stick and saying, 'Hi Lou, Hi Lou,'" he recalled. "There's Richard and Béliveau – I know them all. Of course I give them a wave and wish them good luck in the game. The Leafs come out looking tense – they don't look at anybody – just zoom straight onto the ice."

Captain George Armstrong and defenceman Allan Stanley were confident of the Leafs' chances, knowing that if the old boys could survive Imlach's regular season practices, they could win the Cup. For kids like Ron Ellis, just twenty-two, the atmosphere in the dressing room was electric. Punch Imlach came in bearing a box of money, which represented the team's playoff bonuses. "This is what you're playing for," said Imlach in his characteristically blunt way, which was both true, and a kick to their pride. The Leafs were playing to win.

With less than a minute left in the game, the Leafs were ahead 2–1, and the Canadiens pulled their goalie, Gump Worsley, to send out an extra man for a faceoff in the Toronto zone. It was one of those achingly tense hockey moments where the series outcome could change in seconds, should the Canadiens win the faceoff and score, taking over the momentum, and possibly the Cup.

On the Toronto bench, Allan Stanley listened as Imlach paced up and down, choosing the platoon to take the ice for this final assault. "Kelly, Armstrong, Pulford, Horton," said Imlach. Finally, he said, "Stanley." "I got one foot out of the gate," recalled Stanley, "and he says, 'You take the faceoff.'" The crafty Imlach had put a combined age of 143 years on the ice, with Sawchuk making it 180. And to this depth of experience, he married an old trick: defencemen had had to change their strategy for taking faceoffs because of an interference rule that prevented them using their superior size to charge into their opponent and drive the man off the puck instead of winning the puck with their sticks. Even so, Imlach knew that Stanley would find a way to get that puck – legally or otherwise. "I was always good at anticipating the drop of the puck," said Stanley, "and I always tried one quick-draw back. If it worked, great. If not, I'd put my stick between his legs and drive him out of the circle. I'm thinking, that's the only way I know how to do it."

Stanley won the draw, shovelled the puck back to Red Kelly, then, despite the new rule, stepped into Jean Béliveau. "He was the most surprised guy in the world," said Stanley. Kelly passed to Pulford, who passed to George Armstrong, who had a clear shot at an open net. "And while this is going on," said Stanley, "Jean was yelling to the ref, over and over, 'Faceoff interference! Faceoff interference!' He was hollering at the guy. But no referee in the world is going to make a call like that at a time like that. If he had called that and they tied it up, the whole of Maple Leaf Gardens would have been down on the ice."

The Leafs fans were now cheering themselves hoarse, for the Leafs had won their eleventh, and at this moment – in the Centennial Year, with NHL expansion looming – most important Stanley Cup. Stafford Smythe invited Louis Janetta and his friend to bring their sons to the Leafs dressing room to have a sip of victory, and Janetta, whose mother used to host Terry Sawchuk for dinner, went to congratulate him. But the volatile Sawchuk now saw Janetta as a traitor. "All of a sudden he says, 'Never mind that bullshit! I saw you wish those guys luck before the game. You just lost a friend,'" recalled Janetta. "It got embarrassing, so I congratulated Armstrong and Mahovlich and went out. I saw him later and he said, 'Go fuck yourself.'"

In Montreal, Mayor Jean Drapeau put a philosophic spin on the loss, saying, "The Canadiens gave it a good try – they have merely stepped out of the throne room for a breath of air." But Jean Béliveau and his teammates were in pain. "We had just as good a team as the Leafs," he said. "But they had Terry

The Montreal Canadiens' Genius GM

In his fourteen years as general manager of the Canadiens, Sam Pollock's astute hockey mind provided the team with the chemistry and talent to win nine Stanley Cups and Pollock a place in the Hockey Hall of Fame upon his retirement in 1978. Pollock's genius is tied to that of his mentor, Frank Selke, who came to the Canadiens in 1946 after resigning from the Maple Leafs. Selke pioneered the NHL's farm system of feeder teams, and Pollock was hired by the Canadiens in 1947, coaching and general managing several feeder teams in the Canadiens' stable, before becoming the Habs' GM in 1964. Legend has it that the Canadiens benefited from having a lock on the best talent coming out of Quebec, because of the "cultural option" granted to Montreal on the inauguration of the amateur draft in 1963. The Canadiens were allowed to draft two players of French-Canadian heritage before any other team could make its first draft choice. The cost to Montreal if they exercised this option was that they would have to forgo their regularly scheduled first and second picks in the draft order – and so the Canadiens used their cultural advantage just once, in the spring of 1969. "The only two players we ever got out of that thing were Rejean Houle and Marc Tardif," Pollock recalled, "but all kinds of crazy stories have been written." Pollock's brilliance lay in his eye for, and development of, talent, and his trades, which made the Canadiens even stronger. The cultural option was retired after the 1969 amateur draft, the year the Canadiens won their fourth Stanley Cup of the decade. (Frank Prazak/Hockey Hall of Fame)

Sawchuk, and I remember a save he made in the first period of a game in Toronto. I still try to figure out how he could have stopped that puck. . . . Nineteen sixty-seven hurt me, and I know it hurt my teammates, because we had a good team and we had no reason to lose."

The Stanley Cup parade, once again led by the 48th Highlanders pipe band, now made its way from Maple Leaf Gardens to Toronto's sleek new City Hall. As far as Punch Imlach was concerned, the eyes of the country should turn away from Montreal and its flashy World's Fair to the Leafs and their city in glory. "We sure as hell ruined the Canadiens' plans to display the Cup at Expo," he said, "and completed a very successful Centennial project on our own hook." The devastated Czechs at Expo 67, who were planning a party for the Cup and for Montreal, watched the display move to Ontario's pavilion that July and their Bohemian Crystal Trophy presented to the Leafs' Bob Pulford (who happened to be in Montreal for a meeting in his capacity as president of the new Players' Association), instead of to a victorious Canadien.

On Canada's official birthday, July 1, Pamela Anderson, a future star of American television, became the country's Centennial Baby by being the first

baby born on that day. It was the Summer of Love, and Canadian hockey fans had another hockey prodigy to look forward to as the great hope of the game.

Bobby Orr wore the colours of the Boston Bruins, but his hockey was pure Parry Sound, and he would change everything, remaking the position of defenceman with his weaving, whirling rushes, his creative play, and his ability to take a hit and to give one – with his fists, if need be. And together with lawyer Alan Eagleson, who would make Orr rich and himself richer, he changed the way hockey players did business.

With NHL expansion to six American cities that autumn, hockey was going to become a big-market business, and the prospect of a twelve-team league stoked Canadian fears that "our game" was being taken away. But Canada's hockey power brokers were not looking south to prove who was best at hockey, they were looking behind the Iron Curtain. Just five years after Expo 67, Montreal would host the inaugural game of an international rivalry that pitted western, capitalist Canada against the communist Soviets, to prove who really owned the game on ice. The contest would change the game – and the country.

Bobby Orr, heralded as the saviour of the moribund Boston Bruins franchise when he joined the team in 1966, takes flight as he scores the winning goal in the 1970 Stanley Cup final, to give the Bruins their first Cup championship since 1941. Orr, a defenceman, also won his first Art Ross Trophy as the NHL's leading scorer that same season, as well as the Norris as the league's best defenceman, the Hart as its most valuable player, and the Conn Smythe as the most valuable player of the Stanley Cup playoffs. *(Fred Keenan/Hockey Hall of Fame)*

CHAPTER 7

THE SOUL OF A NATION

In Moscow in January 1972, some hockey fans got together to warm themselves with a little vodka and talk about their favourite sport. One of the men, a Canadian named Gary Smith, who in his spare time played for the Moscow Maple Leafs (a team stocked with Western embassy staff, wearing castoff uniforms donated by their Toronto counterparts), had brought along a highly coveted reel of film: highlights of the 1971 Stanley Cup final between Montreal and Chicago. Though the vodka and the shared love of the game had done much to thaw the mutual mistrust between these capitalists and communists, it left Cold War prejudices frozen solid. "When they saw Bobby Hull skate," recalled Smith, "They thought the film had been speeded up."

Smith was more than a journeyman ringer playing for an embassy team in Moscow, protecting the integrity of Canada's game from assaults by opponents such as the muckers from the Tass News Agency team, or the grinders from Accordion Factory #7. Fluent in Russian, Smith had joined the Department of External Affairs after university and had gone through intensive diplomatic training for life behind the Iron Curtain. He was then dispatched to Moscow with his wife, where he served as the second secretary to the Canadian ambassador. And now Smith was on a diplomatic mission of the highest order.

"We talked about a best versus best series of friendly matches with games played in Canadian cities and some in the Soviet Union," he recalled. "There would be no trophy and no official championship would be at stake. We agreed Canada should be represented by its best professionals."

Three months earlier, Soviet premier Alexei Kosygin had had a first-hand look at Canada's professionals during a state visit, while taking in an NHL game in Vancouver, which had finally made it into the NHL in 1970. On a grey day in late October, the sophomore Canucks rose to the occasion by losing 6–0 to the Montreal Canadiens, establishing two ignominious club records in the process: it was the first time the Canucks were shutout at home and it was their second game in a row without scoring a goal.

Canadian prime minister Pierre Trudeau had brought up the idea of hockey diplomacy with Kosygin earlier that year while on his first state visit to the U.S.S.R. "Both Canadians and Soviets want competition re-established between their national teams," he said in Moscow, with hockey placed on the official cultural agenda. "This process will take some time, but it has begun." Trudeau saw hockey as a way to crowbar open the Iron Curtain a bit farther so that East and West might catch a glimpse of the other in a way that would encourage dialogue and help avert the mutually assured destruction the Cold War promised. "Let our best play your best," he said, "without any conditions."

Possibly more than anything, Trudeau hoped a Canada–U.S.S.R. contest would be a unifying force domestically, for the past year had seen the country rocked by the kidnapping of British trade commissioner James Cross and the murder of Quebec labour minister Pierre Laporte by the radical separatist group the Front de libération du Québec in the name of Quebec independence.

The idea to stage a tournament between the Soviet elite and the NHL was not Pierre Trudeau's, but he had the will and political muscle to make it happen – and his finger on a very sore Canadian spot. Having the country's best players – NHLers – compete internationally would right an injustice that Canadians had felt since the 1950s, when IIHF president John Ahearne refused to allow Canada to use professional players in the world hockey championships. As a result, and despite the noble efforts of Father David Bauer's

Roger Doucet

For a decade beginning in 1971, Roger Doucet was, if not the most famous, then the most mellifluous, voice on *Hockey Night in Canada*, his robust tenor ringing out "O Canada" in both official languages at the Montreal Forum. Formally trained, the versatile Doucet is best remembered by hockey fans as an essential part of the Forum's magic, but historians remember him as the man who changed the words to the national anthem during the run-up to the first Quebec referendum on sovereignty-association in 1980. Doucet asked his friend Prime Minister Pierre Trudeau if he could change the anthem while singing it live, Trudeau said he could, and Doucet struck a dual blow for Canada and for francophones by changing the second last line of the national anthem from "O Canada we stand on guard for thee" to "We stand on guard for rights and liberties." His version can still be heard in some renditions of "O Canada," which was officially proclaimed Canada's national anthem on July 1, 1980 – a century after it was first sung. (*Montreal Gazette/Peter Brosseau*)

national team, Canada had not beaten the Soviets for world hockey gold since the Trail Smoke Eaters upheld the nation's honour in 1961. The long international drought was a source of profound national humiliation.

Despite being the international hockey powerhouse for the past two decades, the Soviets were relatively new to the game. The Russians had played bandy, or field hockey on ice, since the 1890s, and bandy relied on the kind of precision, and coordinated passing for which the Russians would become renowned. To Soviet eyes, Canadian hockey was "bourgeois" because it encouraged individualism over teamwork. Nevertheless, in 1939, the Soviet authorities decided to introduce hockey as part of the regimen at Moscow's Physical Culture Institute, where promising youth were selected to be trained in their sports specialty, and so bring athletic glory to the Soviet Union. In 1954, just twenty-two years after they first saw the Canadian game played, the Soviets made their first appearance at the World Ice Hockey Championships and beat Canada 7–2 to win the gold medal.

The head coach of the Soviet national team was Anatoly Tarasov. A former player, Tarasov guided the Soviet team to three Olympic titles in 1964, 1968, and 1972, nine straight World Championship titles from 1963 to 1971, and eight European Championships in a row. A contradictory character, Tarasov used the theatrical techniques of Stanislavski and the harsh discipline of Stalin to mould his team – on the one hand encouraging creativity, and on the other, having players denounce each other for poor play or moral lassitude. Once, he even expelled the team's captain for smoking.

Tarasov professed an admiration of the Canadian system, and he cast a contest between hockey's two superpowers in the rhetoric of Cold War ideology. "There are two leading hockey schools – the Soviet and the Canadian professional," he said. "Facing the professionals with our team has always been the dream – to show the world that our system is supreme."

Diplomat Gary Smith was the first to begin the practical discussion with the Soviets about how such a tournament could work. Smith had arranged the details of Trudeau's visit to the U.S.S.R., and now one of his embassy duties was to read the Soviet newspapers for messages, hidden and otherwise, about Soviet intent regarding the international series. An article written under the penname the Snowman caught Smith's eye. "The Soviets have grown tired of defeating other nations year after year at the Izvestia Tournament, the World Hockey Championships and the Olympic Games," it said. "They want a new challenge and stronger competition." The Snowman was Boris Fedosov, the sports editor of *Izvestia*, a man in a position to be a conduit of official Soviet strategy. "I knew this is significant," said Smith. "This is big news because nothing appears in the paper without sanctioned political purpose. I phoned Boris Fedosov and he says, 'Come on over – we'll have a vodka and talk.'"

In April 1972, three months after Smith drank vodka and showed the Stanley Cup highlight film to the astonished Soviets in *Izvestia*'s offices, Canadian hockey officials sat down with their Soviet counterparts in Prague to hammer out the terms of what would be announced as the Summit Series – a showdown between the best Soviet and Canadian players, which would begin that September.

First, however, there were some surprises. Tarasov, who proclaimed, "We are disciples of Canadian hockey. . . . This can move world hockey forward," proved to be a loose cannon for Soviet authorities when he deviated from official policy and started speaking the truth. "I have watched the Canadians closely," he said. "We have revised the training process to also train the team for fighting. Yesterday, I was against a brutal and dirty way of playing, but these games of the world's strongest amateurs and professionals should show what's good and what's bad in both styles."

Soviet sports authorities had clashed with Tarasov's egocentric behaviour in the past, and his final unforgivable sin was indulging in capitalism. He had allowed his players to accept two hundred dollars each for a two-game exhibition series after their 1972 Olympic gold medal in Sapporo, Japan. That was enough. The man who had led his country to nine straight world amateur

Anatoly Tarasov, often called the Father of Soviet Hockey, was a great student of the Canadian game and wrote several books on hockey skills and strategies. A reliable, grinding forward on Moscow teams from 1946–53, Tarasov also coached while he played, then turned exclusively to coaching. From 1962–72 he co-coached the Soviet national men's hockey team to three straight Olympic gold medals, nine straight World Championships, and eight European titles. Autocratic toward his players and insubordinate toward his political bosses if he thought it would help the team, Tarasov was dismissed as the Soviet national coach just before the 1972 Summit Series. *(John Wilson/Hockey Hall of Fame)*

titles and three consecutive Olympic gold medals was given a permanent holiday, replaced on the bench by the gifted former player Vsevolod Bobrov.

Team Canada was beset by its own political war, one rife with a bitter irony. Bobby Hull, the Golden Jet, whose speed had astonished the Soviets when they saw him skate on the Stanley Cup highlight reel, was banished from the Canadian squad, also because of capitalism. Hull's sin was that he had left the NHL to play for the upstart World Hockey Association, a rival professional league that wooed the thirty-three-year-old Hull away from the Chicago Black Hawks with a $2.75-million contract, over ten years, to play for the Winnipeg Jets. The Golden Jet joined the WHA on June 27, 1972, accepting a cheque for $1 million as his advance, which was then a staggering sum to spend on a hockey player. Like other upstart professional leagues before it, the WHA had given notice that it would take the fast route to respectability: they would spend lavish amounts of money to lure superstars to their cause.

The NHL responded to Hull's defection by forbidding him to play for Team Canada, and the Canadian public went into attack mode. The *Toronto Sun* parodied the 1963 James Bond film "From Russia With Love" with a "To Russia With Hull" billboard campaign. Inside the newspaper, there was a message for readers to clip and send to the one man who could replace folly with sense: NHL president Clarence Campbell. "Dear Mr. Campbell," the message read, "I want Bobby Hull to play for Canada. Please do everything you can to see that he does. We've waited for the Russia-Canada series for years and it would be a disgrace if we don't put our very best team on the ice. There's an NHL rule that each team has to use its very best players. Shouldn't the same rule apply to Canada?"

Trudeau, who did not need this setback to spoil his hockey diplomacy, sent Campbell a telegram to remind him of "the intense interest which I share with millions of Canadians . . . that Canada should be represented by its best hockey players, including Bobby Hull." Campbell arrogantly told the prime minister he had been "misled," but the truth was that Campbell's bosses, the NHL owners, couldn't afford to allow Bobby Hull to play for Canada as they would effectively be ending their monopoly over premier hockey talent. "This is absolutely crazy," said Hull, speaking for the nation. "I'm a Canadian and I want to play for my country. I don't know why the NHL has to be so petty over this. I want to do this for Canada."

Hull's desire wasn't enough, and he was obliged to watch from the stands, but the hockey gods struck back via another Bobby, the one surnamed Orr, who, at age twenty-four, while playing defence for Boston, had reinvented the game. Orr had been reformulating the game both on and off the ice since he was a boy. In 1960, Boston Bruins' general manager Lynn Patrick, along with

Wren Blair, a coach for their minor league affiliate in Kingston, had been scouting fourteen-year-old players at an Ontario bantam tournament when they spotted a five-foot-two-inch, 110-pound, twelve-year-old Pee Wee who shouldn't have been playing in the older boys' tournament, but was clearly the best player on the ice. Blair hurried down from the stands to find out the boy's name, and whether any NHL team owned his rights.

Robert Gordon Orr was free, but not for long. The Bruins quickly befriended Orr's family in Parry Sound, Ontario, and "protected" Bobby from other teams until 1962, when he signed a "C" form – a standard contract that gave Boston his hockey rights for life. Any player then signing a "C" form could expect a bonus of $100, but the Bruins lavished $2,800 on Orr, including $900 worth of new stucco for the family home, and the promise of a second-hand car – which Bobby was still too young to drive.

In 1963, Alan Eagleson, then a young Toronto lawyer and Tory MPP, spoke at a sports banquet attended by Bobby Orr's father. Eagleson was known to be acting as an agent for some Toronto Maple Leafs players who had begun to explore the world of representation, and Orr's father approached the lawyer to speak about his talented son's future. The relationship that would revolutionize pro hockey had begun, with, as Orr later recalled, a deceptive innocence. "My mother wanted to know what he was going to charge," he said. "I remember Al looking away as if he was adding up figures in his head; then he turned to my mother and said, 'I'll tell you what Mrs. Orr, if Bobby makes some money, then I will make some money.'"

In the summer of 1972, as the nation geared up for the cold war on ice against the Soviets, there was bad news. The man who had won the Calder Trophy as rookie of the year in 1967; three Hart Trophies as league MVP; the first of two Art Ross trophies as NHL scoring leader; and five of his eight straight Norris Trophies as best defenceman, would also be watching from the stands. Orr had suffered a knee injury in his rookie season, the first in a series of knee injuries, surgeries, and shaky recoveries that would see him compared to the Greek warrior Achilles, invulnerable but for one fatal flaw. Although he had gone to Team Canada's training camp and skated with the rest of the team, it was obvious that Orr's knees were not healed enough to let him unleash his whirlwind play against the Soviets.

The Canadian team did not include the Bobbys Hull and Orr, but it boasted an A-list of NHL hockey talent: goalies Ken Dryden and Tony Esposito; defence stars Brad Park, Guy Lapointe, and Serge Savard; and forwards both gritty and gifted in Bobby Clarke, Yvan Cournoyer, Rod Gilbert, Vic Hadfield, Phil Esposito, Jean Ratelle, Ron Ellis, Gilbert Perreault, Paul Henderson, and Frank Mahovlich.

When Alan Eagleson signed Bobby Orr to the Boston Bruins in 1966 for $80,000 over two years, plus a $25,000 signing bonus, it was the richest rookie contract in NHL history and it forever changed the financial landscape for pro hockey players. Orr was Eagleson's meal ticket, and this deal cemented his reputation as *the* sports agent. (*Graphic Artists/Hockey Hall of Fame*)

Although he was a defenceman, Bobby Orr's speed and skill won him two Art Ross Trophies as the NHL's top point scorer. Orr could control the pace of a game, and his end-to-end rushes often looked as if he were skating around pylons. When Gordie Howe was asked what Orr's best move was, he replied, "Just putting on his fucking skates." New York Rangers star Harry Howell, who won the Norris Trophy as the NHL's top defenceman in Orr's rookie season, said, "I'm glad I won it now because it's going to belong to Bobby Orr from now on." Orr won the Norris eight times in his injury-riddled twelve-season NHL career. *(Graphic Artists/Hockey Hall of Fame)*

The Canadian media stoked the nation's belief that the Soviet domination of the world championships was an aberration born of an injustice that would now be corrected by Canada's – and the capitalist world's – glittering professionals: the best of the best league on earth. "Against our boys, the Russians will be trounced," wrote *Globe and Mail* sports columnist Dick Beddoes, who was just one voice in a large national chorus of sportswriters singing the same tune. "Either we take every single game, or I'll eat this column – shredded at high noon in a bowl of borscht on the front steps of the Russian Embassy."

This arrogance also infected Team Canada, whose scouts had gone to Moscow in August 1972 to watch the Soviets train, and had come home dismissive of the twenty-year-old goalie Vladislav Tretiak, calling him a sieve. The Canadian scouts didn't realize they had been tricked. The Soviet team had been split in two, and Tretiak was backstopping the weak half. Tretiak, who was getting married the next day, was also seriously hungover from his stag party the night before. Hockey hadn't been the first thing on his mind.

The Soviets, on the other hand, were humble and nervous. Gary Smith was assigned to fly over with the team, and as the Aeroflot jet made its way to

Tommy Nayler

As the Toronto Maple Leafs' equipment manager for more than a half century, Tommy Nayler was one of the most influential people in hockey. He invented the portable skate sharpener, ankle and tendon guards, designed the goalie trapper and blocker out of baseball gloves, redesigned the skate boot to better fit the foot, altered the skate blade for speed and mobility, and created body armour for players. Nayler's skills were sought by everyone from visiting Soviet teams to hockey equipment manufacturers, who were not embarrassed to copy his designs and mass produce them. "I've never bothered to protect any of it," said Nayler. "The manufacturers would just make one change and go right ahead – I've never made a nickel out of most of it." Nayler's contribution to the development of hockey was profound, and many hockey experts hope he wins a posthumous place in the Hockey Hall of Fame. (*Hockey Hall of Fame*)

Montreal's Dorval Airport, some of the players approached him like wide-eyed tourists. "Most of the young guys just wanted to talk about Bobby Orr, Bobby Hull and the curved stick," Smith said. "I can tell they're in awe and quite uncertain of what to expect." Once in Montreal, the Soviet players were astonished by the huge crowd at the airport that greeted them (and sized them up), and more tellingly, at the creature comforts of the decadent capitalist system they had been taught to reject. "They are very pleased with their accommodations in the Queen Elizabeth Hotel," said Smith, "and the warm reception they've received here. But more than anything, all of the players marvel at the fresh food and fruit offered at breakfast."

The Soviet players were well aware of the derisory things being said about them. It was hard not to be, as it was out in the open. "We could see from their gestures, the way they acted and the remarks they made during our practice, that they didn't consider us worthy opponents," said Alexander Yakushev, a huge Soviet winger nicknamed the Big Yak. "We could hear their laughter. We could feel it – such arrogance."

On top of this hostility came the ugly realities of the Cold War, and in the most banal of ways. A Canadian now living in Montreal, who had been in Czechoslovakia when the Soviets had invaded in August 1968 to liberate it from the reforms begun earlier that year during the Prague Spring, now wanted justice. His car had been destroyed during the invasion, and after failing to be reimbursed by the conquering army, he took the matter to a Quebec court, which issued an order to seize the Soviet team's hockey equipment until the debt of $1,889.00 was paid. After years of hope and months of careful planning, the Summit Series had been stopped in its tracks by history, and the Soviets deeply resented what they saw as political meddling in sport. Hockey Canada and the Trudeau government were caught between a legal precedent and Soviet pressure, but Alan Eagleson was not.

Eagleson was a key figure on the board of Hockey Canada and had been keen to augment his power by making the Summit Series happen. He was not going to let his success be ruined by some wrecked car. So Eagleson did what he had always done, he played by his own rules. On September 2, the morning of the first game, he wrote a personal cheque for the damaged car and gave it to the man's lawyer at the Queen Elizabeth Hotel.

The series was set to begin at 8:00 that evening, with TV cameras in place to beam the predicted slaughter of the Soviet team to tens of millions of viewers in Canada, the United States, Europe, Japan, and the U.S.S.R. Foster Hewitt, the seventy-year-old legend who had called the play-by-play the first time the Soviets played in Canada at Maple Leaf Gardens on November 22, 1957, would be calling his last great assignment, adding another layer of historical import to the event. Even Montreal *Star* columnist John Robertson, who had been one of the few Cassandras in journalism in doubting the Canadians' automatic triumph, was taken by the overwhelming sense of history. "This is the most important hockey event of our time," he wrote. "From the moment the puck is dropped it will dwarf in stature the NHL playoffs, the Stanley Cup, and any other hockey championship you can name. But the long-suffering hockey fan suddenly has something real, something meaningful to get excited about – international hockey, where he can root for a country instead of a corporation of grasping little men."

Pierre Trudeau, his red lapel rose not yet wilting under the oppressive heat in the Forum, must have hoped as he dropped the ceremonial puck that the Soviets wouldn't lose by much, for their humiliation on ice could deep freeze the Canadian-Soviet relations he had worked so hard to thaw. Trudeau's confidence in Canada's victory was such that he had announced a general election the day before, expecting his Liberals to win another term come November from Canadians swelled, in part, by gratitude for his gift to them on ice.

Not everyone was so optimistic, especially when they saw the Russians on the ice for the first time. Creelman MacArthur, an entrepreneur from Nova Scotia, had managed to buy tickets to Game 1 in Montreal and to all four games in the U.S.S.R. "The Russians' warm-up, their tic-tac-toe precision passing is just unbelievable," he told his seatmates, while watching the pre-game practice before the first match. "My seatmates would reply, 'Well, that's fine when they are warming up and that's fine when you're not playing a real game 'cause in a real game it doesn't work that way.'"

Another worrier was Canada's coach, Harry Sinden. He had played against the Russians in the 1957 Canada-Soviet game, and again in the 1958 World Championship as a member of the Whitby Dunlops. He knew all about Soviet skill and discipline, but the trick lay in getting his confident players to believe him. Sinden had a lot of personal stock riding on the series. After quitting his job as the coach of the Boston Bruins over a salary dispute, he had lobbied hard for the Team Canada job as a certain way to raise his hockey worth. When he and his assistant, John Ferguson, had gentlemanly pre-Series drinks with the Soviet coaches, they were astonished to discover the "enemy" knew everything about them. That August, Soviet assistant coach Boris Kulagin had spent two weeks at Maple Leaf Gardens watching every Team Canada training camp practice and intra-squad game, while coach Vsevolod Bobrov had watched films of the 1971 and '72 Stanley Cup playoffs to create profiles of the Canadian players.

It wasn't the intelligence the Soviets had compiled on the Canadians that most concerned Sinden, it was their superior conditioning, born of year-round workouts modelled on the fitness program of Canadian hockey guru Lloyd Percival. Eight years earlier, Percival had assessed Soviet hockey and saw a vastly superior standard than Canada's. "Today, Russian hockey players are skating an average of four miles an hour faster than NHL players and keeping up the faster pace twice as long or more," he said. "The Russian players are not only in far better shape than NHL players, but they are better coached in theory and technique of the game."

Harry Sinden might have disagreed about the coaching and technique, but he was concerned about the Soviets' level of fitness. "I'm nervous as hell," he told journalist John Robertson. "My main worry is the pace they play at." Thirty seconds after the opening faceoff, Sinden must have felt a little better when Phil Esposito scored Team Canada's first goal. When the Toronto Maple Leafs' Paul Henderson scored again six minutes later, it looked as if the prediction by Team Canada scouts of a 15–0 rout might be conservative.

The Soviets thought the opposite. Before Game 1, Bobrov told his nervous players not to panic if the Canadians scored a couple of quick goals. His team could skate and pass better than the Canadians, and if they stuck to their plan, they would win. The great goalie Jacques Plante had even visited their dressing room before the opening faceoff to give Vladislav Tretiak some tips on stopping the Canadians. The Soviets, remembering these lessons, decided to relax – they

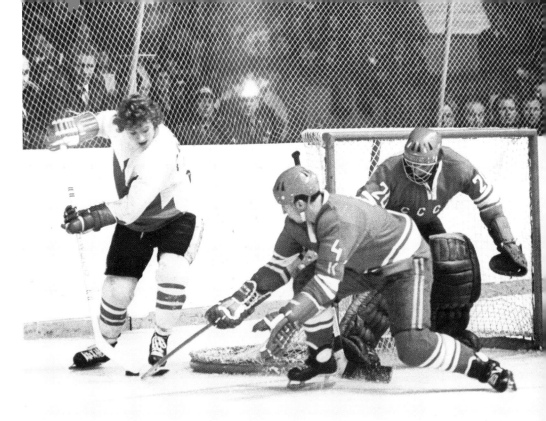

Bobby Clarke (left) was one of only five Team Canada players to play all eight games of the 1972 series. *(Denis Brodeur)*

Valeri Kharlamov (right), a dazzling left-winger who could stickhandle and pass with breathtaking precision, was so fast that he could beat two Canadian defencemen just by skating around them. *(Denis Brodeur)*

Peter Mahovlich, the younger brother of Frank, chases Soviet Alexander Yakushev, nicknamed the Big Yak. A speedy playmaker, Yakushev could blow by Canadian defenders at will.

(*Denis Brodeur*)

Phil Esposito, the series' top point scorer, was the heart of Team Canada, and wore his on the sleeve of his jersey. Here, he reams out Soviet defenceman Alexander Ragulin.

(*Denis Brodeur*)

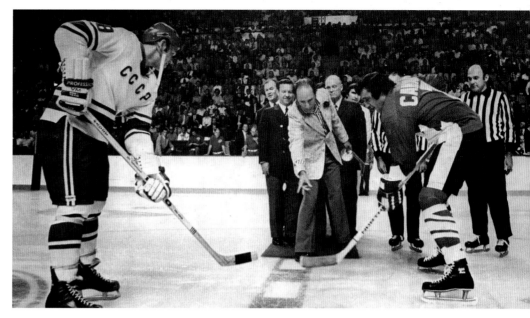

Canada's prime minister Pierre Trudeau, facing re-election, had great hopes for Team Canada in their Summit Series against the Soviets. Trudeau had been crucial in making the historic series happen, seeing the inevitable Canadian victory as something to unite a nation rocked by terrorism in Quebec and discontent in the West. Despite his championing of the national game, Trudeau would win a slim minority government. *(Peter Bregg/Canadian Press)*

had nothing to lose. It was then that the Canadians received a fifty-three-minute lesson in hubris.

The Soviets scored the next four goals of the game, and the stunned Montreal fans, who knew their hockey, began to boo the Canadians and to cheer the Soviets, particularly the speedy, creative line of Alexander Yakushev, Evgeny Zimin, and Vladimir Shadrin, who repeatedly criss-crossed through the Canadian lines, leaving defencemen spinning in their wake. They accounted for two of Team Soviet's onslaught of seven goals.

Some former Canadian National Team members were at the game, including Derek Holmes, who played for Canada in the 1960s and who would become head of Hockey Canada. They knew how good the Soviets were and later said that they had quietly gloated as the game slipped away from Team Canada, who were supposed to accomplish easily what the National Team had failed to do. "We were sitting near the bench," Holmes said. "I remember [that] the Russian Valeri Vasiliev, as he was leaving the ice, winked at me and nodded, as if it were an affirmation. The Canadian players' mouths were open and they were gasping for air."

Even though Bobby Clarke added another goal for Canada, the predicted drubbing was correct, but for the drubbee: the final score was Canada 3, the U.S.S.R. 7. The headline on the front page of the *Globe and Mail* on September 4 spoke to much more than the game, it spoke to a nation in crisis: "Canada Mourns Hockey Myth: Better? Just 100 per cent better." Within the space of three hours the night before, Canada's hockey superiority at the professional level had been humbled beyond belief.

The Canadians approached Game 2 at Maple Leaf Gardens with a ruthless attitude that began at the top: Harry Sinden benched the New York Rangers' star Gilbert–Ratelle–Hadfield line, which the season before had combined for

an NHL record of 312 points. They had also been on the ice for three Soviet goals in Game 1 – one of them shorthanded. The message was clear: the wounded would be shot. The line was not seen again in the series.

In Maple Leaf Gardens, with Canadian flags hanging everywhere like talismans, a nervous sold-out crowd waited to see if Team Canada would show the world that the Soviet victory had been a fluke. Goalie Tony Esposito, replacing Ken Dryden after his disastrous outing, gave the fans hope by making two brilliant saves early in the game, which in turn gave his team confidence. The Canadians remembered how to forecheck, and to backcheck, and to pass. They also remembered how to "take the man," and they seasoned the remembrance with violent abandon. "A lot of high sticks were rubbed under the noses of the Soviets," says Ken Dryden, who had an intimate view of his team's tactics from his seat on the bench. "There were also a few cheap shots. If I had been one of the Russian players, I'd have thought, 'These Canadians must be awfully brutal to be going around and doing these things all the time.'"

Canada's star players came through, and on goals by Cournoyer, the Mahovlich brothers – Frank and Peter – and team captain Phil Esposito, the Canadians evened the series with a 4–1 victory. Peter Mahovlich's goal was particularly effective in building Canadian confidence, for not only had he beaten a Soviet player one-on-one for what seemed like the first time in the series, he had done it while killing a penalty, to give Canada a two-goal lead. Nevertheless, critics said that Canada had just responded to Soviet skill and elegance with thuggery. The team's rough tactics divided the country into two camps: the people who were clamouring for Team Canada to win at all costs against those who had seen – or remembered – how hockey could be played, courtesy of the Soviets.

He scored only one goal in the series, but Peter Mahovlich's short-handed, solo display of virtuosity while notching a third period tally less than a minute after the Soviets had scored cemented the critical Game 2 win for Canada.

(*Graphic Artists/Hockey Hall of Fame*)

For assistant coach John Ferguson, Team Canada's critics were a bunch of ignorant aesthetes. "Hell, these guys can't know much about the game," he said. "That's the way it's been played for the past fifty years, and that's the way it'll be played for another fifty. Has hockey ever been anything else but a street game? After a century, are we going to change it to suit the fine-arts crowd?"

Worrying about violence in hockey would seem self-indulgent by the time the next game was set to go in Winnipeg on September 6. The day before, members of Black September, a terrorist group connected to the Palestine Liberation Organization, had taken Israeli athletes hostage at the Munich Olympic games. By nightfall, eleven Israelis were dead, killed by the terrorists during a gun battle with German police. Before the start of Game 3, fans and players paused in silent remembrance of the dead, but the memorial lasted just thirty seconds, and the Summit Series organizers were swiftly criticized for their parsimonious half-minute gesture toward an act that had stained not just the sporting world but the entire planet, with the blood of the innocent.

That world seemed far away to those who were focused on the third game, believing it would be the one in which Canada would break the "Russian machine" once and for all. The popular press had fed the idea that the Russians were robots, and that once Canada had them on the run, their wiring would short-circuit, and the Summit Series would be over. But Canada's playing style seemed to fit better the communist stereotype: a proletarian dump, chase, and thump style that contrasted poorly with the nimble entrepreneurship showed by the Soviets, who used precision passing, forechecking, and backchecking to create a breakout play, or force a Canadian mistake that could be converted into a goal.

That night, however, the Canadians' style was paying off. When Paul Henderson scored at 13:47 of the second period, Canada had a 4–2 lead. It looked as if they had found their killer instinct, and would head to the next game in Vancouver with a reassuring momentum. The Soviets thought otherwise. Within five minutes their Kid Line (or Headache Line) of twenty-one-year-olds, Lebedev, Bodunov, and Anisin, had added two goals to tie the game, and so it remained. Harry Sinden considered it a lucky escape. "A tie is as exciting as kissing your sister," he said afterward, adding that, "for the last ten minutes tonight that hockey game looked like Raquel Welch to me."

The Series was tied at one win, one loss, and one tie each as the teams took the ice in Vancouver. Even though Vancouver fans were generous and forgiving toward their NHL Canucks, just two seasons old, they showed a hard heart toward Team Canada, and some skeptics even booed them during the pre-game warm-up. On the ice, the Canadians, who desperately wanted to head to the U.S.S.R. with a home-game win, showed their wracked nerves. Bill

Goldsworthy, under orders to keep the Soviets at bay without taking any stupid penalties, took two of them, and boos rang out in the Pacific Coliseum. Then the lethal Soviet power play went to work, and Boris Mikhailov put the Soviets up 2–0 on two almost identical deflections during each man-advantage. The Vancouverites booed at full volume.

The young Buffalo Sabres' star Gilbert Perreault made a flashy end-to-end rush to score, and Rod Gilbert, back in the lineup, appeared to have tied the game, until his goal was disallowed on the grounds that he had kicked it in. The Soviets scored twice more, and now Team Canada's goalie Ken Dryden received mocking cheers when he simply stopped the puck. Sarcasm then gave way to scorn when the Soviets scored again to make it 4–1, and the people in the stands added to their repertoire of displeasure, much to the delight of the Soviets. "Fans started throwing things to show disapproval of Canadian players," said Soviet centre Vladimir Shadrin. "I like Canadian fans because they know hockey. They are experts, they notice the smallest details. That's what makes them different from Soviet fans who are not educated in hockey."

It was not necessary to be a hockey expert to see Canada's 5–2 loss in their final home game as a dark harbinger of things to come, and the Vancouver fans expressed the entire country's bitter disappointment when they lustily booed Team Canada off the ice. Team Canada answered back when their sweaty, drained captain, Phil Esposito, told CTV's Johnny Esaw that the Canadian fans were not helping a cause in which the players still believed. "For the people across Canada: We tried, we gave it our best. For the people who booed us, geez, I'm really – all of us guys are really – disheartened and we're disillusioned and we're disappointed in some of the people. We cannot believe the bad press we've got, the booing in our own buildings. Every one of us guys, thirty-five guys who came out to play for Team Canada, we did it because we love our country." Then Esposito added a parting shot that showed Team Canada thought the booing bordered on being treasonous. "If the fans in Russia boo their players like some of the Canadian fans – I'm not saying all of them – booed us, then I'll come back and apologize to each and every one of the Canadians."

Team Canada's lame march on Moscow was interrupted by games scheduled against Sweden as part of the fiftieth anniversary celebration of Swedish hockey. The Swedes thought of Canadian hockey as Wild West lawlessness on ice, a violent parody of the skilled European game, and just as dangerous after the bloodletting in the arena was over, with Canadian players and their travelling sideshow of fans behaving like modern Barbarians as they celebrated victories by boozing and brawling. The Canadians thought the Swedes were hypocrites at best, that they were players who used their sticks like champion

Tretiak's Mask

Some hockey fans might have been awed by the Soviet goalie's hockey talent, but others thought his "bird cage" mask was a bulky totem of Eastern European dullness. There were also practical reasons to dislike the mask: the helmet shifted during play and wasn't designed to absorb the impact of a puck. By the end of the decade, though, the sleek, moulded fibreglass masks of the NHL had been ruled unsafe by the Canadian Standards Association. After Philadelphia's Vezina Trophy–winning Bernie Parent had to end his career in 1979 after taking a stick to the eye through his moulded mask, many goalies switched to the bird cage. Dave Dryden, the NHL–goaltending brother of Ken, took one of Greg Harrison's classic masks and cut out the face area, replacing it with wire, thus launching the next generation of NHL combination masks. *(Hockey Hall of Fame)*

fencers and flung themselves to the ice like Olympic divers but would never account for their crimes and theatrics in the honest way the Canadians preferred: like boxers. In Game 2, Sweden's Ulf Sterner sliced open Wayne Cashman's tongue so badly with his stick that Cashman was unable to play when the Summit Series resumed in the Soviet Union.

The two-game series in Stockholm was supposed to allow the Canadians to adjust to the new time zone and, more importantly, to the larger European-size ice. The ice surface seemed so huge to Canadian defenceman Pat Stapleton that he called it "Lake Erie with a roof over it." Canada prevailed in the first game and managed to eke out a tie in the final minute of the second. Team Canada could now claim that, so far, they were unbeaten on their road trip, but their play had not been pretty. Even the Canadian ambassador to Sweden called the team hooligans for their rough play both on and off the ice. Team Canada wasn't deaf, and now, hearing that some fans back in Canada were rooting for the Russians, they closed ranks. As many a troubled team had learned before them, and has learned since, a road trip can cure what ails. And the road trip was just getting started.

When the Canadians arrived in Moscow, they encountered a society whose cultural identity was enshrined in monoliths such as the Bolshoi Ballet and Red Square, and whose economic life provided none of the consumer goods that defined the good life for the average Canadian. Even basic food items, such as a tough old chicken, were luxuries there, as it could cost one-twentieth of a teacher's monthly salary.

The three thousand Canadian fans – including hockey icon Cyclone Taylor – who travelled with Team Canada had left home confident that they came from the greatest country in the free world, and arrived to a cold and frightening welcome. Soldiers toting machine-guns patrolled the streets – and the ice rink – and the Canadians were told by the Soviets to keep their patriotism under wraps. But under the surface coldness, the Soviets were passionate about hockey, their national sport. An estimated 50 million people across the fifteen republics constituting the Soviet Union would be watching the series on TV – more than 20 per cent of the total population. Ordinary Soviet citizens could not get a ticket to the game unless they had connections. "The tickets were absolutely not on sale, they were distributed among organizations," says Andrei Petrov, who was just ten when he attended the first Summit game on Russian soil – his first hockey game – along with "prominent people like cosmonauts [who] had a free passage to any sporting event, fans from Canada. My father was lucky enough to win some kind of a 'draw' for two tickets in his organization."

Team Canada went into Game 5 facing a difficult task. In order to win the Series, and reclaim not just international honour, but national respect, they had to win three of the four games. The mood in Moscow's Luzhniki Arena was tense, with armed police patrolling the aisles, and the Canadian fans under a Soviet directive to refrain from any boisterous behaviour, or face expulsion.

The game got off to an ignominious start for the Canadians. Captain Phil Esposito stepped forward as he was introduced, and his skate blade caught the broken stem of one of the flowers handed out to the players. Esposito landed hard on the ice, and the Canadian fans, instead of howling in derision, as they might have done at home, did something extraordinary: they applauded him. It was an affectionate gesture to a beleaguered team. Esposito responded in kind, raising himself to one knee and sweeping the ice with a lavish bow, which provoked even louder cheering from the Canadians. Vladislav Tretiak later said that Esposito's elegant, self-mocking gesture was that of "an artist."

For the first two periods, the Canadians played like kids on a frozen pond, with a creative, devil-may-care attitude that gave them a 3–0 lead – a score that might have been double but for the superb play of goalie Tretiak. But then, despite being up 4–1 almost halfway through the third period, Team Canada let the Soviets back into the game. And with a little more than five minutes left, the Soviet team had a 5–4 lead, and they would not give it up.

Canada, having lost two straight games to the Soviets (interrupted by their Swedish adventure), would now have to win three straight. It seemed impossible that they would, and yet this time, the Canadian fans did not boo their team off the ice. Instead they saluted them. "We gave the team a standing ovation and sang 'O Canada' at the top of our lungs," said fan Brian Gallery, who had made the trip to Moscow. "We feel we're part of Team Canada, too, and we want to do whatever we can to rattle the Russians." That sentiment, combined with the

While being introduced to Moscow fans in Game 5, Phil Esposito slipped on one of the flowers that had been handed to players and landed hard on the seat of his hockey pants. The charismatic, creative Espo promptly gave himself a truer introduction, and turned Soviet laughter into cheers, by taking a bow and blowing a kiss to the crowd, a gesture he later insisted was aimed at the unamused Soviet leader, Leonid Brezhnev. (*Denis Brodeur*)

thousands of telegrams pouring in that wished the players well, lifted Team Canada's spirits. "We knew we were in a corner," said Harry Sinden, but the ovation and the support from fans in Moscow and at home "made us feel as though we just couldn't let the country down."

Team Canada responded, winning the next two games. Their supporters, seeing the players' new-found strength and confidence, began a chant that grew louder and louder: "Da, da Canada! Nyet, nyet Soviet!" (Yes, Canada! No, Soviets!) Winning served to intensify the cold war on ice.

In Game 6, feisty Soviet left-winger Valeri Kharlamov, who had burned the Canadians for six points thus far, was attacked so viciously that the incident is still remembered in the Soviet Union as the great "crime" of the series. After Canada's John Ferguson told the Philadelphia Flyers' scrappy Bobby Clarke to do something about Kharlamov, Clarke hunted down the Soviet star and dealt him a two-handed slash on the left ankle of such ferocity that he fractured it. But the attack paid off: the hobbled Kharlamov would score just one more point – an assist – against the Canadians in the final game.

The Canadians suspected that the Soviets would tilt the lumpy ice of Luzhniki Arena any way they could to make victory theirs, and the cold war on ice became even colder when Gary Smith and other Team Canada officials were invited to a most unusual rendezvous. "We were summoned to a meeting in the basement of the arena. Apparently, one of the referees, the one who was our choice, was unable to work Game 8 and would have to be replaced," says Gary Smith. "Our coaches and management were invited – theirs were not. I knew they were up to something."

On September 28, millions of Canadians tuned in to the game of the century. Television sets were hauled into school gymnasia; offices were shut down;

Dynamic and intense, Phil Esposito notched his most important points by scoring two goals and adding two assists in Game 8, propelling Canada to victory. *(Denis Brodeur)*

travellers paused on their journey to find a way to watch; and it has become enshrined in Series lore that anyone who cannot answer the question "Where were you in '72?" was not yet born, such was the draw of the final game of the Summit Series, now dead even at three wins, three losses, and one tie.

The first period ended with the teams tied at 2, but the referee switch had rattled the Canadians. The crisis came when journeyman left-winger Jean-Paul Parise received a penalty for interference, which he vigorously protested. "You can't be called for interference when the other guy has the puck," he said later, but at the time, he made his point by breaking his stick on the ice.

The West German referee, Josef Kompalla, was as loathed as his country-man and fellow official Franz Baader by the Canadians, who nicknamed them "Badder and Worse." The duo had given Canada nineteen penalties to Sweden's six during the Stockholm interlude, and then struck again in Game 6, giving eight penalties to Canada and just three to the Soviets. Team Canada had been told that they would never see Kompalla again, and now, after being subbed into the game by Soviet machinations, he gave Parise a ten-minute misconduct. Parise went berserk, skating up to Kompalla with his stick raised as if to decapitate the referee, and repeating the gesture. Kompalla tossed him from the game; the Canadian bench tossed two chairs onto the ice. The game was halted.

Gary Smith, watching in horror, saw years of high-level international diplomacy crashing before his eyes, the consequences too awful to contemplate. "After all the effort that had gone into this, and the reasons for the prime minister wanting to have this series, I'm thinking we're headed for a disaster," he said. "Everything is starting to come apart quickly. Let's get the series over."

As the Canadian fans chanted "Let's go home, let's go home," Alan Eagleson tried on the diplomatic mantle and hurried over to the Canadian bench to calm things down. Up in the stands, Gary Smith, sitting with injured defenceman Bobby Orr, was not hopeful. "You can see we're being shafted," Orr said. "Do we have to throw chairs on the ice?" said Smith. "What the hell – this is crazy – do we really have to do this?" Orr replied, "Gary, you've been here too long."

With one period left in Game 8, the Canadians were losing 5–3, and even a tie looked optimistic. And a tie would be no good. Alan Eagleson had learned the awful news during the intermission: the Soviets were going to declare themselves victors on total goals if Game 8 ended in a draw. By the time Team Canada came on the ice in that third period they, too, knew that it was victory or nothing. Phil Esposito – now a favourite of the Soviets because of his spirited play – started the climb back. At 2:27 of the third period, Esposito whacked home his own rebound. Team Canada shifted up a gear, calmly, with purpose, and ten minutes later, Esposito shook off two Soviet players to fire a hard shot at Tretiak. The rebound popped onto the stick of Yvan Cournoyer, and with seven minutes left, the game was tied.

Alan Eagleson, sitting in the front row at centre ice, saw neither the referee signal a goal nor the red flash of the goal light, although the TV replay later showed that the referee had signalled a goal almost immediately. Eagleson didn't have the benefit of replay, but he had recent memory: the same non-signal had happened when Paul Henderson scored the winning goal in the previous game. It looked to Eagleson as if the Soviets were playing dirty. He leapt from his seat and over a five-foot wall into the middle of a group of startled Soviet police. After some bumping and shoving, he was marched away by half a dozen military policemen. The Canadian players were still celebrating the goal, but Pete Mahovlich saw what was happening, as did defenceman Gary Bergman. Charging to Eagleson's defence, the players were joined by Wayne Cashman and Bill Goldsworthy, who had not dressed for the game. Even coach Harry Sinden pitched in as they fought off the police, who, startled by the Canadians' assault, let Eagleson go.

The players led the rescued agent across the ice to the safety of the Canadian bench, and en route, Eagleson raised his middle finger in a crude salute to the goal judge, while another Canadian official, also in jacket and tie, did the same. Moments after his gesture, police reinforcements flooded the arena. "It feels like war on ice. But I see now, it's like a real war: two countries, two systems fighting to show the world who is most powerful," said Soviet right-winger Boris Mikhailov. "We're taught to do what's necessary – to win at all costs."

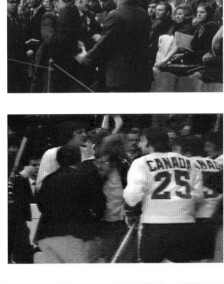

When it looked as if a Canadian tying goal had been disallowed with just over seven minutes left to play in the final game, Alan Eagleson's famous temper erupted. He jumped over the boards to sort out the officials but was seized en route by Soviet militia men. Eagleson was freed by stick-wielding members of Team Canada, and the goal was allowed.

The Chin Family

Paul Henderson received his first set of hockey equipment from the Chin family of Lucknow, Ontario, who ran the town's only Chinese restaurant. Three of the oldest Chin brothers, Albert, George, and Bill, played on a line for Lucknow's Junior B team and were invited to a Toronto Maple Leafs training camp in the mid-1940s. Albert later coached the PeeWee Paul Henderson, who was using rolled up Eaton's catalogues for shin pads, as his father needed all the spare money he had for baseball equipment for the young ballplayers he coached. The Chins saw a worthy cause in the promising Henderson, and their generosity became a gift to the nation when Henderson scored to win the 1972 Series for Canada. *(Imperial Oil – Turofsky/Hockey Hall of Fame)*

With one minute left in the last game, Creelman MacArthur, a fan from Nova Scotia, was sure that the tournament was going to end in failure, and started to make his way out of the arena. "I got out of my seat realizing that there would be a rush to the exits and the buses," he recalled. "I thought, 'This is going to be a tie game, and this is going to be a tie series, so let's go back to the hotel and get in the Romanian champagne.'"

Meanwhile, Sinden wanted to send out the Clarke–Henderson–Ellis line, but Esposito's line wouldn't come off. Henderson shouted three times, and finally Pete Mahovlich came off and Henderson went on, but Cournoyer was on the far side of the ice, and Esposito was a man possessed. He had no intention of leaving the ice unless the police came to take him away too.

Cournoyer fired a long diagonal pass just behind Henderson. With the puck loose in the Soviet corner, Phil Esposito beat three Soviet players to it, then fired it at Tretiak from twelve feet out. There was a rebound. And now Paul Henderson, miraculously alone in front of Tretiak, could win it all for Canada. He shot the puck, and Tretiak made a pad save going down. The puck came back to Henderson, and he shot again.

A cheer went up across Canada, rising on a great wave of pride and relief and elation. Team Canada had not swept the Soviets, as the pundits had so arrogantly predicted but had done something better. They had been at the edge of devastating defeat and in a characteristically Canadian fashion had fought

It is the most famous goal in Canadian hockey history. At 19:26 of the third period in the final game of the series, Toronto Maple Leafs forward Paul Henderson scored his third game-winning goal in a row, and Canada defeated the Soviets. The dramatic goal provided catharsis for the entire country and is remembered as a defining moment for a generation. *(Frank Lennon/Canadian Press)*

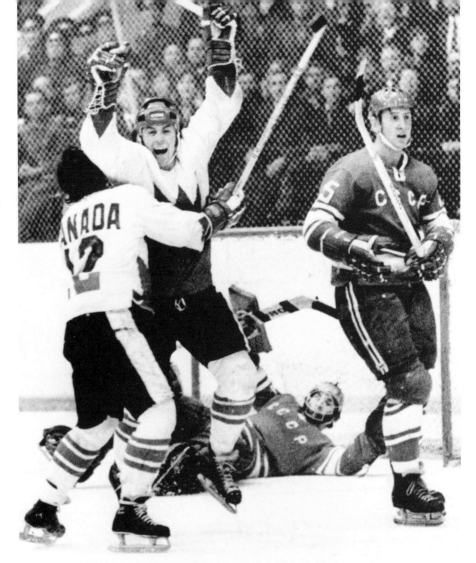

until the end: even though this time the war was on ice, it was still "do or die," and Team Canada had proved the pundits wrong.

Later, Alexander Yakolev, a former Soviet ambassador to Canada, said that the Soviets had won something too, that the 1972 Series was the seed of glasnost and perestroika – the "openness" and "restructuring" of Soviet society that took place under Mikhail Gorbachev's leadership in the 1980s and culminated in the fall of the Berlin Wall in 1989. It had marked the first time the Soviet people had been exposed to so many foreigners who had not come to do them harm, but who had come to share in their mutual love of a game.

Canadians showed their love for Team Canada, treating the players they had sent off with a chorus of boos as conquering heroes. Crowds jammed into Montreal's Dorval airport to greet the team and lined up in the rain in Toronto's Nathan Phillips Square to catch a glimpse of them. And Phil Esposito kept the promise that he made in Vancouver to apologize to the country. "You people have proved me wrong," he told the crowd. "You've proved the rest of us wrong." No one cared about his apology now. The maple leaf was back on top of the hockey world, even though the violence of the series had besmirched it.

As a boy growing up in Winnipeg, Ben Hatskin loved to sketch Canadian one-dollar bills, to the chagrin of his Russian immigrant father, Louis, who had hoped his son would use his drawing lessons for loftier artistic purposes. In the summer of 1972, Ben Hatskin, now a forty-four-year-old multi-millionaire, thanks to his father's successful cardboard and lumber business and his own ventures in real estate, horse racing, timber, and investing, found that lofty purpose. This time, he drew not a dollar bill, but wrote a cheque worth a million of them to Bobby Hull and he presented it to the NHL star in the middle of Winnipeg, on a warm day in late June, signing Hull to a new team in a new league.

Thousands of Winnipeg hockey fans backed up traffic for blocks on three sides of the city's busiest intersection, and when they couldn't see what was happening from the street, they stood on their parked cars. Larry Sekuler, a local hockey fan who was smarting from the NHL's rejection of Winnipeg as an expansion city, saw the event and its portent as nothing less than civic redemption. "Bobby Hull's ceremonial signing at the corner of Portage and Main was the biggest thing that had happened in Winnipeg since the 1967 Pan-American Games," he said. "The feeling there was absolutely electric. Everybody in the big crowd was happy and smiling and looking forward to seeing major-league hockey. It really did put Winnipeg on the map. Wherever I

On June 27, 1972, Chicago Black Hawks superstar Bobby Hull shocked the NHL and delighted Winnipeggers by accepting a $1-million cheque at the city's famous Portage and Main intersection and joining the Jets in the upstart World Hockey Association. Here, Ben Hatskin waves Hull's contract for $2.75 million over ten years, which was the richest to date. The NHL saw its financial future all too clearly and, in retaliation, banned him from playing for Team Canada in the 1972 series. (*Manitoba Sports Hall of Fame and Museum*) would travel in North America, if I said I lived in Winnipeg, people would say 'Bobby Hull.' I think the feeling was that we really showed the NHL."

Bobby Hull was now a Winnipeg icon because of the World Hockey Association, a bold gamble dreamed up by two Californians, lawyer Gary Davidson and entrepreneur Dennis Murphy, who had been behind the founding of the American Basketball Association in 1968 and in 1971 saw an opportunity to take on the NHL's stranglehold on professional talent, unchallenged since 1926. "We felt the NHL's weakness is their arrogance and selfishness," said Dennis Murphy. "They have a monopoly on hockey and have traditionally made lots of money on the backs of exploited players. The NHL thought they had it made and, if they ignored us, we'd go away."

The WHA offered cities across North America that the NHL had over-looked or rejected the hope of joining the big leagues. Ben Hatskin was the perfect candidate for the WHA, for he was an accomplished sportsman as well as a tycoon. The proprietor of Hatskin Farms, his horse-racing stable, Hatskin had won a football scholarship to the University of Oklahoma and two Grey Cups as a centre for the Winnipeg Blue Bombers in 1939 and 1941. He had fall-en in love with hockey as a boy, playing defence on juvenile and junior teams, and in 1967, had brought a junior Winnipeg team, which he called the Jets, into the new Western Canada Hockey League. The WCHL fought with the Canadian Amateur Hockey Association over the same things that rival leagues had fought over for decades – money and power – but the tenacious Hatskin wanted the WCHL to succeed and quietly funded three other teams to help keep the league afloat.

Hatskin had hoped to be part of the NHL's second wave of expansion in 1970, but when he called Clarence Campbell to inquire about a franchise, he, like other would-be owners in what the NHL thought of as small-market cities, was treated as a window-shopper. Campbell told him he'd have to guarantee a 16,000-seat rink and a $7.2-million entry fee.

It was an impossible goal for Winnipeg to achieve, and the NHL knew it. Hatskin, though, became only more determined to see professional hockey in his hometown. "When I have to talk my way through a business deal, I can talk," he said. "If I have to push my way through, I push." Hatskin approached "Wild" Bill Hunter, owner of the WCHL's Edmonton Oil Kings. Hunter had tried to turn the WCHL into a professional league to rival the NHL in the 1960s, and when the WHA opened for business, Hunter took Hatskin to California to meet the future of pro hockey in North America. "When the idea of a second major league originated, I was all for it," said Hatskin. "I fig-ured it was maybe the only chance our city would ever have to go major league in any sport."

For the bargain entry fee of $25,000 (compared to $6 million in the NHL) cities could have their own WHA franchise, though Davidson and Murphy warned prospective owners to be prepared to lose $2 million in the first five years of operation, even with franchises in the big-market cities of Los Angeles and New York. "It didn't take very long before I realized these guys didn't know a damn thing about hockey," said Hunter. "Nothing. It was crazy how little they knew."

At a press conference in New York on November 1, 1971, the WHA announced plans to begin play in October 1972 with ten franchises, including ones in Winnipeg, Edmonton, and Calgary. Shortly afterward New England (Boston) and Ottawa were added, but even before the season began, the Miami franchise was moved to Philadelphia, Dayton's to Houston, and San Francisco's to Quebec City. Canada would have five teams in the new league, but Hatskin knew that the new league needed something more than regional representation: it needed a superstar.

Bobby Hull was the perfect candidate. The Golden Jet was one of the NHL's highest flyers, a player with blistering speed and a wicked shot on the ice, and with a lopsided smile and a magnetic manner off it. After defining the Chicago Black Hawks for more than a decade, scoring more than six hundred goals, leading them to a Stanley Cup, and having just come off a fifty-goal season, the thirty-three-year-old Hull had become embittered by the Hawks' stingy attitude in his recent contract negotiations with them.

Ben Hatskin saw the opening and lobbied Hull's agent, Harvey Wineberg, knowing that the money to sign Hull was safe in the WHA's war chest, to which each franchise had contributed. Hull would be good not just for Winnipeg, but for everybody in the WHA. "Getting a superstar like Hull would mean instant-league in the minds of the public and the news-media," said Hatskin. "Also it would cause other players to take the WHA seriously. There are only three or four superstars in hockey. All but Hull were tied up. He was our trump card. We went after him and got him."

At a time when NHL stars were earning an average salary of $50,000 a season (and lesser lights, half that), Bobby Hull's entry into the WHA was not just a move into another hockey league, but into another financial league. Hull, who had been the NHL's highest paid player at $100,000 a year, would receive, beyond the $1-million signing bonus, $1.75 million over ten years, as well as a house in Winnipeg – and a farm. "In those days, a million dollars might as well have been a billion dollars," Hull recalled. "Nobody had ever heard of a million dollars for a hockey player."

Other NHL players heard the call of money coming from the WHA. The Boston Bruins' star goalie, Gerry Cheevers, signed with the Cleveland Crusaders

In 1973, Gordie Howe came out of uncomfortable retirement at age forty-five to join his sons, Marty and Mark, on the WHA's Houston Aeros. He proved that this first father-son combo in the history of the game was no publicity stunt when he scored a goal just twenty seconds into his first shift. He went on to score one hundred points that season, leading the Aeros to the WHA title, and was named the league's most valuable player.

(*O-Pee-Chee/Hockey Hall of Fame*)

for $1.4 million over seven years, while Montreal's defensive standout J.C. Tremblay received a $125,000 signing bonus and $600,000 over five years from the Quebec Nordiques. In 1973, Mr. Hockey himself, forty-five-year-old Gordie Howe, signed with the Houston Aeros, so he could play pro with his two sons, Mark and Marty. The team even signed his wife, Colleen, as an officer of the club.

The NHL responded to the exodus in the courts, using Gerry Cheevers and his teammate and fellow defector Derek Sanderson to invoke the NHL reserve clause, a feudal mechanism adopted at the league's formation in 1917, which made NHL players the league's property for life. On September 28, 1972, the day of Canada's triumph over the Soviets in a series Bobby Hull had been forbidden to play because of his jump to the WHA (and he, too, couldn't play in the league until the courts ruled), a judge declared the restrictive clause invalid, because it had not been collectively bargained.

Other signings to the WHA followed the ruling, the most unusual being that of Rocket Richard, who was hired to coach the franchise in Quebec City, which had been bought by businessman Marius Fortier and five other local entrepreneurs from San Francisco for $215,000 and renamed the Nordiques.

"We were told time and again that we weren't good enough – that Quebec was a city of second-class citizens," said Fortier. "We were told so often that we decided it was time to try something. Finally, Quebec has its own place in the world of professional hockey."

Quebec City had not seen a professional hockey team since the glory days of Joe Malone, more than half a century earlier, and now, with an icon, Richard, at the helm, the city was poised to take on Montreal in a contest for the affections of hockey fans across the province. But fans in the provincial capital were not convinced that Quebec City had returned to the big time. "It's not the NHL, that's your first thought," said season ticket holder Luc Dupont. "You can't avoid it. There's Coca-Cola and then there's Pepsi. In professional sports, there's the NHL and the other leagues."

Richard lasted just two games as coach, and the Nordiques turned to another hockey legend, goalie Jacques Plante, to coach and manage the team. Soon the team's uniform was changed to reflect the provincial flag: blue, with a white fleur-de-lys cresting the shoulders of the sweater. With Quebec national-ism rising, les Nordiques became what the Montreal Canadiens had been at their inception: a team of francophones, for francophones. "The Nordiques are the people's team. It's becoming a love affair," said Luc Dupont. "The players speak French, they wear the fleur-de-lys on their jersey, and they endure insults from the English-speaking crowd that calls them frogs."

By 1974, the WHA had exploited the opening of hockey borders pioneered by the Summit Series two years earlier and had signed foreign players. The move did not go over well. When the Winnipeg Jets signed Swedish stars Anders Hedberg, Lars-Erik Sjoberg, and Ulf Nilsson, their doom was widely predicted. The Swedes arrived, hoping to season their skills with a little North American toughness. "If you want to be on the leading edge of the plough, you're going to have to get dirty," says Anders Hedberg. "It was a time when teams thought they could win by intimidation. But it wasn't in my personality to be scared. There's no way that was going to bother us, and believe me, lots of people tried." The Swedes teamed up with Bobby Hull, feeding him pucks and more fifty-goal seasons, but they paid the price. "They took a shit-kicking that first year," said Hull. "Those two guys [Hedberg and Nilsson] were the toughest players I ever played with."

The Jets and the Nordiques both went on to win the Avco Cup as champi-ons of the WHA, which slowly but surely transformed the professional game by encouraging more European players to head to North America, and by hiring players whose skills with their fists were more noteworthy than their skills with the puck. The league drafted teenage players who would one day light up the

Ulf Nilsson (left) and Anders Hedberg (right) joined the Winnipeg Jets in 1974–75, thanks to the WHA's smart strategy of recruiting European players at a time when the NHL was focused almost exclusively on North American talent. The duo played on a line with Bobby Hull (centre), who said their sublime hockey skills improved his own game. Hull scored his thousandth point while playing with the two Swedes, and the duo became the WHA's top scorers.

(Mecca/Hockey Hall of Fame)

NHL – Mike Gartner, Ken Linseman, Rick Vaive, Michel Goulet, Rob Ramage – and two who would become legends, Mark Messier and Wayne Gretzky.

Despite the WHA's successes, it was struggling financially, and by 1978, Bobby Hull had become a campaigner for a WHA–NHL merger. The WHA's free spending was not recompensed by gate receipts and, within the first two seasons, some franchises had moved or folded. To make matters worse for the new league, the Canadian NHL franchises in Toronto and Montreal, joined by the previously ill-used Vancouver, ganged up to prevent any sharing of their TV revenue from *Hockey Night in Canada* with the WHA's Canadian franchises in Winnipeg, Edmonton, and Quebec.

As they had done when Vancouver was shut out of NHL expansion in 1967, fans protested by boycotting the products of the Montreal Canadiens' owners, Molson. There was also expensive litigation in the courts between the NHL and the WHA, and the NHL finally got the message when its owners added up the legal tab. On March 22, 1979, at a special meeting of the NHL Board of Governors, the league voted 14–3 to absorb the WHA franchises in Edmonton, Quebec, Winnipeg, and Hartford. They would join the NHL for the 1979–80 season, giving the league twenty-one teams.

The NHL was not generous in victory: they ruled that the WHA clubs could protect only two goalies and two other players from their rosters, while the existing NHL teams, without need for compensation, could reclaim players who had joined the WHA in its seven-year adventure from 1972 to 1979. The WHA clubs would also be bumped to the back of the line in the 1979 entry draft, forced to pick eighteenth through twenty-first on each round, a move designed to give the NHL clubs first shot at junior talent. The new teams also had to pay $125,000 per player they selected in the expansion draft. The message was clearer than ever: the NHL was the only king of hockey in North America. It would not give in to pretenders.

Despite the free-flowing play of the Europeans who had signed with both the WHA and the NHL, professional hockey was not becoming a more skilful game, it was becoming more violent. WHA players Jeff and Steve Carlson and Dave Hanson joined forces as the fictional Hanson Brothers in the 1977 hit film *Slapshot*, a searing look, which some took as satire, at the world of semi-pro hockey, which it depicted as a sideshow where violence trumped skill. The Hanson Brothers were portrayed as simpleton thugs who dragged their knuckles (wrapped in tinfoil, for more effective punching) from game to game, leaving a trail of blood behind them. When he introduced the film's über-thug, Ogie Oglethorpe (based on real-life WHAer Billy Goldthorpe, who once bit the ear of a referee), to the crowd, the rink announcer said, "This young man has had a very trying rookie season, with the litigation, the notoriety, his subsequent deportation to Canada and that country's refusal to accept him, I guess that's more than most twenty-one-year-olds can handle. Number six, Ogie Oglethorpe."

The movie became one of the most popular hockey films ever made, for which a cult following endures, thanks to its hilarious, caustic view of pro hockey, but the violence that had taken centre ice in the NHL was not funny for those who regularly found themselves in the middle of it. "The league had sunk to new depths," says NHL referee Bruce Hood. "The mentality of the game had changed. Coaches would no longer simply sketch out offensive plays for their star players, but would figure out how to best match their goons against those on the other team." The Hanson-esque "goon" characterized the NHL's expansion in the 1970s, and in Philadelphia it was made into a virtue. The Flyers, led by Bobby Clarke, the man who had deliberately broken Soviet star Valeri Kharlamov's ankle in the Summit Series, were now nicknamed the Broad Street Bullies, a team of talent and thuggery which would profoundly change the game.

"If the NHL wants to condone goon squads like the Flyers, if the Canucks are silly enough to play along and the customers are suckers enough to buy it, who am I to say no?" wrote *Vancouver Sun* columnist Jim Taylor after witnessing the Flyers pummel the Canucks in 1973. "There's just one thing that bothers me. The Flyers play butcher shop hockey and succeed by the only measuring stick that counts. They win. Success breeds imitators. If they make it to the Stanley Cup final, how many more goon squads can we expect next season?" The fanatical win-at-all costs Bobby Clarke summed up the Flyers' strategy: "You don't have to be a genius to figure out what we do on the ice. We take the shortest route to the puck and arrive in ill humour." The team's coach, the aphoristic Fred Shero, was even more bloody-minded: "There are things I would do for my players that I wouldn't do for my sons."

Led by the goal-scoring talents of Bill Barber and Rick MacLeish, the netminding genius of Bernie Parent, the fists of Dave "the Hammer" Schultz and Bob "the Hound" Kelly, and the relentlessly ferocious Bobby Clarke, the Flyers made it to the Stanley Cup final four times between 1974 and 1980, and won the Cup twice. There were, however, casualties along the way. During a 1976 play-off series with Toronto, Ontario attorney general Roy McMurtry laid charges against Philadelphia's Mel Bridgman and Don Saleski for possession of a dangerous weapon – a hockey stick – and the charge of common assault against Joe Watson and Bob Kelly. Charges against the first two were stayed, while Watson and Kelly pleaded guilty and were fined.

The Maple Leafs were scouting another Swede (future NHLer Inge Hammarstrom) when they saw Borje Salming play defence and promptly recruited him. Salming became one of the first Europeans to play in the NHL, joining Toronto in the 1973–74 season. The Swede was soon celebrated not just for his skill, but for his shot-blocking toughness and his stamina, regularly playing more than an extraordinary thirty minutes a game. (*Toronto Star*)

McMurtry's brother William, a lawyer and investigator for the Province of Ontario, had, at the request of the provincial government, conducted a study about hockey violence at the amateur level, and his conclusions were scathing. "When you tell six-year-old children that fighting is a healthy part of the game, there's something cathartic about it. More than any language, race, custom, flag or anthem, hockey is the Canadian common denominator," he wrote. "Psychotic behaviour outside the rules is something that should not be rewarded. We know that if we do not act, the situation will deteriorate even further."

McMurtry likely remembered the violent 1971 Memorial Cup junior hockey championship between the St. Catharines Black Hawks and the Quebec Remparts that had been advertised as a contest between cultures, even though

Called the Hammer because of the punishing way he played – and fought – Dave Schultz grew up in a Saskatchewan Mennonite community where he played hockey in the winter and attended Bible camp in the summer. In 1973–74, he set an NHL record by spending 348 minutes in the penalty box, the equivalent of nearly six full games over a seventy-eight-game season. (*Canadian Press*)

the two star players were both francophone. The Remparts were captained by Guy Lafleur, while the Black Hawks were led by Marcel Dionne, who was disparaged in Quebec as a traitor for choosing to play in the Ontario league. The series soon became a savage contest.

St. Catharines had bullied their way on ice all season, and the nasty tone of the series had been established at the outset in Ontario, when a fan threw live frogs on the ice. After exchanging wins in two fight-filled contests, the teams moved to Quebec City, where fourteen thousand fans crammed into the 10,240-seat Colisée to watch a game repeatedly stopped by fights and 102 minutes of penalties, nearly three-quarters of them given to St. Catharines. "There were too many distractions for us to play," said Marcel Dionne. "Things were constantly being thrown on the ice. We fought back."

Fighting erupted in the stands, and after the Remparts won, the Black Hawks had to leave the ice under police escort. When a Quebec fan spat at one of the Ontario players, he tried to hit back with his stick, and instead struck a police officer in the face, sending him to hospital for stitches. "With things getting out of control, police officers had our bus pulled up right against the building, so we walked out the door, right onto the bus," said Black Hawk Brian McKenzie. "Once we're on the bus, then it really starts – rocks, bottles,

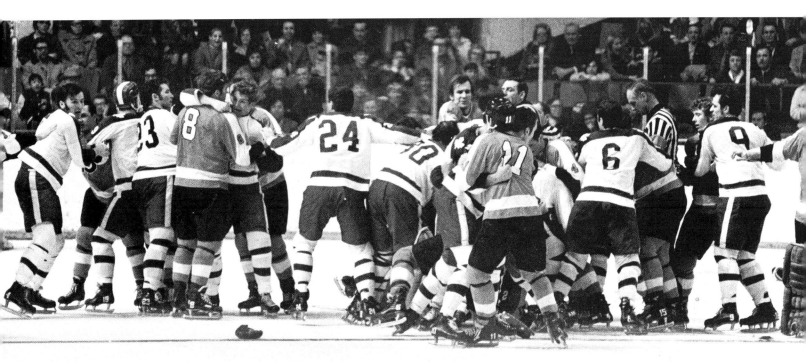

Nicknamed the Broad Street Bullies for their violence on ice, the Philadelphia Flyers took their cue from coach Fred Shero, who had been a boxing champion before turning to hockey. Shero used to have his forwards practise break-aways while being slashed from behind, saying, "Nobody ever lets you score an easy goal in a game. Why practise that way?" The Flyers fought, slashed, and scored their way to two straight Stanley Cup victories in 1974 and 1975.

(*Toronto Star*)

windows breaking." The St. Catharines players were forced to lie face down on the floor of the bus to avoid being hit by the projectiles of the enraged mob. It took five police cars to clear their escape route. Once safely home, the team management held a meeting with players and parents, and after a 15–5 vote, decided to abandon the series. "The bad part was to see how mean and violent people can get," said St. Catharines' Bob Peppler. "I was frightened enough that I wasn't going back to play them in Quebec." The Remparts went on to play the Edmonton Oil Kings for the Memorial Cup, and won junior hockey's highest prize.

NHL president Clarence Campbell had initially shrugged off the violence in the professional game, saying, "We're in the entertainment business – I don't consider I have any moral sort of responsibility," but public outcry at the violence then tarnishing the game at all levels, and government interest in punishing the thugs among the pros, was sufficiently loud to send the NHL a message to do something before outside forces did it for them. Campbell changed the rules to punish the third player entering a fight, to give a game misconduct to any player physically interfering with spectators, a double minor for the first player to leave the team bench during an altercation (as well as a game misconduct and additional fines), and a fifty-dollar fine for a boarding check that caused injury to a player's face or head. Campbell also left the NHL president room to review any incident and add more punishment, if he deemed it warranted.

The NHL Players' Association was rumoured to want to go farther toward eliminating the violence then staining the sport. The association representing the men who had to do the dirty work was advocating the immediate expulsion of players involved in a fight – even one that might have involved only one punch and counterpunch, and game misconduct penalties for players who engaged in stick swinging. The NHL owners, well aware that NBC advertised its Game of the Week by showing clips of a hockey fight, defeated the proposal by a vote of 13–4.

William McMurtry pointed the way to the high road in the conclusion to his report. "Rather than a divisive force, fueled by calculated animosities, it can and should be a bond between participants, with a shared commitment to excellence, and the common love of a game, hockey, which perhaps more than any other can give one a sense of physical exhilaration and sheer joy of participation." It would take the women's game, and the arrival of a remarkable kid, to show how exciting a clean game could be.

The 1972 Summit Series, followed by another in 1974 with a Team Canada made up of WHA players and which the Soviets won; the birth of the Canada Cup in 1976; and the annual World Championships saw men's hockey thrive in international competition, even if the domestic product offered up by the NHL had been weakened by rapid expansion, as some thought it had, and by the riotous – and successful – tactics of the Broad Street Bullies. In the meantime, women's hockey, for decades in and out of official and public favour, was poised to break through to a whole new level of skill and respect on the international stage.

Nancy Dragan was an eighteen-year-old student at the University of Saskatchewan in March of 1978 when her hockey team received an extraordinary invitation: to play at the first North American intercollegiate women's hockey tournament, to be hosted by the University of Minnesota. Dragan had been playing hockey since she was a girl in Indian Head, Saskatchewan. "My mother taught me how to skate when I was three years old," said Dragan. "I spent countless hours on the backyard rink my father built, skating in old figure skates and shooting pucks against the barn." So Marg and Ernie Dragan weren't surprised when their daughter told them she wanted to play hockey. "In this area there were groups of girls interested in playing hockey," Marg Dragan recalled. "So Nancy started very early. We went to country rinks where there were no seats, where you had to stand up around the boards and the roofs would sometimes leak on your head."

Dragan began her hockey career as a left-winger on figure skates on an outdoor rink in the local park, and by Grade 8, had graduated to a girls-only

The 1976 Canada Cup arose from the success of the 1972 Summit Series, though the round-robin tournament also included the United States, Czechoslovakia, Sweden, and Finland. In the run to the first final, Canada's only loss was to the Czechoslovaks, thanks to the brilliant goaltending of Vladimir Dzurilla. The championship game between the same two teams was tied 4–4 in the first overtime period when Maple Leafs centre Darryl Sittler broke in on Dzurilla, faked a slapshot to draw him out of position, then popped the puck into the net to give Canada the inaugural Canada Cup. Here, Sittler (left) shakes hands with Dzurilla, while Maurice Richard watches.

(Frank Prazak/Hockey Hall of Fame)

league playing in small town Saskatchewan. During her last year of high school, she played in the Western Canadian Shield, a tournament for girls held that year in Regina. "The Western Shield used to have representatives from each of the western provinces," she recalls. "It was a very big thing." Dragan had been picked up by the Odessa Cal Gals. "I played with a whole new set of players," she says. "The Odessa team was a better team and I was very proud they picked me. The Melfort Missilettes was the best team."

The following year, Dragan was playing hockey with the Huskies at the University of Saskatchewan, which resurrected its women's hockey program in the 1976–77 season. Like other Canadian university women's programs, just because there was a hockey team didn't mean there was money for it. "Every single time we went to play in a tournament we had to raise funds," she said. "I can't believe what we have to go through to play hockey. We have tenacity on the ice and we work hard to go everywhere." When the University of Minnesota tournament beckoned, "We financed the trip by raffling off bottles of liquor," says Dragan. "We sold tickets at Louie's, which is the university watering hole."

The USask team made the trip to frozen Minnesota in an unheated van. "The weather was bitter cold and stormy through North Dakota," Dragan recalls. "But we drove all night, stopping at all-night restaurants for coffee and cinnamon buns." When they arrived, they and their Canadian colleagues from the universities of Manitoba and Winnipeg were in for a surprise. The United States teams had benefited from Title IX, a law passed by Congress in 1972 that prohibited sex discrimination in educational programs that received federal funding – legislation made possible by the resurgence of the women's movement in the late 1960s. Title IX meant that female hockey players could receive the same money, coaching, and ice time as men got, and the U.S. women's hockey teams had taken off. They surprised Dragan and her teammates with their level of play. "We played those Ivy League colleges and universities and they beat us pretty well," Dragan says. "The University of Chicago, Brown University, and the University of New Hampshire teams were really good. They beat us with something like twenty goals. They were just so good – way more skilled players."

Sue Ring had started the University of Minnesota women's team as a graduate student in 1974, taking advantage of Title IX, and getting ice time for the women three times a week in the early morning, and once a week at night. "We had about forty women playing, and we were divided into an A and B team," says Ring. "My club members were hard core . . . that's all we did: go to school and play hockey." She campaigned for more practice time, better funding, and for hockey tournaments and also became an advocate for European-style hockey. "Eliminating body checking decreases the likelihood of unnecessary fighting and allows team members to develop skating finesse by playing the puck, rather than playing bodies," said Ring. "We don't want to beat them up. We want to beat them clean."

The Minnesota team's superior funding and practice time, as well as their large talent pool, saw them win the inaugural tournament against Saskatchewan. "We were perhaps a little intimidated by the U.S.A. teams," says Dragan. "The University of Chicago had black players on its roster . . . and it was the first time I'd ever played against black players in hockey. Chicago and Minnesota both had strong players and were definitely better organized and disciplined as teams. It all came down to Title IX. That's the difference between Canadian and American players." Still, the Americans learned something from their Canadian rivals. "At first I didn't like playing the Canadians, then I began to enjoy playing against them because they were teaching me things about the game I didn't know," says Ring. "Canadian women were very good at covering man-to-man and good on the boards. Their faceoff was different. In the States we drop the puck, the Canadians threw the puck down on the ice and they hardly ever called icing."

Nancy Dragan also learned a profound lesson from her American experience. "We were so behind at the time, especially in Western Canada. On the way home, I realized that women's hockey needed to be acknowledged and funded by our provincial and national associations," she says. "Only then could we develop minor programs for girls at the grass root levels. Canadian universities also had to realize that women's hockey was here to stay and they needed to organize, develop, and fund programs."

Nancy Dragan was a driving force behind the resurrection of women's hockey at the University of Saskatchewan. In 1978, the left-winger and her Huskies teammates were invited to play at the first North American intercollegiate women's hockey tournament, at the University of Minnesota. Women's hockey was financed so abysmally, the Huskies had to raffle off bottles of liquor to pay for their trip to the tournament in an unheated Volkswagen van. (Nancy Dragan)

The University of Minnesota women's hockey team not only hosted the first intercollegiate women's hockey tournament, they also won it. In 1972, the United States enacted Title IX, a law that established equal funding and practise time for men's and women's varsity sports. As a result, the University of Saskatchewan Huskies women's team were shocked to encounter the high calibre of play from American university teams who had benefited from the new law. (*Nancy Dragan*)

In October 1978, another Western Canadian women's hockey team made a pioneering international trip, one that was lavishly funded by their hosts, the Isetan Department Store in Tokyo, whose owner was president of Japan's hockey federation. The store invited the University of British Columbia women's team to come to Japan for two weeks to show Tokyo's three women's teams how the people who had invented hockey played it.

A year earlier, the UBC men's team had gone to China, which made the Japanese invitation all the more remarkable to UBC women's sports athletic director Marilyn Pomfret. "Because there had been so many sports exchanges between boys' teams, it was quite a coup for somebody to invite the first North American women's team and to be supportive of women." The Japanese were so generous they paid for airfare, lodging, entertainment, and made the players North American–style breakfasts. They also addressed a pressing need for the Canadian women. "Isetan even bought the UBC varsity team new hockey uniforms, including gloves," says goalie Kathleen Corbett. "The jerseys were the proper UBC colours, midnight blue and gold."

Corbett had become a goalie as a fourteen-year-old in 1968 because she didn't know how to skate backward, and after her toes turned black from stopping pucks with her figure skates, her father attached soup cans to the skate fronts as bumpers. Corbett had played intramural hockey at UBC for two years before the university decided to raise the women's game to the varsity level. "We were put on probation, I don't think they thought we could do it,"

Corbett says. "We had to prove we were worth the $1,200 they were giving us. How generous, when the guys get $10,000!"

At the time, just fifty cents of the ten-dollar athletic fee UBC levied on students went to women's sports, the rest went to men's. The women's hockey team's share of the miserly cut barely paid for their ice time, and their first league game was scheduled before they could even have a practice. "We had never played together before," Corbett says. "Some had intramural practice, others had been in leagues in the east, and others had just figure skated. We had a real Heinz variety of talents."

In Japan, the UBC Thunderettes, who had finished in seventh place in a ten-team league in their first season, were treated as celebrities. "We were stars in Japan," says Corbett. "Photographers and TV crews were following us everywhere. We walked into a room and people were clapping at us and looking at us . . . Oh my God, what a feeling! We'd never had that before."

The Thunderettes, who were lodged in Tokyo's Shinagawa Prince Hotel, which featured two Olympic-sized ice rinks, would dress in their hotel rooms then walk down to the rink where they held hockey clinics for the Japanese players. "The girls were all smiles and eager to learn," says Corbett. "Very respectful and kind of in awe because we were Canadian players." The Canadians were faced with the delicate task of playing all three Japanese teams, but not too hard. "There was no need to stack the deck, but neither could you back off because that would have insulted them," says Marilyn Pomfret. "Of course, the score would be very spread out, but not in the extreme. We didn't lay it on by any means."

The Japanese women, however, did lay on the body, which was something new for the Canadian women, whose league play did not allow bodychecking. "They were very polite about it," Corbett says. "They would take you against the boards and give you a hip check and then they'd kind of laugh and apologize and skate away. We just didn't know what to do because we'd never been bodychecked before. We did go home with a few injuries because we didn't know how to bodycheck." The UBC players also went home with the Isetan Cup, a huge glass trophy commemorating the series, in which the Canadians won every game. The women relished their ambassadorial role and being on the vanguard of a sport.

But as the 1970s gave way to a new decade, hockey's premier ambassador of excellence was a man, or rather, a boy, who sprang to national prominence as a thirteen-year-old playing in the Quebec Pee Wee Tournament, a hockey jamboree held every year since 1960 at the close of Quebec's famous Winter Carnival. The tournament had increased its attendance each year, reaching almost 150,000 fans annually during the 1970s, but the 13,000 people who

Even as a slight, shy thirteen-year-old, Wayne Gretzky was famous in Canada, and thirteen thousand people crammed into a ten-thousand-seat arena at the 1974 Quebec Pee Wee tournament to watch his budding genius on ice.

(*Canadian Press*)

crammed into the 10,000-seat arena in 1974 had come to witness the miracle of Brantford, Ontario. "That day, our local paper carried a headline, 'The Gretzky Tornado Is in Town!'" says Gilles Tremblay, the vice president of the Quebec Pee Wee tournament.

Wayne Gretzky was already famous, having been interviewed on national television, in newspapers, and regularly by CKBC in Brantford after one of his multi-goal games, which the station aired. In the 1971–72 season, he had scored 378 goals, and a Canadian Press story that year reported that his scoring feats were presenting "a pleasant problem for the organizers of the novice tournament. The four-foot-four, seventy-pound dynamo has been turning them away at the doors here and didn't disappoint his fans again Wednesday night, scoring nine goals and assisting on two others."

When Gretzky debuted in Quebec, his host family could scarcely believe that this was the player who had loaded his family's living room with so many trophies they had had to build a special room to house them. "A friend of mine called and asked if we would like to billet a few players from Brantford, including this kid who's broken all the minor league records with his slapshot," says Louis Lortie. "He looks as light as a feather; his wrists are as big as my little finger. I think, my God, there's no way this is the kid!"

Gretzky went so far as to trade jackets with a teammate, hoping to get away from the relentless glare of his own celebrity, but when his team beat one from Texas by a score of 25–0, with Gretzky tying Guy Lafleur's record of eleven points, he became, says Gilles Tremblay, "the only story in town." Gretzky's talent alone wasn't enough, and his team lost the semifinal to Oshawa. But a star had been born.

While Canada would lose in humiliating fashion to the Soviets as the new decade began, the country now had Gretzky to take revenge and to fight its hockey battles, not with his fists, but with his extraordinary hockey talent. Known universally as "the Great One," he would become for a long time the standard by which all hockey players were measured.

CHAPTER 8

HOPE AND BETRAYAL

In April 1980, a slender, curly haired young man with an easy smile and an extraordinary mission took the first step of his journey to becoming a Canadian hero. After dipping his left leg, the one not lost to cancer, into the Atlantic Ocean on a cold, misty morning in St. John's, Newfoundland, twenty-one-year-old Terry Fox began his distinctive hop-skip run across the country, hoping to raise a dollar from each of Canada's 26 million people for cancer research, in what he called the Marathon of Hope. Fox logged forty-two kilometres a day, running through Canada's Atlantic Provinces and pausing in Borden, P.E.I., on May 24 to take in a little hockey. "I had a great shower

and watched part of the sixth game of the Stanley Cup playoffs between Philly and the New York Islanders," he wrote in his diary. "Then I drove to Summerside. It is beautiful country. I finally relaxed!"

By the time Fox reached Toronto in July, he was a North American celebrity. When the head of the Ontario branch of the Cancer Society asked Terry if he had any special requests, he said that he wanted to meet Bobby Orr and Darryl Sittler. Sittler, the captain of the Maple Leafs, wanted to meet Fox just as much. Sittler drove to his home in Mississauga to retrieve a gift for Fox, which he put in a brown paper bag and presented to the runner at a huge rally at Toronto's Nathan Phillips Square. When Fox saw that it was Sittler's 1980 NHL All-Star sweater, he proudly pulled on the Number 27 jersey and raised his arms in triumph. "I've been around athletes a long time," said Sittler, "and I've never seen any with his courage and stamina."

Fox's other hero, Bobby Orr, presented him with a cheque for $25,000 from his sponsor, Planter's Peanuts, and Fox wrote in his diary that meeting Orr was the highlight of his trip. But there was more to come. When Fox reached Orr's hometown of Parry Sound, Ontario, Orr's father gave him Bobby's Canada Cup sweater, and Fox was on top of the world. He was close to the halfway point of his extraordinary journey, he had raised $11.4 million, and he had met his two hockey heroes. And then, on September 1, it was over. The cancer had spread to Fox's lungs, and he was forced to abandon his run near Thunder Bay. Darryl Sittler and the Maple Leafs offered to continue on for him, to meet up with him back home in Port Coquitlam, B.C., but Fox said no, he'd get through the next round of therapy and be back on his marathon himself. But the marathon – and soon the hope – were over. A watercolour of Terry Fox by artist Ken Danby was given to Governor General Ed Schreyer at the opening of the championship game between Canada and the Soviets at the 1981 Canada Cup, a game dedicated to Fox, who was remembered with a moment of silence before it began. He had died in June, at the age of twenty-two.

George Smith watched the final game in his Winnipeg trucking office, and he liked Canada's chances. The Soviets and the Canadians were the finalists of the round-robin format of the Canada Cup, which had been delayed a year because of the Soviet invasion of Afghanistan. As the Canadians had defeated the Red Machine with a convincing 7–3 performance in their previous meeting in the tournament, the country was expecting to celebrate another win in 1981.

There wasn't much to celebrate in Canada that year. The country was still wounded from the first Quebec referendum, held the year before, which rejected separation by a mere 60 per cent; and because of fury in oil-rich Alberta over Ottawa's National Energy Policy, in the boardrooms of Calgary, Canada's "blue-eyed sheiks" were also making separatist noises. Meanwhile, interest

In July 1980, Terry Fox's Marathon of Hope reached Toronto's Nathan Phillips Square. The one-legged runner, who had lost his leg to cancer, was thrilled to receive the 1980 All-Star jersey from Maple Leafs captain Darryl Sittler (left).
(*Bill Becker/Canadian Press*)

The NHL Goes to Saskatchewan

In the early 1980s, entrepreneur Bill Hunter, who owned junior teams in Western Canada and brought the Edmonton Oilers into the World Hockey Association, had offered to purchase the NHL's financially moribund St. Louis Blues and planned to move them to Saskatoon. He already had eighteen thousand people in the province that had given so much to the hockey life of the country committed to season's tickets, and plans for a new arena in which to seat them. "Have you heard the news, we're getting the Blues?" was the refrain of a song that was given heavy air-time on the provincial radio stations, unwittingly anticipating the depressing news that the NHL had rejected Bill Hunter's application: Saskatoon was too small and economically shaky to support a franchise, went the reasoning, though the truth was that American markets promised much greater revenue from television.

(*Graphic Artists/Hockey Hall of Fame*)

rates were a crippling 21 per cent. Canadians badly needed something to cheer for, and the Canada Cup gave the country hope of winning a prize that mattered. The Stanley Cup now seemed to be owned by the New York Islanders, who had won it two years in a row. Worse for Canadian pride, the Olympic hockey gold that Canada had not been able to wrest from the Soviets since 1952 had been won the year before by Team USA, with their "Miracle on Ice."

Despite a feisty start by the Canadians in the one-game, winner-take-all 1981 Canada Cup championship, they were on the wrong end of a 3–1 score by the time the second period finished, and had been humiliated 8–1 when the siren sounded in the Montreal Forum at the end of what was quickly named – at the time, innocently – the Montreal Massacre. George Smith watched Prime Minister Pierre Trudeau and Alan Eagleson, the Canada Cup's boss, present the trophy to Valeri Vasiliev, captain of the first foreign team to win the Cup. It was Canada's most humiliating international hockey defeat. "And we thought well, that's done as done," says Smith. But all was not done. "The following morning I woke up at about 5:30 and before I left for work I was watching CTV news and it showed the Montreal police department fighting with the team, the Soviet team, regarding the Canada Cup, to take it away from them. And I said, 'That's a hell of a Goddamn thing.'"

The Soviets, under the impression that the Canada Cup, shaped like half a maple leaf, was theirs to take home, had packed it with their gear for the flight to Moscow. The Cup's custodian, Maurice "Lefty" Reid, discovered this bit of excess baggage, and Alan Eagleson proclaimed that a team had to win the Cup three times before they could keep it, and with the help of some Montreal policemen, took the Cup back from the startled Soviets.

Smith was offended. "If you win something fair and square, you get to keep it," he said. This was not the first time he felt Eagleson had gone too far. He was still smarting from Eagleson's slur on Winnipeggers, whom he had called, Smith says, "a bunch of cheapskates because we weren't willing to pay $30 at that time to watch Finland play Sweden or Czechoslovakia play Finland." Now, with talk that the Soviets would never again play the Canadians, he took action.

After getting a brush-off from the *Winnipeg Free Press*, Smith called Peter Warren's popular hotline show on CJOB to present a remedy for the stain on the nation's honour. "I said 'Hey, this is a great idea, maybe the people of Winnipeg can make a Canada Cup and show the Eagle we're not cheapskates after all.' And the subject changed immediately to the Canada Cup and seventeen out of eighteen people that called in said, 'Hey, that's a great idea, let's go for it.'" That afternoon, Smith was being photographed by the young *Winnipeg Sun* newspaper as the leader of the movement to give the Canada Cup to the Soviets, and his trucking office had become the campaign's national headquarters. Smith told the reporter, "If we get a dollar apiece out of enough people we'll be able to pay for a Canada Cup and do it." The story was picked up by other *Sun* papers and, Smith says, within three or four days he started to receive one-dollar bills. In just three weeks, Smith collected thirty-two thousand dollars from supportive Canadians. "They came from Nova Scotia, New Brunswick, Newfoundland, and B.C. and everywhere in Canada," he recalled. "There was even a letter that came from New York City that sent ten dollars in American money and said 'Screw Eagleson.'"

A foundry in Winkler, Manitoba, offered to replicate the Canada Cup for free, but there was, however, a problem: Alan Eagleson. Smith began receiving threatening letters from the lawyer, and then the RCMP paid him a visit to talk of "patent infringement." Unbowed, Smith made a phone call to his boyhood friend Eddie, now the governor general of Canada – and the custodian of the Canada Cup. Ed Schreyer told Smith that the Cup that Eagleson was preventing the Soviets from taking home was a replica itself, as the original solid-nickel trophy, weighing nearly 140 pounds, was safe in Rideau Hall. "All of a sudden the Mounties backed off and everybody backed, and nobody else bothered us," says Smith.

When the replica Canada Cup was ready, George Smith and three to four thousand people congregated at the intersection of Portage and Main, singing "O Canada," before their trophy was presented by Manitoba's lieutenant-governor, Francis Jobin, to Soviet Embassy counsellor Vladimir Mechulayev. "This is not an endorsement of all the actions of the state of Russia," Jobin cautioned, voicing the hostility toward the Soviet Union felt by Manitoba's Ukrainian-Canadians. The Soviets were not all fans of Canada, either. When triumphant Soviet goalie Vladislav Tretiak arrived back in Moscow, a lady kissed him on the cheek and told him how happy she was that the team "beat those Canadian bastards!"

But on the corner of Portage and Main, Mechulayev was the perfect diplomat, transcending geopolitical turbulence and historical enmity to thank the Canadian people for "an amazing gesture" and "a truly noble act" of understanding and good sportsmanship. The Soviets, he said, would give the trophy a place of honour in the Sports Hall of Fame at the Lenin Stadium in Moscow. Then he presented Smith with a large snowy owl doll, mascot of the Izvestia Cup. Smith modestly refused to take credit for the remarkable reparation of Alan Eagleson's petty tyranny, saying, "It was the people of Canada . . . several thousand who sent in one- and two-dollar bills."

As the replica Cup had been made for free (but for the pattern maker, who kept upping his price as the money rolled in until Smith cut him off at $900), Smith made an equally generous gesture to the sporting world, passing more than $30,000 of the donations he had received to minor hockey associations in North Winnipeg and in Winkler.

The Canada Cup's restoration to its rightful winner was a generous act in the autumn of 1981, and the country took heart from it. And as fans embraced another hockey season, they were buoyed by the hope created by hockey's new young hero. Wayne Gretzky, on whose thin, twenty-year-old shoulders hung the jersey of the NHL's Edmonton Oilers, was the messiah of the ice for whom the country had been waiting since forever. There had never been a player quite like him. And he was just getting started.

As a boy growing up in Galt, a small industrial city in Southwestern Ontario, journalist Peter Gzowski used to play hockey on an outdoor rink in Dickson Park, dreaming of hockey glory. In later years, he said of his boyhood love affair with the sport, "I would sometimes imagine one great outdoor hockey game stretching from just inside the Rockies to the shores of the Atlantic, detouring only around the too temperate climate of a few of the bigger cities. Or perhaps a hundred thousand simultaneous games, all overlapping as our own used to overlap at Dickson Park."

Gzowski called hockey "the game of our lives," a title he gave to his book chronicling the exploits of a dynasty in the making, the Edmonton Oilers, and hockey's prince, Wayne Gretzky. By the time Gzowski spent the 1980–81 season following the Oilers, Gretzky, just twenty years old when the season began, was already famous across the land.

When Wayne Gretzky was just thirteen, he had appeared on Gzowski's CBC radio show, *This Country in the Morning*, and three years earlier he had been profiled in the *Toronto Telegram* as a scoring machine. Gzowski wanted to talk to him about his astonishing record of 988 goals and the looming 1,000 goal milestone, which he passed in 1973–74, after just seven years of playing organized hockey. Gzowski had expected to meet an arrogant, hormone-fuelled superstar-in-the-making, but instead found Gretzky to be a humble, polite teenager, just five-foot-two, whom he said resembled "a solemn squirrel."

In November 1977, during Gzowski's brief detour from radio into the fickle world of television, he profiled the sixteen-year-old Gretzky on his short-lived variety show *90 Minutes Live*. Gretzky had just begun his Junior A career with the Sault Ste. Marie Greyhounds, and after a mere seventeen games, Gretzky already led the league with twenty goals and thirty-five assists. The slender boy wonder, who told Gzowski that his teammates called him "pretzel," showed a remarkable self-awareness. His manner captivated the journalist, and his skill showed him to be the kind of genius who understands the limits of his gift and lets instinct do the rest.

"When I'm out there, I try to think as far ahead as I can," Gretzky said, "even before the play develops, I try to think of where the puck's going to go and where to be. When I go in on goal, I think about everything else but scoring." Then he disarmingly admitted that, despite his mental calculations, sometimes his mind just went blank, as it had a few nights earlier in Ottawa, when he was in alone on a goalie who had decided his best chance was to charge out to cut Gretzky off. Gretzky had just glided around the goalie and scored.

Gretzky had begun skating at age two on the Nith River behind his grandparents' farm, a twenty-minute drive from Brantford. His father, Walter, would flood the family's own backyard each winter to make a rink for Wayne, using a lawn sprinkler to spread the water evenly. One year, when the sprinkler finally succumbed to its unseasonable use, Walter Gretzky asked his wife, Phyllis, to buy a replacement. When she returned home with a new one, she told Walter that he was on his own the next time – the clerks had thought she was crazy for buying a lawn sprinkler in February.

But Walter Gretzky wasn't crazy: to be sure, he wanted his son to excel, but he was simply trying to keep up with the boy who was born to play hockey. Wayne loved the before- and after-dinner drills on the backyard rink strung with lights so they could go late, with Wayne jumping over hockey sticks while his father fed him passes, or shooting at the corners of the net because Walter

While Wayne Gretzky's genes had a lot to do with his hockey genius, so too did endless hours of practising in the backyard rink that his father, Walter, built for him when he was six. It was for self-preservation, Walter said. "I got sick of taking him to the park and sitting there for hours freezing to death." (*Gretzky family/Hockey Hall of Fame*)

had blocked the rest of it with the family picnic table laid on its side. "When the Russians came over here in 1972 and '73," Wayne Gretzky says, "people said 'Wow, this is something incredible.' Not to me it wasn't. I'd been doing those drills since I was three years old. My dad was very smart."

Despite telling Gzowski in the 1977 TV interview that he wanted to finish Grade 13 and then go on to complete university, Gretzky began his professional career less than a year later, after flying with his parents and agent, Gus Badali, in June 1978 to Vancouver to meet entrepreneur Nelson Skalbania, who needed a marquee name for his shaky WHA franchise in Indianapolis. After Badali unsuccessfully tried to snag one of the paintings hanging in Skalbania's luxurious home, where they met – an Utrillo, or perhaps the A.Y. Jackson – Wayne Gretzky signed a personal services contract with the Vancouver high-flyer for $1.75 million over seven years, $250,000 of which was a signing bonus. Gretzky was just seventeen years old.

The following year, Skalbania's Indianapolis franchise was bleeding money and Skalbania initially offered Gretzky up to Winnipeg Jets owner Michael Gobuty for a backgammon game, the winner getting to name his price. Gobuty, not confident in his backgammon skills, turned down the offer, so Skalbania phoned his friend Peter Pocklington, owner of the Edmonton Oilers, then playing in the WHA. Pocklington knew a masterpiece when he saw one, and bought Gretzky's contract, signing him on his eighteenth birthday in January 1979 for twenty-one years and $5 million. At the time, it was the richest contract in the history of sport.

The riches kept coming. After the WHA folded, the Oilers became an NHL team, and in his first season with the league in 1979–80, Gretzky tied Marcel Dionne at 137 points for the NHL lead. Dionne was awarded the scoring title because he had more goals, and Gretzky was awarded the first of his eight consecutive (and nine in total) Hart Trophies as the most valuable player in the

NHL, as well as the first of his five Lady Byng Trophies, for being the most gentlemanly player. The NHL denied him the Calder Trophy as rookie of the year, because he had played in the WHA and had won that league's rookie of the year award, the Lou Kaplan Trophy, the previous season.

On the ice, Gretzky continued to shatter seemingly unbreakable records with ease. In March 1981, he notched three assists in a 5–2 Edmonton win over Pittsburgh to surpass Phil Esposito's record of 152 points. Two days later he broke Bobby Orr's record of 102 assists, on his way to a whopping 164-point season – 55 goals and 109 assists. The following season, he shifted into an even higher gear. On December 30, 1981, he scored 5 goals against Philadelphia, achieving 50 goals in just 39 games, the fastest anyone had scored that many goals in NHL history. While some disparaged his accomplishments as the result of a watered-down league, another scoring virtuoso, Rocket Richard, saw otherwise. "I have now seen Gretzky enough," he said, "to say that in whatever decade he played he would have been the scoring champion." Two months later, in a game against Buffalo, Gretzky scored his seventy-seventh, seventy-eighth, and seventy-ninth goals of the season, breaking Phil Esposito's record of 76 en route to a jaw-dropping 92 goals and 120 assists, becoming the first NHL player to cross the 200-point threshold in a single campaign.

Sportswriters and fans, including new fans he attracted to the game, all had to learn how to watch him play, such was his singularity. Gretzky's genius, honed by thousands of hours of drilling, was to anticipate where the player or the puck was going to be, and either send the puck there, or move into that position himself to take the puck on the fly. Eventually this mixture of talent and skill led him to set up behind opponents' nets in a space that sportswriters began to call his office. There he would design plays while standing still with the puck, watching. If an opponent moved in to check him from the left, he moved out to the right; if two opponents pinched in from both sides, then that left two teammates in the open. Gretzky was a threat even when he seemed to be doing nothing.

Gretzky's contract with the Oilers was soon in need of serious recalibration, and in January 1982, he signed a twenty-one-year contract that would see him earn $20 million over fifteen years, as well as a piece of a shopping mall. The event generated international buzz, as if Gretzky had just had El Dorado land in his lap. On CBC-TV's *The Journal,* host Barbara Frum had to mediate an argument between Peter Gzowski and Dick Beddoes over the deal and Gretzky's merits – or in Beddoes's opinion, lack thereof. "Nobody is worth that, especially a hairy-legged hockey player from Brantford, Ontario," fumed Beddoes, who a year earlier had said Gretzky "just might have made third-string centre on one of the good Leaf teams of the past." Gzowski, testy at Beddoes's devil's advocacy,

In his sophomore season in the NHL in 1980–81, Gretzky proved that his nickname, the Great One, was no exaggeration. He won the first of seven straight Art Ross Trophies as the NHL's top point scorer – beating Bobby Orr's record with 109 assists and Phil Esposito's record with 164 points. The following season, he smashed Esposito's seemingly unbreakable record of seventy-six goals by scoring ninety-two of them.
(*LA Media*)

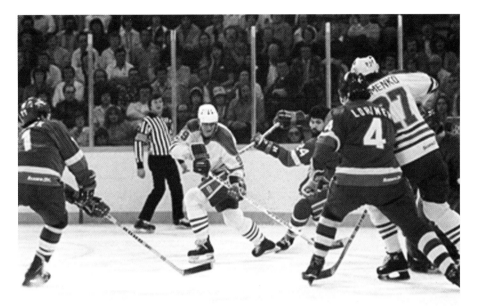

replied, "His legs aren't very hairy, Dick, and he's certainly the best hockey player on the market right now, as even you have to admit."

Two years later, in May 1984, Gretzky led the Oilers to their first Stanley Cup, and that June, he was appointed to the Order of Canada for his outstanding contribution to hockey. But it was in September of that year that the eyes and expectations of the entire country were focused upon Gretzky, as Team Canada entered the 1984 Canada Cup determined to redress their 8–1 drubbing by the Soviets just three years earlier. Only five players from the 1981 team were returning, and the new Team Canada was largely drawn from the champion Edmonton Oilers, including Gretzky, a veteran of the 1981 squad, and his teammates and newcomers Mark Messier, Glenn Anderson, Kevin Lowe, Charlie Huddy, Randy Gregg, and Grant Fuhr.

Things looked grimly familiar for Team Canada when, at the end of the first round, the mighty Soviets had achieved a perfect 5–0 record, while Canada had broken even at 2–2–1. Just as ominous, their embarrassing fourth-place finish in round-robin play had earned Canada a place in the semifinals – against the Soviets. But the outcome looked less bleak when Paul Coffey broke up a Soviet two-on-one in overtime and then took off down the ice, firing a puck at the Soviet goalie that was deflected into the net by teammate Mike Bossy. At 12:29 of the first overtime period, Canada had escaped another national crisis, and now faced Sweden in the two-game final.

Led by Gretzky, Coffey, and John Tonelli of the New York Islanders, the Canadians defeated the Swedes 5–2 and 6–5 to win the Canada Cup and to exorcise the demons of three years earlier. Gretzky was named to the tournament's all-star team, and finished first in scoring, with five goals and seven

Roger Neilson

Roger Neilson, a true hockey original, served as head coach to eight NHL teams. At his last stop, the Ottawa Senators, he was elevated from assistant to head coach for just two games, so he could become the ninth man to coach one thousand NHL games, for a record of 460 wins, 381 losses, and 159 ties. Neilson's legacy was much more than statistics, however, for he was one of hockey's more inventive coaches: the first to use microphones and headsets to communicate with his assistants and the first to use video to study players and games on a regular basis. Neilson was also a keen exploiter of the rule book, and many of the loopholes that he used resulted in the NHL's tightening up the rules. He discovered there was no law against substituting a defenceman for a goalie during a penalty shot and then having the d-man rush the shooter, or against putting too many men on the ice every ten seconds to give his penalty-killing team a break when they had two men in the penalty box and couldn't be penalized further.

Neilson was famously expelled from a Stanley Cup semifinal match in 1982, when his Vancouver Canucks were on the wrong end of an officiating deal against Chicago. "Why don't we throw all of the sticks on the ice?" asked the Canucks' tough guy Tiger Williams when the Canucks got another penalty, and the Hawks scored to put the game out of reach. "No, I've done that before," Neilson replied. "Let's surrender." Neilson took a white towel, draped it on a hockey stick, then waved it at the referee, who ignored him. Other Canucks joined in, and when Canucks captain Stan Smyl made sure the referee saw the mockery, Neilson was bounced. At the next game in Vancouver, thousands of Canucks fans showed up with white towels, which they waved, not to protest, but to cheer the Canucks, who would go on to the Stanley Cup final. Roger Neilson had entered hockey lore as the father of "towel power," now regularly seen in other NHL cities come playoff time. (*Canadian Press/UPI*)

assists over eight games. Canadians now had reason to hope for a long and happy international hockey reign. Gretzky was twenty-three years old.

He was now an asset that needed to be protected. Peter Pocklington said, "There is no price on greatness. They'd have my head if I sold him" – or if anything preventable happened to Gretzky, such as being injured by a malevolent opponent. Walter Gretzky had said that his exceptional son knew how to take a

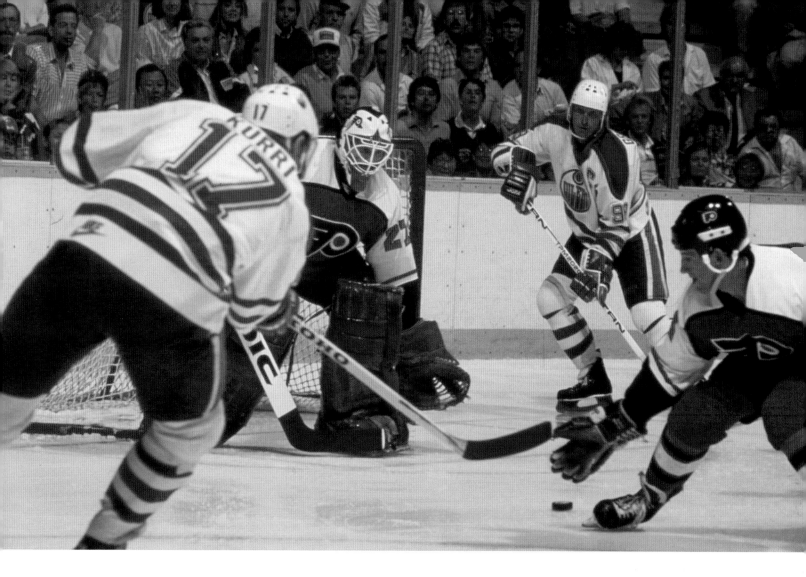

Together, Wayne Gretzky and Jari Kurri formed the deadliest goal-scoring duo in the NHL. Kurri, one of the finest two-way players in the game, was able to defend as well as he could attack, and his favoured method of putting the puck in the net was the quick release shot, which earned him the nickname Master of the One-Timer. In 1983–84, Kurri became the first Finnish-born player to score fifty goals, and the following season, scored seventy-one goals (setting a record for a season's goals by a right-winger) and 135 points – finishing second to Gretzky in the scoring race. (*Paul Bereswill/Hockey Hall of Fame*)

check, and the young Gretzky admitted to Peter Gzowski that, while teams took butt-ended runs at him, his response was "to try to hit them fair." Pocklington didn't want anyone hitting Gretzky, and so the player who had rewritten the record books would now rewrite the rules of superstardom with the help of the Bodyguard.

Hockey had long had enforcers, players such as Montreal's John Ferguson, the designated pugilist for the Montreal Canadiens of the 1960s, or four decades before him, the riotous Sprague Cleghorn. Wayne Gretzky's bodyguard and battle-fighter in Edmonton was left-winger Dave Semenko, who became a one-man, six-foot-three, two-hundred-pound bubble zone around Gretzky.

Hockey's previous most talented players, Rocket Richard, Gordie Howe, and Bobby Orr, fought their own battles with such ferocity that only the foolhardy took them on, but Wayne Gretzky's roughest skirmishes were the scrums around a goalie or in the corners after the whistle had blown, and more often than not he would just skate away. Opposing players soon learned to let him do just that, or else Semenko would be on top of them, threatening to pummel

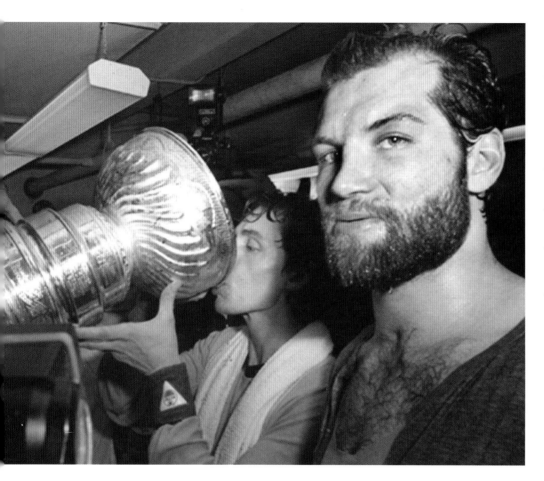

Dave Semenko followed Wayne Gretzky into the NHL and onto the same line when the WHA Oilers merged with the older league in the spring of 1979 and, until he was traded to Hartford in 1986, he was Gretzky's bodyguard on the ice. Semenko's job was to "enforce" the unwritten NHL law that no one took a run at Gretzky; those who transgressed met up with the six-foot-three Semenko's formidable fists. This gave Gretzky, who never fought, a lot of room in which to demonstrate his genius. (*LA Media*)

them into early retirement. Gretzky's bodyguard was his protest that the game's stars should not have to fight when they were put on ice to play hockey.

Like many enforcers, Dave Semenko was happiest when he was playing and not fighting, and skating on a line with Gretzky and Jari Kurri certainly helped his offensive play. During the 1984 playoffs, he earned ten points in nineteen games, excellent numbers for any player, let alone an enforcer. Still, when teammate Mark Messier's uncle, who did PR work for Muhammad Ali, lined up a bout with the Greatest, Semenko trained so seriously that one of Ali's entourage had to warn him not to do "something stupid like trying to take the champ's head off." Semenko got the message, and neither he nor Ali landed any damaging blows in their three-round exhibition bout on June 12, 1983. Opposing NHLers got the message too, so much so that the Oilers deemed Semenko expendable when he insisted he wanted to play and not fight, and traded him to Hartford in the 1986–87 season.

By the time the Oilers had won their first Stanley Cup, and Wayne Gretzky had shredded the record books and stocked the shelves with trophies, he was also stocking his bank account with an astonishing roster of product endorsements: 7-Up, Neilson's Mr. Big chocolate bars, Bic razors, Jofa helmets, Perfecta

Mark Messier, with tears of joy, celebrates his and the Edmonton Oilers' first Stanley Cup win in 1984. Despite playing in Wayne Gretzky's shadow as the centre on the Oilers' second line, Messier emerged as one of the greatest players hockey has known, and one of the game's best leaders. When Gretzky was traded to Los Angeles in 1988, Messier became the Oilers' captain and, in 1990, led them to their fifth Stanley Cup. *(Paul Bereswill/Hockey Hall of Fame)*

skate blades, Titan sticks, and GWG jeans (and later, he would do pizza, car rental, and soft drink advertisements, buy his own restaurant in Toronto, and have his own clothing line). He balanced these endorsements as a spokesman for the Heart Fund, the Red Cross, the Ontario School for the Blind, and then the Canadian Association for the Mentally Retarded (now called "for Community Living"). On top of all that, Gretzky's photograph regularly appeared in magazines, in hockey journals, and in the sports sections of newspapers in the cities in which he played. He seemed to be everywhere. And everywhere seemed to want to be Wayne Gretzky.

Jack Harrington arrived in Milltown, on the south coast of Newfoundland, to teach elementary school in 1981 but soon found that the local kids were taking their lessons from the polite, non-fighting Number 99 of the Edmonton Oilers – a team on the other side of this vast country, and yet right there, on the island. "The kids worshipped Gretzky," Harrington says. "When we were growing up in the '50s and '60s, we wanted a Canadiens jersey, but in the '80s it was Gretzky, Gretzky, Gretzky. They would try to skate around the ice very similar to the way Wayne skated. It wasn't just our community, it was throughout Newfoundland, throughout Canada, and throughout North America and the world."

The ice on which the kids of Milltown skated and played hockey was on the nearby Bay d'Espoir, where people had skated since the late nineteenth century. When Harrington decided to start a minor hockey league in the town, he needed more than a frozen bay – he needed an arena. The town's old sawmill – an open-ended Quonset hut with two corrugated steel walls, a concrete floor, and a roof – made a ready frame for a rink. It just had to be fixed up. The people of Milltown responded to the challenge with muscle, money, and ingenuity. They went door-to-door to get pledges of either labour or cash from their neighbours, then went to work to transform the old sawmill into a hockey palace, logging six thousand trees and hauling them out of the forest by snowmobile, then cutting the logs into enough lumber to build four dressing rooms, a canteen, and bleachers. They installed lights, but didn't have money for artificial ice, so Harrington and his neighbours rigged a pump to fetch water from a nearby pond to flood the ice every night. Their Zamboni was two barrels trailing towels, and they would spray the surface with cold water to aid freezing, though this was not necessary on the nights when the wind would sink the temperature as low as minus 50 Celsius. "When that froze, man, I tell you, that ice was as hard as anything," says Harrington.

In two years, Milltown built a 160-foot by 40-foot covered rink, christened Greenwood Gardens, and Cape Breton folk legend John Allan Cameron played at its official launch. When the town opened registration for the minor hockey program, 200 boys and girls signed up, and another 130 girls registered for figure skating. "With the influence of . . . people like Wayne Gretzky and Mark Messier, parents wanted this for their children and they recognized the benefits of it," says Harrington. "They didn't expect to send all their kids to the NHL, but at least they wanted their children to have the opportunity to have that dream and live that dream. Whoever put on a pair of skates and picked up a hockey stick and just had the feel for the puck, and was able to put the puck in the net, was able to be part of a team and live Canada's national game."

In Edmonton, as in Milltown, the kids were crazy about Wayne Gretzky. Giselle Lavalley, a young aboriginal girl, was trading *The Empire Strikes Back* cards in her schoolyard when another student rushed up to announce that Gretzky and teammate Kevin Lowe were in a sporting goods store just around the corner. "As a swarm, we all ran to the store and jammed ourselves in," Lavalley says. "I couldn't believe I'd met my hockey hero. I lived in the same neighbourhood as Wayne and he immediately became my favourite player."

Despite Gretzky's superstar status, he was not a typical hockey player, and for years, he had heard about it from the critics: his skating was stiff, his body was too thin, his slapshot too weak. Gretzky's achievements despite these drawbacks spoke to every kid who was "too" something, or too "not" something else, making "impossible" just a word. Giselle Lavalley begged her parents to buy her a hockey stick, so she could be a hero too. "As soon as the teams were picked, the squabbling over who got to be the Oilers would begin and two or three kids would always yell, 'I wanna be Gretzky,'" she says. "I was the only girl playing street hockey in a neighbourhood of boys. I tried to emulate Wayne's style of hockey – unselfish and smart, a real team player with a strong work ethic and a lot of passion."

When a friend asked to borrow her Gretzky autograph, she willingly lent it, but after a week, the friend became shifty, and Giselle knew that the autograph had disappeared forever. Wayne Gretzky, however, would not. Wayne Gretzky had become the game, and he belonged to the whole country.

When they ate lunch in their staff cafeteria in Edmonton one day, Jay Peacock and Dave Gridzak thought they were seeing things: the Stanley Cup had just walked into the room with a couple of the Edmonton Oilers. Peacock and Gridzak, who shared a house across the street from Edmonton's Northlands Coliseum, had heard that the champion Oilers would show up in the city's bars with the Cup and fill the jug with booze until all the patrons had sipped from hockey's ultimate trophy. And now, during lunch hour at Gainers Meats, Lord Stanley's Cup was right in front of them. Since neither had ever seen it up close

Peter Pocklington bought the almost bankrupt Edmonton Oilers of the World Hockey Association in 1977 for $1.4 million, and true to his tycoon style, paid with his wife's $150,000 diamond ring, a 1928 Rolls-Royce, two A.Y. Jackson paintings, a Renoir, and real estate. The following year, he bought Wayne Gretzky and two other players from the Indianapolis Racers for $760,000 and rewarded Gretzky's play with a $57,000 black Ferrari. In 1984, Pocklington's investment paid off, for he had his hands on hockey's priceless prize – the Stanley Cup.

(Paul Bereswill/Hockey Hall of Fame)

before, there was only one thing to do. "Dave was wearing his meatpacking clothes and lifted the Cup over his head like Gretzky did," says Peacock. "It was an amazing experience. Everybody was excited and laughing. Nobody ever dared dream they would see the Stanley Cup in their lifetime."

It was something that Edmontonians got used to seeing in the mid-1980s, as Wayne Gretzky and the Oilers seemed to lift the Cup over their heads every spring, and share it with a delirious city. "[Edmonton] came apart at the seams then," says Peacock. "Once they started winning it was expected, and when they won it was like you didn't expect it, but you knew it. It was like having your kid score his first goal and you're so elated. You knew it was coming but you're so happy when it does."

Peter Pocklington was so happy when the Oilers won their first Stanley Cup in 1984 that he had his father's name engraved upon a silver ring of the ever-elongating trophy. Pocklington's gesture was the first time that the name of someone outside the game had ever been etched into the pantheon of the victorious, and in the superstitious world of hockey, some said it would offend the gods and bring down ruin upon Pocklington's lavish house.

Peter Pocklington, a car salesman from Ontario who had parlayed his love of risk and eye for a deal into a multi-million-dollar empire, had no such worries in 1984. As a fan of Ayn Rand, the high priestess of egoism, and a man who considered altruism as the ruin of society, the forty-one-year-old tycoon was writing the script for his own journey to glory, and the Edmonton Oilers were his action heroes. "Hockey is like motherhood and nickel cigars," he said. "It's a ticket to an almost crazy place in the sun. It certainly allows me to talk on things I like to speak out about, and to be recognized." He was also writing the cheques, though true to his flamboyant style, he preferred to pay with his possessions. When he bought the near-bankrupt Oilers off the WHA in 1977, he paid for half the team with his wife's $150,000 seven-carat diamond ring, four paintings, including two A.Y. Jacksons and a Renoir, a half-million dollars' worth of real estate, and a 1928 Rolls-Royce phaeton that had been used in a movie about another ambitious tycoon, *The Great Gatsby*.

Pocklington wore Yves Saint Laurent glasses and gold-buckled Gucci loafers, he owned a Lear jet that he said could climb into the wild blue yonder "like a homesick angel," and Emily Carr's paintings of the muscular West Coast rain forest decorated his penthouse office in Edmonton's Sun Life Place. He went fishing in the Yukon with the man who would become the first President Bush, and with Ken Taylor, the former Canadian ambassador to Iran who helped rescue American hostages during the 1979 Iranian Revolution, and he took his prize, Wayne Gretzky, with him. He had a partnership with actor Paul

Newman in a Can-Am car racing team, and he owned a racing boat, which he crashed, and whose several successors he named, apparently without irony, what he had called the first one, *Free Enterprise.*

In 1978, in a frank display of ego, he mused about his greater ambitions. "There's no question I'd like to run Canada," he said. "I'm just not sure that the prime ministerial office in this country is the best place from which to do it. Perhaps I should just be a corporate giant. Yes, perhaps it would be more constructive to shape Canada from the boardroom than Parliament Hill."

Jay Peacock and Dave Gridzak both worked for Pocklington, who acquired Gainers Meats in a 1978 mega-deal. The two workers played hockey on a company team called the Rascals, and once a year Pocklington would invite the meatpackers to play the desk jockeys in the Oilers' hallowed arena. "Until you've been on that ice you don't know what real ice is like, because it is slick, it's not even cold in there, but the ice is just slick," says Peacock. "And you get in there and you've got them big stands and you were more in awe of playing in the actual coliseum than who you were playing or what you were doing, because even coasting you're coasting fast." Pocklington was generous, on his own terms: There were prime playoff tickets for his workers and promises of profit sharing, and he would even invite the Oilers to the Gainers Christmas party, for after all, everyone worked for him. The professional athletes would rub shoulders with the meatpacking grunts and the secretaries and accountants. While it wasn't quite the same as the Leafs working in Conn Smythe's gravel pit in the off-season, the paternalism displayed by Pocklington seemed to be from an era long past.

"He tried to tie us both in, make us brother and sister companies," says Peacock. "It worked, because that's the way it was, I mean, you don't go to your Christmas party and have the Oilers as part of your Christmas party. It's like, 'What? Okay, the Wayner is going to be there.' You spruce it up a little bit more and be on your best behaviour and you maybe get a chance to talk to Marty McSorley or Kevin McClelland about the fights he was in that year."

Edmonton in the 1980s was a City of Champions. While the Oilers were winning four of their five Stanley Cups in the decade, the Canadian Football League's Edmonton Eskimos won five straight Grey Cups between 1978 and 1983, then added another in 1987. Not to be outdone by their male counterparts, the Edmonton Chimos reached the pinnacle of women's hockey in 1982. Their twenty-nine-year-old captain, Shirley Cameron, a centre, was one of the best hockey players in the country and had honed her talent while growing up on a farm near Bonnyville. "We played in this small area in between the three farms where the three Cameron families lived," she recalled. "So we would gather all the time at the slough and we would play hockey every single night in the winter and on Saturdays and Sundays."

In 1972, a group of Edmonton women who wanted to play hockey and to socialize got together. Though some of them couldn't skate, and some knew little about the game, it was from this group that the Chimos were born. "We were just called the Tuesday night girls' team," said Cameron. "Whenever we went to the bar one of the girls on the team would say that you had to go 'chimo' and have a drink. Because chimo is an Eskimo greeting meaning, 'Hi, how are you doing?' And so the next year we decided that would be our name."

The league began to grow, with one team spelling *women* backward to become the Nemow, and with another called Bon Accord. The Chimos, though, were the better players, and after winning the first league title, were classified an "A" team while the rest of the league was "B," which meant the Chimos couldn't compete within their own league. So they followed a well-skated path and played against the boys – literally, at first, by taking on bantam and midget teams, then barnstorming the province playing men's "old-timers" teams. The Chimos played to arenas packed with people there to enjoy the spectacle of women giving the men a thumping. "They just loved the fact that we would come in there as women and hit the guys. Most of the communities cheered for us over the guys' teams," Cameron says. "It was great fun, but after a while if you're playing female hockey, what you want is to play other females."

The Edmonton Chimos, led by Shirley Cameron (back row, third from left), scored the first goal in the first Canadian national women's hockey championships, the Abby Hoffman Cup, in 1982. Named for the woman who had won international fame as a child playing hockey in a boys' league, the tournament signalled and inspired the resurgence of elite women's hockey in Canada. *(Shirley Cameron)*

The Chimos rejoined the North Alberta Ladies' Hockey League for the 1981–82 season, and after winning nineteen of twenty league games, the Chimos won the provincial playoffs and were off to Brantford, Ontario, to compete for the Abby Hoffman Cup. Hoffman had been recruited along with Maureen McTeer, a lawyer and wife of former prime minister Joe Clark to organize the first national hockey championships for women. Their other task was to give the venture credibility, for women's hockey was still seen as a novelty act by some members of the media, something that Hoffman countered at the press conference prior to the inaugural tournament, pointing out that the swift rise of women's hockey was reflected by the trophy's name. "I thought you had to be dead," she joked, "to have a trophy named after you."

For the Chimos, the trip to Brantford to play for a national title was a heady experience, not just for the chance to compete, but for the social perks that went with it. "They had a championship hotel where the teams stayed, and it was so exciting for us it was unbelievable," says Cameron. "You're talking about coming from nowhere to a national championship." A celebrated hockey mom, Phyllis Gretzky, was tapped for the ceremonial faceoff. "That was pretty exciting for us," Cameron says. "We were from Edmonton and Wayne Gretzky played for us, and here's his mum dropping the puck for the first game."

Thus inspired, the Chimos scored the first goal in the first women's championship, which soon attracted the attention of the media. The CBC even televised highlights and promoted the games during the intermission of *Hockey Night in Canada*. With the Chimos playing Ontario for the national title, the media were keen to interview the Edmonton captain, and Cameron, in her exuberance at being on the national stage, was keen to oblige, but for one small problem. A Canada Post letter carrier, Cameron had been unable to get time off work to attend the historic event, so she had obtained a doctor's note saying that she was injured. Her boss thought she was at home, recuperating, and so she said to the reporter, "'I'll tell you anything you want to know about our team. But please don't write my name,'" Cameron says. "And he asked me why, and I explained to him why and he made a headline out of that in the paper the next day. That was my first experience with the media, and it wasn't a good one." The Chimos lost 3–2 in overtime to the Agincourts of Ontario, and when Cameron returned to Edmonton, her boss suspended her for a week, without pay. By the time, two years later, the Chimos played for the national title at home, in Spruce Grove, Alberta, Cameron's boss had seen the light, and after they won, he gave her a couple of days off.

For Shirley Cameron, the real triumph was how what she and the Chimos had accomplished on the ice would inspire the girls in the stands. "To have our

Swift Current Broncos

Junior hockey teams playing in Western Canada have long complained about the gruelling travel schedule, as road games in far-flung cities mean long bus rides in the dead of winter. On a snowy December 30, 1986, a bus carrying the entire Swift Current Broncos Junior A hockey team, heading to Regina for a Western Hockey League game, slid out of control and into a railway overpass. The bus bounced off the concrete and landed on its side. Joe Sakic was a member of the Broncos and was sitting up front with teammate Sheldon Kennedy. "After everything seemed secure we started to file one-by-one through the windshield – not knowing what happened at the other end of the bus," Sakic later told the *Hockey News*. At the back end of the bus, four players, Trent Kresse, twenty, Scott Kruger, nineteen, Chris Mantyka, nineteen, and Brent Ruff, sixteen, had been playing cards when two of them were thrown from the bus and pinned underneath. When the rest of the team reached the hospital, they learned that their four teammates had died.

Kresse and Kruger had been in the top ten of WHL scoring, Mantyka was a popular enforcer, and Ruff was one of the more promising juniors in the country. The surviving Broncos were given standing ovations of respect in each rink they played in for the remainder of the season, and Sakic was widely thought to have come of age as leader through the tragedy. "Clearly, you grow up in a hurry after something like that," Sakic said. "It changes your whole outlook on life and makes you appreciate what you have even more." (*Regina Leader-Post*)

national championships and have the arena jam-packed was unbelievable for us in our own province. And I think it helped spur a bit of growth in the younger girls to see that there was an opportunity to play."

In the mid-1980s, Canadian hockey fans found themselves with an unprecedented seven NHL teams in the country to cheer for, and this inspired a new fervour for the national religion, for now, with divisional rivalries, Canadian teams could play each other for the Stanley Cup, and between playoffs, they could compete for regional bragging rights.

Wayne Gretzky and the Edmonton Oilers regularly fought their archrival Calgary Flames in the Battle for Alberta, and there was a similar contest in

Quebec, for the wearers of the sacred *bleu, blanc et rouge*, the Montreal Canadiens, now had to contend with the team that wore the provincial emblem, the fleur-de-lys, and who called their temple La Colisée. The Quebec Nordiques had moved to the NHL from the WHA in 1979, and sixty years after the Bulldogs left for Hamilton, the provincial capital finally had another professional franchise.

Their first season was tough for the Nordiques, who finished in last place with just twenty-five wins in an eighty-game schedule. The following season, Czechoslovakian Peter Stastny, spirited to hockey glory in a John le Carré–style defection caper engineered by owner Marcel Aubut, came to the rescue, winning the Calder Trophy as rookie of the year, and scoring 109 points to help lead the Nordiques to the playoffs. Suddenly, a team that some had seen as second-class because of its tenancy in an upstart professional league gained instant legitimacy. Now fans in Quebec had to choose between "*les glorieux*," the Canadiens and the upstart Nordiques.

The McNeils, who lived near Quebec City, were a family divided by hockey loyalties. Karl McNeil was a true believer in the Canadiens and their nearly

Known as the Battle of Alberta, the ongoing competition for provincial hockey supremacy between the Oilers and the Flames began in the 1980s. In 1984, the Flames took the Oilers to seven games in their division final, the closest any team had come to knocking them off. Led by Wayne Gretzky, who frequently set up Oilers' goals from the space behind the net that came to be called his office, the Oilers defeated the Flames en route to their first Stanley Cup victory. (*Paul Bereswill/Hockey Hall of Fame*)

In the early 1980s, Marian, Peter, and Anton Stastny (left to right) escaped to Canada to play for the Quebec Nordiques. The defection caused outrage in their homeland, Czechoslovakia, especially when Peter, who had become a Canadian, played for his adopted country against the Czechs in the 1984 Canada Cup. *(Paul Bereswill/Hockey Hall of Fame)*

seventy-five-year tradition of championship firewagon hockey; his father, Robert, saw the Nordiques as the people's team, wearing the people's emblem, and battling against the uppity Canadiens with their Anglo owners and establishment fans – a team that had stolen Jean Béliveau from Quebec City in the 1950s, a memory that still rankled. The two McNeils' passions were so high, that hockey talk was banned from family gatherings to preserve the peace. "Dad was red, white, and blue deep down and right up to when the Nordiques came on the scene," Karl McNeil says. "Then he became a Nordiques fan. The Canadiens-Nordiques rivalry was really strong, and with my father it was a subject we were best to avoid if we didn't want to argue."

It was a subject hard to avoid in the spring of 1984, when the Nordiques and the Canadiens found themselves playing each other in the Stanley Cup playoffs for the second time, and the air was heavy with revenge. In 1982, the Nordiques had shocked the Canadiens by eliminating them in a best-of-five

series, and then claiming to be *the* French team in the province, even though their lineup now featured Stastny and his brother Anton, as well as a tough and talented Ontario farm boy named Dale Hunter.

By the time the series reached Game 6, appropriately during Passion Week, the Canadiens were poised to win, and emotions were high. Game day fell on Good Friday, a day when the devoutly Catholic Quebec of a generation earlier would have been praying at church, rather than baying for blood in a hockey arena. Which is what they were doing at the end of the second period, for the game had turned into a brawl. Nordiques goalie Clint Malarchuk, the backup that day, rushed onto the ice. "So Richard Sevigny, the Canadiens' backup, and I are throwing punches at each other, really going at it," he says. At one point, Sevigny tried to go after Dale Hunter, the Canadiens' public enemy number one, even though Dale's brother Mark played for Montreal. "I told Sevigny that Hunter would kill him, and he just turned to me and said, 'That's not the point.' He was just like all the other Canadiens: They all wanted to get Hunter. Even Dale Hunter's brother wanted to fight him . . . and he started throwing punches at him. It was brother fighting brother! I don't know if that's ever happened before. It was just a wild scene."

The arrival of the WHA's Quebec Nordiques in the NHL in 1979 gave the Canadiens an instant rival, and fans in the province were passionately for, or against, one or the other team. The players took that rivalry onto the ice, and in 1984, it turned bloody. A Stanley Cup playoff game turned into a bench-clearing brawl at the end of the second period – and again when the players came out for the third period. By the time the game resumed, many of the players had been ejected, and Montreal ended up winning, eliminating the Nordiques from the playoffs.

(*Canadian Press*)

When the officials finally stopped the brawl, they ordered both teams back to their dressing rooms, but the fighting started again as soon as the players returned to the ice for the third period warm-up skate. "It was a mess, but eventually they restored order," says Malarchuk. "There were a lot of ejections. I think ten guys total were thrown out. I think Peter Stastny ended up with a broken nose and got kicked out for us, and that was a big blow because he was a big weapon for us. Dale and myself, and I think Alain Côté, got kicked out. We ended up losing that game and were eliminated."

The intensity of this battle for supremacy in Quebec carried over into the world of fiction, in the hit TV series *Lance et compte*, created by journalist Réjean Tremblay, who used Quebec's new team in the NHL as the template for his imaginary club: les Nationales. Tremblay even filmed episodes at the Colisée, where thousands of Nordiques fans turned up as eager extras, all happy to carry the battle standard as supporters of the Quebec dream team – native sons who can shoot, score, and win in the end.

The series chronicled the career of a young Québécois hockey player named Pierre Lambert in a big-league team, and his unsentimental education in the cauldron of Quebec hockey. It became one of the most popular TV shows ever broadcast in the province, with millions of viewers tuning in to watch the handsome athletes move through the violent, racist, treacherous, and sometimes beautiful world of professional hockey, one that Tremblay realized, with discomfort, he had rendered all too accurately. "*Lance et compte* is probably the greatest reporting ever done on hockey," he says. "But by the time of the seventh, eighth, ninth episodes, when they started censoring certain sequences, I realized that the series had become a kind of monster."

English Canada had its own dramatic TV series about hockey, a non-fiction one. Each week millions of viewers tuned in to *Coach's Corner*, to see just what a bombastic dandy had to say about the state of the national game. Don Cherry, with his garish plaid suits and starched high collars and gaudy ties, was a cross between a nineteenth-century travelling salesman and a good old minor league hockey tough guy who could express his opinions with his fists or his mouth, both equally blunt. "The Swedes sure play tennis well and that's what they should stick to," he once said, expanding upon the stereotype that Swedish players were too delicate to play hockey. And he once summed up the players from an entire continent by saying, "The Europeans couldn't fight their way out of a wet paper bag. The only fighting they do is with their wives."

Francophone Canadians, often by omission, or by deliberate insult, found themselves portrayed by Cherry somewhere between heroic Anglo-Saxon players and perfidious, lily-livered Europeans. "All I can picture is the guys in the beer halls out there, in Saskatchewan or wherever," said Cherry. "Those are my people. I'm a beer hall kind of guy, and I know those are the guys watching me." The remarks reflected Cherry's belief that hockey was an English-Canadian game, fast and bruising but fair, and in which fighting was essential to protect the honour of the team against underhanded opponents.

He practised what he preached as a journeyman minor leaguer in the 1950s, who played just one NHL game in Boston, on March 31, 1955. "I was a tough, stay-at-home defenceman," he said. "I was a plugger. I could fight and I was a sucker puncher. Once when I was nineteen and playing for Hershey, Bobby Baun hit me with a sucker punch while I was watchin' a fight. Nobody ever suckered me after that. I was the gunfighter. If a guy went runnin' at Bronco Horvath of our club, I took care of him." In 1954, on his first date with the woman he would marry, Rose Martini, Cherry took her to a hockey game in which he was playing during his rookie year in Hershey, Pennsylvania. That was his idea of high romance. "It was the first game I'd ever seen," Rose Cherry recalled. "And about two minutes into it, Don was in a brawl. I said, 'These Canadians are barbarians.'"

Coach's Corner debuted by accident in 1980 after Cherry had been fired as an NHL coach by the Boston Bruins, and was on the bubble with the Colorado Rockies who had won just nineteen games, while losing almost fifty and tying thirteen. Amid rumours that he was about to be fired again, Cherry accepted an invitation from CBC-TV to dispense coaching wisdom to the viewers between periods of Stanley Cup games. For Cherry, who had once supplemented his minor-league hockey income with off-season work painting houses, selling cars (or not selling them, once calling himself "the world's worst Cadillac salesman"), and getting up at five-thirty on freezing winter mornings to work a construction jackhammer, the TV offer was a chance to be paid for doing what he loved.

The media already loved Cherry from his Boston tenure, when he not only coached the talented Bruins to four straight first-place finishes, and also for his sartorial boldness, his ability to quote Lord Nelson and Popeye, his tribal mentality, and for saying aloud what other people would not. "I just say the things that everybody else thinks, but is afraid to say," he admits. His critics were quick to say that it wasn't fear that kept their mouths shut, but that they didn't think those things in the first place.

Cherry's popularity soared, and *Coach's Corner*, aired each Saturday night of the hockey season, after the first period of *Hockey Night in Canada*, became must-see TV for Cherry-lovers and those who loved to hate him. With his blustery, often sentimental style, which he wrapped in the flag and delivered with unshakeable conviction and a common touch, Cherry became the moral guide for a generation of hockey players, their parents, and their coaches.

The television personality and former coach Don Cherry played just one game in the NHL, for the Boston Bruins in the 1955 playoffs. He spent his entire playing career in the minors, winning the American Hockey League's Calder Cup as a defenceman with the Springfield Indians in 1960. He would later win two more Calder Cups with the Rochester Americans, in 1965 (above) and 1966. (*Billy Harris*)

Canada was leading the Soviets 4–2 at the 1987 World Junior Hockey championship and was assured of the gold if the team won by at least five goals when a fight between Pavel Kostichkin and Theoren Fleury caused a bench-clearing brawl. The fighting players, including future NHL star Brendan Shanahan, kept battling even when the arena lights were turned off. The game was cancelled, and the IIHF expelled both teams from the tournament and awarded Finland the gold. (*Associated Press*)

In January 1987, Cherry's "take no prisoners" attitude made him a hero to millions. Canadian and Soviet World Junior hockey teams were playing the deciding game in Piestany, Czechoslovakia, and Canada was leading the Soviets 4–2. Canada was assured a medal: gold if they could beat the Soviets by at least five goals, silver if they won by less than five goals, and bronze if they lost the game. Then a fight broke out, and a twenty-minute, bench-clearing brawl followed. Norwegian referee Hans Ronning and his linesmen were unable to stop the fighting, and even left the ice for a time. Desperate tournament organizers turned off the lights in the arena and, eventually, the exhausted players stopped.

In the CBC studio in Toronto, Cherry, acting as commentator, defended the Canadians from host Brian Williams's criticism. "[The Russians] were goading our guys all the time. And we do not accept high sticks, we do . . . spears in the back," Cherry fumed. "It's our Canadian nature not to take that stuff. . . . You people sitting at home in your living rooms, maybe having a pop or two or a sandwich, or something . . . so see something, 'How could this fellow do that?' You don't know what those guys have been through over there, and what they're going through. So don't say it's a black mark against our players, please." Williams persisted, arguing that both teams should be kicked out of the tournament. The International Ice Hockey Federation felt the same way, voting to expel both teams from the tournament and awarding Finland the gold medal. "We knew what we had to do," said Cherry. "I feel bad about it. We had to do it. But we don't take slaps in the face."

Two weeks after the brawl, Cherry was the subject of a *Globe and Mail* feature, and firmly planted his flag in the ground of the "real" Canadian male. "There's a lot of mothers and women who don't like it," he said. "There's a lot of college professors that don't like it. But I'm talkin' to the guy that goes in the beverage hall." Cherry's blue-collar sentiments were making him rich. He owned two bars, was a TV pitchman, and his *Grapeline* radio show was broadcast on ninety stations nationally, and *Grapevine* television show on twenty-six stations. "Every time I drive by those guys that are workin' on the highway with a jackhammer," he said, "I have a guilty feeling that I should be there too."

In 1989, Cherry released the first in a popular series of video titles called *Don Cherry's Rock'em Sock'em Hockey* in which the coach presented a compilation of clips showing what he thought hockey was about: brilliant, fearless playing, and very heavy hitting, with a fight or two thrown in. Writer and

Don Cherry dispenses his hockey wisdom in the company of the genial and insightful Ron MacLean each Saturday night during the first intermission of the first game of CBC's *Hockey Night in Canada* doubleheader. Flamboyant, forthright, and a patriotic traditionalist, Cherry's weekly television performance turned him into a "love him or hate him but don't miss his show" Canadian institution. (*CBC Television Sports*)

journalist Roy MacGregor has commented, "His thinking, and his extraordinary influence, has been the single most destructive influence on the development of Canadian hockey." But St. Louis Blues captain Chris Pronger best sums up Cherry's appeal. "I know people who don't even watch the game on Saturday night," he said, "but just tune in for *Coach's Corner*."

In June 1985, a twelve-year-old hockey player sat down at the family kitchen table in Toronto's Beaches neighbourhood, and with the help of her mother, Caroline, wrote a letter to the *Globe and Mail* about the state of hockey. "Tryout time is here again, and I'm going to hear the same words again: 'Yes, you're good enough. We wish we could use you. But you're a girl,'" Justine Blainey wrote. "I have important reasons to want to play in the boys' hockey league. Girls' hockey offers only two levels of play; the boys have five. I want to play more games at the highest level of competition. Is there an individual or a group that can help me? Is there a lawyer willing to donate his or her time to fight this unfairness? I want to be judged on my ability alone."

Like generations of girls before her, Justine Blainey just wanted to play hockey at a level suited to her talents, and that meant playing with the boys. She had used a now common ruse and played for a season disguised as a boy, dropping the "e" from her name. But the fakery presented problems to a girl approaching puberty. "It's difficult, you know, to pretend you're a boy. It wasn't so easy. If you like certain boys on the team and . . . you just weren't yourself."

Justine's mother believed that publicly funded teams should not bar girls from play if they were good enough to make the cut, and she believed that Canada's new Charter of Rights and Freedoms supported her position. "Every individual is equal before and under the law," reads the Charter's section 15, "and has the right to the equal protection and equal benefit of the law without discrimination and, in particular, without discrimination based on race, national or ethnic origin, colour, religion, sex, age or mental or physical disability."

The City of Toronto agreed, and in April of 1985, threatened to cancel arena permits for minor hockey leagues that refused to let girls play on boys' teams. That same spring, Justine Blainey, just five-foot-one and one hundred pounds, made the Toronto Olympics hockey team after tryouts involving more than sixty players. Her coach, Dan Damario, rated her as the sixth or seventh best player on the team. "She is very competitive, wants to learn and has good basic skills in skating and shooting," he said. "She skates backwards as well or better than anyone her age in the A level. She will be a regular with us, most likely on right defence."

Despite her coach's enthusiasm, Blainey was still barred from play in a league game because the Ontario Hockey Association fought back with a rule preventing mixed play above the age of twelve, a rule supported by the Ontario Human Rights Code, which allowed for gender segregation in sports. Blainey's family and their lawyer, J. Anna Fraser, fought the matter to what was then called the Supreme Court of Ontario, invoking the Charter of Rights to argue their case, but the court disagreed, rendering a decision in record time. "I feel very upset, not only for myself, but for my coach, who now has to find another team player, and for the other little girls who won't be able to play in higher levels of hockey," said Blainey. "I'm doing it for every little girl, not just for myself." The Blaineys and their lawyer appealed the decision to the Supreme Court of Canada.

Ironically, some of Blainey's strongest opponents were women. Fran Rider, president of the Ontario Women's Hockey Association, worried that the proposed changes to the Ontario Human Rights Code, which the provincial government had put into motion, would damage women's hockey by allowing men to invade it. Women's hockey officials, players, and parents began a petition campaign against Blainey that smacked of a witch hunt. "Sometimes a ten-, twelve-, thirteen-year-old would have four or five adults telling them, 'You'd better sign this petition here before Justine Blainey ruins women's hockey,'" Blainey recalled. "'There won't be a place for you to play or your daughter to play if you don't sign this petition.' And players came to me later and apologized for signing it, but they felt coerced."

When Blainey went into the locker room of her Scarborough girls' team and sat down to change, players would get up and move, rather than sit beside her. On the ice, things were worse. "My teammates wouldn't speak to me," she recalled. "I would be on the bench, and coaches would talk about me and how I was ruining women's hockey, not realizing I was right beneath them. And then players wouldn't even sit beside me on the bench. We'd go to tournaments and they would all go out bowling and not take me. It was a very difficult time. I was a very sad teenager." School was just as bad. Her grades plummeted because of the time she was spending in court, her teachers threatened to suspend her, and bizarre accusations swirled around her because of her high public profile. "Every one of my friends were seeing me on TV and all of the sudden they're saying, 'Who do you think you are? You're some kind of hot shot,'" Blainey says. "I was told I was gay, I was sleeping my way to the top, I'd never get married, and I'd never have kids."

On June 26, 1986, a year after starting her legal battle, the Supreme Court of Canada overturned the Ontario decision, ruling that it was unconstitutional for the Ontario Hockey Association to prevent Blainey from playing with boys' teams, and that the clause in the Ontario Human Rights Code allowing for sex segregation in sport was also unconstitutional.

It would take another year and a half before the OHA admitted what it saw as defeat. In January 1988, when Blainey was fifteen years old, she finally took to the ice with the boys. "I'm proud that I was able to fulfill a dream of mine," she said. "I can't wait for my first game." Unfortunately, winning the battle was costly. Blainey never fit in with her new team, and gave up playing boy's hockey less than a year after her historic breakthrough. Even so, her victory allowed other girl players to hope that they, too, could play at as high a level as they needed to. Like her hero, Wayne Gretzky, Blainey had changed the face of the game.

On May 26, 1988, Gretzky was at the top of his world and aiming even higher. As the Oilers sipped champagne from the Stanley Cup for the fourth time in the decade, Gretzky promised a locker room full of friends, family, and reporters, "We're going to be even better next year." Gretzky's optimism was fuelled by happiness off the ice. In January, he announced that he and his girlfriend, Janet Jones, would marry that summer in Edmonton. Gretzky had met Jones in 1981, when he was a celebrity judge for a dance contest show, and the sixteen-year-old Jones was a dancer. Six years later, the two met again by chance at a Los Angeles Lakers–Boston Celtics basketball game, and it was love at second sight.

On July 16, 1988, nearly ten thousand people lined Edmonton's Jasper Avenue to watch what some called "Canada's Royal Wedding" proceed to St. Joseph's Basilica for the biggest social-calendar event in Edmonton history. The Edmonton Symphony Orchestra provided the "food of love," and seven

Her male teammates on the Toronto Olympics supported Justine Blainey's groundbreaking legal fight to be allowed to play on a boy's team and wrote a letter to the *Toronto Star* in January 1986 making their endorsement public. "We are the Toronto Olympics minor peewee hockey team. We would like everyone to know that we think of Justine as a teammate, and we hope she wins her case this time so that she can play in the playoffs. Signed David Gill and 13 other members, Toronto Olympics." *(Justine Blainey)*

hundred people packed the basilica, among them Wayne's idol, Gordie Howe, Soviet star goalie Vladislav Tretiak, Los Angeles–based Canadian actor Alan Thicke, and Alberta premier Don Getty, along with many of the Oilers. They all watched the King of Hockey and his bride, whose white satin gown was rumoured to have cost forty thousand dollars, make their vows.

At the time, Gretzky was already aware his life in Edmonton might soon be over. The day after the Oilers' fourth Stanley Cup triumph, Peter Pocklington had told Gretzky that the Vancouver Canucks were interested in acquiring him. Gretzky's shock had made Pocklington back off the idea of selling his star player, but by the time of the wedding, Gretzky had heard rumours that he was going to Vancouver, to Detroit, or to Los Angeles. Pocklington's attitude toward doing the unthinkable and trading the superstar had evolved during the past two troubled years because of one thing: money.

In June 1986, workers at Pocklington's Gainers meatpacking plant had walked off the job in a strike that lasted six months. It was the latest blow to Pocklington's troubled empire. Fidelity Trust, which he also owned, had collapsed in 1984, he owed $50 million to the Alberta Treasury Branch, his oil investments were suffering because of a sharp drop in oil prices, and the Gainers Strike turned ugly when he received a $209-million bailout of the company and hired replacement workers. "I got arrested four times," says meatpacker Jay Peacock, who had not so long ago skated on Pocklington's ice and drunk beer with the Oilers at the company Christmas party. "Twice the first day, once the second day, and once later on. I was just thrown into the clink for an hour or so and then they let you go. One time it was just for standing on the line. The police just went through and randomly grabbed people. And another time I threw a shopping cart at one of the strike-breaking buses. It bounced off the bus and the shopping cart almost made it past the plant barricade."

With so many debts, Pocklington had examined his remaining assets. Wayne Gretzky belonged to Pocklington, and with each passing year, his value dropped. The idea of Gretzky as a commodity had been put into Pocklington's head in 1986 by Los Angeles Kings and NBA Lakers owner Jerry Buss. He told Pocklington that he needed a Gretzky to sell hockey in Los Angeles. Knowing that Pocklington was loath to part with Gretzky on an emotional level, Buss said that a trade would be just business. Gretzky, he said, was a "depreciating asset." The talks between Buss and Pocklington continued, but in the end Pocklington retreated, saying, as he had said before, that he would be hung if he traded the Great One.

In the summer of 1988, the Kings had been sold to Los Angeles entrepreneur Bruce McNall, and he saw in Gretzky what Buss had seen: the greatest name in the game putting cash into his bank account. Pocklington, his fear of a public lynching tempered by his desperate need for money, saw the same thing, and Gretzky, who was still on his honeymoon, consented to the inevitable. On August 9, the rumour that people found too terrible to believe was confirmed when Number 99 was traded to the Los Angeles Kings along with Mike Krushelnyski and Marty McSorley in return for Jimmy Carson, Martin Gelinas, and the Kings' first-round draft picks for 1989, 1991, and 1993. And $20 million in cash.

At a press conference, a weeping Gretzky said that it was his decision to go, but in the days following, as shock turned to anger, people pointed one finger of blame at Pocklington and another at Gretzky's American wife – and Los Angeles resident – Janet Jones, vilifying her as a Jezebel, or as the "Yoko Ono of the Oilers." Wounded by the accusations, Jones called an *Edmonton Sun* hockey reporter while on her honeymoon to set the record straight. "Wayne told me, 'Janet, all the rumours are false.' This was before the wedding," she explained to Terry Jones. "I brought my car to Edmonton and we had every intention of living the rest of our lives in Edmonton and spending time in Los Angeles in Wayne's off-season and when we could. . . . Five days after the wedding, Wayne received the call from Bruce McNall. McNall told Wayne that he talked to Pocklington and Peter had told him, 'If you can swing him over, you've got him.'"

Jones reported that Gretzky was hurt by the fact that Pocklington, for whom he had done so much, hadn't made the call himself, and instead had gone fishing in the Yukon. But what truly rankled him were Pocklington's remarks after the press conference. "He's a great actor," Pocklington had told a *Los Angeles Times* reporter. "I thought he pulled it off beautifully when he showed how upset he was, but he wants the big dream. . . . Wayne believes he can revive hockey in the U.S. or make it a sport to be watched by millions more. Wayne has an ego the size of Manhattan. I understand that, though. If people had told me how great I was day in and day out for ten years, I'm sure my ego would be a pretty generous size too." In an equally grave insult, Pocklington wagged his finger at the people of Edmonton, the ones who so passionately supported his team. "If they think their king walked the streets of Edmonton without ever having a thought of moving," he said, "they are under a great delusion."

But Edmontonians were under no great delusion about Peter Pocklington. "People started looking at Pocklington as someone else other than just the owner of the Oilers," says Jay Peacock. "He became a ruthless businessman, out for the almighty buck. He was a traitor, he deceived the Oilers, he

When it was announced in August 1988, Wayne Gretzky's trade to the Los Angeles Kings shocked Canadians, and the sight of him then playing against the team whose hockey dynasty he had ruled was even more jarring. Despite predictions that the Oilers would be finished without Gretzky, they won a Stanley Cup in 1990. Gretzky only ever came close to the Cup with Los Angeles, taking them to their first ever Stanley Cup final in 1993, which the Kings lost to Montreal.

(David Klutho/Hockey Hall of Fame)

destroyed them. That was it. People who thought he was great now had a dirty look at him."

Giselle Lavalley, who had first met Gretzky ten years ago, was devastated. Gretzky had remained her hero as she moved across the country with her mother, who was always short of cash. In Peterborough, Ontario, as the only aboriginal girl on her hockey team in 1984, she had felt out of place, but by wearing the same equipment as Gretzky, she had felt connected to his spirit, and was chosen as the most valuable player. Now, at age eighteen, she confessed to her diary emotions that people across the country were feeling: "I still can't believe it. I grew up with him and now he's gone. Tears came to my eyes a few times upon pondering his decision. Hockey is our identity. It's the one thing that allows us to have any sort of sense of superiority over the U.S. All of a sudden I feel there's one more thing they took away from us. It's a real blow. He's one of my favourite players but he also played for my favourite team. Now what's going to happen to the Oilers?"

The Oilers did not fare as badly without Gretzky as some had feared and went on to win another Stanley Cup. In the United States, Gretzky helped to transform NHL hockey into the "coolest game on earth." Fans who once had ranked the sport somewhere below ice fishing were now wearing Kings jerseys on California beaches, with Number 99 and the lustrous brand name "Gretzky" on the back. Celebrities were turning up at the Fabulous Forum in Los Angeles to have some of Gretzky's star quality mix with theirs, and suddenly, hockey was big news in the United States.

Even after he went south, Wayne Gretzky continued to inspire Giselle Lavalley to reach farther than anyone in her family ever had. She became the first to go to university, graduating with two master's degrees, including one in aboriginal studies. She found work in Saskatchewan as an investigator in the Provincial Ombudsman's office, looking for justice, and using hockey as her motivation. "I love hockey," she said. "I love playing it. I've always said I'd keep playing until I was a grandmother or my knees gave out. It's the human struggle at the most primal level. There's someone in your way, trying to stop you from literally achieving your goal, the net. That sense of determination to overcome those who stand in your way, that became my template in life."

In February 2000, on her way to a friend's funeral in Ontario, Giselle had a premonition that she would meet Gretzky again, and just a few days later in Toronto, she noticed a lineup of fans waiting for his autograph at his restaurant. "I got really excited because here's this opportunity that I foresaw a couple of days ago," she said. "His people tried to cut off the line a couple of times, I was scared he was going to leave, but I didn't move and neither did the others ahead of me. Up until I was actually in front of him, I was in a near-panic that I might not get to meet him." But destiny stepped in, and suddenly, Gretzky was autographing her hat, replacing that autograph he had signed for her nearly twenty years earlier, the one that had vanished when she loaned the hat to a friend. When she told him that they were once neighbours in Edmonton, and that he had given her the gift of hockey, he smiled. And then he was gone.

CHAPTER 9

THE WINTER OF OUR DISCONTENT

In January 1993, Toronto Maple Leafs captain Doug Gilmour was skating off the ice after practising with his team when a sportswriter, his face solemn, called out to him, "Hey Doug, have you heard?" The reporter used the familiar tone of one delivering the news that a player has been traded to another team. "Heard what?" asked Gilmour, his hot eyes suspicious. "You've been traded to Anaheim," said the reporter, letting the punchline dangle for a beat, "in exchange for Goofy and Pluto." Everyone laughed, including Gilmour.

A lot of people in hockey thought that the Anaheim Mighty Ducks, an expansion NHL team owned by Disney, a team that would take to the ice in the autumn of 1993, was a joke. Named after Disney's hit 1992 movie about a sleazy lawyer whose conviction for drunk driving earns him a community service sentence as the coach of a misfit hockey team, the Mighty Ducks' arrival upset hockey purists. To them, the team's owners and the NHL's new commissioner, a basketball executive named Gary Bettman, were making a mockery of Canada's national game.

The NHL was expanding into the United States once again. The other new NHL team that coming season was based in Miami. Wayne Huizinga, owner of Blockbuster Video, had paid the NHL $50 million for the right to bring hockey to a place where ice was what you put in your drink. In the corporate world, though, Disney and Blockbuster's entrée into hockey was hailed as a major coup because it would give the NHL access to high-powered marketing machines. And to the Canadian fans, that was the problem: it looked as if Canada's game was slipping away on a tide of American corporate wealth and bad taste.

Even the Ducks' debut press conference was embarrassing. Bettman and Disney boss Michael Eisner blew duck callers, and Eisner said, "This is a quack heard round the world." After blowing another "quack," he added optimistically, "See, this will work. It will work."

Bettman had been hired by the NHL's owners to bring some marketing savvy to a sport that had seemed frozen in time in comparison to the glitzy branding of the NBA, with its smoke machines and thumping courtside music and colourful marquee players. "If you run the business aspect well, the game will take care of itself," he told the *New York Times*, referring to hockey as an "entertainment product."

Gretzky's trade to Los Angeles had redirected professional hockey's sights from Canada and the Rust Belt of the northeastern United States, south to the Sun Belt – that ribbon of palm trees and desert and swamp and savannah that runs from the Pacific to the Atlantic and south to the Gulf of Mexico. Gretzky's coronation as a Los Angeles King in 1988, which verged on a national tragedy in Canada, had turned hockey into a hot ticket in Hollywood. "There was a buzz, the town was excited, this is a star-driven town even in the world of sports," said Alan Thicke, Canadian expatriate and star of the TV series *Growing Pains*, who had acted as Gretzky's welcome guide to Tinseltown. "And so they understood Wayne Gretzky on a celebrity level if not a hockey level."

Among Gretzky's legion of new fans were Goldie Hawn, Kurt Russell, their four-year-old son Wyatt Russell, and Hawn's children, Kate and Oliver Hudson. The family appeared on *Hockey Night in Canada* to tell Canadians

In the autumn of 1993, the Disney Corporation upset hockey purists by icing an NHL expansion team named after one of their movies. The movie was a 1992 hit about a sleazy lawyer who is arrested for drunk driving. He is sentenced to community service as coach of a misfit hockey team called the Mighty Ducks. The team jersey of the real-life Anaheim Mighty Ducks featured an angry duck face and the team played their home games at The Pond. Just the same, the arrival of the Anaheim team was much more than a cute publicity stunt. The NHL was serious about taking the game of hockey to the United States. The Ducks joined two other expansion teams in the States – the San Jose Sharks and the Florida Panthers – as well as a new Senators team in Ottawa, which had a long hockey tradition. Within another ten years, there were teams in a number of locations where hockey was a novelty, such as Nashville and the Carolinas, as well as in hockey-savvy Minnesota and Columbus. (*Canadian Press*)

just how Canada's loss had been their gain. "We are having so much fun, we are having a blast. This is the greatest sport," said Hawn. Young Russell had his eye on the L.A. netminder, telling host Ron MacLean that his favourite player was Kelly Hrudey. Russell would grow up to be a hockey goalie himself, and in order to fulfill his potential, his parents moved for part of the year to Vancouver so that he could play junior.

Michael Eisner's son liked hockey too, and it was while driving from his son's hockey rink in Anaheim that Eisner realized that the new building going up just down the street wasn't an office building, but an arena. He made inquiries and found out that the arena would have ice, but as yet, it had no NHL tenant. Eisner approached Bruce McNall, who not only owned the Los Angeles Kings but was chairman of the NHL Board of Governors. He told Eisner that the NHL was open to supporting another franchise in Southern California. It would be good for McNall too, who would receive $25 million of the Ducks' $50-million expansion fee in compensation for his territorial rights.

Some hockey purists in Canada claimed that the southern United States would never understand hockey, not knowing that it had been played in California for decades. The minor league professional Western Hockey League had had teams in San Francisco and Los Angeles for decades before the arrival of the NHL. In Florida in the 1938–39 season, five teams made up the fancifully named Tropical Hockey League, with one of them representing Havana, Cuba, although it was based in Miami. And in 1992, the NHL had put a franchise in Tampa Bay, Florida, at the same time as it put the Senators back in Ottawa. Still, Canadians worried that adding three southern-based U.S. teams in just two years did not bode well. When the Minnesota North Stars – who were far enough north to be almost Canadian – were relocated to Dallas in 1993, they saw the future all too clearly.

Gary Bettman had been hired to "grow" the game, in the corporate parlance of the day that sought to make business expansion organic, and he knew that placing teams in populous American cities in different time zones would make hockey attractive to the ultimate corporate sponsor: television. By the end of 1993, the NHL had its first national American TV contract in decades, a five-year deal with the brash channel Fox Sports for $31 million.

At the time, Fox had a reputation as a fearless innovator, and it saw hockey as a product in dire need of a TV makeover. It went to work. At first, Fox tampered with the camera angles perfected by decades of experimentation at *Hockey Night in Canada*. Suddenly, fans were watching a power play unfold from a camera placed behind the goalie or in the corner – angles that failed to show the architecture of a power play in full flight, and instead put the TV viewer on the receiving end of an attack. Next, after enough American viewers complained that it was too difficult to follow a black puck on a sheet of white ice (though a speeding white baseball hurtling at close to 100 mph from a pitcher's hand apparently posed no such problem), Fox came up with a solution, which they debuted at the 1996 all-star game in Boston.

For many Canadian fans, having "the Fox Puck" imposed upon the game was sacrilege. The rubber puck was implanted with infrared sensors that enabled especially programmed computers to track its movement and show the puck on-screen as a blue dot or a streaking red comet, depending on its velocity. Fans hated it. "Help, there's something wrong with my TV!" said Michelle Knight of Ottawa to an *Ottawa Citizen* call-in phone poll. Players were even harsher. "That's a bad puck," said Detroit Red Wings' Igor Larionov, a player nicknamed the Professor for his intellectual approach to the game (and for his scholarly, bespectacled appearance off-ice). "It's unbelievable. You can play on bad ice, but the most important thing is the puck. Every time we play Fox games, the puck is not frozen. We've got no feel. You can't make a pass. You can't handle the puck. I think it's heavier. That's what I don't like about Fox games. The puck is not very good."

While the Fox puck was used only during games televised by the U.S. network, and would vanish altogether after Game 1 of the 1998 Stanley Cup playoffs, Fox's enthusiastic attempts to transform hockey into a television-friendly affair had some Canadians feeling as if, suddenly, the country's

As a junior player with the Laval Voisins, Mario Lemieux set his sights on a seemingly impossible task. He wanted to break the 130-goal season record set in 1970–71 by his boyhood idol, Guy Lafleur, when he too played in the Quebec Major Junior League. In 1984, in the last game of his last junior season, Lemieux scored his second goal of the night to tie Lafleur's formidable record – then he added three more goals for an 11-point night, and a superlative 282-point season.

(Quebec Major Junior Hockey League)

national religion had been hijacked by Dr. Faustus: "The National Hockey League would sell its soul to get a large television audience in the United States," wrote *Toronto Sun* sports columnist Al Strachan. The soul of Canadian hockey was in trouble and there was no saviour in sight. The most highly touted player in Canada after Gretzky left was now with a franchise as earthbound as its name: the Penguins.

It had not begun that way when Mario Lemieux was selected first overall in the 1984 amateur draft by the Pittsburgh Penguins. Coming off a staggering 133 goals and 282 points as a junior with the Laval Voisins, Lemieux had expected to go first in the draft. His jersey number, 66, was a modest inversion of his friend and mentor's famous 99. Lemieux had thought about taking that number, until his agent told him it would be a touch presumptuous.

Lemieux had said that he wanted to play for a struggling team like Pittsburgh and turn them around. And Pittsburgh was in serious trouble. Barely a third of the 16,033 seats in its Civic Arena, nicknamed the Igloo, were regularly occupied in 1983–84. The Penguins had endured a woeful season and ended it with a deliberate whimper when they traded away their best defence-man, Randy Carlyle, and put in net a goalie who allowed an average of six goals a game. They lost fifteen of their final eighteen games and ensured themselves the right to pick first. But when they called Lemieux's name first overall, expecting him to march proudly to the podium and pull on his first pro sweater, he refused to go. The problem was money.

Lemieux had been clear about his own worth since agent Bob Perno put a million-dollar price tag on him when he was just fifteen. The Penguins thought so highly of Lemieux they had turned down the trade dangled by Quebec of three Stastny brothers for this son of Montreal, as well as all twelve draft picks offered by the Minnesota North Stars, whose general manager Lou Nanne had said Lemieux was the "type of player you could build a franchise around." They were not, however, prepared to offer an untried eighteen-year-old prospect a million dollars, no matter how good he'd been in junior. The highest they would go was $700,000.

It was a sign of the times in the NHL that $300,000 was now the difference in a salary dispute, and not the salary itself, and that an eighteen-year-old hockey player would be in the middle of it. Lemieux, however, was no stranger to disputes, having made a very public one earlier that year when he refused to play for Team Canada in the World Junior Championships.

Lemieux had played for his country in the 1982 World Juniors, but his talent for offence play didn't suit the all-round requirements of coach Dave King, who benched Lemieux for three games. Lemieux, humiliated and angry, vowed he would never play for Canada in the World Juniors again. When he refused to pull on Team Canada's sweater in the 1984 tournament, he said it was because it meant he'd miss four Quebec Major Junior League games and hurt his chances at winning the QMJL scoring championship and at beating Guy Lafleur's record. The hockey establishment wouldn't tolerate what they thought was disrespect and suspended him – for four games. Lemieux took the matter to the Quebec Supreme Court, which agreed with his claim that he was under contract to the Laval Voisins and not to Team Canada. However, the judge voiced the sentiments of Canadians when he added that as a junior professional, Lemieux must make some sacrifices. Still, Lemieux had won his point, and he beat Lafleur's record, but his refusal to play for his country for what many saw as selfish reasons tarnished his image.

Lemieux had made it very clear he was looking out first and foremost for himself. And, in June 1984, in his hometown of Montreal, with CBC-TV cameras broadcasting live, and eight thousand fans in the Forum cheering him on, he refused to budge from his seat. Envoys from the Penguins came over to him, but the eighteen-year-old star-in-waiting sent them away. In the end, his agent and the Penguins came up with a creative bonus deal that allowed him to earn a million dollars in his rookie season. Now all eyes were on Lemieux, watching for him to show the world that he was worthy of the sobriquet Mario the Magnificent.

Lemieux was used to the attention – and to having a sense of destiny. His mother, Pierrette, used to bring snow into the family home in Montreal's working-class neighbourhood of Ville Émard, and, despite the raised eyebrows of the neighbours, tamp it down in the hallway so Mario and his two older brothers could skate indoors when the winter weather was too harsh. Ron Stephenson, who coached the young Lemieux, first saw him play, he says, "probably at six years old. He was just outstanding. He was just a level above the other kids of that age. Each year he got better, he could do more on the ice. By the time I coached him at age ten, at peewee, he was already an outstanding hockey player." When the Montreal Canadiens' coaching genius, Scotty Bowman, saw Lemieux in action as a twelve-year-old, he said, "He'll be a star in the NHL one day."

Lemieux's reputation had brought people flocking to see him play when he was still a boy. "At the time they would play what you call triple-headers – peewee, bantam, and midget teams would play on the same night," says Stephenson. "And they would charge admission, I think it was a dollar. And it was really packed every night to see Mario play. They stayed the three games, but the drawing factor was Mario." Some of the people who came to watch the Ville Émard phenomenon were consumed with jealousy, and Lemieux, who was a target on the ice because of his excellence, became a target off it. "The problem, especially in the pee-wee, was the adults, adults in the stands," says Stephenson. "He'd come off the ice and women would spit at him. He would go in the arena and adults would push at him. So, a lot of times when we played, not in Ville Émard, but other games in the league, if Mario wanted to go off to get a soft drink, we would have to send other team members with him."

The harassment continued until Lemieux passed the six-foot mark, heading to a formidable six-foot-four, 230-pound form. Now, hostile adults thought twice about pushing him around. The young Lemieux, however, was popular with his teammates, and while he seemed – to those who didn't know him – selfish and aloof, he was a team player. "Mario played to win," says Stephenson. "He didn't play to see how many goals he could score, how many points he could accumulate. I think he learned early that if they went after him, there was somebody open somewhere. Mario's a very generous boy too. He knew that by passing the puck, he had a greater chance of winning. I think he also gained pleasure seeing the other kids score too."

Lemieux scored on his first shift in his first NHL game in 1985, and went on to win the Calder Trophy as rookie of the year. He played so well, he redeemed himself in the eyes of those who thought he had snubbed his country by refusing to play for Canada in the World Junior Championships.

After Canada's humiliation in the 1981 Canada Cup, the country had rebounded, winning a gold medal in 1984, and in 1987, Lemieux found himself on the ice with Wayne Gretzky, wearing the maple leaf – and the hopes of a nation. After losing the first match of the three-game final to the Soviets, Lemieux rose to the occasion in the second game with three goals, all assisted by Gretzky – the hat-trick goal coming dramatically in the tenth minute of the second overtime period. In the championship match at Copps Coliseum in Hamilton, the game was tied at five with less than two minutes left on the clock in regulation time, and Lemieux had yet to find the back of the net. Tension was climbing off the meter as another overtime loomed – the nation's honour at stake. The Soviets won the faceoff, and the puck headed back to Soviet defenceman Igor Kravchuk. Lemieux went after the puck and used his long reach to poke it away from Kravchuk and into the clear for Gretzky. The two superstars took off, with defenceman Larry Murphy joining their three-on-two rush.

The fans were on their feet, screaming as Gretzky crossed the blue line with the puck, hugging the boards, and taking a Soviet player with him. Murphy moved to the net and took another Soviet with him. This meant Lemieux was in the open, and the all-seeing Gretzky fed him a perfect tape-to-tape pass, which Lemieux fired into the top corner, glove side, of the Soviet net. Canada had won in dramatic, last-minute fashion, but just in case Canadians

After refusing to play for Canada at the 1984 World Junior Championships, Mario Lemieux earned widespread condemnation for being selfish. His chance to redeem himself came at the 1987 Canada Cup, and he seized it, scoring both the goal that tied the championship three-game series with the Soviets – and the victory goal.

(*Doug MacLellan/Hockey Hall of Fame*)

hadn't received the message that Lemieux had performed a service for them, and himself, he reminded them after the game. "What can be a greater thrill than scoring the two winning goals against the Russians?" he said. "I think I have answered some questions about me in this tournament."

He continued answering questions about just how good he really was in comparison to Gretzky. The following season, 1987–88, he beat Gretzky in scoring to win the first of his five Art Ross Trophies as the NHL's leading point scorer, and the first of his three Hart Trophies as the league's most valuable player. The season after that, he elevated the Penguins, who had missed the Stanley Cup playoffs for the past five seasons, into second place and a playoff berth. And in 1991, despite suffering a herniated disc that forced him to play in a back brace, he led the Penguins to their first of two consecutive Stanley Cup championships.

Ryan Malone was thirteen years old when the Penguins won their first Stanley Cup, and the hockey-loving Pittsburgh kid took the triumph as a sign that he should look to the game as his future. "There was only one rink to play on when I was growing up," Malone says. "We'd play on one half and then you'd have the seniors playing on the other half. That's how we'd practise. . . . It was winning the Cups in 1991, '92 that really made the difference here, people started saying we've really got something here." Malone's father, Greg, had played for the Penguins in the dark years before Mario the

Mario Lemieux's skill on the ice was always judged against the gold standard: Wayne Gretzky. But Lemieux (right) more than proved his worth, winning in 1988 the first of his five Art Ross Trophies as the NHL's leading point scorer and the first of his three Hart Trophies as the league's most valuable player. In 1991, despite suffering a herniated disc, which forced him to play in a back brace, he led the Penguins to the first of their two consecutive Stanley Cup championships, which revived pro hockey in Pittsburgh.

(Paul Bereswill/Hockey Hall of Fame)

Magnificent, and his job as a scout in the Penguins organization meant Malone could have his picture taken with Lemieux and the Stanley Cup. But if Ryan Malone wanted to hone his hockey skills, he and his teammates had to travel to Canada, where, he says, "You knew you were going to get whupped, but that was rep hockey's idea of training. To play a game you'd have to drive an hour or so just to play another team."

Kids like Malone, inspired by Lemieux, would come to be known as the Mario Generation. Because of Lemieux, hockey rinks were built in Pittsburgh and local players were given serious training. In 2003, the effort paid off when Malone became the first Pittsburgh-born player in the NHL – as a left-winger with the Penguins. Malone says, "In a way, Mario was the guy that made it possible for me to play in the NHL, by turning on this whole area to hockey."

Lemieux's success in the United States still rankled some Canadian fans, who saw it as further evidence of the threat to Canada's hockey status, with the best talent heading south to the land of endless money. Then, in the mid-nineties, the haemorrhage took an alarming turn for the worse, when two NHL teams in Canada's hockey heartland found themselves for sale, with their prospective buyers living in the United States. The city of Winnipeg, with a venerable hockey pedigree, the city that had pioneered hockey in Western Canada a century earlier, and that had seen its Victorias win two Stanley Cups at the turn of the twentieth century, decided it was time to fight back.

On May 16, 1995, thirty-five thousand Manitobans took part in the largest gathering that Winnipeg had ever seen, larger than the throng that had come out to cheer, with tragic innocence, the beginning of the First World War in 1914, or that had, with a bitter sense of betrayal, taken part in the General Strike in 1919. For the crowd that gathered at the Forks in the spring of 1995, Winnipeg was again facing a type of war, and it was inflamed, not by a strike, but by the 103-day lockout that the NHL had endured for most of the first half

Eric Lindros

The strapping six-foot-four, 236-pound Eric Lindros entered the NHL with a roar – of protest, of vilification, but still, in some quarters, of approval. When he was drafted first overall by the Nordiques in 1991, Lindros and his manager parents Carl and Bonnie made it clear that the superstar-in-waiting had no interest in playing in francophone Quebec City, where lucrative endorsement contracts would not be as plentiful as they would be in Toronto or the United States. Lindros was widely perceived to be spoiled and greedy, and a popular Quebec television commercial characterized him as "Bébé Lindros." Others, though, cheered his refusal to subscribe to a system that limited his and other players' choices. Lindros was eventually traded to Philadelphia, but his first appearance at Quebec City's Colisée in the autumn of 1991 was with Team Canada. His former fans had not forgotten and threw pacifiers at Bébé Lindros. At the 1992 Olympics in Albertville, Lindros was Canada's best player, putting on a one-man show to help Canada to a silver medal.

(*Canadian Press*)

of the 1994–95 season. The lockout had particularly hurt the NHL's Winnipeg Jets, whose loss of revenue and whose need for a new building led their government-underwritten ownership group to insist that unless more money could be found, the Jets would be sold, and the buyers would be American.

Efforts by the Manitoba Entertainment Complex to arrange financing to buy the team and build a new arena were stymied by all levels of government, which had sustained the Jets' principal owner Barry Shenkarow. Winnipeggers now considered him a heartless businessman who had drained the public money trough dry and was now bailing on the city. After the Jets failed to make the playoffs, a ceremony was held in the Winnipeg Arena on May 6 to retire Tomas Steen's Number 25, and the team's logo, because the Jets were going to be sold. It was a civic funeral. "It wasn't just about hockey, it was about experiencing something that made us feel exhilarated as a community or down as a community," Jeff Shewaga wrote in a letter to the *Winnipeg Free Press*. "We live in a time where . . . we're prone to feeling a little awkward at the simple task of

The 1990s were a tough time for Canada's hockey heartland, which saw two Canadian NHL franchises decamp to more lucrative markets in the United States. Despite the impassioned protests and rallies of tens of thousands of Winnipeggers, their Jets moved to the desert to become the Phoenix Coyotes in 1996. They followed by a season the departure of the Nordiques for Denver to become the Colorado Avalanche. Their bereft Quebec fans grieved when the Avalanche won the 1996 Stanley Cup and Joe Sakic was awarded the Conn Smythe Trophy for being the most valuable player during the playoffs.

(*Above: Hockey Hall of Fame, right: Winnipeg Free Press*)

saying hello to our neighbours . . . Yet we have no problem high-fiving someone at a hockey game, or weeping with them in the last moments of an era we couldn't believe was really ending."

But Winnipeggers refused to give up hope. On May 9, Operation Grassroots began a campaign to preserve their team, organizing a riverside rally that raised $250,000. The following night, Mark Olson, his wife, Leslie, and friend Michael MacKay, staged an old-fashioned Manitoba social for the Jets. Olson had been at the May 6 tribute to the team, and it had profoundly affected him. "I've got three kids – six, eight and nine. We're doing the wave and one of the kids looks up and says, 'Dad, I just can't stop crying,'" he says. "Hockey is such a part of Canadiana. It's not a right to have a team. You have to keep it, support it, and nourish it."

Leslie Olson came up with the idea of organizing the social on a Friday night, and initially thought of charging guests $10, but Olson thought $100 was more appropriate, for after all, the team needed millions. By Saturday afternoon, the Olsons had secured the Winnipeg Convention Centre, and were planning the social for the following Wednesday. "We had everyone in the world wanting to offer prizes to us for it," says Olson. "Air Canada came in with a free flight to anywhere in Canada, then Northwest Airlines came up with a free flight to anywhere in the world. We had a cottage lot donated at Clear Lake, that's prime cottage country around here. People were coming up with fox and mink stoles, we had everything."

Everything except people buying tickets. By Tuesday morning, the group had sold only forty tickets, but then, Winnipeggers mobilized. Twenty-four hours later, the organizers had sold eight hundred tickets, and the Safeway supermarket was preparing food for that many people when Olson called them that afternoon to say there would now be 1,500 guests for dinner. In the end, 2,000 people showed up. Philadelphia Flyers star Eric Lindros donated a jersey for the raffle, which bumped the social's fundraising total up by $50,000, to $250,000.

The people of Winnipeg moved into high gear, canvassing local corporations and setting up donation centres. In the end, Winnipeggers raised $8 million, and in August, five thousand people showed up at the city's famous intersection of Portage and Main to hear the news that owner Barry Shenkarow's deadline had been met, and that the Jets would be staying. And the Jets did stay – but only for another year while arrangements were made to move them to Phoenix, Arizona.

Mark Olson heard the announcement of the team's sale on the radio. "Of course I was very disappointed, but in a way it was good to have a year to say goodbye, that long goodbye, we really appreciated that, to be able to enjoy them one more time, for one more year," he says. The Jets said farewell to less than capacity crowds, and after squeezing into the playoffs, lost to Detroit in the first round. "Life deals you some harsh blows sometimes, and you bounce back how you can," says Olson, "but you don't always get things to work out the way you want."

That sad resignation was becoming the norm in Canada. With average player salaries skyrocketing by more than 50 per cent after Wayne Gretzky was sold to Los Angeles, NHL hockey had become too expensive for some cities. The term "small-market team" came to mean the kiss of death not just for Winnipeg but for equally hockey-mad Quebec City. "No other NHL team is as close to its community," team owner Marcel Aubut had once said. "This team will forever be in Quebec City."

Aubut and his consortium faced a similar situation to that in Winnipeg, with an outdated arena and insufficient revenues. They wanted tax breaks from the municipal, provincial, and federal governments to build a new arena for a team that was now showing the colours of a Cup contender. In the 1994–95 season, new coach Marc Crawford had guided the Nordiques to the top of the Adams Division, and the team was predicted to do great things in the playoffs. But the predictions were wrong, and the New York Rangers eliminated the Nordiques from the playoffs in six games. On Canada Day, 1995, the Nordiques ownership group announced they had reached terms with the American conglomerate COMSAT Entertainment Group, and the "people's team," who wore the fleur-de-lys on their sweaters, were on their way to Denver, to become the Colorado Avalanche. "Think about all the job losses. It's a very, very sad day," one woman in the street told a TV interviewer. "Marcel Aubut, go to hell. We were there to support you and you didn't appreciate it. You know when the Nordiques were losing we still went to see them play even if they weren't champions. But today, the team is much better . . . and Quebec people are crying." Twisting the knife deeper into Nordiques fans, the Avalanche won the Stanley Cup the following season, though in Quebec City, fans still claimed the Cup for the Nordiques, if only to have the satisfaction of winning the "Battle of Quebec" in their broken hearts.

The Nordiques' archenemies, the Montreal Canadiens, were not immune to loss either, and while the team was staying put, their fabled temple was being deconsecrated and the team moved to a new building. In March 1996, Romeo Paré made the long drive from his home near Trois-Rivières to bid adieu to the Montreal Forum, a place he had cheered his beloved Canadiens in since he was a boy. He was given tickets to their games by Bob Fillion, who played left wing for the Canadiens from 1943–50, and who had once worked for Paré's father in Thetford Mines.

When Paré was a student at the Université de Montréal, he and his penurious student friends would stake out the lobby of the Forum on Thursday nights to buy half-price tickets from season ticket holders who were unable to stay for the game. Occasionally, he would go to Toe Blake's Tavern, an institution from 1952–83, to talk to the players and accept a beer on Toe, who would buy a round when the Canadiens won. "The old Forum was like a hockey shrine for me. It was the place where our national heroes, our hockey star, Maurice Richard, evolved, where he made us all feel so alive during a time where it was the sport that mattered, and not money," says Paré.

On March 15, posing as a journalist, Paré managed to make his way past security at the back of the Forum and entered the building. Once inside, he saw the pantheon of Canadiens "old-timers" waiting to get into the cars that would

On March 16, 1996, after the Montreal Canadiens won 4–1 (defeating not an Original Six team, but the Dallas Stars), the Forum closed with a ceremony that featured the cream of the Canadiens over the years: coach Scotty Bowman, general manager Sam Pollock, players Bob Gainey, Guy Lafleur, Jean Béliveau, Ken Dryden, Frank and Peter Mahovlich, Yvan Cournoyer, Dickie Moore, Gump Worsley, and Henri Richard and his adored older brother, the Rocket. For nearly ten minutes, the fans in the Forum stood in ovation for Maurice Richard, who had once worried that, after he had retired, he would fade from memory. Then Emile "Butch" Bouchard, the oldest living former captain of the Canadiens, who had patrolled their blue line from 1941–56, skated out with a torch and passed it to the Rocket, who in turn passed it to Béliveau, and onward into history. (*Canadian Press*)

carry them in a parade to mark the opening of the Canadiens' new home, the Molson Centre. Leaning against a pillar was Paré's hero, Maurice Richard. "He seemed a little dreamy, he seemed sad," Paré says. "I think he was also getting sick by that time, too. I went to see him, I introduced myself . . . and said, 'So, it's the end of an era,' but I didn't want to get into it too much because I know that he's a sensitive guy."

Paré asked for Richard's autograph, and the seventy-four-year-old Rocket, now ill with cancer, who once could roof the puck into the net with one hand, while using the other to push off the opponent clinging to his back, said he would be pleased to sign, but that he could not write his full name because his hands were too shaky. "For me it was a farewell not just to the Forum, it was a goodbye to Maurice Richard," says Paré. "I had my picture taken with him, I spoke to him as well. He was so simple, gentle and humble. I was all alone with him and I spoke with him. I tell you this now and I get goosebumps, but nowadays I don't know any players who could give me goosebumps."

Less than twenty-four hours after the Forum closed, the Canadiens' management placed the twenty-four Stanley Cup banners that had graced the arena up for auction, promising that they would be replaced by replicas twice as large and better suited to the bigger Molson Centre, where corporate millionaires in luxury boxes could gaze at them, and the action on the ice, between making deals.

Three years later, Toronto lost its hockey temple when Maple Leaf Gardens closed its doors after nearly seven decades as home to what Conn Smythe had originally envisioned as "Canada's Team." The Leafs moved to the bigger, plusher,

European Players Flock to the NHL

The fall of the Berlin Wall in 1989 and the subsequent collapse of Communism in Eastern Europe had a major effect on professional hockey. The most talented players from former Communist countries were now free to test their skills in the world's greatest hockey market, the NHL, and to earn its lucrative salaries. In 1989, Sergei Priakin became the first Soviet player to join an NHL club when he signed with the Calgary Flames, following Alexander Mogilny, who had been the first to defect, when he fled Russia to sign with Buffalo earlier that year. Soon Russian stars such as Sergei Makarov, Igor Larionov, Slava Fetisov, Sergei Fedorov, and Pavel Bure, along with Czechs Dominik Hasek and Jaromir Jagr, were lighting up the NHL and changing the North American game. When, in 1997, the Detroit Red Wings won their first Stanley Cup since 1955, they featured an all-Russian five-man unit. These pioneers in turn were followed by the next generation of Eastern European stars: Pavel Datsyuk, Marian Hossa, Ilya Kovalchuk, and Alexander Ovechkin. In an ironic turn of events, during the NHL lockout of 2004–5, many NHLers went to Eastern Europe to play professional hockey. (*Hockey Hall of Fame*)

and much pricier Air Canada Centre, which boasted 115 luxury boxes. When Leafs coach Pat Quinn was asked if he feared losing the blue-collar fan, his reply was swift and brutal in its honesty. "We've already lost the blue-collar fan," he said, well aware of the cost of taking the family to an NHL game, where four prime tickets could easily tally $400, with parking and food adding another $100. "I'm worried about the white-collar fan."

There were also worries on the ice. NHL owners were squeezing teams out of cities and ordinary fans out of rinks in the service of profit and exorbitantly rising player salaries, for hockey players were now seeing the NHL not just as the best league in the world, but as a rink iced with gold.

The opening of the Iron Curtain in 1989, and more than two decades of international hockey play, had allowed a generation of young European players to be seduced by the money and the chance to play in the NHL that success in Canadian junior hockey promised. One such young player was Pavel Kubina, who left Ostrava in the Czech Republic when he was just nineteen years old. Less than a day later, he was in southern Saskatchewan, ready to play defence for the Moose Jaw Warriors of the Western Hockey League. "I knew if I want to play in the NHL I'm going to have to go as a young guy to learn different life, different language, and especially different hockey," Kubina says. "I was very nervous because I didn't speak English and I knew I'm going to miss my parents and my family and my friends. But I was also excited because my dream was to play NHL. You know, I was trying to make my dream come true."

Kubina's dream began harshly, as he knew no one in Canada when he arrived at the house where he was billeted one cold day in October 1996. "I saw a small town in the middle of nowhere," he said. "Snow everywhere . . . It was so cold outside, and I saw their house and I just met them. And the first couple of days, I was almost crying because they were trying, trying to talk to me, and I didn't understand one word." Kubina says that his host family, Cam and Marie King, and their infant son, Zach, "were very nice to me, and anything I asked for, they took care of that. They always took me, if they had a dinner with their family or friends. So, I was the younger brother or older son, and that's how they make me feel at home."

The Kings soon learned that they would have to begin at the beginning with Kubina. "The funniest part about the first night here was Brice, the other player living with us, trying to tell Pavel to take his clothes off or to find out if he had a bathing suit to go into the hot tub," says Cam King, who was still building a bedroom in his house for Kubina when he arrived. "And Pavel had no idea what he was talking about. We spent a lot of time in the hot tub the first couple of weeks just talking to him and getting him adjusted."

When it came to hockey, the rangy Kubina, six-foot-four and 229 pounds, needed no adjustment. He already spoke the language of the game with uncommon fluency. In his first of sixty-one games that season for the Warriors, he scored a goal and two assists in a winning cause and broke the ice with the locals. "The first game I played well, and I can say, the people, they loved me right away," he says. Fans loved Kubina's skill with the puck, something he learned back home in drills that taught him puck control and strategic movement. "He was always trying to get the puck moving up the ice, whereas they play more of a defensive system in Canada," says King. "We talked about it a lot. He goes, you Canadians, all you do is skate, none of you can handle the puck." Kubina still learned much from his Canadian colleagues, especially the desire to win. "I saw the guys, their intensity, even in practice," he says. "They worked hard in the practice, and they worked even harder in a game. And their intensity, their heart, they always played with a lot of passion, and they play like that's the last game for them."

By 1995, European players in the NHL had passed the 20 per cent mark, and that same year Czech-born Jaromir Jagr became the first European to lead the NHL. In 1997, King and Kubina watched the NHL All-Star Game

Hockey fans called Jaromir Jagr "Mario Jr." when he came to the Pittsburgh Penguins from his home in the Czech Republic in October 1990 – not just because it was an anagram of his name, but because he was in the same class as teammate Mario Lemieux. Jagr, as skilled with the puck as he is strong, led all rookies in playoff scoring that season and won his first Stanley Cup. In 1995, he became the first European-born player to lead the league in scoring, winning the first of four Art Ross Trophies as the league's top scorer. *(Hockey Hall of Fame)*

together. For the first time it was either being beamed live or on tape delay to 150 countries. European players were now among the league's brightest lights, and later that year, Kubina was selected in the seventh round of the amateur draft and played ten games for the Tampa Bay Lightning. By 2004, he had become an NHL All-Star himself, and a key component of Tampa Bay's Stanley Cup victory that season. The day after the Lightning won the Stanley Cup, Kubina phoned Cam King and told him, "I just wanted to thank you and Marie, because if it wasn't for you guys, I would have gone home after the first week. I was so scared."

Canadian scouts were now flocking to Europe in search of skilled players, now a valuable commodity for the North American game. The Europeans were equally eager to compliment their "skilled" game by mastering the physical aspects of the "Canadian" game, where punishing brawn had become so accepted that players as young as twelve were kicked out of leagues if they weren't big enough. And other Canadian skills, along with skilled players and beloved teams, continued to disappear.

In 1905, the Hespeler Wood Specialty Company began making their legendary sticks in the Southwestern Ontario town of Hespeler, providing a living for people in the region who, in turn, provided the nation with hockey's key tool. The district had been a centre of hockey equipment manufacturing ever since, and its products fuelled the dreams of generations of players young and old, amateur and pro, who fantasized achieving hockey glory with a Hespeler stick in hand, or one from E.B. Salyerd and Sons Ltd, which began making sticks in nearby Preston in 1887. And on their feet they had Bauer skates, first made locally in Kitchener.

Leigh Martin was the union president for the Bauer skate factory when word came in 1994 that American corporate giant Nike had bought both the Hespeler stick factory and the Bauer skate plant. The company threw the employees a celebratory party in Kitchener's Bingemans Park, and told them their jobs were safe. Martin and her colleagues were not so sure, for if professional hockey teams could pick up and leave the country for more profitable places, so too could hockey equipment companies. "A lot of us were like, 'Uh-oh, don't think this is too good,'" Martin says, "because we knew their reputation. Nike doesn't have a good record. And this was a good place to work. We had more than 400 people working there, making good wages. In Taiwan and those places they pay somebody $2 to $2.50 a day and then the skates go for way over $100. So we thought, 'They're not going to pay us these good wages.'"

Three years later, in April 1997, on the same day that negotiations for a new collective agreement were to start, the regional head blew a whistle, just like a hockey referee, and summoned all the workers. "I knew something serious was up then, for them to stop production like that," Martin says. "He didn't beat around the bush at all. He just told us the plant was shutting down and we all had one year left. I felt sick to my stomach. We all did."

A year later, Martin's job, and those of her co-workers, migrated to Asia, though Bauer kept some skate-making jobs at its Quebec factory. When Nike shut down the stick factory in 2004, the Hespeler employees rallied, pooling their money to buy their factory and to keep their jobs – and their skills – in Canada, calling themselves Heritage Wood Specialties. But the message was clear: Canada was having trouble competing with the world, and not for reasons of talent, or desire, but for reasons of money. Money and the United States would also be what ended another Canadian tradition, although this time, there would be cheering.

Pavel Kubina (left) was just nineteen when he left his home in the Czech Republic to pursue his hockey dream in Canada. At first, his lack of English and the bleak winter landscape of Moose Jaw, Saskatchewan, where he played junior hockey with the town's Warriors, almost sent him packing. But the support of his host family and the civic warmth of Moose Jaw convinced him not only to tough it out, but to excel. Kubina went on to play defence with the Tampa Bay Lightning in the NHL, winning a Stanley Cup in 2004, a gold medal at the 2005 World Championship for the Czech Republic, and a bronze at the 2006 Winter Olympics in Turin.

(*Dave Sandford/Hockey Hall of Fame*)

On the afternoon of November 16, 1994, Ian McClelland, Reform MP for Edmonton Southwest, rose in the House of Commons and asked a pointed question about hockey, one he had been asking various members of the government, including Prime Minister Jean Chrétien, for months, without answer: "Mr. Speaker, in March of this year the House was informed that the RCMP was involved in an ongoing investigation into the activities of Hockey Canada and Mr. Alan Eagleson," he said. "Since then a U.S. grand jury has brought down a thirty-four-point indictment and the Law Society of Upper Canada a forty-one-point complaint against Mr. Eagleson. The RCMP in this time has not even contacted the primary source of information to the FBI and the Law Society of Upper Canada, Mr. Russ Conway of Lawrence, Massachusetts. My question is for the Solicitor General. Why has the RCMP not even interviewed Mr. Conway and why is the RCMP not pursuing this investigation with vigour and commitment?"

The Solicitor General of Canada, Herb Gray, sought to reassure McClelland after the usual caution about a man in his position commenting on an ongoing case, saying, "The investigation continues. I am sure it will be carried out with the professionalism that we associate with the RCMP."

Alan Eagleson, superagent, hockey czar, friend of the mighty and the famous, the man whom ex-NHLer Carl Brewer once called "the most powerful man in Canada" was in deep trouble, thanks not to the vigilance of the RCMP, nor of the government of Canada, but to some disgruntled hockey players and the dogged investigative work of Russ Conway, a chain-smoking reporter for the Lawrence, Massachusetts, *Eagle-Tribune*.

A few months before this extraordinary parliamentary exchange about hockey's woes, Bruce McNall, the man who had bought Wayne Gretzky for the Los Angeles Kings and had spent a fortune to make hockey cool in the heat of Southern California, had declared personal bankruptcy in the wake of a flurry of criminal investigations into his rare-coin business and his relationship with the banks. In December, McNall pleaded guilty to two counts of bank fraud, one count of conspiracy, and one count of wire fraud. He was sentenced to seventy months in jail for the massive shell game that was his empire.

The Kings had made it to the Stanley Cup final the season before, only to lose to the Montreal Canadiens. After the game Wayne Gretzky hinted that his back problems might speed the end of his brilliant career, one made very lucrative by the pioneering work of R. Alan Eagleson.

Until Eagleson's arrival on the scene in the 1960s as a defender of NHL players and their right to make much more money from their labours, professional hockey players had been at the mercy of rapacious owners and of their own insecure hierarchy. For decades, the NHL owners had treated the players as glorified but replaceable servants, something that the Original Six era of the NHL encouraged with its low supply of jobs and high supply of players. Original Six heroes such as Gordie Howe, and to a lesser extent Maurice Richard, were accused of keeping hockey salaries artificially low, because no player would dare ask for more money than was being paid to the best players in the best league. Not that the other players knew how much money Howe and Richard earned. The NHL was obsessed with keeping salaries secret, a far cry from the day when Cyclone Taylor's earnings were published in newspapers on both sides of the border. But during hockey's "golden years" in the 1950s and 1960s, the owners knew that they were underpaying their stars. They also knew that if the players found out, there would be far less profit for themselves, and they thought they were the ones taking the real risk.

So each season, Gordie Howe would take his $1,000 raise and believe the fiction that the rest of the Red Wings were receiving only a quarter of that because Howe was four times better than anyone on his team. It was a system that worked to feed the stars' egos, and the owners' bank accounts, until the day in 1968 when Bob Baun, the new president of the Players' Association, was traded to Detroit. Howe asked Baun how much he thought he was making, and Baun's answer – $49,500 – was very close to the true amount. Then Baun stunned Howe by telling him that he, a good defenceman but no league superstar, was earning $67,000. Baun also told Howe that, as the best player in the league, he should go at once to see the Wings' owner, Bruce Norris, and demand $150,000. Howe was angry, but he was also nervous – Howe had always felt intimidated by those he thought were his social or intellectual superiors. So Howe asked for only $100,000, but Norris agreed, shocking the man known as Mr. Hockey. When Howe asked why – after twenty-two seasons – Norris was only now agreeing to a huge raise, Norris answered for the entire league. "Gordie," he said, "you never asked for anything more. I'm a businessman."

Bob Baun and fellow Maple Leafs Carl Brewer and Bob Pulford were the first to hire their childhood friend Alan Eagleson to negotiate their contracts. Profane, pugnacious, and competitive, Eagleson could speak the lingo of a barroom brawl or that of the NHL Board of Governors. He had a University of Toronto law degree, he wore a suit, and he mixed easily with the owners at their country clubs. He also had an attitude that he would win at all costs, one that eventually cost him his livelihood, and his reputation.

At the height of his power, Alan Eagleson represented 350 athletes, almost all of them hockey players, but his first prize was Bobby Orr. One bitter discovery Orr made when he retired early at age thirty in 1978 because of his crippling knee injuries was how little money he really had. Eagleson had been fond of joking that he and Orr divided ninety-ten what the hockey superstar earned, pausing

Brothers in Hockey

For ball hockey, pond hockey, and pick-up hockey, many a sibling has been drafted into a game to make up numbers. Even the professional game has seen dozens of brothers take to the ice together – or in opposition. At the turn of the last century, brothers Frank and Lester Patrick brought the pro game to the Pacific Coast of North America, and in the 1920s and 1930s, Charlie Conacher starred for the Toronto Maple Leafs, while his adored older brother Lionel played for Montreal's Maroons, as well as in Pittsburgh, New York, and Chicago. In the 1940s, the small but speedy Max and Doug Bentley made a potent combination for Chicago, as did Bobby and Dennis Hull in the 1960s, while the decade in between saw Maurice "Rocket" Richard and his younger brother Henri, "the Pocket Rocket," dazzle the NHL with the Montreal Canadiens. Sibling rivalry on the ice was at its most intense in the 1970s, when Chicago goalie Tony Esposito tried to stop the Boston sniper – his brother Phil – from rewriting the goal-scoring record book. In the same decade, Frank and Peter Mahovlich were reunited, first on the Detroit Red Wings and then on the Canadiens. Both the Espositos and the Mahovliches wore the maple leaf in the historic 1972 Summit Series against the Soviets. Since then, the NHL has seen other illustrious brother combinations, including Pavel and Valeri Bure, a trio of Stastny and Hunter brothers, and, remarkably, six of seven Sutter brothers. In the 2003 Stanley Cup final, Anaheim's Rob Niedermayer faced off against his brother Scott of the New Jersey Devils, the Cup winners. Whenever their mother was asked for whom she was cheering, she kept peace in the family by simply saying, "My sons." (*Canadian Press*)

before delivering the punch line: "Orr lives very well on the ten per cent." It turned out to be no joke at all.

When Bobby Orr signed with Chicago on June 9, 1976, Eagleson publicly accused the Bruins of stopping their negotiations with Orr the previous December, when he had re-injured his knee. The truth was that the Bruins had been desperate to sign Orr, and in January 1976 had offered him an 18.5 per cent ownership stake in the team that he had led to two Stanley Cup championships. If Orr had taken the offer, it would have made him a "millionaire by the time he was thirty" as Eagleson boasted when Orr signed what his agent called a "guaranteed $3 million" contract with Chicago.

In 1980, Orr formally severed his relationship with Alan Eagleson, after signing a document saying that his affairs had been handled in a competent manner. Orr felt he had little choice but to sign, because he was ruined. He had assets of $454,000, but his legal and tax bills alone amounted to $469,000. Orr's later sale of Bobby Orr Enterprises (to Eagleson) and his settlement with the Chicago Blackhawks barely covered his debts. It wasn't until 1990 that Orr could bring himself to speak publicly about Alan Eagleson's hand in his ruin. Eagleson responded, with characteristic hubris, that Orr had done himself in with profligate living. Other players knew that this wasn't true – Orr was modest to a fault, a man who, far from being a nocturnal playboy, would slip into the wards of children's hospitals at the height of his fame to spend time with young and terribly ill fans. Those same former players also knew that their meager pension fund, overseen by Alan Eagleson, wouldn't let them live like libertines.

Eagleson's boast that he had negotiated an excellent deal for the players who had made him rich was untrue: by the late 1980s and early 1990s, NHL pensions were the worst in professional sport: Gordie Howe, who had played for twenty-six years and had been one of the greatest stars the game had ever known, was collecting a pension of less than $14,000 a year. Bobby Hull received $10,500, and Phil Esposito, with eighteen years in the pension plan, was getting $10,800. Rocket Richard got just $7,200.

In 1990, at a twenty-year reunion of the Bruins' Stanley Cup team, reporter Russ Conway was surprised to learn how little the players were making from their pensions, and how Eagleson had kept them in the dark about how the pension fund worked, the one to which they had contributed, through their salaries, and through the proceeds from all-star games and international tournaments such as the Canada Cup. Conway eventually convinced Toronto CBC-TV sports reporter Bruce Dowbiggin that there was a story here, and Dowbiggin became one of the few Canadian journalists willing to look into the dark corners cast by Eagleson's powerful shadow. "I couldn't believe somebody who was that well connected and that powerful would be so brazen and leave himself open to these things," says Dowbiggin. "And yet, I kept seeing stories where players had had their disability insurance taken away from them by Alan Eagleson. I kept seeing stories where Alan Eagleson had represented management and players in the same negotiation. On and on the list of conflicts were there. I kept thinking, 'Who am I to do this? Why isn't anyone else doing this? This is a great story.'"

Carl Brewer, an All-Star defenceman who won three Stanley Cups with the Toronto Maple Leafs, was deeply troubled by Eagleson's apparent conflicts of interest. He and his partner, Sue Foster, decided to find out as much as possible about just how Eagleson was cheating the men he represented. They soon discovered that Eagleson's influence was far-reaching. "There was absolute reluctance among Canadian reporters," said Sue Foster. "Eagleson

In 1995, former NHLers Carl Brewer, Bobby Hull, and Gordie Howe, who had launched a lawsuit against the NHL over their pensions, were vindicated when the court ruled they had been "grossly short-changed" and awarded them $40 million. A year earlier, in a Boston courtroom, a U.S. grand jury had indicted Alan Eagleson on thirty-two counts of racketeering, fraud, embezzlement, kickbacks, and obstruction of justice. In 1998, a plea bargain ended in Eagleson pleading guilty for a fine of about seven hundred thousand dollars and an eighteen-month prison sentence for robbing the players – such as Bobby Orr – who had made him the most powerful man in hockey. Eagleson served just six months of his sentence. Above, Milt Schmidt (left), Bobby Orr (centre), and John Bucyk, all former Boston Bruins, are on their way to attend Eagleson's trial. *(Canadian Press)*

had compromised everybody . . . He had surrounded himself and insulated himself with prime ministers, former prime ministers, premiers of provinces, Supreme Court justices, chiefs of police, the top lawyers in the land. And he really thought he was untouchable. He was part of the old boys' network and he just didn't think anyone was ever going to stop him."

In 1991, David Cruise and Alison Griffiths published *Net Worth: Exploding the Myths of Pro Hockey*, a book that took on many of the powerful figures, both past and present, in the NHL and lent journalistic support to the players' case. "It was the first real explanation of Alan Eagleson's conflicts," says Dowbiggin. "I remember reading the manuscript and thinking, Where have I been all these years? I'm supposed to be a journalist. I got in touch with several people who knew Al Eagleson very well [including] Carl Brewer, the retired player who had always been trying to alert the world about Alan Eagleson."

That same year seven NHL veterans, Carl Brewer, Bobby Hull, and Gordie Howe among them, took the NHL to court to try and recover at least $40 million in pension funds that they believed belonged to the players. Eddie Shack was one of the ex-NHLers who put his name on the lawsuit. He and his wife, Norma, along with Keith McCreary, had worked the phones to rally the retired players to take the league to court. "It was Carl Brewer and his partner, Sue Foster, who first got the ball rolling about this," says Norma Shack. "So it wasn't hard to get the players to come to a meeting, especially when some of the big names like Gordie Howe and Bobby Hull agreed to be there." Public support for the former players grew when the NHL threatened to sue Howe and Orr for talking about pension problems. But "it was still very scary," says Shack, "seven of us going up against the powerful NHL."

Meanwhile, Russ Conway was compiling a catalogue of Eagleson's crimes that became the basis for an FBI investigation into his activities as head of the NHL Players' Association. When Conway's series, which first ran in the *Eagle-Tribune*, was reprinted in the *Globe and Mail* in 1994, ex-Boston Bruin Mike Gillis became suspicious of his own dealings with Eagleson. Gillis had seen his career end in 1984 after he broke a leg in training camp. Eagleson, his agent, had charged him more than forty thousand dollars for additional legal help to negotiate his disability payment with the insurers. Gillis had since become a lawyer, and in 1994, he took up Eagleson's offer to take possession of his own files, a gesture Eagleson said he was making so that the snooping RCMP wouldn't be able to poke their noses into his files on the players' private business. But in the files he gave to Gillis, Eagleson mistakenly included papers about the disability money that Eagleson had charged Gillis to collect on his behalf. Gillis's wife found the smoking gun: a receipt showing that Gillis's insurers, Lloyds of London, had agreed to pay his claim without contest. Eagleson had stolen $41,250 from a disabled player. Gillis eventually won $570,000 in damages against Eagleson and this encouraged him to go on to become one of the most respected player agents in professional hockey.

In 1995, the players who had launched the pension lawsuit were vindicated when the Supreme Court of Canada ruled that they had been "grossly short-changed," and awarded them a settlement of $40 million. In a Boston courtroom, a U.S. grand jury indicted Eagleson on thirty-two counts of racketeering, fraud, embezzlement, kickbacks, and obstruction of justice.

The indictment against Eagleson detailing just how he had stolen from the men who made him rich was appalling. He was alleged to have defrauded the National Hockey League Players' Association of hundreds of thousands of dollars in airline passes that belonged to the NHLPA for personal trips. He

Hazel McCallion

The first organized women's world hockey tournament was held in North York, Ontario, in April 1987, and the Hamilton Golden Hawks, representing Canada, won the gold medal and the Hazel McCallion Cup with their 6–0 record. Hazel McCallion, mayor of Mississauga, helped organize the tournament and was also its honorary chair. Before turning to municipal politics, McCallion had been a professional hockey player, earning five dollars a game as a fleet centre with Kik Cola, one of three teams in a Montreal women's league, for which she played in 1942–43. Long after her playing days ended, she remained active as a board member of the Ontario Women's Hockey League, helping local women's teams to get ice time by spurring Mississauga to build the Hershey Centre sports complex. (*Hazel McCallion*)

was alleged to have stolen money from the five Canada Cup tournaments he organized and to have embezzled money from the NHLPA by submitting expense claims for $250,000 for tickets to the theatre, the ballet, and the Wimbledon tennis tournament. He also used the players' money to buy gifts for customs officials and to throw lavish dinner parties for Canadian judges and politicians. Between 1981 and 1991 he was alleged to have used NHLPA money to loan millions of dollars to friends and business associates, and to have received benefits for these transactions. He was also alleged to have defrauded two former NHLers, Glen Sharpley and Bob Dailey, of five thousand dollars each as he processed their disability claims and to have taken kickbacks on the disability insurance he bought for the NHLPA. He was even alleged to have interfered with witnesses called before the grand jury, exhorting one to destroy documents and another not to testify. He had used his position, the indictment said, "for the purpose of acquiring personal wealth and profits." Asked for his reaction to the allegations, Carl Brewer, who had worked for two decades to achieve this moment, said, "It's not that I'd be happy to see him go to jail. It's just that I wanted him stopped."

In November 1994, the Law Society of Upper Canada subsequently charged Eagleson with a variety of offences termed "professional misconduct," ranging from unauthorized loans of union funds to embezzlement of airline tickets to collusion with NHL owners. And the RCMP, after years of inaction, finally laid criminal charges against Eagleson in December 1996. A year later,

The world's first international women's hockey tournament took place in Ottawa in March 1990, featuring teams from Sweden, Finland, Norway, West Germany, Switzerland, Japan, and the United States, and was covered by journalists from eighty-five countries. When Canada's team first saw their country's jerseys, they were horrified. In what someone thought a cute publicity ploy, the jerseys were pink. By the time the tournament was over, the Pink Ladies had proved that the best publicity was excellence, outscoring their European opponents 32–1, defeating Japan 18–0, and beating the United States 5–2 to win the gold. (*France St. Louis*)

on January 7, 1998, Eagleson pleaded guilty in a plea bargain in Boston, and received a fine of $1 million Canadian and an eighteen-month prison sentence. Norma Shack said that the frustrated U.S. judge told Eagleson that "if it were not for the unusual international plea bargained arrangement of this sentence, I would be sending you to a U.S. prison for a very long time."

Despite the light sentence (Eagleson would serve just six months), Carl Brewer felt vindicated. "I remember Carl Brewer standing up in the court room and, you know, with that bald gleaming head, he looks so intimidating, and he stood up and he said, 'Your honour, I have one thing to say which is, God bless America because if it wasn't for the United States of America, none of this would be happening today,'" says Bruce Dowbiggin. "What Carl Brewer was saying is that if it had not been for the U.S. Justice Department and the FBI, Alan Eagleson would still be a member of the [Hockey] Hall of Fame. He'd be a member of the Order of Canada. He'd probably still have some kind of role in hockey."

Goalie Manon Rheaume became the first woman to play a game in the NHL when she tended goal for the Tampa Bay Lightning in an exhibition game against the St. Louis Blues on September 23, 1992. In her one period in net, Rheaume faced nine shots and allowed two goals, an accomplishment that rapidly focused attention on the women's game. She made history again when she became the first woman to sign a professional hockey contract, with the Atlanta Knights, the Lightning's farm club, making her debut on December 3, 1992.

(M.R. Photography)

In 1998, for the first time ever, the Olympic Games, held in Nagano, Japan, included women's hockey. Much was expected of the Canadian women's team as they had just won four world championships in a row. And, with NHLers making up the men's Olympic hockey team for the first time, it looked as if Canadian hockey might end its troubled decade with a gold medal.

The Canadian women played the Americans thirteen times before the Olympics, and the U.S. beat them in five out of seven matches in the two months preceding the Games, and once in the pre-medal round. Now they were facing each other once more, in the gold-medal game.

Manon Rheaume was outstanding in net, but still let the puck through twice. It wasn't until midway through the third period that Canada finally scored to make it 2–1. Then Team USA scored into an empty net in the last minute. Team Canada stood with silver medals around their necks, sobbing as the "Star Spangled Banner" boomed over the PA to confirm the USA's 3–1 victory. Only then was it revealed that Canada's best player, Hayley Wickenheiser had been hampered by two injuries, a strained knee ligament, and a cut on and possible fracture of her right elbow. But what was truly broken were Team Canada's hearts, for the women had expected to skate away as Olympic champions. "All I can remember is I'm crying," says France St. Louis. "I'm looking beside me, everybody's crying. We don't, we can't look at them in front, you know, we couldn't really understand what happened. We lost the biggest game in our lives, you know."

For the rest of the country there was still hope for hockey gold. The biggest game, the Canadian men's contest against the Czechs in the semifinal, remained to be played. For the first time since 1952, Canada expected nothing less than a gold medal in men's Olympic hockey, thanks to their collection of NHL stars, led by Wayne Gretzky. And more than a million Canadians watched in horror as Team Canada lost in an overtime shootout 2–1. Coach Marc Crawford had chosen not to use Gretzky, who, by his own admission was weak on breakaways, in the shootout. The defining image of the men's bitter loss came at the end – an ashen Gretzky, stapled in disbelief to the Canadian bench. The stunned team went on to lose the bronze-medal match to Finland, and come home filled with thoughts of revenge. "Any time you put on the uniform, anything less than the gold medal is unacceptable," said Gretzky. "This is the only country in the world where that's true."

The following year, Wayne Gretzky retired. He was given standing ovations in Ottawa during his last game in Canada, and a grand farewell during his last game in New York as he waved goodbye to the fans, and they applauded the most remarkable player hockey had ever known. It was a bittersweet ending

for the Great One, for while he had popularized the game in the United States and among kids throughout the continent, and while he was richer than he could ever have imagined, he had not won a Stanley Cup since he left Canada.

In 2002, he was back at the Olympic Games as Team Canada's general manager. Although he was in the stands now, not on the ice, Canadian fans hoped that the force of his hockey genius and the weight of his presence would inspire the players to reclaim the honour of the nation. Once again, the country was looking to Wayne Gretzky to be a saviour.

Women's hockey made its Olympic debut at the 1998 Winter Games in Nagano, Japan, and Canada's team, as winners of four world championships in a row, had their sights set on gold. But injuries and penalty trouble led to their 3–1 defeat by the United States in the championship game. (Left to right: Stacy Wilson, Thérèse Brisson, and Danielle Goyette.) (*Canadian Press*)

CHAPTER 10

RECLAIMING THE GAME

During Game 7 of the Stanley Cup semifinal between the Dallas Stars and the Colorado Avalanche on May 27, 2000, the broadcast was interrupted by breaking news, or rather, heartbreaking news. Maurice Richard had died, at age seventy-eight.

More than 100,000 people filed past Richard's casket before his funeral, just as thousands had done for another great Canadiens' hero, Howie Morenz, more than sixty years earlier. Morenz had lain in the Forum, the temple that he and Richard had anointed with their genius, but the Rocket made his final appearance at centre ice of the Molson Centre.

Those who came to pay their respects to the Rocket were joined in their grief: mothers with babies, weeping twentysomethings who had only seen Richard play on video tributes, fans old and new, and Canadiens' greats from the past, Émile Bouchard, Jean Béliveau, and the Rocket's little brother, Henri, nicknamed the Pocket Rocket. Richard's children were there too, his real family among the thousands who felt themselves part of the Rocket's hockey family. Many of those paying their respects were named Maurice because of him.

As the Rocket's cortège made its way to Nôtre Dame Basilica, people lined Ste. Catherine Street shouting "Maurice! Maurice!" as if to urge him on just one more time. They applauded when his hearse pulled up to the church, and the bells tolled nine times for Montreal's last and, to most, only Number 9. His fellow *glorieux* Jean Béliveau, Dickie Moore, and Elmer Lach, steered his coffin into the basilica, leading Montreal *Gazette* writer John Meagher to observe, "Probably for the first time since he left his mother's arms as a babe, the Rocket – who once led teammates to victory with opponents draped on his back – needed someone to carry him."

Inside the church, 2,700 mourners filled the pews – 1,000 seats in the upper galleries having been set aside by the Richard family for the ordinary people whom Richard called his own. And so the prime minister sat with the separatist premier, skinheads with bankers, francophones with anglos, and hockey players who had once worn the *bleu, blanc et rouge* with those who had worn the blue and white of Toronto. Another Number 9 paid his respects, Gordie Howe, the Rocket's greatest rival, his hair now white with age. "We didn't like him because he beat us, but we still respected him," said Howe. "The Rocket would live it, right to the end."

Richard's friend, Montreal's Roman Catholic archbishop Cardinal Jean-Claude Turcotte, wondered aloud at this diversity in his sermon. "How can it be that Maurice Richard, who is only a hockey player, be a subject of such love and admiration?" he asked. Everyone, including the archbishop, knew that Richard was much more than "only a hockey player," even though that's all he thought himself to be. Indeed, his family had politely refused an offer from the Quebec provincial government to drape Richard's casket with the provincial fleur-de-lys, a potent nationalist symbol. All through his long career, Richard had refused to allow his name to be used for any political cause. He felt he was put on earth

Maurice Richard's death on May 27, 2000, at age seventy-eight, was the end of an era both for older fans who remembered his hot eyes gleaming as he raced in on another terrified goalie, and for the young who had seen his glory only on old highlight reels. More than one hundred thousand people filed past Richard's casket before his funeral, though their fallen hero lay in state not in the Forum, the rink he had lit up with his brilliance, but in the Molson Centre, a place he had never played, but which his beloved Canadiens now called home. Here, Rocket Boily and his son, Maurice Richard Boily, pay their respects to the hockey hero.

(*Canadian Press*)

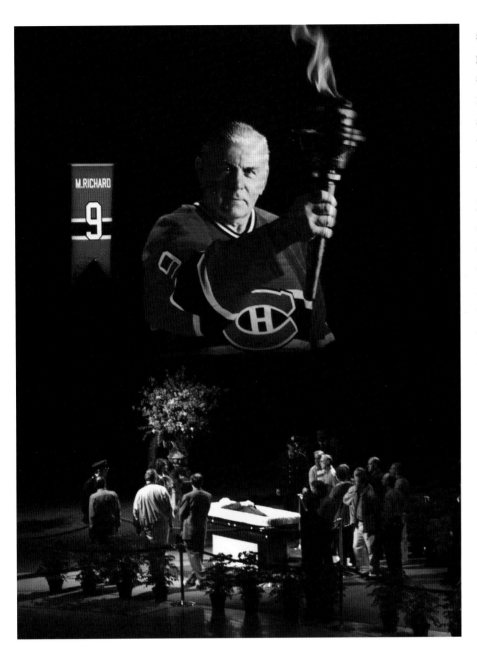

simply to put hockey pucks past goalies, and to do it straight up. "He always said what he felt, and people identified with him for that reason," said Guy Lafleur. "You couldn't buy the Rocket . . . he was his own man." And now he was gone.

Maurice Richard's death at the dawn of the new millennium seemed an ominous sign for hockey. For more than a century, Canada had worshipped the game that it had given to the world, but faith in hockey had waned as the 1990s drew to a close, partly due to its own success.

Wayne Gretzky had inspired a generation of children, and by the mid-nineties, more than half a million boys and girls were registered with the nation's minor hockey associations. This led to intense competition for quality ice time and skilled coaches, and intense and sometimes ugly competition on the ice. In a thoughtful and disturbing report on the hockey program at the University of Moncton, author, lawyer, and former NHL star Ken Dryden wrote in June 1996: "Once sports existed in an idealized world apart, with its own special, *higher*, code of behaviour – sportsmanship and fair play. It was a way for the rich – because only the rich had the time and energy to play games – to teach life's lessons to their children, lessons of hard work, morality, and discipline. Lessons to build character, to build empires. But in time, as money, celebrity, and national prestige came to enter sports, as sports became more like real life, we came to behave in sports as in real life."

The incident that led to Dryden's report happened on February 24, 1996, when the Université de Moncton's men's varsity team, the Aigles Bleus, were playing the second game of a best of three playoff series against the University of Prince Edward Island Panthers, in Charlottetown. With the score tied at two, in overtime, the UPEI forward made a shot on goal and the goal light flashed on. When referee Brian Carragher made no signal, it quickly went off.

Some of the UPEI players began to celebrate, and Carragher blew his whistle to stop the play, making the washout sign, which can mean that play has been called, or that a goal has been waved off. A few UPEI players assumed the latter and skated over to the referee to protest. He in turn skated away to confer with his linesman and the goal judge. Both the goal judge and a linesman told Carragher that they had seen the puck hit the rear bar of the net. It was a goal.

The Aigles Bleus were furious. They had seen the referee make the no-goal signal. They had assumed the goal judge had turned the goal light off quickly because he was in error. Suddenly, Carragher was surrounded

It became his signature pose: Ken Dryden leaning on his goal stick during stops in play. Dryden's stature as all-star goalie for the Montreal Canadiens led people to compare the scholar-athlete's stance to Auguste Rodin's famous statue "The Thinker." *(Frank Prazak/ Hockey Hall of Fame)*

by angry Moncton players, and then there was a punch, followed by two more. "It frightened me," said Dryden. "I also felt a sense of violation as I watched. You do not touch a referee. It didn't matter the circumstance, no explanation could obscure the point. You didn't do it. Period."

While the game was not broadcast live, a Radio-Canada crew was present to collect highlights, and soon, images of the violent swarming of a hockey referee by university hockey players were broadcast across North America. Hockey fans, already distressed by constant reports of enraged hockey parents and coaches attacking hockey referees, were shocked.

Ken Dryden was the perfect man to examine this disturbing incident, for he had more in common with the scholar-athletes of a century earlier, of men who viewed sport as an expression of the higher self, than with thugs let loose in pursuit of a bloody victory. After retiring from the Montreal Canadiens as the winner of five Stanley Cups, one Calder Trophy as rookie of the year, and three Vezina Trophies as the NHL's top goalie, he had become a writer, penning two bestselling books on hockey, *The Game* and *Home Game*. He also wrote a book on the country's education system, *In School*, after spending a year in a suburban Toronto high school. By the time he reported on that game in Charlottetown, he had worked for the Ontario Ministry of Education, he had taught at the University of Toronto, and he was a lawyer and had an arsenal of experience to interpret what went wrong that night, and to explain how the game might be fixed.

Dryden said that the heat needed to be turned down, not to the point of turning what was fun and exciting about hockey into tepid predictability, but enough that the heat had less chance of exploding into the flame of irredeemable violation. "The purpose of minor sports, of high school and post-secondary sports, is surely to learn," he wrote. "But sports itself is neutral. You learn what you experience, and what you are taught, and it is parents, coaches and administrators who establish the direction, create the environment, and set the tone."

The Université de Moncton had responded hotly to the incident, with what Dryden called a mentality of "locking someone up and throwing away the key." It suspended three players for five years, one for two years, and one for one year, and handed multiple-game suspensions to the coaches. Upon appeal to the Commission of Ethics of the Atlantic Universities Athletic Association, the suspensions were reduced and tied to community service. "These students are, in many respects, model citizens," the Commission wrote. "It was the kind of mistake which they have never made before and it is considered highly unlikely that they will ever make . . . again."

The Canadian Hockey Association disagreed. It scolded the Ethics Commission for "bad judgment" and reimposed the original suspensions, even though one of the accused players had been cleared by the Charlottetown police, who had charged several other Aigles Bleus with assault. The other accused players had pleaded guilty and were given fines and conditional discharges provided they completed fifty hours of community service during their twelve-month probation period.

Dryden had several recommendations, but the most surprising was that the Université de Moncton should put its hockey program on probation for two years, while it and other universities asked what the proper place of sports was within their communities. By extension, he was asking the rest of the hockey world to ask itself the same question. "The heat of the action is everybody's business," he wrote.

Three years later, Dryden's quest had expanded, for so too had the problem. After the Aigles Bleus' transgression, after the country's golden hockey hopes at the 1998 Nagano Olympics turned to silver for Canada's women, and to dust for Canada's men, after "rink rage" had entered popular parlance as a glib description of the thuggish behaviour prevalent at minor hockey rinks, Dryden called on Hockey Canada to stage another Summit on Ice.

He had been a member of the Summit Series in 1972, the year Canadian innocence about its primacy in the game received an unsentimental education from the Soviets despite victory. "And though we had won," said Dryden, "we would never feel the same about ourselves again." He spoke those words at his inaugural address to a hockey brain trust in Toronto in the summer of 1999, which, as a sign of the corporate times the game now lived in, was called "The Molson Open Ice Summit on Hockey." For three days in late August, more than one hundred of the key players in Canadian hockey, representing the National Hockey League and its teams, as well as minor hockey parents, coaches, association branch presidents, and Canadian Hockey Association board members and administrators, met to discuss the future of the game they loved, now so badly served by violence. They wrestled with ways not just to reclaim the game from the dark end of the ice to where it was sliding, but to take its transformative beauty and power, its expression of "Canadianness," proudly into the next century.

"Why don't we pass more and better? . . . Why do we play so many games and practise so little? . . . What about the body contact in our game, the stickwork, hits and fighting?" Dryden asked the delegates in his opening speech. "Do we need it? Is it spontaneous and natural, or is it just us? Does it get in the way of our developing other skills? You don't put a kid in the water with sharks when he's learning to swim. Then he can't focus on swimming. Then he'll just learn to tread water."

Dryden's theme was progressive change. He outlined the innovations that hockey had seen in the past century, from the forward pass to the goalie mask to Wayne Gretzky's style of play, and pointed out they had "not usually come first from institutions, from those who govern the game, but from individuals – players, coaches, owners."

He reminded delegates in hockey's next century "how we do on the ice will have to do with what we do off it," and they responded by drawing from the past to build the future. They recommended programs to train and mentor master coaches, to increase practice time and decrease game time, and to teach fundamental skills lost in the pursuit of winning at all costs. By teaching respect and tolerance, Canadians would rediscover the pleasure of the sport, and in that rediscovery lay the future of the game.

One of the delegates attending the summit was Steve Larmer, a former Calder Trophy winner for the Chicago Blackhawks, who, at the end of his

All-Star NHL right-winger Steve Larmer was also a hockey visionary – or, revisionary. After attending the Open Ice Summit on Hockey, which met in the summer of 1999 to find ways to improve the game, Larmer joined forces with a coaching friend in his hometown of Peterborough, Ontario, and launched a powerfully simple teaching tool he knew well: bring the pond hockey game back for eight-year-olds, allowing them to be creative and free, not bound by rules and coaches obsessed with winning.

(*O-Pee-Chee/Hockey Hall of Fame*)

career was dealt to the New York Rangers and whose twenty-one goal season had helped lead them to their 1994 Stanley Cup – the team's first in fifty-four years. Larmer believed that the element now missing from the game was what had made him want to play it in the first place: fun.

After the summit, he joined forces with Ed Arnold, a newspaper editor in Larmer's hometown of Peterborough, Ontario, and a veteran coach in the OHL's Peterborough Petes' system. Their plan was brilliantly simple: bring back the pond game for eight-year-olds. There would be few rules, a loose structure, and players would rotate positions so that everyone could play everything. There would be no such thing as a mistake. "Nobody wants to yell," explained Larmer. "If you yell, they'll get scared and then they'll be scared to

Hockey Songs

"The Hockey Song," a between-play fixture of Canadian arenas written and performed by Stompin' Tom Connors, is possibly the best-known hymn to the game, and it is just one of a lively roster of songs dedicated to hockey and its history. The Tragically Hip's "Fifty-Mission Cap," tells the sad story of Maple Leaf Bill Barilko; Jane Siberry's wistful "Hockey" recalls Sunday afternoons on the frozen ponds of childhood; and Warren Zevon's "Hit Somebody" speaks for the inner dreams of all enforcers. The most eloquent hockey song could be the one without lyrics, first aired in 1968 as the theme song to *Hockey Night in Canada* and now regarded as the country's second national anthem by many hockey enthusiasts, who play it at weddings and bar mitzvahs and wakes – and as the ring tone on their cellphones. On May 30, 2004, more than nine hundred saxophonists joined the Shuffle Demons jazz band in Toronto's Dundas Square to play a sax version, setting a world record in the name of one of the country's most beloved tunes. (*Shuffle Demons*)

make that mistake again and then they won't do anything at all. We don't care if these kids make a mistake. If it doesn't work this time, it might work the next. Keep that attitude of I can, I can, I can."

When Richard Jamieson returned home to Montreal after coaching hockey for eighteen years in Europe, he was shocked by how Quebec minor hockey players were playing the game. "It was like a punch in the nose," he said. "It was physical, rough, and intimidating. If you don't have three or four big guys, you couldn't even think about winning. Players were afraid to play the game." Jamieson had coached major junior teams in Canada, and professional teams in the United States over a forty-year career. Upon his return home, he became the coach of Petit-Nation, a team of fifteen-year-olds playing in the Outaouais region of western Quebec. He quickly introduced a new system designed to bring respect back to the game.

The system was called "Franc Jeu" or fair play. In an attempt to reduce the violence plaguing minor hockey, Hockey Quebec came up with an innovative concept: teams were rewarded for playing within the rules of the game. Even a team that lost a game could earn an extra point in the standings if they stayed under a certain number of penalty minutes during a game. Conversely, they'd lose a point if they won the game but had piled up too many penalty minutes in their quest for victory.

"It's another way of seeing the game, and Franc Jeu allows us to give the pleasure of playing the game back to the kids," said Jamieson. "Because what I saw before was the coach controlled too much. They had too much power in using players for this type of intimidation, and finally you got 10, 12, 20 penalties. Often it didn't bother them because there was no price to pay for this. . . . My philosophy from the start was to say, 'Franc Jeu is ours, and you own the results of the game on the ice. If we respect each other and understand each other, each one of us will make the necessary effort so that our teammates succeed.' This is team spirit."

The team spirit that Jamieson and Franc Jeu players found was not seen as such by those who believe that penalties are a strategic part of the game. This is the "good penalty" philosophy that considers tripping a player who has a breakaway to be a smart move, better than coaching goalies to stop breakaways. But Jamieson's biggest problem turned out to be the parents of the players – a group hockey's future depends upon. "I think Franc Jeu is good, but the day when parents applaud beautiful things and stop criticizing the referee, a lot of the violence will disappear," Jamieson said. "That's why I say that Franc Jeu is an important tool, but we must go farther."

Montreal's École Secondaire Édouard-Montpetit had gone farther, having already addressed a key point that would be made by the Open Ice Summit's delegates: to introduce hockey more intelligently into the education system. Rinks at schools often went unused between 9 a.m. and 4 p.m., and students were far more likely to learn basketball or gymnastics in their physical education classes, if they had physical education classes at all.

Édouard-Montpetit had become a "Sport-Étude" school, one of a few scattered across Quebec that combined academic studies in the mornings with sports in the afternoon, with an emphasis not on competition but on creation. Students can apply what they learn at school by playing in outside leagues, but they must maintain a 75 per cent average over a full academic course of study or else they are removed from the program.

The school's approach to sporting and academic excellence produced several graduates who made it to the NHL, including players as different as journeyman defenceman Patrick Traverse who has played for the Montreal Canadiens and the Dallas Stars, hard-nosed right-winger Ian Laperriere of Colorado, and Edmonton's talented enforcer Georges Laraque. Édouard-Montpetit's biggest star has been baseball's Eric Gagné, an ace relief pitcher with the Los Angeles Dodgers, who was also a fine hockey player – hockey and baseball being the two sports on which Édouard-Montpetit concentrates.

One of the prime movers behind Édouard-Montpetit was Benoît Barbeau, who began coaching hockey when the school became a "Sport-Étude" in 1989.

Barbeau, a hockey strategist, holds many degrees: a bachelor's in physical education, specializing in hockey; a master's in sports administration from the University of Montreal; and a certificate in psychosocial intervention from the University of Quebec at Montreal.

In 1986, he became a technical adviser to Hockey-Quebec, and in the 1993–94 season, he created the innovative Barbeau Method, which he calls a "non-traditional modern pedagogy," which is another way of saying that students are given the freedom to make mistakes. "Hockey was always an area where teaching was a lot about orders: 'Do this and you will see that it works,' 'Stand there, you must be there,' without necessarily teaching kids how to understand by themselves where to place themselves and what moves to make," he said, outlining the difference between his method and that of most coaches.

"For example, you come to take the puck away from me. I have a problem. I have to solve this problem. In other words, what am I going to do so you don't take it away from me? There are means that have been put in their tool box and they are going to use them. There aren't two kids who will do it exactly the same way, but they will respect the rules, precise rules, principles of the game."

Barbeau also anticipated another prime Open Ice Summit recommendation – the better training and mentoring of coaches. "A volunteer coach will be with his team two or three times more each week than our phys-ed instructors,

Benoît Barbeau has been a hockey coach and prime architect of Montreal's Édouard-Montpetit high school since it became a "Sport-Étude" academy in 1989. The school allows promising athletes to learn their sport while taking a full academic course load, and its athletic emphasis is on practising and experimenting, not on competition. The Barbeau Method is celebrated for its encouragement of an athlete's imagination, by giving students a problem to solve relevant to their sport, then letting them solve it creatively, and not by prescription. (*Édouard-Montpetit School*) who have four years of university education," he said. "Can you imagine that? Yet that's the situation we have."

The Sport-Étude schools use professional coaches, and one of them had an impeccable hockey pedigree as both a player and a teacher. Hockey pioneer France St. Louis, an original member of Canada's women's national and Olympic teams, had seen profound changes to the women's game over her twenty-year playing career. When she began her career in 1978 at age nineteen, there was no Canadian women's national hockey team, and when she retired at age thirty-nine, she had won a silver medal with Team Canada at the 1998 Nagano Olympics.

A physical education teacher, St. Louis started a Sport-Étude program for girls at the École Secondaire De Mortagne in Boucherville, just outside Montreal, hoping to offer them not only a chance to extend their education through sport, but to stay in Canada to do so. "They can go to college and university and be able to study and play hockey at the same time," said St. Louis. "So I think it's great, but we are losing a lot of players going to the States. It's our fault. We need to work on that and make sure they stay here in Quebec because we do have good hockey players."

The reason that both male and female Canadian hockey players were moving south was because of the comprehensive, well-funded university athletic scholarship system in the States. Many male players, when given the option of leaving home at age fourteen to play Canadian Junior A hockey and losing their scholarship eligibility, or taking an offer from a U.S. college and forgoing the junior route took the doubly sure thing: an education and the chance of being spotted by the professional scouts who take U.S. college hockey seriously. Three Canadian junior leagues responded to the loss of players to the States by offering scholarships of their own, paying a player's room and board while he played junior hockey, and then tuition at a Canadian university if the player was not among the lucky few to make the NHL when his junior career officially ended at age twenty.

While the program persuaded more Canadian players to stay home, there was a catch for any talented player who, at age eighteen, decided to go to a Canadian university. He was faced with the prospect of extensive bench time, as older vets from Junior A formed the core of the college team. The country that had given the world hockey still had not worked out a foolproof way to keep its hockey talent at home, and happy to be there, playing with the best, and looking out for the future.

So, as the 2002 Salt Lake City Olympics approached, Canadian hockey had something to prove on many levels, despite the deep introspection and innovative teaching tactics and programs that combined sport with education. The painful memory of Nagano still drove the country's elite players. The country needed more than self-searching and pedagogy. It needed heroes.

When Hayley Wickenheiser was just fifteen, she was invited to join the Canadian women's national hockey team. Nicknamed "High Chair" Hayley because of her youth, Wickenheiser won a gold medal at the 1994 world championships with her Canadian teammates, the oldest of whom, thirty-five-year-old France St. Louis, Wickenheiser called mom.

A centre and forward, Wickenheiser boasted a classic Canadian hockey pedigree. She grew up in Shaunavon, Saskatchewan, and took her first steps on the ice at age two, when she was given her first pair of skates. On Saturday nights, like millions of other Canadian kids, she would watch *Hockey Night in Canada*, and cheer the playmaking genius of Wayne Gretzky and the muscular vitality of Mark Messier as they and the Edmonton Oilers built their dynasty in the 1980s. Between periods and after the game, she would skate on the back-yard rink that the father of a friend had made, trying – like all the other kids on the block – to become like Gretzky. She was in love with the game.

"It just combines so many elements," she said in explaining the attraction to hockey felt by her, and by millions. "You need to be strong, fast. You need to be smart, you need to be creative. I loved the movement, the action, that it's different every time you stepped onto the ice. It played on all those things that I liked when I was a kid. And the other thing is that it was a great challenge. I was at a young age, the only girl, besides my best friend Danielle, who played hockey in our community. And that was what we did. I just loved it."

This idyllic hockey childhood was also classic in another sense, for when Wickenheiser wanted to play organized hockey at age five, she had to play with the boys. As other girls had found out before her, the problems, when they came, were not with her fellow players, but with their parents. "I still remember one mother," said Wickenheiser. "She told me, 'You don't belong here. You should do something else.'"

When Wickenheiser was twelve, her teacher parents decided to move the family to Calgary. While leaving behind friends at the onset of teenage life was difficult for her, the move was critical for Wickenheiser's development as a player. For the first time, she could play in a girls' league and gauge her abilities against her peers. "It was fun to finally be with a bunch of girls and feel more comfortable," she said. "You didn't have to change by yourself all the time. You got to be in the dressing room with the girls. So, that was kind of an exciting time."

Her hockey talent, a potent mix of strength and speed and creativity, soon made it clear that Wickenheiser had no female peer, and she found herself

Hayley Wickenheiser was just fifteen in 1994 when she was invited to join the Canadian women's national hockey team, which went on to win a gold medal at the world championships. A strong forward of exceptional talent, Wickenheiser won a silver medal in women's hockey at the 1998 Winter Olympic Games in Nagano and gold medals at Salt Lake City in 2002 and Turin in 2006. Her superlative talent caught the eye of the NHL, and she attended two rookie camps for the Philadelphia Flyers. In 2003, during the first game of a three-game tryout in Finland, Wickenheiser became the first woman to score a point in a men's pro hockey league. She said she played in the men's league not to make history, but to test herself against the best, to make the women's game even better.

(*Dave Sandford/IIHF/Hockey Hall of Fame*)

again playing with the boys – on a top-level bantam team, where, in her second season, she did something extraordinary. She won the league's most valuable player award. "That was a pretty special moment," Wickenheiser says. "That was a moment for women in hockey because you would have never thought that a girl could get that at that time. There were a lot of people who didn't want me to play in that league. I was a target. It was now full hitting, so every time I stepped onto the ice, I knew I had to be ready and be one of the best players in order to play well, to play at the level that I needed to survive."

Not only did Wickenheiser survive, she became the best female hockey player in the country, a young woman whose natural ability put paid to the so-called limitations of gender. Even in the disappointment of losing the gold medal at the Nagano Olympics, and even while playing with an arm injury, Wickenheiser was the best player on the ice, and it was not a publicity stunt when Philadelphia Flyers GM Bobby Clarke offered her a tryout at the team's prospects camp in July 1998 and again the following year.

There Wickenheiser held her own with NHL–rated talent, but was modest – and prophetic – in her aspirations. "I'm basically just seeing it as a chance to improve my game," she said, while expressing the hope that one day soon, there would a professional women's hockey league for her and other talented female players.

In 2000, Wickenheiser found herself back at the Olympic Games, though this time her sport was baseball, making her the third woman, after skier and kayaker Sue Holloway, and cyclist and speed skater Clara Hughes, to compete in both summer and winter Olympic Games for Canada. But it was the elusive gold medal for hockey that still haunted Wickenheiser, and she credited the lessons she'd learned swinging at pitches on the softball diamond for giving her perspective on Canadians' expectations for revenge at the 2002 Salt Lake City Olympics. "I've learned a lot about patience and timing," she said, "and how it feels to be on the bubble."

Another Canadian hockey hero who knew all too well the feeling of being in a place where winning was the only option was Mario Lemieux. After all, he had already won battles in several arenas, for his Stanley Cup and Canada Cup triumphs on the ice had been shaded with pain. His chronic back problems had kept him in agony, sometimes unable to bend to tie his skates or out of the lineup altogether. Then, in December 1992, he went to see the doctor about a lump on his neck and a sore throat, and was diagnosed with Hodgkin's disease, a form of cancer.

Lemieux had two uncles who had died of cancer, and he had also served as honorary chairman of the Pittsburgh Cancer Institute for five years, not just playing in charity golf tournaments, but visiting very ill children who did not have the same odds of survival that he faced. His cancer had been diagnosed early; he had a 95 per cent chance of being cured.

For the next four weeks, Lemieux underwent daily radiation treatment from Monday to Friday, and while such therapy can produce side effects such as debilitating fatigue, Lemieux's superior conditioning and his will to win served him well. After his final treatment on March 2, 1993, the radiation burn mark still fresh on his neck, Lemieux flew to Philadelphia to rejoin the Penguins, and that night, after a ninety-second ovation from the tough Philadelphia fans, celebrated his survival by scoring a goal and adding an assist.

Lemieux retired at age thirty-one in 1997, after scoring on his last shift of his last game. The Hockey Hall of Fame waived its usual waiting period and admitted him to the pantheon that autumn. But then he was handed another blow when the financially troubled Pittsburgh franchise told him it could not pay him the $33 million remaining on the $42-million contract he had signed in 1992. After unsuccessful attempts to remedy the matter in the courts, Lemieux did something that no other professional sports player had yet done: he bought his old team as part of an ownership group. In order to raise the value of the franchise, he pulled his Number 66 jersey down from the rafters where it had been retired and went back on the ice.

"It was tough early in the workouts," he said about his comeback. "I was having some problems skating and getting tired very quickly. Obviously I was out of shape, but after a couple of weeks I started to skate better, I started

Pond Hockey

In January 2002, the first-ever World Pond Hockey Championships were held in Plaster Rock, New Brunswick. Community development officer Danny Braun thought up the idea of a pond-hockey jamboree to raise money for a new recreation facility, and the inaugural tournament saw forty teams from the Maritimes and Maine play a round-robin weekend slate of thirty games in the hope they would be the ones to win the wooden replica of the Stanley Cup. By the 2005 tournament, ninety-six teams arrived from across Canada, and as far away as the Cayman Islands, to play on twenty-four side-by-side outdoor rinks on Roulston Lake, preserving the heritage of the game by taking it back to its first rink, the one run by Nature. (*Brian Smith/Village of Plaster Rock*)

to feel a lot better, not only skating-wise, but handling the puck and that's when I knew that I had a pretty good chance to come back and play again."

Lemieux's return to the NHL on December 27, 2000, came after a forty-four-month retirement. He was now thirty-five years old, and he made clear his intentions just thirty-three seconds into the game against Toronto, by setting up a goal, and later, by scoring one as the Penguins shut out the Leafs 5–0. "He's a suit-wearing executive by day," said a Penguins executive. "At night he puts on his cape and plays."

After their disastrous showing at the 1998 Nagano Olympic Games, Canada's men's hockey team needed just such a caped hero on the ice. They already had Wayne Gretzky serving as the team's executive director, and Gretzky knew there was only one man who could lead Canada to do what he had not been able to do in Japan: Mario Lemieux would now become Captain Canada, his mission to find gold in the ice and bring it home. And it would take something golden in the ice to do it.

As captain of Canada's men's hockey team at the 2002 Winter Olympic Games in Salt Lake City, Mario Lemieux shouldered much of the weight of the country's hopes for gold. The 2002 Games marked the second time that NHLers were allowed to compete, and after much-vaunted Team Canada's failure to bring home a medal of any colour from the Nagano games in 1998, Lemieux and his teammates faced enormous pressure. But Lemieux, who had survived a bout with cancer, crippling back problems, and had come out of retirement to save the Pittsburgh Penguins as both a player and majority owner, knew all about pressure. He scored six points in five games and led Canada to its first men's hockey gold medal since 1952.

(Dave Sandford/IIHF/Hockey Hall of Fame)

Trent Evans knew about ice. As an ice-maker for the Edmonton Oilers, Evans and his crew were famous throughout the NHL for the quality of their ice: hard, fast, smooth. "We like to think that our ice here lends to the fast game that fans like to see," he said. "The game is a skating game, and it's shooting and passing, and the ice is a huge part of it."

Part art, part science, and part luck of geography, the quality of the ice can make or break a hockey game, and the organizers of the 2002 Salt Lake City Olympics' did not want poor ice to be the deciding factor in gold-medal matches. So they invited Evans and a couple of his Canadian colleagues down to Salt Lake City to become part of an elite international crew of ice-makers and Zamboni drivers who would ensure that the best hockey players in the world had the best ice on which to go for the gold. What neither they, nor Evans, counted on was that there would also be gold beneath the ice.

The Salt Lake City Olympics' premier hockey venue was the E Center, and as an international ice surface, it was fifteen feet wider than in an NHL arena. As the Salt Lake logo on the ice had no centre-ice mark, Evans had to find a way to gauge the measurements of the arena to ensure that the nets and other markings were in the right place. After painting the ice white, he said, "We drew a string through the centre of the goals and both nets and made sure that we were square." Normally, Evans would fix a screw into a lead insert to make centre ice, but he didn't have one. So he reached into his pocket and pulled out

Superstition

The one-dollar Canadian coin that became known as the Lucky Loonie after its presence beneath centre ice at the 2002 Salt Lake City Olympics was credited with helping both the Canadian men's and women's hockey teams to win gold medals is part of a long tradition of hockey superstition. In 1950–51, after the New York Rangers lost several games in a row, a local restaurant owner devised a "magic potion" that players drank before games, and the team's fortunes turned into a winning streak. But it took them fifty-four years to undo "the curse" inflicted on the team in 1940 when their management committed sacrilege by burning the mortgage to Madison Square Garden in the bowl of the Stanley Cup. The Rangers finally broke the spell by defeating Vancouver for the Cup in 1994.

Many hockey players have long believed that putting on their equipment a certain way, or performing ritual actions during the warm-up, has a direct bearing on their game. Wayne Gretzky wouldn't allow any sticks to cross over each other, or to touch other players' sticks, and goalie Patrick Roy would juggle pucks between periods, then hide them to ward off bad luck. In the 1970s, the Philadelphia Flyers believed that singer Kate Smith and her version of "God Bless America" – taped or live, in place of the national anthem – gave them an edge. Toronto Maple Leafs defensive star "Red" Kelly, as coach of the 1975–76 Leafs, put crystal pyramids in the dressing room and under the players' bench, hoping that the "energy" given off by the pyramids' points would propel the Leafs to Stanley Cup glory. After defeating Pittsburgh, Toronto took on their fierce rivals, the Philadelphia Flyers, who eventually won a tough seven–game series – with the help of Kate Smith. (*DiMaggio-Kalish/Hockey Hall of Fame*)

a dime, "knowing that a coin from my pocket, being warm, would melt into the ice and it would stay there at centre."

That night, he and fellow Edmonton ice-maker Duncan Muire concluded that a dime was not the right solution. "We both agreed that it would be better to have the gold of a loonie . . . because we wanted the teams to win gold, and not the silver of a dime."

The following day, Evans went out and placed a loonie, named for the indigenous Canadian loon bird on its obverse, on top of the dime at centre ice, and because he was responsible for flooding the arena, he was the one to seal – but not conceal – his handiwork in the ice. "You could tell visually over top of

The gold-medal-winning women on Team Canada at the 2002 Winter Olympic Games sneak a look at the lucky golden loonie buried beneath centre ice. They were soon hurried away by teammates – Canada's men still had to play their gold-medal game, and they didn't want Canada's secret weapon dug up by Olympic officials.

(Dave Sandford/IIHF/Hockey Hall of Fame)

it that it was definitely a Canadian loonie," he said. That was a problem for the people supervising Evans, who told him to remove the loonie. "They just thought it was, being Canadian, an unfair advantage," he said. "It's not like it's had any bearing on the game. So that's why I didn't think of it as being a huge issue to take it out."

Evans secretly hoped that the coin would have a bearing on Canada's Olympic hockey fortunes, and instead of removing the loonie, he daubed yellow paint over the ice above it. Now he had to let the Canadian teams know. He went to the Canadian Pavilion and introduced himself to Bob Nicholson, president of the Canadian Hockey Association. After hearing the story, Nicholson "was so excited he actually pulled me into a VIP room and he wanted me to tell the story again to Pat Quinn and his wife and some of the Canadian trainers," Evans says.

Evans delivered the news himself to the Canadian women's team, who would be skating for the gold medal against their nemesis, the United States, and now the loonie became a battle standard for the teams. "It was rah-rah, come on girls, we're skating on top of the Canadian loonie, let's do Canada proud."

The Canadian women came into the gold-medal game as underdogs, having lost eight straight pre-Olympic matches to the United States. They had trouble with Finland in the semifinal, before rallying for a come-from-behind, and convincing, 7–3 win in the third period.

Canada's women's hockey team had expected gold but came away with silver at the Winter Olympic Games in Nagano in 1998. Helped by the golden one-dollar Canadian coin – the Lucky Loonie – and by their own roster of talent and desire, Canada's women survived a rash of dubious penalty calls and a third-period surge by their arch-rivals from the USA to win 3–2 and take the country's first Olympic women's hockey gold medal. (*Canadian Press*)

Canadian veteran Thérèse Brisson used an American classic to put her team's task into perspective, e-mailing a friend at home to say that she and her teammates felt like Dorothy in the *Wizard of Oz*. "So we came here with some friends, a Scarecrow, Tin Man, Lion, looking for some brains – brains for me especially (she had suffered a concussion a few months earlier) – heart, courage, and Dorothy found the Wizard and he told her, 'You have what it takes to do it.'"

But now they were playing the United States on home ice, and it seemed to the Canadians as if the Olympic ideal might be trumped by unbridled nationalism. The referee, an American, called thirteen penalties against Canada – eight of them in a row – while giving Team USA only six. "She might as well have had an American jersey on today," defenceman Geraldine Heaney said after the game.

With four minutes left, the women wearing the Maple Leaf had a two-goal lead when Karyn Bye, who had wrapped herself in an American flag in celebration after winning gold at Nagano, closed the gap to one, and it looked like the momentum might have shifted. But the Canadians had the golden loonie beneath them, and then gold around their necks as they avenged their loss at Nagano, and proved they were who they thought they were: the golden girls. "It was the most emotional moment in my life," said Wickenheiser, who had scored one of Canada's goals, and would be named MVP. "Everything I had worked for, hoped for, came together at that moment. I was the happiest person on earth."

In their elation, the Canadian women now saw the buried loonie as a real part of their triumph, and some of them wanted a closer look. Trent Evans was near the bench and saw that what was now a true talisman could be the wrong kind of history – the vanished kind – if they gave away the secret. "I said to Bob Nicholson, you have to get the girls away from centre ice. We need this secret to be carried forward to the men's game as well."

Up in the stands, Wayne Gretzky was thinking the same thing. Team Canada's executive director was on his cellphone, urgently trying to find someone to move the women's team away from centre ice. In the end, Wickenheiser got the message and skated out to disperse her teammates, with no apparent damage done to the secret weapon. But the women were not quite finished with the good-luck loonie. When the E Center was dark and empty, and Team Canada were wearing flip-flops and not skates, they all trooped out to centre ice. "They saluted the loonie," said Evans, "and had a beer with the loonie that night."

The fates were tempted again when CBC-TV's Peter Jordan, known for his whimsical insider pieces, did a story about ice-making at the Olympics and learned about the buried loonie. For a journalist, the story was too good to hold, and despite Evans's efforts to embargo the piece, the story aired just before the men's gold medal game, which already had enough drama as it, too, pitted Canada against the United States.

Evans, cautious, and now very superstitious, was sure that the jig was up. "That's why the Sunday morning of the gold-medal game, I did go out and confirm . . . I thought that it would be gone so I had a spare loonie in hand – if it was out, I was going to try to get another loonie in."

The loonie was still there, and while the Canadian men's team knew about it, most of the millions of Canadians who were watching on the afternoon of February 24, 2002, didn't know that the puck was being dropped on such a powerful good-luck charm. All they knew was that this one game was as big as Game 8 of the 1972 Series, or perhaps it was even bigger: it could mark the first time that Canada claimed gold in men's Olympic hockey, since the Edmonton Mercurys won at the 1952 games, a half century earlier.

At home and abroad, Canadians both old and new stopped what they were doing to watch the game, hoping that what they believed was true: Team Canada was the best. Jerry Jabson, a recent immigrant from the basketball-crazy Philippines, joined friends in front of the TV. Six months earlier he had traded the sun of Manila and his job as an engineer for the snow of Scarborough, Ontario, and a job on an assembly line to earn enough money to bring his family over to this new country obsessed with this strange game. "We did not know the rules," said Jabson. "The only thing we know is that you shoot the puck in the net to score. It's the first thing you have to do, whatever happens. And you can run on the ice using this skating shoe. It's really special this kind of game because you have a special shoe and you can go fast."

Jabson was keeping his appointment with this game because he knew he had to understand it to become a true Canadian. "Hockey is the national game of the country," he said. "Everywhere you go in Canada, they always talk about hockey, in bars, restaurants, at parties. Especially when your team is in the finals. Sometimes they don't even go to work, just to watch the game."

Geographically close in Caledonia, Ontario, but a world away from the immigrant experience, museum curator Karen Richardson and her family watched the game through the prism of an impeccable hockey pedigree. "We were almost all born with skates on and a hockey stick in hand," she said. Her husband, Rick, served as a director of the Ontario Hockey Association, and she had grown up playing the game on the Grand River in Southwestern Ontario, and her mother had played for a women's team in the 1970s. Both her sons had played minor and junior hockey and continued to coach as adults in a recreational league, and her two young grandsons had just begun their hockey-playing lives.

To capture this historic day for a family and sport, the Richardsons video-taped their extended hockey family watching the hockey game of the century. "As the excitement began to mount we all sat on the edge of our seats savouring every minute of the game," Richardson says. "The cheers and flags would go up every time we scored and of course there was my mother, on the edge of her seat, practically playing every play along with the team."

Half a world away, in the dangerous war-scarred landscape of Kandahar, Afghanistan, Sgt. Lorne Ford sat in a trench in the middle of the night, thinking of hockey. Ford was in a war that looked as if it belonged to an earlier century, with trenches and warlords and an enemy on horseback. That night, he and his fellow NCOs and officers had taken over operational duty to let the enlisted men watch the Olympic game.

As he sat guarding his base camp from hostiles, he could hear the game coming from the radios the Canadian troops carried and from the TVs that those who were not on duty were watching inside a nearby tent. "You could hear the goals being scored from where I was, from the tent," he said. "It was something we'd all wanted to see for fifty years. From the Motorolas that everybody had, they would say that Canada just scored. Within seconds, everybody knew what was going on in the game, throughout the whole line. I don't know if it was happening in the American lines or not. I highly doubt it. I mean, we know where hockey lies closer."

Canadians everywhere stopped what they were doing on February 24, 2002, to watch the most important men's hockey game since the 1972 Summit Series. To the nation's delight, Team Canada defeated the USA 5–2 at Salt Lake City to win Canada's first Olympic gold medal in fifty years.

(*Canadian Press*)

The game fulfilled all its hype, and by the third period, its hope, too – for Canada had a 3–2 lead, and for fans watching across the nation and abroad, no meter ever devised could measure their tension.

Team USA put a scare into Canadian hearts and hope into American when Brett Hull got a glorious chance on a power play, but Martin Brodeur coolly stopped him. Then, with four minutes left, Canada's Jarome Iginla snapped a shot that U.S. goalie Mike Richter – sliding across the crease – had to reach back to stop. The puck hit his glove and spun end over end toward the empty net. Joe Sakic, Iginla's centreman, tried to deflect the puck, but missed. U.S. defenceman Tom Poti tried to sweep it out of harm's way, but he missed. And when the puck dropped inside the post, Canadians everywhere joined Team Canada, and their managers Wayne Gretzky, Kevin Lowe, and Steve Tambellini in leaping up with a fist-pumping roar. The game wasn't over yet but it was now Canada's to lose, and Joe Sakic made fools of any doubters with another goal, giving the Canadians – and an ecstatic nation – a convincing 5–2 gold-medal win.

In Kandahar, Sgt. Ford had been relieved from his trench duty so he could watch the end of the game. He says, "It was just, it was incredible. The tent was just going wild." The victory was just as passionate for Karen Richardson's family back in Ontario. "Several times I am sure the whole neighbourhood could hear the screams from our living room," she said. "Then the final moment when we knew it was ours . . . and there was my mother, jumping up, screaming . . . It truly was a magical moment."

"In my profession I am always telling people that history isn't about dates and events so much as it's the stories of people . . . ordinary people," says Richardson. "The memory of sharing that time with the whole family will be one we will all cherish forever."

After witnessing the Canadian triumph and the horn-honking and flag-waving of his ecstatic Scarborough neighbours, Jerry Jabson understood his new homeland better. "Back in my country, we are a bit conservative," he said. "We don't express our feelings the same way. It makes you feel good when your team wins. It's human instinct."

In Salt Lake City, another maple leaf was being cheered. While Team Canada was celebrating its victory after the final whistle, ice-maker and loonie master Trent Evans grabbed a screwdriver and seized his chance. "Within ten seconds I had melted a hole over top of the loonie," he said. "I used the screwdriver to lift it out." Now, in an impromptu press conference, he handed the doubly golden loonie to Wayne Gretzky. "This loonie is going to the Hockey Hall of Fame," said Team Canada's visibly relieved boss. "It brought a little bit of luck to the men's and women's teams. It brought them gold."

In 2004, professional hockey celebrated its centenary. It had come a long way from Houghton, Michigan, but then again, it hadn't. In June, a small-market team from Calgary played a hot-market team from Tampa Bay for the Stanley Cup and delighted fans of every vintage with the most exciting series in years.

When Tampa Bay won the Cup, its citizens, who, in the very recent past, used to get free tickets to Lightning games by spending ten dollars on gasoline, went out into a joyous throng to buy Tampa Bay Stanley Cup gear – including copies of a local newspaper, where someone had prematurely sent the composing room an editorial congratulating the Lightning on a good try in a losing effort, and better luck next year.

But next year was on the collective mind of the hockey world, for there was labour trouble in the air as the September 15 expiry date for the contract between the NHL and its players ticked down. Canadians worried that the World Cup, played that September, would be their last glimpse of their NHL heroes for – if dire predictions came true – a long time. On September 14, Canada fulfilled the hopes of the country by defeating Finland 3–2 to win the World Cup, but it was a bittersweet victory. In the Canadian locker room a sign summed up the triumph: "Practice is cancelled tomorrow. No one else left to beat." But more than practice was cancelled the following day. The NHL locked out its players after concluding that it could not forge a new collective bargaining agreement with the union.

Over the next few months there was acrimony, and apathy, and then, on February 16, 2005, when rumours of an eleventh-hour agreement between the NHL and the players proved false, the NHL became the first professional sports league in history to cancel an entire season. Radio and TV reports gave voice to disappointed fans, but Wayne Gretzky, now a team owner, made perhaps the most revealing comment. "The Canadian fans will always come back to the game," he said. "It's the American fans we have to worry about."

Canadian fans spent the almost sixteen months between Game 7 of the 2004 Stanley Cup final and opening night of the 2005–6 season by returning to the junior and amateur games, and by debating just how hockey now fit into the Canadian landscape. The focus of this debate came via a legal challenge to the NHL's "ownership" of the Stanley Cup, first by an Edmonton group calling itself "Free Stanley." They were joined by a Toronto group who took the matter to the Ontario Superior Court in February 2005. The would-be liberators of Lord Stanley's Dominion Challenge Trophy emphasized the "challenge" in Stanley's endowment of his trophy, and took argument with the NHL's claim that by taking possession of the Cup in 1947, it effectively owned it.

A hockey-starved media took up, if not the cause of the little guys, then the story, and Canadians – and Americans – weighed in on the debate by proposing

As if to prove wrong the hockey pundits who said "small-market" teams were the way of the past, the 2004 Stanley Cup final between the Calgary Flames and the Tampa Bay Lightning was one of the most exciting in years, with the two teams trading wins until their dramatic showdown in Game 7 – the first time in a decade a Stanley Cup final had gone to seven games. Tampa Bay led 2–0 when a Flames' power-play goal midway through the final period put the Cup in Calgary's reach, but they couldn't beat Tampa's netminder, Nikolai Khabibulin. The Lightning, who had only made it into the post-season twice before since their NHL debut in 1992, took home the Stanley Cup. Here, Andreychuk (left) and Iginla (right) battle it out.

(Dave Sandford/Hockey Hall of Fame)

the 2005 Stanley Cup should be competed for by college leagues, by the American Hockey League, by the senior leagues challenging for the Allan Cup, and by the national and international women's league. The current governor general, Adrienne Clarkson, supported the challenge to the challenge trophy and promised to award women hockey players a trophy of their own.

The Cup debate focused attention on hockey at all levels in Canada and beyond. While many NHL players had decamped to Europe during the lockout to keep in shape both physically and financially by playing for European clubs, the fans kept their eye on the game. A fan website poll showed that nearly half of those queried supported the use of replacement players should there still be

During his rookie season of 1985–86, Patrick Roy quickly established himself as one of professional hockey's premier goalies, backstopping the Montreal Canadiens to a Stanley Cup championship and winning the first of his three Conn Smythe Trophies as the most valuable player in the playoffs. Recognition of his excellence grew with the first of his three Vezina Trophy wins in 1989, and as his reputation swelled, so did the size of his goaltending equipment. By the time Roy retired in 2003 with 551 career wins – the most in NHL history – his early gear makes him seem comparatively unprotected. The NHL would redraft rules to diminish the size of goalies' equipment in 2005 to encourage more goal scoring. (*Left: Hockey Hall of Fame, right: Dave Sandford/Hockey Hall of Fame*)

no contract by the start of the 2005–6 season. Even in its absence, the NHL still occupied people's attention.

In July 2005, the players and the league finally reached an agreement, their minds no doubt concentrated by the possibility of destroying the NHL by losing another season if they didn't act. Hitherto non-negotiable items from the players' perspective, such as a salary cap limiting team expenditure on player salaries and connecting them to league revenue, were now in the books. So too was a 24 per cent, across-the-board player salary rollback.

There was also good news for the players, with time limits reduced on free agency eligibility, revenue sharing between teams and the league, and good

news for the fans, with rule changes designed to speed up the game. Goalie equipment, which in recent years had rivalled the padding of the Michelin Man, became smaller, and so too did the zone around the net in which goalies could handle the puck.

Games still tied after a five-minute overtime period would see a shootout, to encourage teams to play flat-out for a win, as shootout victories – and losses – might be exciting for the fans but they ring hollow with the players. The NHL also promised to crack down on obstruction, so that the league's skilled players could shine, helped by an elimination of the red line. Now a defenceman could fire a pass from beside his own goal net all the way to his teammate at the opponent's blue line, and it would be a legal play. The change would open up the game and reward speed and skill, while making life tougher for defencemen who used grabbing and hooking to guard their zones.

"Let's drop the puck on a fresh start and a wonderful future for the National Hockey League," said NHL president Gary Bettman, but there was still bitterness. "At the end of the day, everybody lost," said Wayne Gretzky, now the managing partner of the Phoenix Coyotes. "We almost crippled our industry. It was very disappointing what happened."

On NHL opening night, October 5, 2005, all was, if not forgiven, then filed away for future reference as the world's premier professional hockey league got back in action. Indeed, the hockey world saw some familiar faces in new roles. Wayne Gretzky was now also a coach, directing his Coyotes from both the front office and behind the bench. Pittsburgh's Mario Lemieux, also an owner, was back in uniform as the mentor to the Penguins' number-one draft choice,

They call him the Next One, playing off the nickname the Great One, owned by Wayne Gretzky, the player to whom Sidney Crosby has been, and will be, compared throughout his career. While he has the same will to win as Gretzky, and the same genius at seeing the ice, Crosby differs in that he enjoys waging physical battles to get the puck and put it in the net. (*Canadian Press*)

On October 5, 2005, after a sixteen-month lockout of players by the NHL, the first professional sports league to lose an entire season due to a labour dispute, professional hockey, returned to North America, and once again there was life in winter. On opening night, old rivalries resumed between Ottawa and Toronto, Edmonton and Calgary, and Montreal and Boston, while the Vancouver Canucks took on the future, playing the Phoenix Coyotes, now co-owned and coached by Wayne Gretzky.

(*Graig Abel Photography*)

the kid called The Next One, Sidney Crosby. In the 2005–6 season, Crosby showed that the hype surrounding him had merit, emerging as one of the league's brightest new stars. He was poised to take on the mantle of Mario Lemieux, who retired for good in January 2006. The Vancouver Canucks' Todd Bertuzzi, who had been suspended in March 2004 for his attack on Colorado Avalanche player Steve Moore, was allowed back on the ice, and in his contrition promised to redeem himself by bringing a Cup to Vancouver, still waiting for another one since its first – and last – in 1915. The hockey establishment welcomed him back into the fold by nominating him for the 2006 Olympic hockey team.

As ever, hope was in the air for hockey fans across the country, that this season would be *the* season of triumph for their NHL team, for the record TV ratings of the opening week showed that fans were back to the league and the game they had missed. "Game on," the universal cry of hockey players and fans everywhere, was heard across the land, and the glinting of a trophy donated more than a century ago to encourage the spread of hockey was once again the gleam in the eye of hockey fans not just in Canada, but around the world, fuelling the winter dreams and the springtime hopes of players from Shediac to Shawinigan to Salmon Arm, from Stockholm to St. Petersburg, both the one in Russia and the one in Florida. Canada's game now belonged to the world.

However, the 2006 Olympics were notable for Canada's men only in the team's failure to make the medal standings. Once again, the hockey-loving nation asked itself if it was still the best at the game that it gave the world. Before long, there was a corollary to that question. Did reigning supreme on the ice even matter, when the country was mired in the global financial crisis and people were asking themselves where they would find the money to meet the mortgage and the weekly grocery bill? As it had done in dark times past, the game came to represent something luminous and beckoning in the face of the financial market storm. And, with the 2010 Winter Olympics taking place at home, in Vancouver–Whistler, hockey more urgently belonged to the people who gave it to the world: something to watch, to play, to cheer for, and to believe in.

CHAPTER 11

GAME ON

—————

Downtown Toronto at midnight wasn't the time or place you'd expect to see a six-year-old boy, not even one in the company of his father. But for this father, Karl Subban, who came to Canada from Jamaica at age eleven and learned the game in a Hab-crazy francophone neighbourhood in Sudbury, Ontario, the outdoor shinny rink in front of City Hall under the light of the winter moon was the closest he could get to providing his son with a frozen backyard pond. His own parents hadn't been able to afford to put him in a hockey league, but that had done nothing to lessen Karl's love of the game. Now, in the 1990s, he would spend hours in the library researching hockey drills in books, then take his son Pernell Karl (known as P.K.) to the finest classroom he knew and teach him the ways of the ice.

Hockey Night in Canada gets a new theme

In June 2008, hockey fans across Canada were grappling with the news that the rights to the theme song to *Hockey Night in Canada* would not be renewed. The tune had heralded the arrival of our game on CBC TV since 1968, and had become as much a part of the national fabric as the national anthem. To the great dismay of fans, Dolores Claman's iconic theme moved to TSN's NHL hockey broadcast, and the CBC launched a national competition for a new hockey theme. "Anthem Challenge" attracted nearly 15,000 entries, from serious composers to garage bands and teenage whiz kids – many of them motivated by the $100,000 prize on offer, and by the chance for their tune to become part of a national tradition. With fans voting for the shortlisted song on-line, the final showdown was a reflection of the widespread appeal of the contest; "Sticks to the Ice" by thirteen-year-old Torontonian Robert Fraser Burke was facing off against "Canadian Gold" by Colin Oberst, an Edmonton elementary school teacher. The rivals stood side-by-side as Don Cherry announced the winner to a live studio audience in Toronto in October 2008, and Oberst's winning entry – of the five he submitted – then took to the ice as the new theme of all *Hockey Night in Canada* telecasts. A thrilled Oberst said the prize money could not compare to his place in hockey lore. "I'm married, I've got two young kids and a mortgage so, as far as the kids' education and my house, I think [the prize money] will go pretty quick."

Karl Subban was an elementary school administrator in Toronto who worked nights as the vice-principal of a continuing education program at Runnymede Collegiate, where he also taught a business course. He'd arrive home late, wake up his sleeping kindergartener, then drive him over to the outdoor rink at Nathan Phillips Square to join in shinny games that would sometimes last until the clock chimed two.

"It wasn't child abuse," Karl laughingly told a Toronto reporter in the winter of 2007. P.K. loved every moment he spent on the ice. His mother, Maria, recalls him telling his father after watching *Hockey Night in Canada*, "Dad, I want to be one of those guys on TV." He was just four at the time. And so, just as shinny games have been for fathers and sons for more than a century, the midnight games in the core of Canada's largest city were fuel for Karl and P.K.'s hockey dreams.

Reporters were paying attention to what P.K. Subban's family thought about the national sport in the winter of 2007 because Subban had been chosen to join Canada's squad to compete in the 2008 World Junior Hockey Tournament. The tournament is a showcase of the world's elite under-twenty-year-old male hockey players, one that fills Canadian hockey hearts with patriotic hope – and the country's TV screens with more than a few heart-stopping moments – every year from Boxing Day through to New Year's.

Subban, a defenceman with the Belleville Bulls, helped the junior squad to claim their fourth consecutive gold medal in a thrilling overtime win against Sweden in Pardubice, Czech Republic (and to be named "team of the year" by the Canadian Press). But it was back home in 2009 that he came into his own on a junior men's team not only rich in talent, but in expectation.

"We're probably not ranked at the top," said head coach Pat Quinn as the team prepared to defend its title. "We'll be favourites here simply because we're Canada and we're expected to win all the time."

The Canadians were led by John Tavares, a pure goalscorer who had notched 183 goals in three-and-a-half Ontario Hockey League seasons, with Subban on defence, Dustin Tokarski in net, and "character" players Cody Hodgson and Thomas Hickey, both talented leaders. The squad's high morale was bolstered further by the feel-good stories of how two other players had made the team. Angelo Esposito had made the team on his fourth try after three heartbreaking cuts, and Evander Kane, the seventeen-year-old Vancouver Giants' star, had been one of the team's last cuts, and was then summoned back to the squad when another player was injured.

However, the Canadians had not won five straight junior hockey gold medals since their domination of the tournament in the years 1993–1997, and were well aware of what happened after that magical run: no more gold until 2005, the year that began the streak they were now expected to continue.

To prepare a collection of talented young players from across the continent for the intense pressures they'd face as a team both on and off the ice, Eugene Melnyk, the Ottawa Senators owner and chair of the host organizing committee, pitched a short, sharp team-building exercise that was starkly outside the usual realm of such bonding ventures: the junior squad would begin their brief life together at a Canadian army base.

"Whether you are a hockey player on Team Canada or a front-line soldier on the Canadian Forces, there exists a bond defined by national pride and a driving desire to succeed on behalf of our country," said Melnyk. "With Hockey Canada's decision to select CFB Petawawa as a training site, we know that bond will be part of the winning formula to bring home the gold in 2009."

The equation of sport and war seemed to come from an age long passed, from the soldier teams and sportsmen's battalions of the First World War and from Conn Smythe's athlete-stocked anti-aircraft battery of the Second World War. Suddenly, young men who lived in a world where the words *warrior* and *battle* described fighting for the puck, and where failure just meant a loss on the score sheet, found themselves immersed in a world where failure could mean death.

Under the supervision of Afghanistan vets, the hockey players' two days at CFB Petawawa began with parachute training known as the "Jump of Fear," a harnessed leap from a ten-metre wooden tower that put a lofty spin on the meaning of "taking one for the team."

"When I first hooked up I was like, this is easy," said Subban. "But once you get up there and look down, I kind of debated whether I should take my harness off and go back down. But it was too late when I got up there – Johnny T [John Tavares] and the boys were shouting, 'You gotta go! You gotta go!' and I had to jump."

Next, the junior squad carried a wounded colleague (in this case a dummy) down the banks of the Ottawa River, and then hopped into Zodiac boats for a trip upriver – straight into an ambush.

"They didn't really give us an idea it was coming," said Thomas Hickey, Canada's team captain. "They just said, 'Look around, use your ears and everything, and communicate with each other.' Then all of a sudden there was smoke flying everywhere and the sounds of guns going off."

That evening, the players were choppered into an "enemy village" and, armed with plastic assault rifles and night vision goggles, were ordered to attack it. "Having the talent is one thing," said coach Quinn. "But to make them a team, that's the issue. We're here to understand the basic concepts of teamwork, trust, and believing in our people and equipment."

The distinction between game and war lost all subtlety when the players were having lunch and heard the news that a Canadian Forces plane had arrived at CFB Trenton to the south, bearing the coffins of three soldiers killed in Afghanistan – the fourth, fifth, and sixth soldiers to die in the past ten days. Even so, the base's commanding officer saw the players – not much younger than many of his soldiers – as a morale booster for the troops.

"To have them here, to have the opportunity to put them through some team-building events, on ice and in a military uniform, is phenomenal," said Lt.-Col. Bill Moore. "The military is all about putting soldiers through adversity to come together as a team and build confidence in each other, and that's what these young players need, as well."

For the preliminary round of the tournament, the Canadians' confidence soared, as the team outscored opponents 35–6 over four games. Their first chance to truly employ their military team spirit came in the final preliminary match when the United States scored on their first shot of the game and were up 3–0 by 12:35 of the first period. After the Americans' third goal, John Tavares, the highly touted Oshawa Generals centre, rallied the Canadians during a timeout.

"I just said we should play our game," Tavares said. "I thought our emotions were getting the better of us. I said to the guys to relax."

Team Canada's defensive star P.K. Subban patrols the ice during the second period of Canada's 8-1 romp over the Czech Republic in the preliminary round of the 2009 World Junior Championships. Team Canada would go on to win its fifth consecutive gold medal at the tournament.

(*Andre Ringuette/Hockey Hall of Fame*)

Tavares then played *his* game, scoring back-to-back goals less than a minute apart, with Jordan Eberle, a right-winger with the Regina Pats, adding the tying marker at the end of the period, and P.K. Subban setting up the comeback with two assists. Tavares would add another empty net goal, and Subban another assist, in a 7–4 Canadian win.

Those who had followed Canada in international hockey knew all too well that the team had won nothing but a lesson in adversity, one that the country never seemed to tire of learning on the ice. The win was also a salutary reminder about the ever-shifting fortunes of the sport: Canada's opponents in the semi-final would be their old Cold War nemeses, the Russians.

Even though twelve of the twenty-two-man Canadian squad were not yet born when the Berlin Wall fell in November 1989 (and the oldest of those alive at the time was nine-month-old Thomas Hickey), the team was all too aware that the Russians had long given the Canadians grief on the ice, having beaten Canada three times for the gold since 1999. They knew from the legacy of the 1972 Summit Series never to underestimate a Russian team.

This time, the very right to play in the gold medal match was at stake, with the loser having to play for the bronze – and maybe going home with nothing. For Canada, playing at home in Ottawa, the prospect – as Samuel Johnson famously wrote about the fate of being hanged in the morning – concentrated their minds wonderfully.

"You could argue about skills this year or that year, just like you could Muhammad Ali versus George Chuvalo," said coach Quinn, "but our intention is to win a gold medal and all the other stuff doesn't mean a darn thing right now."

The Canadians were leading 3–2 going into the third period, but then the Russians struck quickly, tying the game just fifty-one seconds into the final frame. Canada regained the lead when Angelo Esposito scored, but the Russians answered back with two goals, their fifth coming with just two minutes and twenty seconds left in the game – a dagger that seemed to have punctured Canada's gold medal dream.

With nearly 2.7 million viewers watching on television, and another capacity crowd of more than 20,000 people in Scotiabank Place, the Canadians took all their Petawawa warrior team-building and unleashed it, coming at the Russians like the Canadian team had done so many times before: as if the fate of the nation depended on it.

With time painfully, dramatically running out, the clock now ticking down from ten seconds, John Tavares took a quick shot on goal, which a Russian defenceman tried to cover. Jordan Eberle reached in, poked the puck loose – then slipped it past the Russian goalie.

With 5.4 seconds left in the third period, Canada had tied the game. After ten minutes of overtime failed to break the tie, the Canadians – led again by Tavares, Eberle, and goalie Tokarski – won the match with two shootout goals to none for the Russians. "When we tied the game it was an unbelievable feeling," Subban said, "even more than winning the tournament."

In the end, Team Canada had endured its trial by fire in the U.S. and Russia games. The final game, watched by 3.7 million TV viewers, and 20,383 fans in Ottawa – including Prime Minister Stephen Harper – saw the

Martin Brodeur's record

On March 17, 2009 – appropriately, St. Patrick's Day – New Jersey Devils all-star goaltender Martin Brodeur eclipsed the record of his boyhood idol, "Saint" Patrick Roy, by backstopping his 552nd victory. With the 3–2 win over Chicago, Brodeur became owner of the NHL record for most career wins, an achievement the Montreal-born netminder added to his 1994 Calder Memorial Trophy for rookie of the year, his four Vezina Trophies as the NHL premier net-minder, his ten All-Star appearances, and his three Stanley Cups. At the final buzzer of the game – after stopping a potential game-tying goal with a pad save against Chicago's Troy Brouwer – Brodeur jumped into the air, pumping his right arm. Afterward, he told reporters, "When I heard the buzzer, I was like, *Wow, it's over now*. This is good." Then he found a pair of scissors and cut the netting out of the net he had defended for two periods – the kind of milestone memento only a goalie could love.

Canadians play a tough and chippy Swedish team, taking a tense 2–0 lead into the third period before opening it up to a 5–1 victory, and their fifth consecutive junior gold medal.

Subban seemed to be everywhere on the ice in that game, rallying his team-mates, shutting down the Swedes, and even scoring a goal – the game's first, an attention-getting kind of goal on the power play just thirty-eight seconds into the match. "We've been blessed since Day One," he told an interviewer after the game. "We started our trek in Petawawa as a bunch of individuals; we came to Ottawa as one team, one nation, on one mission."

In addition to winning two junior hockey world championship gold medals, Subban made a dream come true for both he and his father when he was selected forty-third overall in the 2007 NHL entry draft by the team his father had worshipped as a young immigrant, and whose banner still hung on P.K.'s bedroom wall: the Montreal Canadiens.

As the juniors were celebrating their gold medal, the Montreal Canadiens were jubilant, too. The team that had been invented for Montreal's francophone community in a mixture of revenge and entrepreneurship turned one hundred years old in 2009. While they hadn't won a Stanley Cup since 1993, the Canadiens remained one of the world's most successful professional sports franchises, with fifty-four former Canadiens elected to the Hockey Hall of

Fame, fifteen retired jerseys, and twenty-four Stanley Cup banners hanging from the rafters of the Bell Centre arena.

Even the Royal Canadian Mint joined the homage to the storied team, issuing a series of commemorative coins honouring the Canadiens' achievement. Despite their national and global appeal, the Canadiens' century of francophone triumph and tragedy is still so essential to Quebecois culture that in January 2009 the Université de Montréal began offering a sixteen-week graduate course to future clerics called "The Religion of the Montréal Canadiens."

Today, *les Canadiens* are a polyglot bunch, as is the rest of the NHL, with Russian and Czechs and Finns playing alongside Franco- and Anglo-Canadians, and a few Americans. But the Habs' hope of adding another Cup banner to the rafters is pinned to a Canadian player: Carey Price, a twenty-year-old netminder from Anahim Lake, B.C., whose mother, Lynda, is chief of the Ulkatcho First Nation.

Like P.K. Subban, Price learned the game from his father, though Jerry Price did not teach himself hockey drills in the library and haul his son out to play in the middle of the night. Jerry was a goalie who was skilled enough to be drafted in 1978 by the Philadelphia Flyers, and who once bought an airplane so he could fly Carey from their remote northern community of Anahim Lake, population 1,500, to play in games in Williams Lake, B.C., 320 kilometres away.

Jerry Price never did play in the NHL, and instead wound up in the minor leagues, but his hockey genes and teaching skills helped make Carey Price into one of the professional game's most promising players. Price entered the NHL in 2005 with huge expectations as the Canadiens' first round, fifth overall draft pick, bearing a pedigree that dazzled even when compared to the goalies in the Canadiens' well-stocked pantheon.

In 2007, Price became the only goalie in the history of hockey to win, all in the same year, the Canadian Hockey League's goaltender of the year award, the American Hockey League's Jack A. Butterfield Trophy as the most valuable player, en route to his team's Calder Cup championship, and a gold medal with the Canadian junior team, in a tournament where he was also named the most valuable player.

He made his NHL debut with the Canadiens in October 2007, and won his first game. By the end of the 2007–08 season, Price led all rookie goalies with twenty-four wins, a .920 save percentage, and three shutouts. In the first round of the playoffs against Boston, Price recorded the first shutout by a Canadiens goalie since Patrick Roy notched one in 1986 – a year before Price was born.

Though the Canadiens would be eliminated in the second round of the playoffs, in the mind of Habs fans Price's success linked him inextricably to Roy, known to them as "Saint Patrick." And, not surprisingly for a team so rich in religious transference that it calls its iconic red, white, and blue jersey "Sainte-Flanelle," the holy jersey, it wasn't long before people were calling the young net-minder "Jesus" Price.

Like his biblical namesake, Price performed his miracles calmly and serenely, nothing like the mercurial Roy, who used to talk to his goalposts and refused to skate over blue lines, preferring to jump over them instead. Roy was even known to throw a punch or two at rival goalies, though on the goalie eccentricity graph, he lies well below former New York Ranger Gilles Gratton, who believed himself a reincarnation of a Spanish conquistador, and wouldn't play if the moon was in the wrong part of the sky.

A measure of Price's sang-froid came during a playoff game against Philadelphia in the spring of 2008, when Price misplayed the puck behind his own net and set off a chain reaction of players crashing into each other in pursuit of it. Price's friend and teammate Josh Gorges recalled: "I'm at the bottom of the pile, and Carey's on top of me somewhere and I can hear him laughing, so I say to him, 'How could you be laughing at a time like this?' And all he said was, 'That was a close one, eh?' I didn't know how to react to that, so I just started laughing, too."

However, when the Canadiens were eliminated from the playoffs, the volatile and vast hockey punditry that inhabits Montreal was not amused, venturing that Price was too passive, too loose, and a perhaps a little too well padded, a result of his fondness for late night burgers and sweets. Perhaps, mused the hindsight visionaries, he didn't really have the desire to be the Number One goaltender for *les Glorieux*. The criticism stung the young goalie.

Price hadn't wound up wearing the "Sainte-Flanelle" by accident, and his competitive flame helped him burn nearly thirty pounds off his six-foot three frame during the off-season, recalibrate his diet, and come back to the team in the best shape of his life, ready to live up to the promise of his rookie year. When Montreal hosted the NHL All-Star Game on January 26, 2009, Price was the Eastern Conference's starting goalie, fresh off rehab for an ankle injury that he'd suffered on December 30. He allowed two goals on eleven shots in his one period of play, and made a couple of fine stops – including one on a shot deflected by his second cousin, Shane Doan of the Phoenix Coyotes – before the East won the game 12–11 in a shootout.

Few aboriginal players have ever made it to the professional game, and Price is acutely aware of the responsibilities his achievement places on him, especially to aboriginal youth. When the Canadiens made their only appearance at GM Place in Vancouver in February 2009, more than one thousand people from among Price's family, friends, and B.C.'s wider aboriginal communities came to the city to congratulate him.

The Clarkson Cup

During the NHL lockout in 2004–05, the question of what to do with the Stanley Cup became an issue, with some arguing that the Cup truly belonged to hockey, as Lord Stanley had decreed when he gave the game his trophy in 1892, and not to the NHL, which didn't exist until 1917. Adrienne Clarkson, Canada's Governor General, suggested that since there was no men's professional hockey, the Cup could be awarded that year to the national women's hockey champion. The idea didn't catch on, but it led her to create and donate the Clarkson Cup, a women's hockey championship trophy. Designed at the Nunavut Arctic College in Iqaluit, the Cup is a silver bowl on a slender stem with two strong handles, the form of a powerful woman with her hands on her hips.

Perhaps fittingly, as the idea was born during a labour dispute, a labour dispute also dogged the Clarkson Cup's creation, when Hockey Canada said that it could not award the Cup to the women's hockey champion if there were any "strings attached" – Hockey Canada wanted to own the Cup outright. The Cup's principal artist, the silversmith Beth Briggs, protested that a licensing arrangement was needed to recognize the intellectual property rights of herself and the cup's three Inuit designers, Therese Ukaliannuk, Pootoogook Qiatsuk, and Okpik Pitseolak. "They talk about a cup with no strings attached," she told the press, "but those strings happen to be the laws of Canada to compensate artists."

It took almost three years for a financial arrangement to be successfully negotiated among all parties, and the Cup finally found a home when the best in the east met the best in the west in Kingston on March 21, 2009. The Minnesota Whitecaps of the Western Women's Hockey League played the Montreal Stars of the Canadian Women's Hockey League for the right to be the Cup's first winner as elite women's hockey champions of North America. Adrienne Clarkson dropped the puck in a ceremonial faceoff, and then joined Mississauga mayor Hazel McCallion, a longtime supporter of women's hockey, and House of Commons speaker Peter Milliken, the Member of Parliament for the Kingston area, to watch as Montreal defeated Minnesota 3–1 to keep the Cup in Canada. In the end, the lengthy dispute was trumped by the sense of history that the players felt. "We are really happy to win the Clarkson Cup for the first time ever," said Stars captain Lisa-Marie Breton. "It's something we'll remember forever."

The fan club had been organized by Gino Odjick, a former Canuck and Canadien player, who works with the NHL Players' Association's Goals and Dreams program, which outfits kids with hockey gear, and emphasizes the importance of staying in school and having a goal beyond it. "We all know the First Nations' way out of poverty is through education," Odjick said at the celebration. "We really push for that."

"Gino is a first-class guy," Price said, in appreciation of the gesture. "He's been a real role model for myself, being a First Nations guy playing in the NHL. He's really done a lot for the First Nations community, especially here in Vancouver."

Kids decked out in Canadiens' sweaters cheered Price in the game-day skate and mobbed him for autographs afterward. "A lot of those faces were familiar,"

Price said afterward. "A lot of those kids were me – I was in that exact position growing up, in a small community just off the reservation. It was good to see a lot of young kids show up and be happy."

It was also a bitter homecoming, for Price had been struggling to regain his inspiring form since his All-Star appearance, and was scheduled to watch from the bench for his home province debut. However, thanks to the score, and a sporting gesture from Habs' coach Guy Carbonneau (who would be fired a month later as the team woes continued), Price was put in goal late in the third period, when the Canucks were leading 4–1. His appearance generated a huge cheer, and in his nine minutes in net he posted a shutout, even though Montreal lost 4–2. "I've just got to make sure I let the kids know what's important," Price said. "Keep your head high and work really hard. If you do that, there's no limit."

Odjick agreed, telling a reporter after Price had departed that aboriginal teens had been inspired by seeing such a success story in the flesh. "A couple came over and said they were going to finish their degree or go to university or try harder, outside of hockey," Odjick said. "If we can get a few to start thinking like that and spread the word, it makes this all worthwhile."

Just as Carey Price's NHL success has inspired youngsters, the NHL's success inspired professional players to imagine a career beyond the league. Once more, the NHL's exclusive hold on the professional game was challenged when the Kontinental Hockey League debuted in 2008. The NHL, launched in 1917, had been the world's reigning pro hockey league since the collapse of the Patrick brothers' Western Hockey League in 1926, its only serious challenge coming from the World Hockey Association between 1972 and 1979.

With twenty-four teams from Russia, Belarus, Latvia, and Kazakhstan, and plans to expand to the Czech Republic, the KHL was more than an ambitious parvenu. It emerged from the Russian Superleague, which itself had succeeded the Soviet Hockey League, founded in 1946. The KHL, proud of its heritage, named its four divisions after Russian hockey legends: players Bobrov and Kharlamov, and coaches Chernyshev and Tarasov. To cap the nationalist message, the KHL's championship trophy, the Gagarin Cup, was named after Yuri Gagarin, the first human to venture into outer space, and orbit the earth.

The KHL saw itself as not merely a pioneering and patriotic enterprise, but as a long overdue commercial response to the NHL, which it viewed as both a source of talent and the enemy. Even before the dismantling of the USSR, the NHL had been a magnet for Russia's hockey-playing elite, and the Russian hockey trust felt that the NHL had raided some of the country's best talent without giving much back other than a paltry $200,000 transfer fee and a brief

glimpse of the Stanley Cup, whenever a Russian member of the winning team brought it home for a whirlwind visit.

When KHL founder and president Alexander Medvedev said that KHL clubs wouldn't count the salaries of NHL players they had signed against their salary cap of 562,500,000 rubles (US$24.2 million), the gauntlet was dropped.

In July, NHL president Gary Bettman sent a delegation to meet with European leagues and the International Ice Hockey Federation in Zurich, to try to calm the Russian bear. However, Medvedev, deputy chairman of Gazprom, the world's largest natural gas refiner and distributor, and a deep-pocketed KHL sponsor, was confident that pro players regarded the new league not as a fallback to the NHL, but as an equal.

The KHL attracted NHL "cup of coffee" players, including Ivan Baranka, who'd played one game with the New York Rangers and signed with Spartak

Alexander Radulov and his teammates celebrate their 2008 triumph at the Men's World Hockey Championships after defeating Canada 5-4 to claim Russia's first gold medal at the event since 1993.

(Matthew Manor/Hockey Hall of Fame)

Moscow, and the talented but troubled Ottawa goalie Ray Emery, who signed a one-year deal with Atlant Moscow for in excess of US$2 million, plus bonuses. The KHL's real coup was signing a bona fide if ageing superstar in thirty-six-year-old Jaromir Jagr, who signed a contract for US$14 million over two years with the Siberian team Avangard Omsk.

It was rising star Alexander Radulov, though, who put the ambition and the threat of the KHL into perspective. The Russian-born Radulov, who was selected fifteenth overall by the Nashville Predators, and had just come off a sophomore NHL season that saw him score twenty-six goals and thirty-eight assists, signed with Salavat Yulaev in Ufa, capital of the Republic of Bashkortostan, part of the Russian Federation. One of his teammates was former Team Canada World Junior captain Steve McCarthy.

Radulov's defection outraged the NHL brass, as he still had one year left on his contract with the Predators. The KHL executive responded that Radulov had signed his KHL contract in a most timely fashion – on the day before the NHL signed a deal with the International Ice Hockey Federation to ensure that all players honoured their existing contracts. This infuriated the NHL even more, and they suspended Radulov from the Predators without pay for the 2008–09 season. This hardly hurt Radulov, though; he'd signed a three-year deal with the KHL for US$13 million.

Despite the fat salaries it was offering and its aggressive play, the KHL soon found itself skating on thin ice. The global economic meltdown hit it particularly hard in late 2008. After rumours of its demise began to surface, league president Medvedev announced in February 2009 that the salary cap would drop by more than a quarter, to US$17.4 million, as clubs struggled to meet their payrolls after the ruble lost a third of its value, setting an eleven-year low. Enigmatic goalie Ray Emery even quit his Moscow team in a dispute over the true exchange rate, but later rejoined the squad in time for the playoffs.

After his team was eliminated from the Gagarin Cup playoffs in March 2009, speculation arose that Alexander Radulov would be welcomed back to the Nashville Predators, to help them with their NHL playoff push. Radulov's agent dismissed the idea, but it was true that the Predators were in need of help, being one of ten NHL teams identified as particularly suffering from the recession.

When the 2004–05 NHL season was cancelled, hockey's Cassandras predicted that the professional NHL game would never be the same, but the NHL came back with vigour, with greater parity between teams, and even a 5 per cent rise in the league's revenue in 2008. The players were prospering as well, with the average salary rising under the Collective Bargaining Agreement from $1.8 million in 2003–04 to roughly $2.2 million in 2008–09. One of the reasons the players didn't opt to reopen the CBA in 2009 was because the salary cap had risen from US$39.5 million immediately after the lockout to $56.7 million.

In January 2008, Alexander Ovechkin of the Washington Capitals signed a US$124 million, thirteen-year contract; the Detroit Red Wings' Henrik Zetterberg signed a twelve-year deal worth US$73 million; and, a year later, the Vancouver Canucks signed Mats Sundin, a thirty-eight-year-old warhorse, for a pro-rated US$8.6 million for one season (i.e. $5 million for three months, and the playoffs).

There were, however, signs of major trouble in paradise as the global recession took hold and some financial shenanigans were uncovered. In June 2008, Henry Samueli, owner of the Anaheim Ducks, pleaded guilty to lying to the U.S. Securities and Exchange Commission during its investigation of a stock manipulation at his company, and he now faces a prison term. Several investor lawsuits were launched against Silicon Valley venture capitalist William "Boots" Del Biaggio, who, with commissioner Gary Bettman's encouragement, had long been trying to gain control of an NHL team. Del Biaggio once owned a small percentage of the San Jose Sharks, and had bought a majority stake in the Nashville Predators in 2007, only to be discovered to be using money that wasn't his. He has since been indicted in the United States on federal fraud charges. As an ironic and sad coda, the once rich and mighty Peter Pocklington, flamboyant ex-owner of the Edmonton Oilers, and the man who brought Wayne Gretzky to the NHL, was arrested and charged in California in March 2009 for making false statements on his accounts when he filed for bankruptcy. He owed his creditors $20 million and claimed assets of just $2,900.

Teams were also cast in the cold realities of the balance sheet. Those in the Sun Belt that had been struggling to build a profitable fan base now found themselves in the epicentre of the mortgage crisis. Wayne Gretzky's Phoenix Coyotes, losing millions, even offered free tickets to their April 7 game to people who bought a 1.75 litre bottle of Smirnoff Ice vodka, and were rumoured to be heading back to their origins in Winnipeg. They were not the only team in jeopardy. The Nashville Predators explored the possibility of buying up empty seats in their building so that they could qualify for revenue sharing, which requires a 14,000 paid attendance average for home games in order to be eligible for a full share of the NHL revenue pie. The Atlanta Thrashers, Tampa Bay Lightning, and the Florida Panthers all saw thousands of fans staying away from the rink. It was hard to pay for hockey games when your house was under foreclosure.

Things were so bad in Florida that the team offered fans the "Panthers Promise Plan" – a chance to buy tickets to four games now in exchange for the promise of four free tickets to games next season, should the Panthers fail to make the playoffs. Those fans who took the leap of faith were rewarded when the Panthers lost a dogfight for a playoff spot at the bottom of the Eastern Conference, but the victory may be worthless as there is no guarantee the Panthers will even be in Miami come October 2009.

It wasn't just the expansion teams that were suffering, for the Montreal Canadiens' centennial celebrations were darkened in March 2009 when reports surfaced that the team and its home arena, the Bell Centre, were for sale. It was widely known that the majority owner, George Gillett, urgently needed $600 million to pay back a loan he and Dallas Stars owner Tom Hicks had taken out to buy 50 per cent of another fabled sports franchise, Liverpool Football Club.

When asked whether he thought that the sale of the Canadiens might see the team leave Montreal, Mayor Gérald Tremblay's response was categorical. "It would be impossible because the fans will never let it happen," he said, "and I will do everything that is humanly possible to ensure that it doesn't happen."

La Presse mused that the Canadiens could be kept in Quebec by the deep pockets of the founder of Cirque du Soleil, Guy Laliberté, or even those of singer Céline Dion and her husband, René Angélil. Despite the economic crisis, the franchise was still valued at $334 million – third in the NHL after the Toronto Maple Leafs and the New York Rangers – by *Forbes* magazine in October 2008, and it's unlikely the Habs will be going anywhere, such is their bond to Montreal, and to francophone cultural identity.

That is not the case for the rest of the NHL. The Players Association president Paul Kelly has said, "I would not at all be surprised to see a team move in the next five years. Maybe more than one." It was a prediction that riled NHL commissioner Gary Bettman, who countered by saying, "We try not to abandon our franchises. If there's a problem, we try to fix [it]. I just urge a little restraint on suggesting we're contracting because we're not and that teams are going to relocate because they're not."

Even so, NHL players have raised the portion of their salary that goes into escrow – an emergency trust account – in the event of a financial shortfall. The players, who put aside thirteen of their paycheques at the beginning of the 2008–09 season, were committing to escrow a staggering 22.5 per cent by spring of 2009, clearly betting that the league's fortunes were going to get worse before they got better.

When NHL general managers met in Florida in March 2009, the financial crisis was not the only matter weighing heavily on their minds. Also on their agenda was an issue that has polarized hockey since Charles Masson killed Owen McCourt in a hockey brawl in 1908 – the place of fighting in the game.

The GM's discussion was made all the more urgent and sombre by the death of York University student Don Sanderson, a twenty-year-old forward for the Whitby Dunlops of Major League Hockey, who died three weeks after hitting his unprotected head on the ice during a fight on December 12, 2008. Sanderson's death renewed calls for a ban on fighting in hockey. Anti-fighting advocates once again argued there was plenty of evidence that the absence of fighting would have no deleterious effect on the integrity of the game. Fighting is a rare beast during the NHL playoffs and in the world junior tournament, and is punishable by ejection in pee wee, college, European, Olympic, and women's hockey. The ban, they contended, should be extended to regular season play.

Hockey commentator Don Cherry, who regularly shows video footage of fights in his various media enterprises and praises the combatants, upbraided the media for asking him about fighting when he attended Sanderson's funeral. "I can't believe that some people in the anti-fighting group would take advantage of something like this to make their point," Cherry said, without irony.

His point, and that of those who support hockey fighting, is that without preventive medicine, the so-called skilled players will be attacked and harmed by less skilled players. Fighting ensures that such behaviour from lesser mortals will be punished.

Fighting's opponents argue that enforcing the rule book and issuing stiff penalties for fighting – ejection, suspension, banishment – will put a stop to the violence, both real and staged. The Western Hockey League, the roughest of the junior leagues, promised to eliminate "unnecessary fighting" of the staged ilk, where players plan to fight in advance, and to crack down even further on obstruction fouls. As a result, this junior hockey league saw major penalties for fighting drop to 1.3 fights per game, down from the record of 2.1 fights per game set in 1986–87.

The NHL's commissioner Gary Bettman seemed to disagree that the fighting should stop. Following a meeting of the NHL Board of Governors during the 2009 All-Star weekend in Montreal, Bettman spoke to the notion that hockey has outgrown fighting. We're not going to have any immediate knee-jerk reactions," he said. "We're going to have to study things before we make changes, if we decide to make changes. I don't think that there's any appetite to abolish fighting from the game, and there are lots of reasons for that, including the fact that it's been a part of the game."

Don Sanderson's father, Michael, took issue with this logical fallacy – that hockey fighting should continue to exist because it's always existed – when he spoke to Michael Enright on CBC Radio One's *Sunday Edition* in March 2009. "Let's make the rules so if somebody wants to fight then go ahead and fight," he said. "But there is the catch: let them have to serve the consequences. If I am a player and I have to fight, let's make the rules so that I get thrown out of the game, but if you're my teammate and you're on the ice with me, you now have to serve my five minutes of penalty."

The NHL's general managers had come up with no such powerful solution by the time they adjourned their Florida meetings. They had considered banning staged fights, and agreed to mull over a rule requiring players to keep helmets on during fights, something Toronto's GM Brian Burke, an advocate of fighting, saw as problematic. "The helmet is a detriment injury-wise during a fight until [the fighting player] falls," Burke said. "We've had far more broken hands and knuckles and cuts from helmets. The helmet is a more of a problem of man-games lost until he hits the ice. Once a player hits the ice, it is far more catastrophic, or has the potential to be . . . So it's not that simple."

Just how complicated the NHL would choose to make a solution was revealed when the league suggested that since players who fought while wearing visors accounted for some of those broken bones and cuts, perhaps inventing an easily removable visor for fighting purposes might be a way forward.

Despite widespread media predictions that the NHL was finally ready to crack down on fighting, the GMs wound up recommending that, beginning in 2009–10, fights that happen just after a faceoff – staged fights – be penalized with an additional ten-minute misconduct, and that the instigator penalty be used with greater frequency when a player attacks another player for delivering a clean hit. At the time of the GMs' meeting, the instigator penalty had been called in just 6 per cent of NHL fights in the 2008–09 season, where nearly a quarter of those fights resulted from a player trying to protect a teammate. And in more than 80 per cent of those fights, the player challenged to drop his gloves had delivered a clean hit, or at least wasn't penalized for it.

It could be that the NHL was simply reflecting the zeitgeist, at least that of those who watch professional hockey. A Harris Decima poll taken after Sanderson's death found that 54 per cent of Canadians thought fighting should be banished from the NHL – but 68 per cent of those who considered themselves fans and followed the game "closely" thought that it should remain.

Fighting is banned in the Olympic game, though the Canadian men's hockey team at the 2006 Turin Games may well have wanted "a word" with chief ice-maker Dan Craig, after he refused to put a lucky loonie at centre ice in the hockey arena. "My job is to make the ice for everybody," said Craig, firmly sticking to the letter of fair play. "I can't have the Czechs come up to me and say `What the heck?' I can't have the Swedes, Finns, you name it, come to me and say I did something to favour Canada." The "lucky loonie" had entered Canada's hockey mythology after icemaker Trent Evans inserted one beneath centre ice at the

2002 Salt Lake City Winter Olympics, and both the Canadian men's and women's hockey teams came home with gold medals.

Canadians were hoping for repeat victories at Turin, but the men's team entered the tournament with a bereaved and beleaguered executive director, for Wayne Gretzky had lost his mother to cancer just before Christmas, and his maternal grandmother to a heart attack just after New Year's. Those deep personal losses were shadowed by gambling allegations that followed him to Turin. Not only was Gretzky's wife, Janet Jones, alleged to have bet $100,000 through a gambling ring, but a New Jersey newspaper reported that wiretap evidence revealed Gretzky speaking about the ring, and that at least one NHL team owner and more than a dozen NHL players made bets through it. One of the ringleaders was alleged to be Gretzky's assistant coach and close friend Rick Tocchet. On May 25, 2007, Tocchet agreed to a plea bargain in a New Jersey court on counts of promoting gambling and conspiracy to promote gambling, and was sentenced to two years probation. He was reinstated as an NHL coach in February 2008.

Gretzky denied involvement in the gambling ring, but the strain of death and the proximity to disgrace seemed to filter down from him to the ice, where the men's team was sluggish and vulnerable. After beating Italy and Germany, the Canadians were shut out twice in a row, first by Switzerland, then by Finland. They rallied to beat the Czechs 3−2 to win a place in the quarter-finals, and then were shut out again, this time by the Russians, and finished far from the medals in a woeful seventh. Gretzky took the blame. "I feel tremendously responsible that we didn't win," he said in a news conference following Canada's loss to Russia.

Then, as he had done as a player when his Los Angeles Kings lost the Stanley Cup Final to Montreal in 1993, Gretzky surprised everyone by musing that his time was up. "I'm going to re-assess where I fit and what I'm going to do in the future," he said. "Hockey Canada is wonderful, my country is great, and I love it dearly. But I'm also human, too. It's tough and it's nerve-wracking. It's not fun when you don't win."

Gretzky wasn't just trying to redirect the spotlight of judgment away from his underachieving team. In October 2008, former Detroit Red Wings captain Steve Yzerman took over as executive director of Team Canada. Yzerman had managed Canada's entry in the 2007 World Championships to a gold medal, and had been a key player on Canada's gold medal team in 2002.

The women's team at Turin was unaffected by the men's poor showing. They blasted through the preliminary round, outscoring their three opponents 36−1, the only goal against them coming from the Swedes. After shutting out the Finns 6−0 in the semi-finals, the Canadians were surprised and disappointed

James Creighton's Headstone

When venerable hockey historian Bill Fitsell visited Ottawa's Beechwood Cemetery in the summer of 2007, he was saddened when he came across the grave of James Creighton. "There's nothing there, just empty space," said Fitsell. "It gave me an empty feeling to think that this man was a pioneer of our national sport and yet has been overlooked. It was a real disappointment."

Creighton was the man who staged the world's first indoor hockey match in Montreal in 1875, formulated the game's rules, and played with the Rideau Rebels alongside two sons of the man who would give hockey its greatest prize, Governor General Lord Stanley. "Creighton is the closest thing hockey has to a founding father," said noted hockey buff and Canadian Prime Minister Stephen Harper in 2008, echoing the thinking of many historians.

Creighton, who was modest to the point of silence on his role in organized hockey's birth, collapsed and died of a heart attack at Ottawa's Rideau Club on June 27, 1930, two weeks after his eightieth birthday. His wife, Eleanor Platt, died a week later. They had no children to memorialize them, and no one thought to mark Creighton's grave with a headstone, let alone a monument.

So Fitsell and other hockey historians – who have been trying for years to win Creighton a place in the Hockey Hall of Fame, without success – have decided to give hockey's founding father a permanent memorial. "We're looking to put up a modest marker, date of birth and so on, maybe one sentence about his role in the history of hockey – and a couple of crossed sticks," said Fitsell. They estimate that it will cost $2500, and are hoping that the government of a hockey obsessed nation will help them.

to learn that they weren't going to meet their arch-rival, the U.S. team, in the gold medal match as expected – the Americans had lost to Sweden 3–2 in a stunning shootout upset.

In the gold medal game, Canadian Gillian Apps, granddaughter of Maple Leafs legend Syl Apps, and daughter of NHLer Syl Apps Jr., scored at 3:15 of the first period on a blind backhand shot. By the end of the second period, Canada was up 4–0, and early in the third, the Swedes scored on the Canadians, but this was the last goal of the game. They couldn't prevent Canada's women from taking their second Olympic gold medal.

"To defend the gold for our team and every Canadian back home is huge," said Hayley Wickenheiser, the tournament MVP. "For us, it's all gold or nothing.

There's no other medal to win in this tournament. That's the pressure we put on ourselves. We're just happy we can land in Canada with everybody smiling."

Wickenheiser, who at age thirty has spent half her life in women's hockey at the highest level, will return to represent Canada at the 2010 Winter Olympics in Vancouver, though this time both the men and women will be hoping to accomplish something no other Canadian hockey team has ever done: win an Olympic hockey gold at home.

The Canadian Olympic Committee expects nothing less. It launched an "Own the Podium" campaign in January 2005 with the stated aim of seeing Canada finish first in medals in Vancouver, and among the top three in the gold medal count at the Paralympic Games that follow. While Vancouverites are caught up in the Olympic excitement – and endless construction detours and ballooning financial costs and protests from anti-poverty and tax payer groups – they, along with the rest of the country, know that "owning the podium" will ring hollow if Canada's men and women hockey teams win anything less than gold.

The Canadian women's hockey team that will be trying to win the highest place on that podium will also likely be younger. When Team Canada won a silver medal at the IIHF World Championships in 2008, fifteen of the team's twenty-two players were born before 1983, eight of them in the 1970s. However, the national team chosen to play in the World Championships in Finland in April 2009 was a harbinger of the Olympic squad, with six of the twenty-one players under the age of twenty.

"You don't stay on the national team for 10 years like it once was," captain Hayley Wickenheiser said after learning that long-time teammate and double Olympic gold medal winner Cheryl Pounder had been cut. "Especially being an older, veteran player, young players coming up are always pushing. If you have a bad season or a few bad camps, that could be the end for you."

One of the most promising young players on Team Canada is Marie-Philip Poulin, who was born in 1991, the same year that then-thirteen-year-old Wickenheiser played for Team Alberta in the Canada Winter Games – scoring the gold-medal-winning goal in the Under-17 Girls' competition, and winning game MVP honours. Often called "The Next One," Poulin, a sturdy 5'6" and 161 pounds, turned eighteen shortly before the 2009 World Championships. Poulin is inspired by Hayley Wickenheiser and her gold medal performance in the 2002 Winter Olympics, and is often compared to Wickenheiser for both her power forward skills and her precocious debut on the national stage.

Like Wickenheiser, Poulin played boys hockey into her teens, trading in her figure skates for hockey skates at age five, and playing first with her brothers, then with AA and Pee Wee boys' teams. She made her first national team

Marie-Philip Poulin scored a hat trick in the first ever Women's World Under-18 Championships in January 2008, leading Team Canada to an 11–2 rout of the Czech Republic, and an eventual silver medal.

(Pekka Mononen/Hockey Hall of Fame)

appearance as a sixteen-year-old with the Under 18 squad in a three-game exhibition against the United States in 2007. She went on to win a silver medal for Canada at the Under 18 World Championships in 2008, and took the tournament's "top forward" honours as well. In the 2007–08 season of the Canadian Women's Hockey League, she also led all rookies with twenty-two goals and twenty-one assists during her first season with the Montreal Stars, and was named Rookie of the Year.

Head coach Melody Davidson is careful not to let the young player's early success stop her from developing even further. "Marie-Philip has a lot of tools, but in my opinion I feel like she's got to settle into a good solid power-forward role," Davidson explained. "She's fortunate enough that she has the hands and the skills to be a bit of a finesse player, but her size and skating alludes to the fact she should be a strong power forward who can put the puck in the net."

Poulin, from the small town of Beauceville (pop. 7000), near Quebec City, moved to Montreal to attend high school and improve her English, recognizing that she needed to learn the language to have a successful shot at the national team. Now she's being wooed by elite Anglo bastions such as Harvard, who would like to see her winning on the ice in their crimson. But first comes Vancouver, and 2010.

"It's been a dream in my head growing up," Poulin said, after winning a place on the national team. "Maybe I have a little chance to go in 2010. I just have to be confident in myself and do my thing."

One thing is certain for both the men's and women's hockey teams at the 2010 Olympics: ninety years after the Winnipeg Falcons in their maple-leafed jerseys won the first Olympic hockey gold at Antwerp, the Canadian teams will take to the ice bearing a new logo. The IOC has decreed the current logo of a player skating inside a maple leaf to be a corporate logo, and thus, forbidden as Olympic wear lest it corrupt the amateur ideal. Ontario MPP Rick Bartolucci was so upset at the news that he launched an online petition to persuade the IOC and the Canadian Olympic Committee to reconsider. "I cannot fathom an Olympic hockey game without the Hockey Canada logo," he said. "It is the heart of who and what we are in Canadian hockey."

But that heart is a Protean one, and since the first indoor game in Montreal in 1875, it has seen many changes. Indeed, one of the most potent comes from the world of the currently "new media," which today sees bloggers and tweeters opining on all aspects of hockey, from pee wee to the pros.

Technorati.com, the search engine for searching blogs, has pointed out that at least 94 per cent of the 133 million blogs it has identified since it began indexing them in 2002 have gone dormant, with many of the rest being taken over by professionals or conglomerates. The world of hockey blogging, however, is so robust that all the major television network carriers of the 2009 Stanley Cup playoffs – TSN, ESPN, NBC, and CBC – have added blogs or used existing ones to enhance their "traditional" coverage.

Of the four networks, CBC has been the one to most recognize the power of the blogosphere. Before the 2009 Stanley Cup playoffs began, the network dedicated a prime-time hour to the upcoming quest for the Cup. During the show they unveiled their new I-Desk, an interactive website featuring live blogging and tweeting that would run throughout the playoffs, in addition to the blogs and tweets from its own reporters, and blogs covering each of the Stanley Cup series.

They also recast their Hot Stove segment – which originated in 1939 with sportswriters talking about the game – to showcase three of hockey's premier and most credible bloggers: Tom Benjamin of Canucks Corner, Greg Wyshynski of Puck Daddy, and Paul Kukla of Kukla's Korner. The trio spoke of how their unique perspective gave them a fresh take on the sport, with

Benjamin in particular taking pride in his status as an outsider, pointing out that the mainstream media often has a detrimentally cozy relationship with the NHL teams they cover.

It's a perspective that Alanah McGinley knows well, as she writes "Canucks and Beyond" for Kukla's Korner. McGinley says that the increase in credible hockey blogging and podcasting in the past five years has been a powerful one, not only in reaching a wider audience, but also in changing the way hockey is covered by mainstream media.

"Interesting to me is how the rise of hockey blogging has impacted journalists themselves, and how they seem to have relaxed their own lofty professional standards in order to compete," McGinley notes. "For instance, pie-in-the-sky hockey rumors that once would never have been considered in mainstream news media, are now sometimes being *started* by mainstream news media, not because they have any substance, but simply to generate controversy and instant website traffic."

While the newspapers see themselves in competition with cyberspace to get breaking news out to the market fast, and ideally, first, McGinley points out that more news is not, by default, better news. "Hockey blogging has made for much broader coverage, but not necessarily more *honest* coverage. For one thing, hockey bloggers themselves are typically fans, not journalists. They spread their passion for the game, but don't have the benefit (or hindrance) of journalistic standards or big media employers to govern what they print. They simply write for their own selves and their readers. Which is fine – that's their mandate and what they enjoy."

By the same token, though, McGinley thinks that the niche-like aspect of blogging gives it more commercial firepower. "It's a direct line to the consumer of the product without the interference of 'journalists' [getting] in the way of their message," she says. "You can consider social applications like Twitter, too, which allow executives in the NHL's head office to have a constant dialogue with the league's fans. Half a dozen or more NHL executives dialogue directly with fans on Twitter all day, every day."

Bloggers and podcasters are now being taken much more seriously by the NHL, for the league understands the immediacy and the reach that these Internet writers have, and the issues that interest their fans. Many have received accreditation from the NHL to attend games, and are beginning to have a more traditional relationship with a team in terms of access to media information. McGinley's own podcasts are even featured on the Vancouver Canucks website, which, like all the other NHL websites, is administered by the league itself.

However, the 2010 Winter Olympics will be a different story for bloggers. VANOC has struggled to find a place for bloggers amidst the global mainstream media juggernaut that will muscle into Vancouver, though McGinley thinks the solution could be quite simple. "Most bloggers would be happy to simply get access to press conferences on the sports they cover, or simply just receiving press *releases* updating them and their readers about events. If VANOC can make some effort to keep those bloggers in the loop, they also help themselves by influencing those writers and their readers with their own spin on daily events. Everyone benefits."

Despite this problem, bloggers will be in Vancouver, and they may well be chronicling the last time that NHL players participate in the Winter Olympics. The NHL's executive branch has said that the Olympic schedule puts too much of a dent in the regular season (both physically and financially) to be worthwhile, but the most pressing problem seems to be that of insurance.

At the 2008 World Championships for men, insurance costs for Russian superstar Alexander Ovechkin ran from $500,000 to $800,000 – a function of the fact that Ovechkin is paid $124-million over thirteen years. The Russian hockey federation paid the premium, helped by then–deep-pocketed billionaires of the Kontinental Hockey League. In the end their investment bore fruit, as the Russians beat the Canadians 5–4 in overtime to take the gold medal and win the 950,000 Swiss francs in prize money, then worth about US$900,000.

Bob Nicholson, the president of Hockey Canada, said the cost of insuring the Canadian team soared from $250,000 in 2007 to $600,000 at the 2008 championships, and expressed hope that international sporting bodies would direct more prize money to offset the costs. A more dramatic solution mooted by many NHL executives is simply to stop having NHL players take part in international tournaments. The 2010 Olympics could mark the end of the twelve-year experiment that sees the NHL's best going for gold.

In those twelve years, hockey has become the focus for Canadian pride at the Winter Olympics. If the NHL pulls out, will Canada return to the days of Father David Bauer, whose team of scholar athletes made respectable but not triumphal showings on the world ice hockey stage? Or does it mean that Hockey Canada will develop a team specifically for the Olympics, much like it develops its other international tournament teams with an eye to winning Olympic gold?

It would be difficult to keep NHL prospects from playing professional, but not impossible. Many NHLers are now drafted out of four-year college programs, and the commitment to an Olympic team could be attractive to them and Hockey Canada in terms of time commitment and insurance premiums, as the players would not yet have signed multi-million dollar NHL contracts. It would, though, mean that Canada drafts a team made up of much younger

Olympic players. But as the country's world champion junior squads have so convincingly proven, the kids are alright.

And so are the hundreds of thousands of kids who play Timbits hockey, and Canadian Tire hockey, and pond hockey; who root for their town to become Hockeyville, or whose towns host the annual CBC celebration of our game, Hockey Day in Canada. Canada gave the world the game, the world plays it, and in 2010, many countries will play it in Vancouver aiming to be the best in the world. But being the best only means that someone will always try to be better. It's the nature of the game. What won't change is the place of the sport in the country that invented it, for hockey still moves the nation to ecstasy and agony – each spring with the Stanley Cup, each winter with the Juniors, every four years with the Olympics, and pretty much every day in between.

And "Game on!" – the *cri-de-jeu* of players and fans alike – is now heard around the globe, and the glinting of a trophy donated more than a century ago to encourage the spread of hockey, like the glinting of a golden Olympic medal first awarded in 1920 is now the gleam in the eyes of hockey fans around the world, fuelling the winter dreams and the springtime hopes of players from Shediac to Shawinigan to Salmon Arm, from Stockholm to St. Petersburg, both the one in Russia and the other in Florida. Canada's game now belongs to the world – for as long as we have life in winter.

ACKNOWLEDGEMENTS

This book was made possible, and better, by the work of many teams. At the CBC, Karen Bower invited me to the game, and then kept it going with her big-league managerial expertise and her countless kindnesses. The vision of Mark Starowicz and Sue Dando inspired the creative talents of writers, producers, and directors Michael Claydon, Laine Drewery, Peter Ingles, Claude Berrardelli, Jo-Ann Demers, Wayne Chong, David Langer, Lynne Chichakian, Lynda Baril, David Wells, Rob MacAskill, Terry Walker, Roberto Verdecchia, and Michael Drapack. They, and many others in front of and behind the cameras, inspired me. Special thanks to producer Lesley Cameron for always having a pint of champagne on hand when inspiration needed more fuel between periods.

I am particularly grateful for the hard work in the corners by research aces Angela Comelli, Paul Patskou, Ron Krant, and Natalie Tedesco, and for their catching my mistakes so gracefully; and to David York, Carolyn Bell Farrell, Andrew Bergant, Lisa Jakobsen, and Barbara Shearer, for their hospitality to the visiting team when I was in Toronto.

The all-star editorial stickhandling of Dinah Forbes and Jenny Bradshaw at McClelland & Stewart made writing this book like skating on open ice. Thanks to them for gently pointing out those times when the puck wasn't going in the net – or even near it.

As ever, my wife, Nancy Merritt Bell, and my daughter, Rose, reminded me that in the end it's not the score that counts, but how you play the game. It has been an honour and a privilege to play it with such a brilliant and generous team.

Michael McKinley is an author, documentary filmmaker, and screenwriter. He was educated at the University of British Columbia, and then at the University of Oxford, where he was also associate editor of the *Oxford Dictionary of Modern Quotations*. Since then he has written many feature articles for numerous magazines and newspapers in Canada and the United States, among them the *National Post*, *Saturday Night*, the *Los Angeles Times*, and the *New York Daily News*, and has written and produced three feature television documentaries for CNN. He is the author of four books, *Legends of Hockey* (1993); *Etched in Ice* (1998); *Putting a Roof on Winter* (2000); and *The Magnificent One: The Story of Mario Lemieux* (2002); and is co-author of *The Autobiography of Willie O'Ree: Hockey's Black Pioneer* (1999). He is also the author of *Ice Time*, a book for children, published by Tundra Books in 2006. In 2010, *The Penalty Killing*, his first novel in a hockey mystery series, is being published. A hockey maven, McKinley appears in the CBC Television series *Hockey: A People's History*. He and his family live in Vancouver.